Democratic
Repairman

Democratic Repairman

*The Political Life
of J. Howard McGrath*

Debra A. Mulligan

McFarland & Company, Inc., Publishers
Jefferson, North Carolina

LIBRARY OF CONGRESS CATALOGUING-IN-PUBLICATION DATA

Names: Mulligan, Debra A., 1960– author.
Title: Democratic Repairman : The Political Life of J. Howard
    McGrath / Debra A. Mulligan.
Description: Jefferson, North Carolina : McFarland & Company, Inc.,
    Publishers, 2019 | Includes bibliographical references and index.
Identifiers: LCCN 2018044670 | ISBN 9780786498277 (softcover :
    acid free paper) ∞
Subjects: LCSH: McGrath, J. Howard (James Howard), 1903–1966. |
    Legislators—United States—Biography. | United States. Congress.
    Senate—Biography. | Cabinet officers—United States—Biography. |
    Governors—Rhode Island—Biography. | Rhode Island—Politics
    and government—1865–1950. | United States—Politics and
    government—1945–1989.
Classification: LCC E748.M14857 M85 2019 | DDC 328.73/092 [B] —dc23
LC record available at https://lccn.loc.gov/2018044670

BRITISH LIBRARY CATALOGUING DATA ARE AVAILABLE

ISBN (print) 978-0-7864-9827-7
ISBN (ebook) 978-1-4766-3408-1

Front cover: painting of J. Howard McGrath (Department of Justice)

Printed in the United States of America

McFarland & Company, Inc., Publishers
  Box 611, Jefferson, North Carolina 28640
  www.mcfarlandpub.com

Table of Contents

Acknowledgments

My grandfather Pietro (Pete) Cardullo owned a barbershop in Providence, not far from the Rhode Island State House, which overlooks the heart of the city. He was well respected and provided a necessary service to his diverse clientele, among them some of the more illustrious Rhode Island statesmen of the period, including Judge Luigi Cappelli, Governor Christopher Del Sesto, and Director of Motor Vehicles Archibald Kenyon. Although I have no recollection of Pietro Cardullo, I choose to dedicate this book to his memory, and to the memory of the old-time politicians, the ward healers, the small-time entrepreneurs, like my grandfather, who trusted in their representatives to honor the traditions of grass roots democracy.

Maureen Moakley and Elmer Cornwell, authors of *Rhode Island Politics and Government*, described Rhode Island politics as "incestuous," which this text will substantiate.[1] Since most Rhode Islanders are connected to one another somehow, individual stories like that of my grandfather become interlaced within the political landscape of the state. Throughout, the reader will become acquainted with some colorful figures, some honorable, and others roguish. In all, this book speaks to my grandfather's generation, to those who took pride in the democratic infrastructure, and who, through their participation, helped to strengthen its core. Although the system revealed some serious flaws, as evidenced by the political life of J. Howard McGrath and others who were schooled in the tradition of machine-based politics, it also provided the ethnically diverse state with a parochial sense of security; elections may have been rigged, and candidates may have been tainted by a corrupt system, but at the same time, those who represented their constituency were homegrown. Throughout the Great Depression and the world wars, these crusaders fought for reform to ease the suffering of their neighbors, the poor laborers, the immigrants, and the proprietors who owned local retail establishments like my grandfather. Through the stories of these lesser-known figures emerges the foundation of the modern political system in America.

This book could not have been completed without the assistance of many caring, exceptional friends and colleagues who assisted me in my journey. To my many, eager undergraduate students at Roger Williams University who performed the tedious tasks of categorizing, collating, and fine-tuning my research and who helped broaden my understanding of Rhode Island history, I extend my heartiest thanks and good wishes.

A special acknowledgment is due the university's Provost's Foundation to Promote Research and Scholarship, which funded a sizable portion of my several research trips to Independence, Missouri; Hyde Park, New York; Washington, D.C.; and my visit to Clemson, South Carolina. Without the university's support, this book would not have been possible. I also owe a debt of gratitude to my many colleagues, especially Associate Provost Robert Shea, Professors Mel Topf, Barbara Kenney, Lindsey Gumb, Karen Bilotti, Sue McMullen, Deans Roberta Adams and Jeffrey Meriwether, Chairman Sargon Donabed, and the History and American Studies Department at Roger Williams University, who either read portions of my manuscript or provided me with sound advice on how to balance the demands of university life with research and publication.

It would be remiss of me to omit the distinguished historians who I have met as a result of my participation in the Northern Great Plains History Conference. I also owe a debt of gratitude to the dedicated and caring archivists and library staff at the Harry Truman Presidential Library in Independence, Missouri, where I have spent the last eleven summers. They have followed the pattern set by the late Elizabeth Safly, who was the first to greet me when I arrived in Independence. These professionals have proven that while research may be arduous, it does not have to be painful. My travels also brought me into contact with many engaging scholars on the cutting edge of research, graduate students just beginning their doctoral work, and other more seasoned veterans all united in a common goal to preserve the history of Harry Truman and his presidency.

Harry is everywhere present in Independence, in the lifeblood of the people, from the octogenarians who remember him fondly, to the younger population who have heard stories of the always well-dressed former President, enjoying his morning walk or his evening respite on the back porch with his dear wife, Bess. It was during these summers in Independence that I learned the stark contrast between Harry Truman and J. Howard McGrath. The President lived simply, never quite comfortable with the fast-paced, gossip-mongering inner circle of Washington, D.C. On the other hand, McGrath seemed to thrive on it, fully partaking in the social scene of America's political hub, hosting lavish gatherings into the wee hours of the morning.

The staff at the Special and Archival Collections at Providence College have provided me with many years of invaluable support, guidance, and friendship. When my mentor Dr. Patrick T. Conley assigned "World War II years of Governor J. Howard McGrath" to me in 1985, I immediately sought assistance of the then archivist and assistant archivist, Mr. Matthew Smith and Ms. Jane Jackson, respectively. At first, unfamiliar with the political environment in Rhode Island, I was tutored by Mr. Smith and Ms. Jackson who patiently provided me with the context necessary to understand the inner workings of the state's Democratic and Republican parties.

Since then, Archivists Russell Franks and Robin Raincourt have graciously responded to my many inquiries as I continued to explore the political life of J. Howard McGrath. To all at Providence College, I am sincerely and deeply grateful. Dr. Conley, in particular, continued to offer wisdom and guidance throughout this undertaking. Finally, I hold a very special place for my aunt, Phyllis Cardullo, who has read many, many versions of my manuscript, with patient and meticulous care. Barbara Carroll assisted me in so many ways; I benefited from her vast knowledge of the McGrath and May genealogies.

Although most of J. Howard McGrath's contemporaries have since passed on, I had the fortune of becoming acquainted with the Honorable Rae Condon and Mrs. Barbara Carroll, both tangentially related in some way to the period. A most gracious and brilliant observer of the political and legal landscape of Rhode Island, Rae Condon invited me into her home and spoke lovingly and perceptively of her father, Judge Francis Condon, and the environment in which he practiced law.

I extend sincere gratitude to my editor Gaelen Adam, who has an uncanny ability to streamline my narrative into very readable prose, while retaining the heart of the work. Additionally, Hannah Goodman provided me with invaluable advice on the publishing industry, while ensuring that I remained on task. Dr. Robert Cvornyek of Rhode Island College agreed to read my rough draft for its historical context, and through his affirmation and support and helpful critique, assisted me in my quest for obtaining the truth.

I also want to offer my appreciation to the dedicated staffs at the Rhode Island Historical Society, the Providence Public Library, the Boston Public Library, the Clemson University Archives, the Library of Congress, the National Archives in Waltham and Washington, D.C., and most especially to the archivists at the Franklin Delano Roosevelt Presidential Library. Professor Emeritus Athan Theoharis, a noted scholar of the period, provided a wealth of source material, and his collection of Federal documents allowed me to delve more deeply into the lives of McGrath and his contemporaries.

Finally, a special thank you to my wonderful family and close friends who patiently endured the occasional periods of self-doubt, when I worried that this project might never reach its conclusion. To my parents, whose love and support I cherish, especially my dad who regaled me with many stories of his youth, sharing memories of his father's patrons, including Archie Kenyon, who greeted them every morning with a song and a smile. To my husband, David, my daughter, Katie, my son-in-law, Todd, and my dear friend Cynthia Booth Ricciardi, a sincere thank you for reading or listening to many drafts of this biography. My friends Beth Shinn, and Cherine Whitney proved to be very formidable cheerleaders, and for that I am eternally grateful.

The acquisitions editor at McFarland and the staff there have been most gracious, professional, and patient, especially when my academic responsibilities necessitated an adjustment to my original deadline.

In undertaking this project, I could never have anticipated the journey that lay ahead. I soon realized that the saga of J. Howard McGrath is ongoing, and, as such, may not be fully articulated in this initial presentation. Even after fifteen years, I have merely scratched the surface of McGrath's life. My hope is to offer the reader a brief introduction into the life of this complicated individual and provide a foundation for young scholars to build upon as new evidence becomes available. For, as I tell my students, historical analysis is multi-faceted, and one must be open to new possibilities, which may confirm or perhaps even refute previously held perceptions.

Timeline of Important Dates

July 8, 1663—Dr. John Clarke secures a charter from King Charles II incorporating Rhode Island and Providence plantations

November 1843—Rhode Island Constitution ratified by a vote of 7,032 to 59

June 1872—John G. May immigrates to New York via the Portland Steamship Line

June 3, 1887—*Kansas* arrives in Boston with McGrath's father and uncles

April 1888—Amendment VII annuls the property qualifications for "naturalized citizens" but maintains that citizens must own $134.70 in property to vote in city council elections

1890—The McGrath brothers settle in Woonsocket, RI

1901—The Brayton Act, named for Charles, the "Blind Boss" Brayton, stripping the Governor of his veto power

September 5, 1901—James J. McGrath marries Ida Eleanor May in Providence, RI

November 28, 1903—J. Howard McGrath is born in Woonsocket, RI, to James J. and Ida (May) McGrath

1909—Amendment to the RI Constitution increases the number of representatives in the lower house from 72 to 100 members

April 1917—U.S. enters World War I

January 18, 1919—Older brother John Edmund McGrath dies of Spanish flu

January 16, 1920—Eighteenth Amendment to the U.S. Constitution effective nationwide

January/June 1924—Democratic filibuster in the RI General Assembly after Republicans refuse to introduce bill calling for a constitutional convention to amend the RI Constitution

June 1926—J. Howard McGrath graduates from Providence College with a Bachelor of Philosophy degree

1926—McGrath begins law school at Boston University

November 6, 1928—Amendments to the RI Constitution: Article XVII (registration), Article XIX (State Senate redistricting), and Article X (change in qualifications for voting)

June 1929—McGrath graduates Boston University

November 1929—McGrath passes the Bar

November 28, 1929—McGrath marries Estelle Cadorette in Providence

1929—McGrath is elected Vice-Chairman of the state Democratic Party

October 1930—McGrath is elected Chairman of the state Democratic Party

1930–1934—McGrath serves as Democratic State Chairman

1931—McGrath is elected City Solicitor of Central Falls, RI

1931—McGrath supports state-run police commission in Central Falls, RI

October 1931—Death of James J. McGrath

December 1934—McGrath is appointed district attorney by President Franklin Delano Roosevelt

January 23, 1935—Robbery of mail trucks in Fall River, MA, by Carl Rettich and his gang

April 1935—Body of Andino Merola discovered at Lake Pearl, Wrentham, MA

July 1935—Carl Rettich taken down by J. Howard McGrath, Francis Ford, et al.

March 1937—McGrath represents RI department stores' interests in a workers' strike

1938—McGrath is reappointed district attorney

1940—Vanderbilt wiretapping case

November 5, 1940—McGrath wins race for RI governor over William Henry Vanderbilt

January 7, 1941—McGrath delivers first inaugural message as governor

May 1, 1941—McGrath authorizes civil service bill, which calls for state employees to sit for qualifying exam

July 14, 1941—Commissioning of Quonset Naval Air Base

December 8, 1941—McGrath issues seven-point plan to protect citizens of RI following Japanese attack on Pearl Harbor

1941–1945—Mcgrath serves as Rhode Island governor

April 1942—General Assembly grants governor "broad and extraordinary powers"

April 28, 1942—McGrath signs into law the Cash Sickness Bill

October 1943—OPA Director Del Sesto commences campaign against state's black market

March 1944—McGrath signs RI Soldier Vote Bill into law

April 6, 1944—McGrath signs Juvenile Court Bill into law

May 12, 1944—McGrath addresses Tri-State Hospital Assembly

May 30, 1944—McGrath attends National Conference of Governors and urges the end of overlapping of federal and state taxes

October 14, 1944—FDR endorses plan for 400-bed veterans' hospital in RI

November 1944—McGrath wins third term as RI governor over Norman MacLeod

January 2, 1945—McGrath delivers Third Inaugural Address as governor

January 1945—McGrath establishes Veterans' Retraining and Reemployment Committee

July 1945—McGrath attends important New England Governors' Convention at Mackinac Island Conference

August–September 1945—McGrath is appointed to the board of the Rhode Island Charitable Trust

September 29, 1945—McGrath accepts position of U.S. solicitor general under President Truman

December 1945—Philippines War Tribunal; prosecution of General Yamashita Tomoyuki

1946—President Truman issues report on civil rights: *To Secure these Rights*

October 1946—McGrath resigns as Solicitor General to run for Senator

1946–1949—McGrath serves as U.S. Senator

August 1947—McGrath is elected Democratic national chairman after Robert Hannegan steps down

August 1947—McGrath desegregates the Democratic national committee

October 1947—McGrath and four other senators of the Subcommittee of the Judiciary Committee visit displaced persons camps throughout Europe

February 2, 1948—President Truman delivers message on civil rights

February 23, 1948—McGrath meets with Southern governors

March 8, 1948—Harry S Truman officially announces his bid for the Presidential nomination

May 12, 1948—McGrath and Senator Carl Hatch (D–New Mexico) introduce legislation to amend the 1948 Displaced Persons Act

June 25, 1948—President Truman reluctantly signs the Displaced Persons Act (Wiley-Revercomb Bill), which authorizes the entrance of 200,000 displaced persons in a two-year period

July 12, 1948—McGrath delivers opening speech at the Democratic National Convention

July 16, 1948—McGrath is reelected Democratic National Chairman

July 17, 1948—Southern delegation bolts the Democratic convention and establishes the Dixiecrat Party

September 1948—McGrath drafts political analysis memorandum for President Truman

September–October 1948—Whistle Stop Campaign. President Truman visits 48 cities across the United States

September 22, 1948—Textron under investigation by Subcommittee of Committee on Interstate Foreign Commerce

October 1948—McGrath travels to meet 11 Western Democratic Chairmen in Salt Lake City, Utah

November 3, 1948—Harry S Truman declared winner of Presidential election at 2:00 a.m.

November 1948—McGrath denies complicity in Textron scandal

March 1949—McGrath is engaged in verbal fight with Walter White

1949—McGrath introduces McGrath–Neely Displaced Persons Bill in the Senate

August 24, 1949—McGrath becomes the 60th Attorney General

1949–1952—McGrath serves as Attorney General

March 27, 1950—McGrath appears before Subcommittee of Foreign Affairs Committee with J. Edgar Hoover

December 25, 1950—McGrath receives threatening letter from National Park Service aspirant

February 15, 1951—McGrath confers with Judge George H. Moore about the grand jury tax probe

November 17, 1951—President Truman fires Assistant Attorney General Tax Division Theron Lamar Caudle

January 4, 1952—McGrath meets with President Truman regarding investigation of corruption within Department of Justice, but McGrath's position is retained

March 16, 1952—McGrath delivers controversial speech to Sons and Daughters of Eire in RI

March 19, 1952—McGrath begins testimony before Chairman Stephen Mitchell regarding corruption in Justice Department; refuses access to department cases that had been delayed or denied

April 3, 1952—President Truman asks for McGrath's resignation

December 1952—Chelf Committee issues report citing negligence on the part of Attorneys General Clark and McGrath

1955—In an interview, McGrath denies personal blame for his ouster as Attorney General

1960—McGrath loses Senate nomination to Claiborne Pell of Newport

September 3, 1966—McGrath dies unexpectedly at his Sunnybrook Farm home in Narragansett, RI

October 1966—Ida (May) McGrath dies in her Providence home

Preface

He consulted with FBI Director J. Edgar Hoover, campaigned with Post-master General James Farley, conferred with New Dealer Thomas "the Cork" Corcoran, sailed with Governor of New York Franklin Delano Roosevelt, and lunched with President Harry Truman and his daughter Margaret. He also earned the wrath of Senator James Strom Thurmond of South Carolina and the praise of civil rights activist Mary McLeod Bethune. Appearing weekly, sometimes daily, in leading newspapers and magazines from 1945 to 1952, Rhode Island Governor (1941–1945), U.S. Senator (1946–1949), and Attorney General (1949–1952) James Howard McGrath seemed destined for a permanent place in the postwar federal government.

Yet, at the peak of his career, McGrath suffered personal and political ruin, retiring in April 1952 amidst a cloud of scandal and controversy just three years after he accepted the post of United States attorney general. What accounted for this turnabout? This book will examine this question by analyzing McGrath's unique role in state and national politics as a local machine politician who sought to break free from this stereotype as he entered the national stage.

Although state historians have explored a number of significant historical topics in nineteenth- and twentieth-century Rhode Island history, including immigration, Prohibition, labor, and political history, none have focused exclusively on McGrath, whose life encompasses all of these aspects. This volume will fill that gap.

Significance

This study analyzes the transformation of McGrath from local and state politician to local and state politician to national leader, then follows his untimely fall from power, which in retrospect does not detract from his legacy in state and national politics. McGrath's biography allows for a better understanding of both the political history of and the relationship between state and national government during the early twentieth century. James Howard McGrath, like many children of immigrants, faced an ever-changing and often confusing America, first as a rising young Democratic state chairman (1930–1934), then as an upwardly mobile politician mastering the science of statecraft, and finally as a national figure attaining prominence and success. Through a study of this man, we witness the transition from the age of personal, familial machine politics to the modern political infrastructure.

The idea for this project arose from my interest in Rhode Island history and my desire to integrate the state's story into the overall framework of twentieth-century national political history. My decision to focus on J. Howard McGrath emerged from my discovery that, although he is emblematic of the change in Rhode Island and in the country as a whole, McGrath has attracted relatively little attention from historians.

McGrath's ability to take advantage of his political ties was central to his career. Rooted in a traditional Irish Catholic family and community, McGrath relied on this heritage and its requisite principles of honor, loyalty, and unity to pave the way for his rise in politics. However, his failure to adhere to these standards ultimately led to his fall.

McGrath's elevation to state chairman in 1930 provides an early example of this pattern. Using family and community connections, McGrath became the youngest Democratic state chairman in the country,[1] but because of his inexperience and his brash and uncompromising temperament, it did not take him long to alienate many within his party. His support in 1931 for the passage of a Republican proposal for a state-run Police Commission in ethnically diverse Central Falls put him in direct conflict with local politicians, who scrambled to grab the pay-offs and patronage that the Democratic Party had to offer. As he would continue to do throughout his career, McGrath allied himself with the most powerful factions of his party. Thus, even though the bill undermined local rule and allowed bootleggers and other nefarious figures to run roughshod over the city, McGrath's behind-the-scenes maneuvering would yield positive results to the extent that he did not destroy his career. Nevertheless, this fateful decision nearly caused irreparable damage to Party cohesion by intensifying antagonism among the Democrats. However, establishing a pattern that would recur throughout McGrath's career, then–Governor Theodore Francis Green salvaged the situation, taming the impulsiveness of his young protégé and guiding him in a more appropriate direction.

In recommending McGrath's elevation to United States district attorney in 1933, Green provided the young McGrath with an opportunity to tap into his abilities as a legal officer, as well as an escape from the political maelstrom that he had created. McGrath's tenure as United States district attorney proved to be the gateway to a mercurial career. His investigation of New York gangster Carl Rettich and his gang in 1935, for example, not only commanded national attention but also alerted the law enforcement profession to the fact that New England represented a nexus of felonious activity, much of which was concentrated in Rhode Island and Massachusetts. With the repeal of the Eighteenth Amendment in March 1933, former bootleggers like New Jersey–born Rettich were forced to diversify in order to maintain their illicit lifestyles.[2] Already a noted mobster before his move to Rhode Island in 1927 to partner with Danny Walsh, Rettich ultimately became a powerful underworld figure. District Attorney J. Howard McGrath's role in Rettich's incarceration brought him national acclaim, while at the same time called into question the jurisdiction of state and national government.

Another highlight of McGrath's tenure as district attorney was his exposure of Republican governor William Henry Vanderbilt's (1939–1941) hiring of a private detective agency to tap the phones of Democratic mayor of Pawtucket Thomas McCoy and Republican attorney general of Rhode Island Louis Jackvony. McGrath and Theodore Francis Green succeeded in persuading leading senators to endorse a national investigation on wiretapping throughout the country, with the Rhode Island case serving as an integral component in their probe. William Henry Vanderbilt, disgraced by state and national exposure of his role in the wiretapping case, nearly lost the Republican nomination for governor in 1940 and was trounced by McGrath in the Rhode Island election that November.

As governor of the State of Rhode Island, McGrath ably guided his constituency through the dark days of the Second World War. He was not a New Deal Democrat in the strictest sense of the word, but McGrath was able to achieve major inroads as a social reformer while simultaneously facilitating the expansion of state government. One important piece of liberal social legislation intended to improve the lives of Rhode Island residents was McGrath's cash sickness plan. It became the first health care plan in the nation that allotted funding to employees not injured in the workplace and was the foundation for total disability insurance, one of the few programs of its kind still in existence.

Although McGrath guarded against excessive federal intervention, he supported President Roosevelt's concept of a "rights-based" economy, namely the right of every citizen to a healthy and secure existence as articulated in the Second Bill of Rights in 1944.[3] McGrath worked toward achieving these ends through his health care initiatives and his efforts on behalf of a juvenile court, despite Republican opposition in the Rhode Island Senate. Like Roosevelt, McGrath was determined to "[win] the peace" by ensuring that families had the opportunity to reap the benefits of American democracy.

On the other hand, McGrath was exasperated by the General Assembly's failure to grant him emergency war powers until 1942, as well as by their obstruction of important social legislation, especially the Juvenile Court Act, which finally passed in April 1944. His work on behalf of juvenile justice and the cash sickness plan were among his most notable achievements; they paralleled President Roosevelt's call for a Second Bill of Rights, and for increasing the role of state bureaucracy with the war powers bill.

In addition to social legislation, Governor McGrath reformed the state's tax structure and reorganized its government. McGrath was determined that Rhode Island should be able to protect itself against threats from abroad and at home. These actions earned him the trust of the people of the state, who reelected him by substantial pluralities in 1942 and 1944.[4] His nearly three terms as governor of the state had solidified his place in Rhode Island's history, but McGrath was eager to move to a national stage.

Unfortunately, the beginning of the Cold War in 1945 brought mixed results for J. Howard McGrath, and his passage from the state to the national scene brought more scrutiny, and, ultimately, exposed his personal and professional weaknesses. At home in the small state of Rhode Island, Governor McGrath met each crisis with skill and aplomb. He could rely on the personal and political allies he'd tapped to lead each department. More integral to his success were his relationship with the powerful Green and with Green's well-connected executive secretary Edward "Eddie" J. Higgins, both of whom assisted him in circumventing potential crises. Green, a keen judge of talent and a political manipulator in his own right, steadfastly encouraged his protégé to strive to greater heights.

Securing the nomination for United States senator after another former mentor, Peter Goelet Gerry, stepped down, McGrath was one of a handful of Democrats nationally who could claim victory in the off-year election of 1946. His close relationship to the leading power brokers in the state, both Republican and Democrat, enabled him to prevail over some formidable contenders for Gerry's seat, including Robert "Fighting Bob" Quinn (governor, 1937–1939), Dennis Roberts (mayor of Providence, 1941–1951), and James Kiernan (Speaker of the Rhode Island House of Representatives, 1937–1938).

As the junior senator from Rhode Island, McGrath captured the attention of the new president Harry Truman. McGrath was one of three who seconded Truman's nomination for vice-president at the 1944 National Convention in Chicago. His reward came in 1947, when President Truman sanctioned his election as Democratic national chairman, upon the resignation of the ailing Robert Hannegan.

Although McGrath's efforts as Democratic national chairman (1947–1949) during the campaign of 1948 contributed to victory for the party and earned the praise of many throughout the country, the Democratic Party he led was weakened, as Roosevelt's tenuous alliance with Southern Democrats was severed and party coffers were nearly empty. McGrath, who had been the favored son on the local scene, was forced to play a secondary role alongside a host of presidential intimates when he moved to Washington. Most notable among them was Truman's closest adviser Clark Clifford, the co-author of the much-heralded "Clifford-Rowe" Memorandum, which outlined presidential strategy for the 1948 election.

Senator McGrath's 99 percent approval of Harry Truman's legislation smacked of opportunism, although it elicited the president's gratitude during critical junctures in Congress. While McGrath's loyalty served him well as senator, it was not enough to excuse his apathetic response to rampant corruption in the Department of Justice after he was appointed attorney general of the United States in 1949. When evidence surfaced that several key officers in these agencies had violated the sacred trust of the country, the president, his cabinet, and the American people required a more forthright response from the attorney general. Instead, McGrath's passive, evasive attitude and his continued support of his subordinates despite their questionable activities ultimately exposed the Department of Justice and its subdivisions to damaging investigations. McGrath seemed to have lost his fighting spirit. The House investigation of the Department of Justice, led by Frank Chelf of Kentucky and Kenneth B. Keating of New York, revealed a department suffering from poor leadership that failed to halt rampant corruption. In essence, the committee charged McGrath, the Department of Justice's leader, with negligence. Chelf's conclusion that McGrath showed a "remarkable lack of knowledge" of his own department sealed the fate of the now beleaguered attorney general for the historical record, overshadowing his achievements as governor, senator, and Democratic party chairman. A much-diminished McGrath made a final bid for the Senate in 1960, finishing a poor third against victor Claiborne Pell of Newport, and his old sparring partner Dennis Roberts. For McGrath, who had devoted his life to politics, this loss was too much to bear, and would ultimately end his public career.

Scholarship of the Truman era has been particularly harsh toward Rhode Island's wayward politician. Most historians and journalists have either ignored McGrath's impact on the national scene or denounced his performance. In chronicling McGrath's rise to the top in 1951, *Providence Journal* columnist Henry H. Smith offered one possible reason, opining that "McGrath has never devoted time to evolving a political philosophy—except perhaps the philosophy of practical politics; he has never stood out as the imaginative creator of bold, well-documented plans for public service for social welfare, or for governmental betterment."[5]

McGrath himself provided another. In a scripted conversation over the state's radio station WPRO in 1943, then-governor McGrath engaged with Christopher Del Sesto, his local director of the Office of Price Administration

(OPA), on the necessity of war rationing. Stating categorically that he was "not a pedagogue,"[6] McGrath unintentionally revealed a shortcoming that would limit his success as he entered the national stage. In an era of growing media coverage, suave and urbane intellectuals like self-promoter Clark Clifford, Truman's advisor and close confidant, moved seamlessly among the members of the president's Missourian "kitchen cabinet," the Washington social scene, and the Ivy League Brahmans. McGrath did not.

McGrath was a political and geographical outsider. While McGrath and Truman had a fondness for one another, the Rhode Islander was never considered part of the inner circle. McGrath filled a necessary void in the Truman administration, but would become expendable while Clark Clifford and Tom Clark, the latter elevated to the Supreme Court, proved indispensable. The days of machine politicians were past, and so too was McGrath's value as a serious force on the national scene. McGrath's success in 1948, and President Truman's for that matter, signaled the end of an era.

In summation, McGrath's strengths lay not in his innovation, but in his ability to gauge the political scene and employ the best and the brightest to promote the Democratic platform. This strategy worked well in Rhode Island: by 1940, McGrath had effectively silenced most of his political detractors, and in December 1941 Japan's attack on Pearl Harbor forced the rest to embrace unity in the face of imminent hostilities. Locally McGrath maintained a healthy balance between business and labor in the state, while at the same time assuring his constituency that Rhode Island would weather the storms of war.

His political daring during the early part of the century enabled the Democrats to wrest control of the state from the Republicans. McGrath's loyalty to his heritage and his constituency led ultimately to more equitable representation for Rhode Islanders marginalized by the system, including immigrants who had been shut out by outmoded and exclusionary laws forced upon them by the state's leaders.

The student of political history can learn a great deal from the story of this man, who was swept up by the game and enthralled by the contest. Ever strategizing his next move, planning his last great performance, James Howard McGrath lived out a political story that mirrors the changing face of America through the turbulent first half of the twentieth century.

Featured prominently in the living room of J. Howard McGrath's summer home in Sunnybrook Farm in Narragansett, Rhode Island, was a letter written and signed by President Truman shortly after McGrath's ouster in April 1952. The president wrote, "I want you to know that my fondness for you has not changed one bit. Political situations sometimes cause one much pain."[7] The president's words offered McGrath comfort in his final years, but they could never erase the damage that had been done.

A Note on the Title

As Democratic national chairman, J. Howard McGrath reached the pinnacle of his career, and consequently appeared on the cover of several leading publications of the period, including *Colliers Weekly Magazine*. The editors of *Colliers* branded him "Democratic Repairman,"[8] a position that McGrath embraced.

Thus, I chose this rather telling quotation as a title for my book to indicate the high expectations the press had for the new political star from Rhode Island. Three years later, the media would hold a different view of McGrath, at that point a failed public official in need of repair.

1

Cheers to Eire
Irish Immigration

The life of James Howard McGrath and the development of Rhode Island's Democratic Party was predicated on the response of the Rhode Island Republicans to the immigration of thousands of Irish refugees, which followed a devastating famine in Ireland in the nineteenth century.

In his study on the nineteenth-century political machine,[1] political scientist Elmer E. Cornwell argues, "the classic machine would probably not have been possible, and certainly would not have been so prominent a feature of the American political landscape, without the immigrant."[2] Political and religious historian Evelyn Savidge Sterne counters that "machines, for their part, were neither capable of nor interested in mobilizing large sectors of the foreign-born population."[3] Nevertheless, the influx of Irish immigrants had a profound impact on both the Republican and Democratic machines in Rhode Island. The immigrants and their relationship to the political machine were at the core of Rhode Island's political and social history in the nineteenth and twentieth centuries and informed the development of Irishmen and sons of Irishmen like James Howard McGrath and his father, James J. McGrath.

The brief background that follows will reinforce the following themes that recur throughout this study: First, the plight of Irish Catholics, as represented by the personal journeys of families like the McGraths and the Mays (James Howard McGrath's maternal ancestors), was woven deeply into the fabric of Rhode Island's social and political makeup. Whether they hailed from County Monaghan in the north, County Sligo or County Waterford on the Atlantic seaboard, or whether they braved the rocky trail from Newfoundland or Nova Scotia, the Irish transported their unique ethnic experiences to their new surroundings. Equally significant, their travel, while communally based in many ways, was also an intensely personal experience, which affected each subsequent generation differently.

Second, Rhode Island's exceptional beginnings had laid the foundation for its social, political, and economic growth. Founded on the tenets of "soul liberty," as embodied by separatist Roger Williams in 1636, the colony early on served as a refuge for religious seekers and political outcasts. This political and social foundation encouraged members of the Jewish faith and various denominations of Protestantism, which included a vocal group of fiscally minded Quakers, to make their homes in Rhode Island. While the Reverend Williams' journey in the seventeenth century may seem far removed from the plight of the Irish immigrant in the nineteenth century, the two are connected in one significant respect: the religious tolerance espoused by Williams drew nineteenth-century immigrants seeking to escape the economic, political, and social hardship in their home country. Williams and Dr. John Clarke, who was responsible for negotiating the terms of the 1663 charter with King Charles II, established a model for true religious freedom. While other colonies may have espoused religious toleration, Rhode Island explicitly set forth in its charter this tenet of "soul liberty." Williams reasoned that a community would discover the true nature of God through open and unmolested worship of all faiths.

By the eighteenth century, however, this once trailblazing document had become unworkable. While unique in its protection of individual religious freedom, the drafters of the Charter of 1663 had made no provision for amendment. As the colony grew in size, this omission led to growing ethnic and religious repression, which diverged markedly from the original intent of Williams and Clarke. Rhode Island, with its ideal location along the coast, had drawn enterprising entrepreneurs to its shores. Samuel Slater had transported (via his photographic memory) the blueprints for Richard Arkwright's spinning wheel to Rhode Island in 1790, and from that foundation inventor Richard Gilmore constructed the power loom in 1815. Coupled with its physical geography, Rhode Island's business climate was conducive to invention and industry. Thus, Rhode Island was transformed from the small religious haven of the seventeenth century to a center of industrialization in the eighteenth.[4] A class of merchant elites thrived, all competing for profit through their trade in commodities, slaves, and fisheries.[5] As the coffers of these private merchants and businessmen grew, so too did their demand for the protection of their social, economic, and political status. This rising middle class sought to insulate themselves from the laborers they employed. Among these laborers was a growing number of Irish immigrants, who were illiterate, poor, and Catholic, the latter most problematic for the Protestant merchants.

By the mid-nineteenth century, poor Irish farmers, fleeing their native land as a result of several devastating potato famines, were swarming into the state. The fiercest of these famines occurred in 1845–1846, driving Irish farmers to pillage wheat and oat crops, rob cattle ranchers of their prize stock, or pack their bags for overseas destinations. Landlords, unable or unwilling to interfere in nature's grand design, encouraged the farmers to seek refuge abroad, thereby draining the source of Ireland's economic growth. According to local historian Robert Wheeler, over a million Irish had emigrated by 1849–1850.[6]

Even before the onset of the agricultural blight, the Irish of the western coastal towns from Cork to Donegal endured unimaginable poverty.[7] The rocky coastline and barren farmland proved nearly uninhabitable when compared to the "neat, pretty, cheerful looking cottages" and affluence of the northern counties.[8]

When the English Parliament, serving the landlords who wanted to purge Ireland of the poverty stricken, lowered passenger fees to Canada,[9] the Irish farmers had little recourse and great incentive to seek their fortunes elsewhere. Consequently, the Irish fled to the major cities of the United States, including New York, Philadelphia, and Boston, as well as to Rhode Island, including the cities of Providence, Woonsocket, Warwick, and Pawtucket. As a result, Rhode Island soon became among the most densely populated states. The first Federal Census of 1850 indicated that 15,944 of a total population of 147,545 in Rhode Island were Irish. Just over 30 years later, 92,700 citizens recorded that one or both parents were born in Ireland.[10]

The sheer magnitude of this influx becomes more real when one considers the small physical size of the state (1,250 square miles in total). By mid-century, the Irish transplants had become another burden on an already populous state.[11]

Their economic and political livelihood at stake, the native Rhode Islanders decided that these newcomers were a threat that needed to be silenced politically. The rise in Irish Catholicism in the heretofore Protestant stronghold alarmed native Rhode Islanders who feared that the immigrants, unfamiliar with the state's government and traditions, would endanger their political, social, and economic livelihood.

The chauvinism that characterized the state's response to this mass immigration was exacerbated by the poisoned pen of "Boss" Henry Anthony, leader of the Whig and later Republican faction, and owner and editor of the *Providence Journal*. In an odious indictment against Irish immigrants, Anthony contended,

> The immigration from Europe is not largely composed of the most intelligent and cultivated classes ... [the immigrants have come to us] from the almshouses and prisons of Europe, are admitted to the full rights of American citizenship before they have been in the country long enough to have learned to perjure themselves in intelligible English.[12]

Determined to bar Irish immigrants from the vote, Anthony used the pages of the *Providence Journal* to mount a successful anti–Irish campaign. His supporters, dubbed the "Journal Ring," believed that America must reserve citizenship to those who were conversant in American history and culture.

Not exceptional in his attitude, he nonetheless possessed the means (through the *Journal*) to spread his bigotry throughout the state. His conclusions were irrefutable; immigrants held no loyalty to the state and possessed no knowledge of Rhode Island's political system. Although foreigners would be useful as menial laborers in the state's growing factories, he conceded, he refused to believe that they would ever possess the requisite education or loyalty to earn a voting privilege.[13]

"Boss" Anthony, who assumed editorship of the *Journal* at the tender age of 23, wielded his vituperations against the "Irish vagabonds" in full force before, during, and after the infamous Dorr Rebellion, which occurred from 1841 to 1843. Led by Thomas Wilson Dorr, the conflict erupted when the landholding elite refused to drop the property qualification requirement for voting. Dorr sought to replace the antiquated Charter of 1663 (which had not kept pace with the emerging industrialism and growth of cities like Providence) with a People's Constitution, which would favor the inclusion of Irish immigrants, who had settled in burgeoning cities like Providence, Pawtucket, Central Falls, and Warwick. Dorr's objectives were to remove the onerous property qualification clause set at $134 in 1798 and more equitably reapportion voting districts to account for the growing urbanization of the state. Although the movement failed, it marked an important milestone on the road to the expansion of suffrage rights.

In the meantime, "Boss" Anthony had become a prominent United States senator in 1859, wielding much influence in the state. His literary eloquence and political cunning encouraged the development of a one-party state, dominated by Yankee business industrialists who shared Anthony's viewpoint.

At this same time, the state witnessed the rise of the American, or Know Nothing, Party, which emerged for a brief but epochal period. Fading into obscurity by 1857, the party reinforced ethnocentrism in the state, as evidenced by their campaign against immigration. The Know Nothings captured important local and state offices, including the governorship when William Hoppin won the election with a plurality of 8,342 in 1855. More importantly, its anti-immigration creed provided the foundation for the rise of the Republican Party, giving them a sounding board from which to level vituperations against the newcomers and any reform-minded Rhode Island citizen who supported immigrant citizenship.[14]

The new Republican coalition emerged from the ashes of the old. Uniting former Whigs, nativist Know Nothings, and rogue Democrats, the Republicans had become the most powerful political organization in the state by 1854. The coalition attracted industrialists like former Whig Anthony, who with his Protestant cohorts succeeded in maintaining a political hold on the state in some fashion for nearly eighty years. The efforts of these early Republicans figured prominently in the political battle between Democrats and Republicans during the next century.

These factors encouraged up-and-coming Irish Americans in Rhode Island as they looked with hope to a new century. This included legal mind Charles Gorman, who became Speaker of the House; Patrick Henry and his nephew, "Fighting Bob" Emmet Quinn, the former central to the establishment of West Warwick in 1913 and later governor of Rhode Island; Pawtucket mayors James H. Higgins (1903) and later Thomas P. McCoy (1936–1945) and the young J. Howard McGrath (1903–1966); Dennis J. Roberts; and John E. Fogarty, known as a staunch advocate of public health, all of whom fought to break out of the repressive environment created by the Republican Party.[15]

Rhode Island's unwelcoming social, political, and economic environment did not dissuade the more tenacious Irish Catholics like James Howard McGrath's father, James J. McGrath, from establishing residence in the state. Upon arrival, Irish Catholics, like the elder McGrath gravitated to the state's urban centers, including Providence, Newport, Pawtucket, Central Falls, Lincoln, Cumberland, and Woonsocket. Anti–Catholic Republicans, primarily native-born citizens, saw to it that the newcomers would remain in low paying employment and sub-standard living conditions.[16]

This anti–Catholicism dogged Irishmen like James J. and his brothers. The unfortunate scars of racial and ethnic exclusion against Irish Catholics would haunt James' son J. Howard throughout his life, and eventually contribute to his undoing in 1952. As historians Kerby Miller and Paul Wagner point out, "Even those immigrants who achieved security or success in the United States passed on to their children and grandchildren a heritage tinged with bitterness."[17] On the other hand, the tenacity of his Irish forbears also strengthened McGrath's spirit and guided his future political career. This duality helps to explain why second-generation Irish American politicians like J. Howard McGrath were resolute in their determination to succeed against the domination of Yankee Protestantism in urban America. In addition, McGrath drew strength from his family and friends; even in later years J. Howard could count many of the sons of Eire among his closest allies.

Ancestry: The McGraths

James Howard McGrath's paternal ancestry can be traced to the eastern shores of Ireland in County Waterford. Throughout history, County Waterford endured invasions by the fierce Viking explorers and then by the equally formidable, land-hungry Normans. In response, its people sought protection through the construction of a series of strategically placed walls designed to dissuade potential enemies. Despite the presence of these fortifications,

Waterford did not escape the legendary sacking engineered by the Anglo-Normans in 1170, a siege forever etched in the memory of these proud Irish. Artist Daniel Maclise was so moved by the suffering of his forbears that he immortalized the battle in *The Marriage of Strongbow and Aoife*, painted in 1854, which now hangs as a reminder to all in the National Gallery of Ireland.[18] Waterford's principal city of the same name had enjoyed the sobriquet "gateway to Europe" because of its inviting harbor. After its unfortunate subjugation by the Normans, it struggled to regain its importance until the eighteenth century, when George and William Penrose established the fine crystal industry that allowed the city to thrive once more. At the time of McGrath's parents' emigration, the McGrath name was listed among the most prominent in the area.

Edmund McGrath and his wife, the former Mary Fanning of County Waterford, Ireland, with their sons John (15 years old), James J. (14 years old, later to be father of J. Howard McGrath), Thomas (11 years old) and Patrick (10 years old), boarded the ship *Kansas* from Queenstown, Ireland. Bound for the United States, they docked in Liverpool, then arrived in Boston on June 3, 1887. By this time, travel had become less grueling than during the famine period, when a journey to America could take nearly three weeks. Now, the voyage took approximately 10 to 14 days.[19] Disembarking in Boston, Massachusetts, the McGrath brothers discovered a vibrant, industrial city teeming with possibilities. An up-and-coming manufacturing center, the city had seen its population climb to 70,000 in 1880; as Stephen Puleo noted in *A City So Grand: The Rise of an American Metropolis, Boston 1850–1900*, "for the remainder of the nineteenth century, the Irish reshaped Boston."[20] Although post-famine immigration between 1870 and 1900 did not reach earlier levels, more than 50,000 Irish continued to journey to America each year during that period. The *Boston Courant*, like Anthony's *Providence Journal*, warned that Irish Catholics would ruin the American spirit and undermine the Protestant ethic and sense of order, ultimately subjugating the United States to the vile control of the "Holy See" of Rome.[21]

Likely more interested in employment rather than religious domination, James J. McGrath and his brothers soon left Boston to find employment in the thriving mill towns in northern Rhode Island. They lived in nearby Millville, Massachusetts, for a short time before they eventually settled in Woonsocket, Rhode Island, in 1890. Upon the naturalization of James J. McGrath on October 15, 1894, his sponsor, Fred N. Talbot, noted that the 20-year-old, "a mere boy," had arrived in the United States at 16 and maintained good standing in his community.[22] The McGraths found a growing city quite different from their Irish homeland. Woonsocket, or "Thunder Mist," was originally settled by the Eastern Woodland Native American groups, the Nipmucs, Wampanoag, and Narragansett, who named it for its breathtaking waterfalls. Forcing the native peoples out, Europeans had overrun the area in the seventeenth and eighteenth centuries. With the success of Slater's textile mills along the Blackstone River in neighboring Pawtucket, enterprising merchants in Woonsocket established Social Manufacturing Company, which at the height of its influence employed 1,712 laborers. By 1930, a year before the untimely death of James J. McGrath, Woonsocket had become the leading textile manufacturer, with its 24 operating mills, 262,484 spindles, and 676 looms; Providence followed closely behind with 18 textile mills. It was during this period that the Blackstone Valley would emerge as one of the earliest centers of industry, attracting a growing number of Irish immigrants to its villages and towns.[23]

James J. McGrath found Woonsocket inviting for other reasons, as well. Sixty years before the McGrath brothers made their way from Boston to Woonsocket, another industrious laborer had paved the way. Michael Reddy arrived in Woonsocket in 1823, fortuitously encountering entrepreneur Edward Carrington en route. Carrington was fortified with ready capital and an even greater vision, namely to develop an immense waterway along the Blackstone River. Reddy acted as liaison between Carrington and the Irish and native-born laborers to ensure that Carrington's dream would come true. Reddy and his fellow workers commenced activity in the summer of 1825, and by the following year the project was completed. Through the ambition and foresight of Carrington, and the industry and devotion of Reddy, Woonsocket acquired the waterway it needed to become home to thousands of laborers of foreign as well as domestic birth.

Reddy's chance meeting with Carrington laid the foundation for future immigration to the resource-rich city. His foresight also influenced immigrant workers in another important area. Anxious to worship God under the auspices of the pope, Michael Reddy and a small band convinced Catholic Father Robert D. Woodley, DD, who was visiting Rhode Island from South Carolina, to celebrate mass with them. From the community's enthusiastic response to that mass, the first Catholic Church was built.[24]

This third wave of immigration, which included James J. McGrath and his brothers, relied on associations, such as the Independent Order of Foresters and the Ancient Order of Hibernians for aid in advancing politically and socially in their adopted homeland. These organizations, developed by earlier arrivals, enabled James J. to develop skills in labor union organization. According to Miller and Wagner, "hundreds of thousands of both skilled and unskilled Irish Americans joined the Knights of Labor" and the American Federation of Labor as well.[25] Young James J. McGrath evidently saw the social influence of these groups, and gravitated toward political and labor union membership as a means to achieve status in America. Encountering nativism, which barred him initially from voting in his new home, he nevertheless rose to the position of foreman in Woonsocket's Glenark Mills, acted as organizer for twenty local unions in the region, and eventually became city council secretary for the Democratic Party.[26] James J. also served as a representative of the Tenth Ward and became a well-respected officer in the Independent Order of Foresters, a fraternal organization popular among the Irish and French Canadians.

The maternal lineage of James Howard McGrath followed a more circuitous route to Rhode Island. Ida May McGrath's father, John Gideon May, had immigrated to New York City fifteen years before the McGraths departed their homeland. Born in Pictou, Nova Scotia, on October 3, 1846, John Gideon was the sixth of seven children, and the second of three sons, of William Mahy and Elizabeth Catherine Carmichael. Arriving in New York in 1871, aboard a ship owned by the Portland Steamship Company, John married Mary Ann McCarthy in New York City on June 25, 1872.[27] His distinct blend of English, French, and Irish ethnicity and culture was typical of the immigrant experience in Rhode Island, introducing the rich traditions of the small, but sturdy, seafaring community of St. John to the industrialized urban communities of Rhode Island.[28]

May's hometown in Nova Scotia, the original Indian name of which was "Kajeboogwek," also played a significant role in the history of Rhode Island. Founded by Frederick Des Barres in the 1760s, and formally established by George and John Patriquin in 1785, the settlement of River John listed twelve inhabitants in 1806, with another fourteen petitioning for a title to property three years later.[29]

The earliest Mahy (the name was later changed to May) in River John was John Gideon's grandfather William, who first appeared in the census of 1838. William, of West River, was born on November 20, 1801, the same year that England and Ireland forged an uneasy union. In 1829 he married Elizabeth Carmichael, daughter of a prominent Pictou family, in Belle Vue Presbyterian Church.[30]

Although source material is spotty, existing documents show that William arrived from Guernsey in the Channel Islands and earned his keep as a cordwainer. The 1851 census indicates that William and Elizabeth had three boys, one under the age of six years and two between the ages of six and fourteen, one girl under the age of six, and a teenage girl over the age of fourteen. That the Mahys had achieved respectable status in their own right is indicated by the records of their substantial holdings.[31] They purchased a plot of land from George and Martha Mitchell for five pounds in 1856 and sold it thirteen years later for 140 pounds to shipbuilder James Kitchen, Esquire. William and Elizabeth sent their children to the local schoolhouse for a primary education, and the family celebrated religious service with others in the community at the local Presbyterian church. By appearances, then, the Mahys had profited financially despite the economic slump precipitated by the decline in the shipbuilding industry, which paralleled the devastating famine that occurred in Ireland during the 1840s.

Mary gave birth to ten children, eight of whom survived to adulthood. Their second child, Ida Eleanor May, born January 3, 1875, in Providence, Rhode Island, worked as a stenographer before she married 28-year old James J. McGrath. Witnessed by James's younger brother Thomas and Ida's sister Maud, who stood as witnesses, the couple was married by Father Thomas J. McGee at St. Joseph's Church in Providence, Rhode Island, on September 5, 1901.[32] James J. and Ida's first child, John Edmund, named for his paternal grandfather, was born nine months later on June 15, 1902, with James Howard, their second son, following on November 28, 1903. A third son, Thomas Russell, came soon after, in 1906. After the three boys, the young couple had three girls: Anna, Eleanor, and Josephine. Following the birth of James Howard, the McGraths moved from Woonsocket to Providence to live with Ida's parents in the two-family home on the east side of the city.

Both the employment and community activities of James J. McGrath and his father-in-law John Gideon May paved the way for their children and grandchildren to succeed in the United States. Through the elder McGrath's employment in the knitting mills of Millville and then Woonsocket and his affiliation as the high secretary of the Independent Order of Foresters, James J. earned enough to ensure that his children would receive a solid Catholic education. In turn, his sons John Edmund and James Howard forged the path for their siblings by first attending the Cleary Catholic School and then LaSalle Academy, both in Providence.

James J. McGrath and the Independent Order of Foresters

James J. worked continuously to earn enough money to support his growing family. Employed by Glenark Mills in Woonsocket, James J. soon became a supervisor and joined the Knitter's Labor Union to petition for better hours and wages. Following his move to Providence and eager to increase his salary and standing in the community, James J. also joined the Independent Order of Foresters (IOF) in 1904. He served as manager for the Rhode Island and Connecticut branches, later becoming one of its most energetic insurance agents.[33] That James worked hard for the Independent Order of Foresters is evidenced by his wife, Ida McGrath, who said of her husband that he "sold insurance twenty-four hours a day."[34]

The IOF society's purpose, to promote "benevolence and friendship" as demonstrated by their commitment to "visit the sick, relieve the distressed, bury the dead, protect the widow, and educate the orphan,"[35] enabled James

J. to bring health and healing to his fellow Foresters. At the same time, he established lasting alliances with prominent members of the French Canadian and Irish communities. The ties that he established through his philanthropy would pave the way for his second son James Howard to achieve a solid place in the state's Democratic Party.

Because of the society's rapid expansion in America, it was able to establish insurance benefits through the nominal contributions of all living members. James J. McGrath took pride in his association with the Foresters, and served eventually as chief ranger. Proudly wearing the multi-colored collar of the ranger (a yellow star adorned with yellow lace, which clasped a red, white, and green collar), a symbol of his emerging status among his fellow Foresters, James J. took advantage of the friendships forged through the society, which brought him into contact with men of means like French Canadians Joseph Cadorette. James J. was also able to establish an important alliance between Irish and French Canadians Catholic immigrants and sons of immigrants, which proved fortuitous not only for the future of the Democratic Party, but specifically for his son James Howard. Through these ties in the Blackstone Valley, the Democratic Party finally gained a political foothold in the local city councils. The union of Irish and French Canadians through the IOF provided Catholics with a solid community in which to swear an oath to Christian

McGrath follows the path of most Irish Catholic schoolboys in Rhode Island by attending parochial school. He is shown here with a teacher (not identified) in front of Cleary School (St. Joseph's), Providence, circa 1915 (courtesy Special and Archival Collections, Providence College).

brotherhood on the one hand and build support for their political future on the other.[36]

James J. forged a small, respectable niche through his tireless advocacy of the Foresters. In turn, the society provided him with a means to achieve a political voice, which he bequeathed to his offspring. His most eager son, James Howard, would follow the path cultivated by his father. Throughout his life, James Howard would take pride in his Irish Catholic heritage, and look with favor on the various accolades accorded him by the Irish societies. Like his father before him, James Howard McGrath was brought up to value hard work and public service. By the time he was sixteen, he could "out orate" his father, which would contribute to his success as an adult.[37]

The Youth of James Howard McGrath and the Death of His Brother

As supporters and critics alike would later note, J. Howard McGrath early on exhibited characteristics that were unlike those of many of his contemporaries. He always kept his eye on his future ambitions and refused to partake in activities that would pull him away from his ultimate goals. Other than spending a few hours swimming in the Seekonk River with his brothers when they lived on Pitman Street in Providence, McGrath counted few carefree hours during his youth, in part because his early life would be marked by tragedy.

His older brother, John Edmund, died on January 18, 1919, the result of complications of Spanish influenza. While the heartache of his passing changed the whole family, it particularly affected James Howard.[38] Raised in a family that valued industry, Irish Catholic tradition, and responsibility, J. Howard's early path was both typical of many Catholic boys of the period and unique in several ways.

John Edmund, born in 1902, and J. Howard, born the following year, had nearly completed their grammar school training at the Cleary Catholic School in Providence when World War I erupted throughout Europe, following the assassination of Archduke Franz Ferdinand in June 1914. Nearly three years later, on April 2, 1917, President Woodrow Wilson appeared before a joint session of Congress to ask for a declaration of war. He explained,

> It is a war against all nations. American ships have been sunk, American lives taken … the challenge is to all mankind. Each nation must decide for itself how it will meet it.… Our motive will not be revenge or the victorious assertion of the physical might of the nation, but only the vindication of right, of human right, of which we are only a single champion.[39]

After the Armistice was signed, and the American boys marched home from the fields of Verdun, the Marne, and the Meuse-Argonne. They were hoping to put the conflict behind them, but they returned to face additional tragedy. Before the cessation of hostilities in Europe, a deadly virus had begun another kind of offensive on military camps throughout the United States and Europe. Although medical experts were initially slow to recognize the epidemic, it was to confront the growing realization that a pandemic had infiltrated America's shores. Spanish influenza, the disease that had traveled from Europe to America, would soon spread from the military to the civilian population.

In Rhode Island, Dr. Charles V. Chapin, a slight, bespectacled man whose passion for public health proved fortuitous for Rhode Islanders, was able to halt the spread of disease, but not before many had lost their lives. As superintendent of health from 1884 to 1931, Chapin lectured throughout the country and conducted painstaking research on epidemic disease in South Africa and England. His notes, compiled a few years after the epidemic, reveal a man determined to overcome the ignorance of nineteenth-century medical standards, which had only just begun to consider the effects of airborne pathogens on the spread of disease. Chapin would later codify proper medical procedures during a possible epidemic, writing that the medical staff should maintain "as little contact as possible" with those infected, should handle "nothing from patient unless disinfected at once," and should sterilize. Additionally "nurses [should] wear same dress all the time [and] keep [that] gown in the room."[40]

However, even he saw no initial cause for alarm when isolated articles appeared in local and national newspapers, describing what first appeared to be a rather virulent strain of the "grippe." After an emergency meeting with his team of experts in late September 1918, Governor R. Livingston Beeckman, Dr. Chapin and Byron V. Richards, the secretary of the State Board of Health, concluded that the state was in no immediate danger and should not prematurely close theaters, churches, or schools. This, they argued, would only alarm the citizenry unnecessarily. Nonetheless, mounting casualties were being recorded by the day. For example, two weeks earlier, on September 11, 1918, a "Quidneck Resident," 62-year-old Eliza Lamb, who had recently lost her husband Albert, passed away from an unexplained illness. In an attempt to limit the spread of the disease, the *Providence News*, a local news source that rivaled the Republican-backed *Providence Journal*, recommended that those stricken should "REST" comfortably "on the porch or in a tent or in a room which is ventilated."[41]

In the ensuing weeks, concern turned to anxiety and then to desperation; the swift pace of events called for a more aggressive response from the governor and his team of medical professionals. References to deaths caused by influenza and concomitant lobar pneumonia were appearing more frequently in the papers; they were interwoven among reports of final Allied troop movements in France and Belgium on the international scene, and heated political debate on the local front between area Republicans and Democrats.

Rhode Island, home to the Newport Naval Base, was a primary landing site for the virus, which spread throughout the state indiscriminately. It infected wealthy businessmen, poor laborers, widowers, and school children. It struck Protestant ministers and Catholic clergy, and it took the life of John Edmund McGrath, a promising high school junior, who on the day of his death on January 18, 1919, was lauded in the *Providence Visitor* as a promising Catholic boy who had earned a combined grade point average of "94" in all subjects—only four points shy of the top scorer, who had earned a "98." Tucked away with a respectable "87," freshman James Howard McGrath appeared last on the list of the brightest young men at the academy.[42] Overshadowed by his brother in life and death, young James Howard strove never to finish last again.[43]

In Rhode Island's immigrant enclaves, the influenza epidemic brought heartache and dislocation. On the other hand, it also strengthened ties to God and country. The church assumed a central role for first- and second-generation immigrants, who looked to their faith and faith-based organizations to sustain them in their time of need. For James and Ida McGrath and their children, young John Edmund's death bound them to their Catholic faith. The elder McGrath's growing involvement in the organization also supported him and his family throughout this period.

One can only surmise the effect the death of his older brother had on young James Howard. Judging by his aloof public demeanor and by the reticence of his family, the tragedy affected him profoundly. Now the eldest, James was thrust into the role of family guardian, as the son who would make good on the family name.

James Howard's serious, unrelenting work ethic, already evident during his elementary and high school years, now became his signature. He always strove to appear calm, calculating, and unruffled on the outside, but his hands, ever in motion, and his stare, taut and steely, reminded one of an overwound clock. According to K. S. Bartlett, of the *Daily Boston Globe*, "There's a story in Providence that when he was seven he and the daughter of a neighbor hired a horse and tried selling apples from door to door at a local beach resort."[44]

James J. also grounded his son in a good Irish work ethic. According to the *Saturday Evening Post*, "McGrath has been overworking most of his life," and his father was largely responsible. In addition to selling insurance, James J. McGrath, as a high-ranking Forester, was required to attend all social functions, including clam bakes, club socials, and any and all outside activities. As a dutiful son, young J. Howard was expected to accompany his father.[45]

Because of the society's rapid expansion in America, the Independent Order of Foresters was able to establish an insurance program throughout the country, which required nominal contributions from all living members. James J. McGrath assumed the duties of insurance agent for the society, selling policies to its members throughout Rhode Island and Connecticut. His achievements in this area prompted praise from thousands of Foresters in the New England region.

Rising to the position of chief ranger, one of the highest-ranking officers, he proudly donned the multi-colored collar. James J. took advantage of the friendships forged through the society, which brought him into contact with men of means like French Canadian Joseph Cadorette, future mayor of Central Falls. Through these and similar ties with the Blackstone Valley, the Democratic Party finally gained a political foothold in the local city councils.

The elder McGrath contributed to his son's drive to succeed and encouraged his son's active participation in the Foresters. Young J. Howard, who officially joined the order at sixteen, took advantage of his father's tutelage and became an accomplished orator while still in high school.

James J. McGrath wanted his son to achieve a place in the United States. Laying the groundwork for his son's success, James "worked 24 hours a day" as a Forester, union steward, and Democratic councilman. He earned the respect and admiration of his fellow Foresters as a man of vision, propriety, and industry. Not given to demonstrations of affection, James and Ida focused on teaching their children how to get along in America.

A notation, which accompanied his senior class picture in the 1922 yearbook at LaSalle Academy, hinted at his promising political future. Beside his senior photograph, the yearbook caption thanked "our good friend Howard" for his "fine samples of oratory in public speaking contests." It says he has "shown us that he knows" how to organize and lead "class meetings." The observation also highlighted McGrath's skill in securing the "financial success of the *Maroon and White* [the yearbook] throughout the year."[46] Years later, K.S. Bartlett of the *Daily Globe* added, "He learned a lot about pleasing and managing people…. That's an art for which he seems to have a natural gift."[47] John Edmund's death coupled with his father's unrelenting work ethic drove young James Howard, or "Mac," as his LaSalle Academy classmates had come to call him.[48]

While other boys his age roughhoused throughout the ethnic neighborhoods of Providence to offset the discipline of the rigorous classical education of the Brothers at LaSalle Academy and the Dominican friars at Providence College, James Howard stood apart in purpose and action. He never strayed from his ultimate goal: wealth, power, and prestige. While the death of Edmund was rarely discussed in the McGrath family, the effects of the young boy's premature passing instilled in his younger brother the importance of God, family, and industry. Young Catholic boys who graduated from LaSalle

Academy experienced a more seamless transition into Providence College than boys from other schools. According to the Dominican fathers who established the institution, young men from LaSalle and "High Schools of approved standing" were exempted from sitting for an examination, while the board insisted that other applicants pass a prescribed test in order to "giv[e] evidence ... of [their] ability to pursue the courses of study of the Freshman year."[49]

Founded in 1917 by visionary the Right Reverend Matthew Harkins, DD, Bishop of Providence and educational visionary, Providence College served as the stepping-stone for many young, ambitious Catholic sons of Irish men and women. Bishop Harkins had petitioned the Dominican fathers of St. Joseph's Province for permission to establish the school and then appealed to all Providence diocesan parishes to contribute to the development of this project in Catholic higher education. He declared, "The need for a college, catholic in spirit and under catholic auspices, is most evident, considering especially the steady growth in the number of the inhabitants of the diocese during the last twenty years."[50]

His petition was so successful that donations ran well above $200,000. The Charter, which was affirmed in the Rhode Island General Assembly in January 1917, and signed by Governor R. Livingston Beeckman, sets forth the beneficent mission of the school "to promote virtue and piety and learning in such of the languages and of the liberal arts and sciences."[51] Yearly tuition was set at $100 in 1922 with an increase to $150 for the 1925–1926 academic year, which commenced on Thursday, September 17, allowing for the registration of courses and entrance examinations on Saturday, the 19th.[52]

By McGrath's graduation in 1926, the number of faculty had grown from fifteen to twenty Dominican fathers. At that time, Providence College offered incoming freshmen three possible courses of study: a Bachelor of Arts, Bachelor of Philosophy or Letters, or a Bachelor of Science. By 1920, the college established a fourth track: a two-year, pre-medical curriculum, which met the standards of the American Medical Association. Young James pursued a Bachelor of Philosophy (PhB), with emphasis on Classical Studies, including Christian doctrine, English literature, history, philosophy, and public speaking. In preparation for his future career in law, McGrath studied elementary, business, and Roman law, beginning in his junior year. According to the 1924 catalog, the offerings were expanded for young men considering careers in law, medicine, and pedagogy. With a "wider latitude and a large degree of substitution for prescribed studies," the Providence College graduate would succeed in his chosen field of study.[53]

Unlike his brother T. Russell, who graduated a year later in 1927, J. Howard had chosen to immerse himself in the political life of the state, rather

McGrath graduates from Providence College with a Bachelor of Philosophy (PhB), 1926 (courtesy Harry S Truman Presidential Library and Museum, Independence, Missouri, and the Special and Archival Collections, Providence College).

than in the undergraduate life of the school. While T. Russell and Edward "Gael" Sullivan wrote about the weekly activities of the Dominican institution, J. Howard dove into Rhode Island politics with a determination unmatched by his peers.

McGrath partook in college activities that he deemed advantageous to his career, such as the debate team, but he preferred to engage in activities that would reap immediate benefits for his political future. With Gael Sullivan, he established the Young Men's Democratic League of Rhode Island while matriculating at Providence College. Both boys were second generation Irish Americans and had attended LaSalle Academy before Providence College; they sustained a healthy (and sometimes not so healthy) rivalry throughout their adult lives. According to James MacGregor Burns, "the average American politician follows a well-trod path to elective office. He strikes deep roots in a likely community. He joins countless organizations where he can make useful contacts."[54] McGrath eagerly followed this prescription. The establishment of the Young Men's Democratic League of Rhode Island was as beneficial to McGrath as his education. As the up-and-coming leaders of the party, McGrath and his cohorts hosted events and sharpened their skills as orators and organizers. His work for the league, coupled with his classical Providence College education, prepared J. Howard McGrath for a future in Rhode Island politics as well.

As J. Howard diligently studied and continued to assist his father with duties at the Foresters, he also supplemented the family income with employment at Kresge's Department Store.[55]

McGrath developed a personal connection with the *Providence News-Tribune,* recently purchased by wealthy senator Peter Goelet Gerry, when it held a contest to boost subscriptions. Young James Howard McGrath captured the attention of the senator by selling nearly 4,000 subscriptions to the *News-Tribune,* placing second in the "Help Yourself Club" contest.[56] McGrath won a Packard Six Sedan, which listed for $3,980–$4,500, but more importantly secured a position in Gerry's organization.[57] Taking advantage of his father's ties to the Foresters, he gained access to the 4,000 members, which enabled him to gain a foothold into the ranks of the Democratic Party.[58] Years later, he mused, "In politics, I could foresee endless possibilities of advancement and constructive work, and to that end I settled on it for a career."[59] This remark may have downplayed McGrath's voracious appetite for political life— for J. Howard McGrath never "settled" on politics; rather, he thrived on it, and during his early years plunged into the center of political life, relying on his family, political, and personal alliances to sustain him.

In accordance with tradition, McGrath's senior class paraded through the streets of downtown Providence before entering the campus for the graduation exercises, which included a High Mass officiated by the Right Reverend Felix Couturier, OP, DD, ORE, Bishop of Alexandria, Ontario. Appearing before the graduates, Father Couturier emphasized the importance of faith, which "is the rock upon which true education is founded." A former World War I army chaplain, Couturier reminded his young audience that while ambition is important, it must be rooted in God: "And the rain fell and the flood came and the wind blew and they beat upon the house, but it fell not, for it was built upon the rock."[60]

McGrath and his classmates then marched in procession to receive their degrees: the Bachelor of Philosophy students designated by blue mortarboard caps were first in line, followed by the yellow-tasseled Bachelor of Science graduates, and finally by those representing the arts, who were clothed in black and white.[61]

After McGrath's graduation in 1926 from Providence College, he attended law school at Boston University, where he learned the "fundamental principles of the law" and the "technique of the profession"[62] in order to prepare him for his varied career to follow. At a ceremonial dinner 20 years later, one of his admirers and former mentors, Dean Elwood H. Hettrick, praised "the boy who entered Boston University School of Law in 1926, while simultaneously working at California Insurance Company, serving the Democratic Party as its Vice Chairman, and assisting his father as the latter fulfilled his duties as Secretary of the Independent Order of Foresters." Lauding young McGrath's scholarship, Dean Hettrick also cited a letter written to the school in late December 1927 by the freshman law student,

> There seems to be some misapprehension concerning the date of the reopening of school. Some of the boys seem to think Monday, January 2nd, is the opening date, while others are of the opinion that Tuesday, January 3rd, is the date…. Will you please answer this inquiry on the enclosed card and return it to me?[63]

Impressed by the boy's solicitude, attention to detail, and propriety, Dean Hettrick and the several guests noted McGrath's phenomenal rise to high office. Graduating with a law degree in June 1929, McGrath passed the bar that November. According to records later maintained by the Federal Bureau of Investigation, J. Howard McGrath earned a respectable grade point average of "80" during his matriculation as a law school student.[64] Law would provide him with a means to an end, but it was political life that drove the young man to excel. While still attending law school, McGrath was brought on as vice-chairman of the Democratic Party, advancing over other more seasoned and loyal politicians. In order to strengthen his position, J. Howard married Estelle Cadorette, the daughter of one of the Blackstone Valley's most prominent local figures: state senator and fellow Independent Forester Joseph Cadorette, who would later become mayor of Central Falls. When J. Howard courted the young French Canadian Estelle in his shiny Packard, he found that she eagerly supported him in his chosen profession. The *News-Tribune* publicized the wedding with a lovely picture of the young bride attired in a scoop-necked cotton dress and adorned with a string of pearls. Whether theirs was a match made in heaven or brokered in the backroom of a Democratic caucus meeting, J. Howard and Estelle remained partners for life, and she stood by him through both success and tribulation.

McGrath and Estelle married on November 28, 1929, at St. Charles Catholic Church in Providence, Rhode Island. The new Mrs. McGrath would provide strength and continuity for her marriage and family, as well as more practical aid. As a member of the Young Women's Democratic League of Rhode Island, she was placed in charge of organizing an engagement party for State Democratic Chairman Luigi DePasquale and his fiancée. In this task, Estelle showed that she understood the importance of forging ties with all factions of the coalition; she too had been groomed in the manner of public life, and assumed this role gracefully.[65] Estelle instinctively knew when to take the initiative and when to step aside, and while quietly, and by all appearances seamlessly, weathering the highs and lows of public life, she was able to hold on to her traditional beliefs of home and hearth.

Within six months, J. Howard McGrath was unanimously elected chairman of the Democratic State Central Committee, replacing the esteemed Theodore Francis Green, who stepped down to run for governor. Both Peter Gerry and Green recognized the talents of young McGrath and took advantage of his willingness to please them at all costs. In addition, as McGrath himself would later admit, his father's ties to the Independent Order of Foresters brought to the party a growing number of reliable, elite citizens of the state. McGrath was launched.

2

A Young Man in a Hurry

Born during the height of Republican dominance, McGrath would play a major role in its precipitous decline in the middle of the twentieth century. On the other hand, he also bears some responsibility for the near abandonment of party principles, which nearly broke the Democratic coalition during one of the most crucial periods in Rhode Island political history. An up-and-coming force from within political ranks, his exuberance at times revealed his inexperience and questionable judgment.

The restrictive nature of Rhode Island politics complicated the already factious political environment in the state in the late nineteenth and early twentieth centuries, but also served to forge a path for the modern period. The Democrats, attempting to negotiate their place in this emerging modern state, hoped that the postwar period would usher in a change for the better: a Democratic ascendancy achieved through the dedication, cunning, and grassroots efforts of the state's most talented and ambitious Democrats.

Hoping to capitalize on the nationwide reform movement that commenced with the elevation of Theodore Roosevelt to the presidency in 1901, activists like Theodore Francis Green campaigned in 1906. Green initially ran as a member of the Lincoln Party, which was composed of well-to-do dissenters who opposed politics as usual in the state.[1] Eventually the more reform-minded members, Green among them, would join forces with the Democrats to overthrow what they saw as Republican oppression. The work of these early reformers enabled second-generation Party men, like McGrath, to exert influence on the Rhode Island political scene.

In the nineteenth and early twentieth centuries, Rhode Island's coalition remained underrepresented in the city and town councils, where local power resided, and in the General Assembly. The Democrats' minority status meant that eager party members from the more populated cities were competing for relatively few available positions.

The Rhode Island Constitution, which went into effect in 1843, guaranteed Republican domination in the General Assembly through an onerous clause, which retained property qualifications for voting in state and local elections. This allowed power brokers like Henry Bowen Anthony, and his lieutenant Nelson Aldrich—the latter according to muckraker Lincoln Steffens, the "boss of the United States"—to wield unchecked power upon the laborer, both native and foreign-born.

Another infamous Rhode Island icon, General Charles R. "the Blind Boss" Brayton, dominated his native Warwick's politics until his death in 1911, and more importantly cajoled the General Assembly into passing multiple bills, including one that stripped the governor of the veto power, and another that redistricted the state's map. This redistricting effort ensured that rural districts, which had been reduced to a minority demographically, would retain their political dominance through legal and extralegal means. In Brayton's estimation, "I help them [politicians on the dole] to get elected, and, naturally, many warm friendships result, then when they are in a position to repay me they are glad to do it."[2] The bill increased the lower house of the Assembly, originally set at 72 members, to 100 members in 1909 and stipulated that each city or town was entitled to no less than one and no more than 25 representatives. This ensured that Rhode Island's smallest cities and towns (28 out of 39 total), composed primarily of Republican Protestants, turned out a majority in every election. Despite the expansion in the lower house, heavily populated cities like Providence, with 43 percent of the state's population, and Pawtucket were still underrepresented.

Republicans guarded the upper house with even more conviction as each city and town was allotted one senator, regardless of population. Although Brayton's hold was loosened with the adoption in April 1888 of the Bourn Amendment, which expanded suffrage to include non-property holders for all city and town elections, as long as they could prove "residence[y] and home in this state for two years,"[3] it still mandated that persons voting on financial matters must own "134.00 worth of property."[4] As the 1920s approached, however, the Democrats looked to a strategy that would topple Republican dominance once and for all.[5] The key to a Democratic takeover, they determined, was to eliminate all restrictions for voting except the most essential and restructure Rhode Island government, especially by reapportioning the 39 cities and towns to account more accurately for the state's demographic changes, thereby offering them a fighting chance at the polls.[6]

Specifically, the Democratic strategy included legislation to

  (a) remove the property qualification restriction for voting for city councilors and town budgets,
  (b) eliminate the so-called "rotten borough" districting, which favored Republican-dominated rural districts, and

(c) bring the vote directly to the people by calling a constitutional convention.[7]

Although Rhode Island's political environment initially appeared impervious to Progressive reform, a new breed of politician was entering the stage: young, confident, and brazen, ready to challenge their Republican opponents. Most of these young reformers were of Irish origin. Despite the inauspicious beginnings outlined in the previous chapter, Irish immigrants and their offspring gravitated to the state's political infrastructure. In their homeland, one in six Irish male adults could vote. Disenfranchised Irishmen joined organizations in support of an Irish Free State. Sponsored by rebel Daniel O'Connell, the clubs nurtured the innate political acumen of the Irish émigrés.[8] In Rhode Island, the fruits of their labor would begin to take root in the 1920s.

McGrath's political mentors and some of his adversaries emerged on the scene when J. Howard was still an undergraduate at Providence College. Fiery West Warwick legislator Bob Quinn, sometimes ally and sometimes nemesis of McGrath and nephew of vocal committeeman Patrick Quinn, worked with his fellow Democrats to orchestrate a filibuster in 1924 to break the logjam in the assembly. Patrick Quinn, born on December 16, 1869, in the Phenix section of Warwick, Rhode Island, was educated through its public-school system, completing the equivalent of a grammar school education in 1881. Forced to suspend his education in order to help support his family, he nevertheless became a trusted spokesman for the Knights of Labor, earning praise from its leader Terence V. Powderly. An avid reader, though largely self-taught, he passed the bar successfully in 1895. Admitted to the Rhode Island Supreme Court in August, and to the United States Circuit Court in January 1897, he quickly earned praise as a fair and honest judge of character, and as an ardent spokesperson for the Democratic Party and the Irish immigrants.

Tired of fighting a losing battle in Republican-dominated Warwick, Pawtuxet Valley reformers Patrick Quinn, Alberic Archambault, Charles A. Wilson, William P. Sheffield, and Oliver A. Langevin presided over the successful partitioning of Warwick and West Warwick, the latter populated primarily by working class Democrats, many of whom were first-and second-generation immigrants. Governor Aram Pothier's signature officially incorporated West Warwick in 1913. From then on, Quinn served the new town as a member of its local council. He later became a well-respected member of the Democratic State Central Committee.[9]

In 1918, Patrick Quinn welcomed his son, Bob, into his law firm of Ganon and Quinn, instructing him on the most effective means to promote democratic government. Tutored in the culture of the Pawtuxet Valley, an enclave that attracted Irish, Polish, and French Canadian immigrants to its textile mills, young Bob Quinn was determined to win for all West Warwick citizens, whether native-born or naturalized, proper representation in the General Assembly.

The 1924 filibuster was Rhode Island's introduction to the inventive strategy of Bob Quinn. During the previous year, the party had a dress rehearsal with the 1923 filibuster, which proved moderately successful, although the Democrats failed to dismantle the Republican program.[10] The following June, Democrats regrouped in preparation for a second offensive against their formidable political adversary. This filibuster would showcase the resolve of the Democrats, and provide young undergraduates J. Howard McGrath and Gael Sullivan with a fine example of the fighting spirit that had become the cornerstone of Democratic ideals. McGrath, Sullivan. and fellow PC undergraduates would capitalize on this strength in launching the Young Men's Democratic League in 1924.

On June 17, 1924, Democratic senators, already in the sixth month of the filibuster, delivered a laborious reading of Hamlet and an equally interminable recitation of the *Encyclopædia Britannica*, hoping to wear down their opponents. Eager to pass legislation calling for a constitutional convention, amending the Rhode Island Constitution, thereby eliminating the odious property qualifications for voting, the Democrats vowed to fight until they saw positive results.[11] At one point, senators, with "Fighting Bob" at the center of the fray, resorted to fisticuffs. Young Bob was nearly thrown over the rail by a rather imposing 250-pound assemblyman, Woonsocket senator John Letendre.[12] The Providence police were called in to quell the disturbance.

Republican State Chairman William Pelkey trumped these antics with a counteroffensive. By the fifty-third hour of the filibuster, he had secretly enlisted the service of three disreputable characters from Boston, ordering them to use whatever means necessary to crush the insurgency. "Toots" Murray complied by placing a cloth laced with a bromine gas solution between the pages of the *Providence Journal* directly beneath Senate President Felix Toupin's rostrum.[13] Following the explosion, senators began to run helter skelter, with five fainting from the fumes' odious effects. Lieutenant Governor Felix Toupin remained at his post throughout the ordeal, but then fled the scene following the explosion and refused to reenter the chamber, fearing an adverse reaction to the gaseous odors. With that in mind, he finally called off the filibuster on June 19.

Woozy from the aftereffects of the bomb, the afflicted Republicans withdrew to Rutland, Massachusetts, on June 22 and did not return to the assembly until the following January, their absence obstructing legislative action. Without a quorum from which to pass their reform legislation, the Democrats' program went down to defeat. Democratic governor William Flynn and his Lieutenant Governor Felix Toupin, shielded from the bomb's malodorous effects, emerged unscathed physically. Their health intact, they nevertheless suffered politically as the *Providence Journal* mistakenly blamed them for the plot. In one stroke, Pelkey had dismantled the Democratic coup.

The incident was emblematic of Rhode Island's chaotic political state, and the lengths to which Republicans would stoop to protect the status quo. This lesson was hard-won for the Democrats and alerted future young reformers of the party, including McGrath, that much had to be accomplished before high office would be theirs. As the president of the Young Men's Democratic League, established by McGrath and fellow Rhode Islander Gael Sullivan, McGrath addressed his fellow students and hosted Governor William S. Flynn, who explained to the youth why 22 Republican senators had retreated to Rutland, Massachusetts.[14]

Within the next ten years, however, Democrats had begun to chip away at the power of the Republican machine bosses. In 1928, passage of the Twentieth Amendment to the state constitution removed property qualifications for voting in city council elections, and the legislators had laid down plans to redistrict the 39 cities and towns to reflect more accurately the state's changing demographics.

The Democrats saw for the first time an opportunity to take hold of the state. Their antics, at times unwieldy and chaotic, actually paved the way for the party's notable achievement in the coming years. At this point, the Democrats needed a strong leader to unite their ethnic, geographic, and political factions and create a solid coalition, a task that proved daunting given the organization's internal jealousies and deep-seated rivalries.

According to Matthew Smith, from the turn of the century, the Democratic Party was divided into "four major factions." The so-called Providence coalition, led by Senator Peter Gerry, was the strongest and most financially secure. It controlled state's party coffers, but Gerry was parsimonious in doling out what little patronage he had at his disposal, angering many local Democrats.[15]

The second, led by Theodore Francis Green, would by the 1930s gain more control of the party, especially after the nomination of Franklin Delano Roosevelt over Gerry's favorite Al Smith, at the Democratic National Convention in Chicago in 1932. Although technically distinct groups, the Green and Gerry bloc would unite for important issues, like redistricting. Occasionally throughout the first half of the 20th century, however, Gerry and Green's alliance became more tenuous, especially when their allegiance to national presidential candidates diverged.

No one person appeared more removed from the common man than Peter Gerry. Great-great-grandson of Elbridge Gerry, signer of the Declaration of Independence, he had lived in the exclusive Manhattan section of New York before relocating to Newport, Rhode Island, in order to run for the Senate. Personally distant with limited voter appeal, his vast economic resources compensated for his narrow support. Peter Gerry's father Elbridge had sent his personal lawyer and confidante, Tammany Hall's General Henry deWitt Hamilton to Rhode Island to ensure the election of his son to the upper house. In New York, Hamilton had allied with Tammany's "Boss" Murphy, whose handpicked governor William Sultzer[16] named him adjutant general in 1913. There, Hamilton earned a reputation as an exacting taskmaster who saved the local guard thousands of dollars in waste following the First World War.[17]

In 1916, Hamilton managed Gerry's Senate race, helping him defeat Republican Henry F. Lippitt, 47,000 to 30,000.[18] Eight years later in 1924, Gerry purchased the nearly defunct *Providence News* from former backers, James Carr Garrison and John A. Hennessy, both of New York. Gerry named Hamilton president and leading editor of the *News*. The paper, which gave voice to the rising Democratic Party in the state, proved especially helpful for young J. Howard McGrath and his family. It offered an alternative to the powerful, Republican-backed *Providence Journal*, assuring the Rhode Island Democratic Party considerable financial backing in creating a political machine to rival the Republicans.

Nonetheless, Gerry and Hamilton were discouraged in their attempts to transport Tammany Hall's machine tactics to Rhode Island—a state whose independent and rebellious citizens balked at what they considered an alien, unworkable strategy, ill-suited to the political climate of the New England state. To Rhode Island's home-grown Democrats, the Tammany immigrants like Gerry and Hamilton, appeared insensitive to the needs of the state coalition, and instead concentrated on their own narrow interests. Evidence supports this contention, but Rhode Island's political leaders, such as General Hamilton and Peter Gerry, were inexorably linked to the New York machine, as their allegiance to presidential candidate, Al Smith, would later prove.

Theodore Francis Green, in some respects, was as removed from the common man in temperament and background as Peter Gerry. However, he had solid ties to Rhode Island, including a lineage dating to the colony's founding in 1636. According to Robert S. Allen and William V. Shannon, writing in 1950 on the Green/McGrath coalition, Green, "this amazing eighty-three-year-old gentleman possesses one of the wisest and most acute political intellects in the country." Marveling at Green's acuity, Allen and Shannon continue, "it is accurate testimony to his ability that in those four decades Rhode Island has been transformed from one of the most moss-bound Republican states into the most tightly organized, rigidly controlled, one-party Democratic stronghold outside the Solid South."[19]

Passionate in his quest for reform, Green sought to improve the lives of the downtrodden in the state. While exacting in his retribution against adversaries, whether Republican or Democrat, he nonetheless laid a foundation for the Democratic Party that stressed economic recovery and equality for all Rhode Islanders, regardless of their station or ethnic background.

Educated in the finest schools of the state, he also studied abroad at the Universities of Berlin and Bonn, Germany, before serving in the Spanish-American War. In the reform tradition of Thomas Wilson Dorr and Thomas Woodrow Wilson, Green sought to tame the juggernaut of Republicanism and big business by demanding accountability from its leaders.

Gerry, Hamilton, and Green saw in Irish American James Howard McGrath raw talent and naked ambition, which would prove useful to them in solidifying their power. Not afraid to upset more seasoned members of the party, McGrath would serve as their first line of defense by performing the more unpleasant tasks essential to secure power for his mentors. As Green biographer Erwin Levine would later note, McGrath's admonishment of the party's rank and file streamlined the organization and deflected negative attention from Green.[20] On the other hand, Green often found himself soothing ruffled feathers on all fronts as Gerry, Hamilton, and McGrath launched a full frontal assault on the other factions of the party, a role he would continue to play throughout McGrath's career.

Colonel Patrick Quinn, Alberic Archambault, and Luigi DePasquale, comprising the Pawtuxet Valley faction of the party, chafed under Gerry's narrow, self-seeking leadership. Quinn used his significant political weight to publicly denounce Gerry on more than one occasion.[21] Years later, his nephew, "Fighting Bob," commented on the relationship, "My uncle at first supported Gerry, but their relationship soured as the decade wore on." Patrick Quinn's fight with Gerry was legion; at one point, he accused the wealthy senator of forging an alliance with the Ku Klux Klan, and of using his power and wealth to advance his Senate race, rather than the Democratic ticket as a whole.[22]

The final faction, from the Blackstone Valley, was led by Thomas P. McCoy of Pawtucket, who was schooled in the art of "bossism," and became the official leader of the Valley, which was composed of Pawtucket, Central Falls, and Woonsocket. Throughout the 1930s, McCoy and the Providence faction would attempt to rid the party of the other through intimidation, and political intrigue.

Only recently admitted to the Rhode Island Bar, McGrath was elected vice-chairman of his party in 1929 and chairman in October 1930 at the age of 26—the youngest in the nation—following Theodore Francis Green's decision to step down in order to run for governor. Throwing his support behind McGrath, Green demanded that all Democrats follow in kind, and despite the *News-Tribune*'s claim that McGrath was chosen "unanimously" by the Democratic State Committee, his elevation to the post incurred the wrath of several qualified and experienced candidates. These men comprised formidable, vocal coalitions that were openly critical of the state organization, dominated by Gerry and Green.[23]

Two former State Central Committee chairmen, French Canadian Alberic Archambault and Italian Luigi DePasquale, for example, had in 1928 opposed Theodore Francis Green's candidacy for state chairman against Providence senator John J. McGrane.[24] According to disgruntled Democrat Frank Sullivan, "It should cause no surprise that the candidacy of Mr. DePasquale for Lieutenant Governor was thrust aside, as it appears citizens of Italian, Irish and French extractions are only to be used and not allowed to hold high office in the Gerry 'State' organization."[25]

The fight, which was especially bitter, exacerbated the divisions that existed within the Democratic Party. DePasquale and Archambault, representative of the Pawtuxet or Warwick faction of the party, campaigning rigorously for McGrane, but had again felt betrayed as the Providence faction, dominated by Gerry, Green, and McGrath, triumphed in election for state chairman.[26]

Responsible for doling out funds, Gerry, who provided his lieutenants, which included McGrath, more than $13,000 incurred wrath from Italian American wards in North Providence and Johnston for their alleged favoritism in giving funds to cities over towns, and for interfering in local elections to ensure that Democrats friendly to the state organization were chosen.[27] Luigi DePasquale, the hero of the Italian wards, especially the newly redistricted Ward 13, believed Gerry's organization ignored the importance of supporting Democrats of all ethnic backgrounds.

Vocal criticism was heard from the Blackstone Valley coalition, especially congressman and future Rhode Island Supreme Court judge Francis Condon and Mayor Thomas P. McCoy, who expressed their disdain for Gerry, Hamilton, and their protégé McGrath. Thus, this period in McGrath's life was marked by controversy and factionalism. His encouragement of and participation in several political battles among the Democratic cliques nearly cost him his career.

The root of the problem lay in the jealousies incurred by Colonel Patrick Quinn and McCoy toward the wealthy Gerry, who they believed used his limitless income to advance his interests at the expense of party cohesion. Writing to New York Democrat Franklin Delano Roosevelt in December 1924, Quinn complained, "Our Democratic National Committee has never properly functioned, to my way of thinking" since the organization only represented "about half the voters of the country."[28] Contending that Gerry's refusal to consider the Democratic Party, as a whole would ruin its chances of a successful bid against the Republicans that year, he complained that the Democratic state organization was purposely ignoring ethnic minorities in favor of its wealthy, Yankee-Protestant coalition of Gerry and Green. He observed, "a man need not be a tramp to qualify for membership in the Democratic Party but neither need he be an extremely high-hat variety of citizen."[29]

In spite of or perhaps because of his wealth and power, Gerry was reproached by local Democrats who resented his disregard for certain party enclaves and factions when it came time to divide the party coffers. Either unable or unwilling to diffuse opposition, Gerry and Hamilton instead lashed out in the pages of the *News* at rival Democrats, charging them with disloyalty and corruption. This public volleying, especially between Gerry and Quinn and Charles Hall of North Providence, brought the Gerry faction under scrutiny by less verbal detractors.[30]

According to vaudevillian and occasional politician Eddie Dowling, writing in 1934 to Roosevelt's advisor, Louis Howe, "I was in Rhode Island last week. They had two thousand in the Armory to see me, at a dollar a hand, and the sentiment is pretty much against 'Gerry.' Its [*sic*] a rotten mess and the Republican candidate proposes to call the voters [*sic*] attention to Gerry's not being wanted by the White House."[31]

Despite the bitter infighting, a concerted effort was undertaken by party organizers to register those previously disenfranchised voters. While still vice-chairman, McGrath was charged by the Democratic State Committee under the direction of Gerry to organize the "first voters" of the state. Young Gerry lieutenants, such as Henry A. Benoit, Harvey Almy Baker, and McGrath, dutifully urged voters to pledge their support for national Democratic candidate Al Smith in 1928 and again in 1932. As former president of the Young Men's Democratic League of Rhode Island, McGrath was able to enlist the aid of novice party men and women to scour the state for potential voters. By the end of that year, the numbers of those registered, including legions of newly enfranchised women, swelled from 199,030 to 265,017.[32] Their efforts had resulted in a widening political base, with admittance of the previously disenfranchised lower class, including many women and immigrants who turned out in support of the party and the Democratic presidential nominee Al Smith, the first Catholic candidate to successfully win the nomination for president on the Democratic ticket.

Following the Democrats' successes in expanding their voter rolls and their resulting control of important cities like Providence, Central Falls, and Woonsocket, GOP Chairman William Pelkey and his cohorts began to redraw the state map to again secure Republican dominance in the General Assembly. As a result, three redistricting bills were introduced into the lower house in March 1930. The more important provisions of each added four senate districts in Providence and transferred a representative from traditionally Democratic strongholds of Newport, Central Falls, and Burrillville to Republican-dominated Cranston, East Providence, and Warwick. Lastly, the Republican measure increased the number of wards in Providence from 10 to 13. Although Republicans sold these bills as reform measures, the legislation in truth maximized Republican ascendancy by careful redistricting cities and towns to protect the status quo.

On March 21, 1930, the day of the House vote, six Democrats were conspicuously absent from roll, and, as a result, the Republicans were assured the necessary numbers to pass their measures. Disgusted by the turn of events, Newport Democrat James J. Martin sarcastically "congratulated" Pelkey for "keeping so many Democrats away."[33] Providence alderman Frank J. Duffy concurred, warning the six absent members, "Some Democratic members have still in mind the 'Lazarus of old' who was content with the crumbs that fell from the table."[34] McGrath, accompanied by Green on the House floor, witnessed the destruction of the Democratic opposition firsthand.

At the North Providence Democrat Club meeting the following day, McGrath leveled the most scathing condemnation of all. Accusing the six of succumbing to Pelkey's bribery, McGrath marked them as "traitors" who "sold themselves for a measly pittance, some trifling favor or for their self-protection."[35] His "Speech of Stigmatism" against the errant six threatened to drive a permanent wedge among the various factions of the party. Already suspicious and resentful of the Gerry organization, North Providence and Johnston Italians looked askance at McGrath's heavy-handed response and began to criticize him publicly.[36]

Henry Benoit, a prominent member of Gerry's organization, privately complained to Harvey Almy Baker that McGrath's harsh reproach would ultimately cause "more harm" to the party than a more circumspect response would have. To Benoit, McGrath's outburst sent the wrong message to Democrats. By publicly challenging the integrity of the six defectors, McGrath, according to Benoit, would drive them away permanently.[37] His analysis would prove prescient.

Veteran Italian American representative Vincent J. Berarducci of Providence, a funeral director by trade, voiced public indignation at McGrath's accusation, justifying his absence and support for the Republican bills, by stating that the legislation "suit[ed]" him. He further denied that he was a "Pelkey" Democrat, as McGrath had charged, and announced that "no money" could "buy" him.[38]

More scathing, however, was the reaction of a fellow Irish American from Providence: J. Frank Sullivan, a World War I veteran and a representative in good standing since 1923, who was enraged by McGrath's allegations and attacked him in the General Assembly. Sullivan retorted that McGrath was a "political hack, making his livelihood working for a private political machine [Gerry and Green]." He denied McGrath's charge of "selling out" to the opposition, claiming to be ill in bed, fighting off possible pneumonia, and further alleged that McGrath knew of his illness and simply resorted to sensationalism in order to steal the headlines.

Sullivan described the events thus: "My physicians did not know what my illness was but feared it was pneumonia." McGrath then "worked his way into my bedroom," and informed him about rumors that he planned to be absent on the day of the important vote. "Seeing that I was ill this investigator and snooper, slunked from my bedroom and like a whipped cur" delivered his speech to the North Providence gathering the following day.[39] Sullivan's charges drew applause from the Assembly's Republican members.

He remarked: "Never in my eight years in this House have I arisen to speak on a point of personal privilege, but this matter is one that cannot be overlooked. I believe that in politics we should be able to take things on the chin and that by barking back to a dog you lower yourself to his level." Even so, Sullivan was compelled to respond to "this contemptible creature, McGrath," who would "rue the day" he challenged the more experienced legislator.[40]

A more circumspect and politically astute response was offered by fellow Democrats James Kiernan and Edmund Flynn, who focused on the injustice of the Republican measure, rather than on the disaffection of the Providence Six.[41]

McGrath continued to provoke ire within the rank and file of the party. When Mary Keenan, sister of recently deceased Gerry ally, Luke Keenan, ran against the town's endorsed candidate, Francis Manzi, in 1930, John Votolato, leader of the Taxpayers' Improvement Association in Johnston, berated McGrath and the state coalition for interfering in the local caucus. Votolato expressed frustration with McGrath, complaining that "The Democratic party in Johnston is broken to pieces as a result of the attitude of the Democratic State officials."[42]

In a comic-tragic turn of events, Mary Keenan held the caucus vote in her home. Although required by town law to open the doors at 7:00 p.m., she waited an additional thirty minutes while tempers of anxious town Democrats seethed. As soon as the doors opened, chaos ensued. In the process of stuffing ballot boxes, a Keenan supporter was pummeled with a pocketbook, and another woman was "knocked unconscious" and found lying on the front lawn. Ballots were strewn everywhere, and the state police was called in to quell the disturbance. Accordingly, 500 people were turned away from the caucus, unable to cast their votes.

McGrath ignored the town's refusal to endorse Keenan as the head of the local party, opting instead to follow the sympathy of his generous benefactor, declaring, "I am for Mary, first, last and all the time."[43] To Italian Americans in Johnston, McGrath's failure to recognize the will of the people divided rather than united the party. Disgusted by the turn of events and by the failure of the state organization to honor home rule, local Democrats Francis Manzi and Michael Iannuccilli, resigned from the Johnston board in 1932.[44]

The Democrat state organization also fared poorly in their handling of state monies. In North Providence, another town with a strong Italian American base, Charles Hall, leader of the North Providence City Committee, protested vehemently when Peter Gerry refused to advance him $2,500 to cover expenses for voter registration. Local Italian American council members, including Placido Caranci, threatened to repudiate Gerry's campaign if funding was not forthcoming. Hall further denounced Gerry as "the gilded scion of Tammany Hall" who "is not as yet the emperor of a self-respecting party of Democrats."[45]

In another indictment, Hall accused Gerry of concentrating on his personal campaign for the Senate at the expense of party unity. He complained that Gerry "wrote off" towns like North Providence as Republican,[46] and focused instead on the cities where he had a better chance of securing votes in the next election. Instead of downplaying the incident, Gerry published Hall's letter to General Hamilton in his News-Tribune and included an incriminating trailer: "the following letter explains the activity of Charles M. Hall of North Providence in [on] behalf of the Republican machine."[47]

By ostracizing Hall, Gerry, with McGrath's willing assistance,[48] drove the North Providence faction into the camp of Quinn, DePasquale, and other anti–Gerry notables. Hall's well-known support of DePasquale for Lieutenant Governor in 1930 strengthened the anti–Gerry forces. Quinn lambasted Gerry for isolating DePasquale who was "popular not only with the Italian people, but with all classes." He continued by warning Democrats to seek representation from all ethnic groups: French, Italians, and Irish. Otherwise, the Green and Gerry ticket would go down to defeat, which it ultimately did with a vote of 108,558 for Green and 112,070 for the incumbent, Republican Norman Case. Gerry lost his Senate seat to Republican Jesse H. Metcalf of Providence by only 2,515 votes.[49]

While historians might dismiss them as examples of botched political maneuvers by inexperienced, naïve town Democrats, these incidents revealed the widening gap between state and local officials and the deepening mistrust Italian Americans held for Gerry and his organization. They also serve as an example of McGrath's blind acceptance of party directives that would haunt him later in life.

Equally disturbing, it sent a message to fellow Irish Americans that the "Yankee" bloc of the party was indifferent to all but a small group of elite supporters and illustrated the growth of state power in America. Whether they knew it or not, localized politics, though important to the Democratic coalition for years to come, were losing ground to the more centralized, efficient state machine.

Fortunately for McGrath, Green, unlike Gerry and Hamilton, moved him away from the center of controversy and instead toward more productive endeavors. Green's Declaration of Principles, drawn up before his 1930 defeat, for example, outlined his commitment to progressive legislation and elevated the party's rhetoric. By focusing on such measures as restructuring state government, elimination of unnecessary bureaucracy, the establishment of state-funded elderly pensions, the enactment of a more equitable provision for workman's compensation, and the repeal of Prohibition, Green's plan outlined a set of attainable goals and minimized the petty squabbles that plagued the party. His clearly defined statement of purpose set Rhode Island on a path toward reform and identified Democrats as the party willing to achieve economic recovery for all citizens of Rhode Island, both natural- and foreign-born.

Green would eventually appoint DePasquale as Providence's sixth District Court judge and chose Quinn's nephew "Fighting Bob" as his running mate during his successful gubernatorial bid in 1932–1934. Determined to eliminate the animosity that Gerry and Hamilton had incurred, Green encouraged his lieutenants, especially McGrath, to embrace non–Irish ethnic groups lest they defect to the Republican camp. He also sought to repair the deepening rupture between the state organization and the Blackstone Valley, represented by the local machine boss, McCoy. This rift, however, proved formidable, especially after Hamilton and McGrath's involvement in the Police Commission Scandal was leaked to the rank and file of the Democratic Party. The scandal, which violated home rule, rocked the Blackstone Valley for years and threatened to permanently divide the already tenuous alliance.

3

"With Howard, Howard comes first"[1]

Carved out of the town of Lincoln and incorporated in 1895, Central Falls is spread across 1.2 square miles of the Blackstone Valley. The small city's location and its burgeoning textile industry attracted many groups of immigrants, so that by the first few decades of the twentieth century the city had become a potpourri of ethnicities.

During the Great Depression, Central Falls, according to the *Providence Journal*, was "wide open" to crime, as liquor dealers brazenly shared prime stock with known members of organized crime. Bootlegger James Lavell, who had already served time in the Atlanta Penitentiary, and his confederate, "agent" Andrew Sherry, organized a "Franco-Polish" bloc to wrest control of the Central Falls police department and city government from the wealthy, Republican Brahmins.

As a means to this end, a police commission was proposed. Composed of three commissioners wholly subservient to Sherry and Lavell, the commission authorized the establishment of saloons throughout the city as Rhode Island Republicans, and a faction of Democrats, turned a blind eye to the growing graft, corruption, and crime.[2]

J. Howard McGrath's tenure as Rhode Island's Democratic state chairman was compromised by his role in the resulting scandal, which was masterminded by his mentor, and former senator Peter Gerry's lieutenant, General Henry DeWitt Hamilton. On December 21, 1933, Raymond Kennedy, a disgruntled Democrat, revealed to the *Providence Journal* the details of this controversial bipartisan agreement begun nearly three years earlier, threatening to undermine the already tenuous cohesion of the rising Democratic Party.[3]

According to Kennedy, he had, as the Central Fall representative, introduced a bill into the state legislature that disqualified candidates from running for office in cities or towns where they did not reside. This bill effectively prohibited the incumbent Republican Lawrence F. Nolan of Pawtucket from reelection as city solicitor of Central Falls and ensured that J. Howard McGrath, then Democratic state chairman and favorite of the powerful Providence faction of the party, would be elected by the predominantly Democratic city council.[4] McGrath's election would ensure that the Providence faction of the party, led by Gerry and Green, would gain a foothold into the Blackstone Valley, a bloc previously controlled by local machine boss and McGrath nemesis: Democrat Thomas P. McCoy of Pawtucket.[5]

Because the non-residency bill stood little chance of passage by the Republican-dominated General Assembly, Hamilton masterminded a deal with Rhode Island Republican state chairman William Pelkey whereby the Republicans would ensure passage of Kennedy's legislation in exchange for the Democratic Party's secret compliance with the formation of a bipartisan police commission in Central Falls.

Kennedy later explained that, when introduced to Hamilton and the idea, he was "dumbfounded ... [at] hearing such a proposition coming from a Democratic leader" and refused to become involved at first. Kennedy predicted, correctly, as it turned out, that this move would cut short his political career. But he acquiesced when McGrath and Hamilton promised him an appointment on the newly created commission. Based on the word of McGrath and Hamilton, Kennedy agreed to introduce the Police Commission Bill as well. Although sentiment against that bill ran high in Democratic wards, it was passed in February by a vote of 52 to 42.[6]

The Police Commission Bill, an amended version of a previous act, granted the governor power to "appoint, remove for cause and control the chief of police." It stipulated that a board should be created and that it should have three members, "no more than two of whom shall be members of the same political party." The act further directed the governor to appoint the three members within ten days after the bill's passage. The mayor must also designate one of the three as chairman. According to section two, no member of the commission "shall be removed without cause and without an opportunity to be heard in his own defense." This section became particularly relevant as events unfolded, since the party that controlled the governorship controlled the police department, and whoever directed the department would reap a significant profit from the liberal flow of moonshine.[7]

In supporting the state-run police commission in Central Falls, McGrath and his co-conspirators laid the groundwork for the illegal flow of bootleg whiskey throughout the Blackstone Valley, and in an instant struck a blow at home rule by placing the city's police force under the control of a handpicked, state-run organization. Thus, they undermined a major cornerstone of the Democratic Party: home rule, which guaranteed cities and towns a level of independence from the state organization, whether Democrat or Republican.

Upon passage of the bill in 1931, notorious bootlegger James Lavell and local Republican boss Andrew Sherry took control of the newly established police commission, whose three commissioners would serve at their command. In essence, the Blackstone Valley was reduced to a den of iniquity. On the political stage, Lavell and Sherry organized a "Franco-Polish" bloc, aimed primarily at toppling the domination of native Protestant blue bloods in the GOP. They influenced a number of Rhode Island Republicans and a faction of Democrats who were incensed by the encroachment of the national government in city and state liquor traffic.[8]

J. Howard McGrath's role in this scandal revealed an abandonment of party principles, and a move, albeit unknowingly, toward establishing the political state. To discerning observers and critics of the state organization, like Colonel Patrick H. Quinn and future judge Francis B. Condon, he had sacrificed the ideals fought for by leading Democrats for the sake of power.

Republican governor Norman Case reluctantly signed the measure in early March, and, as planned, sent three names, including Kennedy's, to the Senate for confirmation. Following the bill's passage, Senator Joseph Cadorette, McGrath's father-in-law, contacted the governor and urged him to seriously consider Kennedy for membership on the commission.[9] According to his later interview with the *Journal,* Case claimed that he named Kennedy only after he was assured that the remaining two members would show "favor or privilege to no one."[10]

Opposition immediately emerged from state and local Democrats; the most strident emanating from Colonel Patrick Quinn and Congressman Francis B. Condon, an ally of Thomas McCoy. Quinn, who resented Gerry's financial and political dominance in state ranks, publicly criticized Hamilton's methods as "entirely foreign to Rhode Island." Stating that the police commission in Central Falls had "a very suspicious appearance," Quinn suspected that Hamilton had conspired with Lavell.[11]

On McGrath, Quinn was more conciliatory, believing that "this young man" was used by Hamilton to mask his behind-the-scenes machinations with Lavell, Sherry, and Republican William Pelkey. McGrath resented the implication, and retorted, "I respect his age and experience, but I despise the numerous attempts to use his position to the party's detriment."[12]

In a subsequent meeting of Democratic notables at the Narragansett Hotel in late 1931, Quinn went so far as to accuse Hamilton of conspiring with members of the Ku Klux Klan. These accusations outraged Senator Peter Gerry, Hamilton's most ardent supporter. Despite harsh words and political volleying with Gerry and his lieutenants throughout the year, Quinn allegedly fell in line with the party when his nephew, "Fighting Bob" Quinn, was placed on the state ticket as lieutenant governor in 1932. The Green/Quinn combination would make for some equally lively copy during the mid–1930s, including their roles in the famous "Bloodless Revolution" of 1935.[13]

The other formidable opposition emerged from the Condon/McCoy bloc. Francis Condon cautioned Kennedy to table the bill, lest the Central Falls representative be ostracized from the party. Kennedy's refusal upset Condon, who rallied Democrats in the General Assembly to oppose the police commission measure as "subversive of home rule." Unnerved by the protest, Kennedy showed McGrath the letter from Condon advising Kennedy to table the bill. In response, McGrath snapped, "To hell with Condon. We will take care of him later."[14] Kennedy was surprised at this reaction, knowing that he could ill afford to be so cavalier, since he did not have powerful backers. As a minor appendage to the party, he feared, quite rightly, that he would ultimately serve as an unwilling scapegoat. Not trusting McGrath's and Hamilton's assurances that he would not be thrown out of the party, he threatened to reveal the origins of the bill should political harm come to him.[15]

However, Kennedy was appointed to the commission as promised, and he was able to provide the Democratic and Republican conspirators with the results they desired. Within a month, Kennedy succeeded in persuading one of the other commissioners, Republican George MacKenzie, to support Lavell's bootleg interests by dismissing police officers who refused to submit to Sherry's will. Police Chief Joseph A. Chaput was among the first casualties.[16]

Shortly after the bill's passage, the *Providence Journal* sent two reporters to assess the situation in Central Falls. They were able to see firsthand the results of Kennedy's efforts. According to the study, grave inequities were apparent in the commission's handling of liquor violators. While Sherry's "Moonshine Valley" was "wide open," other saloons were either restricted to beer or deemed inoperative. In the moonshine district, Lavell's cohorts continued to enjoy pecuniary success as "legitimate" businessmen under the sympathetic watch of the new police chief, George Collette. Meanwhile, curious construction commenced in nearby Pawtucket where the old Hand Brewery, bought at an auction in 1929 by James Lavell's son-in-law J. Clifden O'Reilly, was remodeled as the Rhode Island Brewing Company.[17]

McGrath denied complicity in the scandal: "While it is not my duty to speak for *The News-Tribune*, it is, nevertheless, fitting that I should place in proper light, those men and institutions which, I know, have as their sole objective the triumph of Democratic principles…. The *News-Tribune* has condemned in no uncertain terms the passage of the police commission bill."[18]

After the commission's removal of Chaput as police chief, Case incurred severe criticism from Democrats and Republicans alike for initially signing the bill and appointing the commission. Therefore, in June of 1931, he authorized the superintendent of the State Police to look into the problem in Central Falls. Superintendent Everitte St. John Chaffee's report convinced Case to remove MacKenzie and Kennedy, name a new commission, and reinstate

Chaput. By that time, however, McGrath and Hamilton had achieved the political inroad into the Blackstone Valley that was their initial goal. McGrath had been elected city solicitor of Central Falls.[19] This episode represented a nadir for the party and left bitter feelings among party regulars who feared that the rift caused by the police commission plot would destroy any chances of unity among the Democratic factions.

In November 1932, Green was elected governor, and McGrath abandoned his promise to return Kennedy to the commission. He allegedly told Kennedy that he "did all that he could" but "he [Green] wouldn't listen to me."[20] Embittered and disheartened, Kennedy confessed his story to the *Providence Journal*. Knowing the *Journal*'s penchant for gossip against the Democrats, Kennedy hoped to smear those who had betrayed him. However, even with the respected testimony of Governor Case to substantiate his story, Kennedy's confession was overshadowed by the Green administration's proposal to dismantle the commission, regardless of its origins. He argued that Rhode Island was not ready for the more centralized government that the police commission represented.

Green's supporters urged the new governor to wash his hands of the controversy by abandoning Gerry and his lieutenants. However, Green chose not to alienate a strong source of his power. Thus, he stood firmly behind McGrath and Mayor Cadorette, while simultaneously denying his own participation in the scandal. When pressed by *Journal* reporters for a comment on whether or not McGrath approached him about appointing Kennedy, Green replied, "The fact speaks for itself that I did not appoint Kennedy."[21]

At the time of Kennedy's death in 1939, his exposè had been the highlight of his career, and revealed the lengths that the Democratic machine, especially Hamilton and his protégé McGrath would go to secure their desired goals. As a pawn of the Central Falls political hierarchy, Kennedy was easily expendable while McGrath appeared to escape relatively unscathed and, in fact, was promoted from Central Falls city solicitor to United States district attorney for the state of Rhode Island in 1934.

Green named a new commission in April 1933, while pledging to end corruption in Central Falls and return cities and towns to "home rule." As the newly elected governor, Green was able to soothe ruffled feathers by doling out patronage to his most vocal critics, a skill he would use to hoist McGrath's career many times during the succeeding years.

By the following January, Green had emerged the hero, by fulfilling his promise to disband the commission. Thus, home rule returned to Central Falls in April of 1934, and the police force came under the direct control of the city council.[22] Now, Democratic leaders focused on the repeal of Prohibition and on recovering from the economic hardship caused by the Great Depression.

In the final analysis, passage of the Police Commission Bill in Central Falls was a means to an end. Although the legislation violated home rule and revealed an abandonment of Democratic principles on the part of its participants, it did not permanently damage the gains made by the Democratic Party during the 1920s and 1930s. It did, however, signal an attempt to move toward a more centralized bureaucracy, with paltry results. To his credit, Green's effective leadership, his appeasement of the contentious factions of his party, and his association with a strong, winning Democratic ticket nationally saved his party from unraveling after Kennedy revealed the plot in December 1933. In the end, the hapless Kennedy was the only real loser.

Viewed from a different lens, however, the real pawn may, in fact, have been McGrath. Recognizing the young man's hunger for a position in the inner circle of the state organization, Hamilton used McGrath to gain a foothold into the Blackstone Valley. Nonetheless, McGrath's volatile reaction to noncompliant Democrats on the state and local level and his complicity in the police commission scandal showed the young politician that he could outmaneuver his enemies to achieve the ultimate prize: wealth and power. By latching onto Governor Green and slowly distancing himself from Hamilton and Gerry, McGrath would learn to be more circumspect. Thanks to Green's maneuvering, he soon secured the position of United States district attorney for the state.

Rhode Island Democrats: State and National Election, 1932

The national political campaign and determination to repeal Prohibition combined to overshadow the controversy surrounding the police commission. Rhode Island Democrats publicly pledged support for the candidacy of Al Smith in 1932, but party leaders, especially Theodore Francis Green and later J. Howard McGrath, began to detect waning interest in the "Happy Warrior." The potential rift caused by this shift in allegiance threatened to divide the two leading Democrats of the Providence coalition: Peter Gerry, an avowed Smith supporter, and Theodore Francis Green, who moved steadily toward the dynamic candidacy of Franklin Delano Roosevelt.

In 1928, Rhode Islanders were energized by the former governor of New York. By identifying Prohibition with the plight of the immigrant, Smith had been able to build a solid base in the state. Although Smith's bid in 1928 failed to win him the presidency, it succeeded in forging a bond among the several ethnic groups in the state who came out to support him. Early Democratic and some Republican reformers opposed Prohibition because they believed that the Constitution should protect the rights of sovereign states against a dominant federal government. Most Rhode Island legislators fought long and hard to overturn the Eighteenth Amendment.

Four years later, Al Smith had worn out his welcome. His poor education, Tammany roots, and devastating defeat against Hoover would prove too great a liability in 1932. While Rhode Island Democrats, led by McGrath, endorsed Al Smith at the Democratic National Convention in Chicago that July, reformers like Green began a strategic move to disengage from the Smith candidacy.

As state chairman, McGrath had publicly led a coalition of Democrats to encourage local cities and towns to form "Smith Clubs," but by 1932 he also privately began to express doubts about the "Warrior's" ability to win in November. Roosevelt publicly accepted Rhode Island's support of Smith at the National Convention, but behind the scenes he made a concerted effort to court the state's party men. Gerry, who had been defeated in the Senate race in 1930, denied the rumor that "my friends and myself have assured Mr. Louis Howe, political secretary to Gov. Franklin D. Roosevelt, that the Rhode Island delegates to the Democratic National Convention, although outwardly for ex-Gov. Alfred E. Smith, would 'be for Roosevelt in spirit.'"[23]

By that May, Gerry, along with J. Howard McGrath and 12 other delegates or alternates to the Democratic National Convention, which would be held in Chicago, pledged their support for Smith. Just as Gerry feared, however, Green and McGrath secretly began working on behalf of Roosevelt.[24] Roosevelt, visiting in July 1932, took Rhode Island's Democratic leaders, including McGrath, sailing along the waters around Stonington, Connecticut, and posed for pictures with them.[25] Rhode Island's loyalty to Smith was "understandable," he said, but as the Democratic nominee he had every faith that Rhode Island would shift its allegiance to him. Convinced that Roosevelt would lead the nation out of the Depression and Rhode Island Democrats to solid victory, Green moved the party behind Roosevelt, encouraging McGrath to follow suit. This move threatened the Green-Gerry coalition, since the latter's ties to Smith preceded his move to Rhode Island. Gerry refused at first to transfer allegiance to Governor Roosevelt, and, despite his eventual acquiescence, he maintained an animosity toward Roosevelt throughout his life.[26]

Roosevelt, however, was slow to authorize a "wet" platform. Unlike Smith, who, under the direction of the rabidly anti–Prohibitionist Democratic National Chairman John Raskob, pushed exclusively for repeal, Roosevelt waited to announce his position on the matter.[27] In Chicago, however, FDR realized that sidestepping the issue would be political suicide, so on June 29 he emphatically declared, "This convention wants repeal; your candidate wants repeal."[28] This decision, coupled with his new economic recovery program, won over Rhode Island Democrats in 1932, completing the shift that had taken place within the Democratic Party in Rhode Island over the last

State Chairman J. Howard McGrath was instrumental in the shift of Rhode Island Democrats from Al Smith to Governor Franklin Delano Roosevelt. Here he is (left) with the presidential nominee onboard Roosevelt's yacht, the *Myth II*, Stonington, Connecticut, July 12, 1932 (courtesy Special and Archival Collections, Providence College).

four years.[29] The Party, under Green's adroit counsel, focused on national recovery and repeal, rather than on local bickering and bootlegging.[30]

This period was witness to a personal transformation for McGrath, as well. Following Green's example, McGrath gradually moved closer to Roosevelt. To the *News-Tribune*, he responded to Roosevelt's victory by explaining that "we Rhode Islanders felt a debt of gratitude to Gov. Smith…. We always looked on Gov. Roosevelt as our second choice."[31] Although McGrath always remained publicly loyal to Gerry, he saw that Green's ability to mollify the opposition could prove more beneficial in the long run. Gerry was often recalcitrant and remote. Photographs of Gerry reveal his uneasy relationship with the public. Always maintaining distance and unable to compromise on matters of patronage, he failed to communicate effectively with his constituency and was unsuccessful at uniting them during this most crucial period in the party's history.

According to Erwin L. Levine, Green was neither bold nor innovative, but instead "came to epitomize the loyal, dependable northern Democrat.

Moreover, he evinced a loyalty to President Roosevelt and his programs—later largely transferred to President Truman—that was at least unusual, if not unique, in a congressman or senator." The same would later be said of J. Howard McGrath.[32]

Because Rhode Islanders supported a "wet" plank, Green inserted a clause into the Democratic state platform advocating repeal.[33] As far back as March 1931, Rhode Island legislators in the lower house had voted against the Eighteenth Amendment, 88 to 1. A year later they shot down the "Baby Volstead," or Sherwood Act, which had been signed into law in 1922. Named for Republican senator Herbert Montague Sherwood of Providence, the bill permitted the consumption of beer with 3 percent alcoholic content and authorized Rhode Island law enforcement officials to prosecute those in violation of the prohibition amendment.[34]

As Democratic state chairman, McGrath endorsed the state platform, which was based on the previous generation's Progressive reform. The Rhode Island Democratic manifesto emphasized the regulation of hours for women and children, reform of the workmen's compensation law, the creation of a state fund for emergencies, the prohibition of yellow dog contracts, and, most importantly, the repeal of the Eighteenth Amendment to the U.S. Constitution. Specifically included in that legislation was a bill to amend the Volstead Act to allow the sale of beer and wine.[35]

When Green became governor, he brought Robert Quinn on as lieutenant governor. Although Italian American supporters of former Democratic state chairman Luigi DePasquale initially balked at Green's election, they rallied behind him when he appointed the Italian American judge of the Sixth District Court. To further appease the Italian coalition, Green named Louis Cappelli secretary of state. Like the Republicans before him, Green and the Democrats practiced "recognition politics" or key placement of candidates of diverse ethnic origins to smooth party rivalries.

The governor then negotiated with Cranston Republican Senate majority leader Harry Bodwell for a bipartisan commission to look into the control of licenses once the liquor ban had been lifted. Along with four other distinguished members of their respective parties, Green chose J McGrath, former conspirator in the police commission scandal, as one of the members of the body.[36] In effect, by standing behind his man, Green effectively played down opposition and moved his party to more constructive endeavors.[37]

In the January 1933 session of the General Assembly, a process was established to choose delegates for a state ratifying convention. Candidates for the convention were required to declare their position on the repeal of Prohibition before their eligibility could be determined. After representative town clerks and canvassers recorded the list of candidates, a special election was held. By May 1933, the process was completed and 31 delegates unanimously approved of the Twenty-First Amendment to the U.S. Constitution. As one of two states that had initially opposed the Eighteenth Amendment, Rhode Island took the lead in supporting its repeal, the third state to do so after Michigan and Wisconsin. As acting chairman of the ratifying convention, Governor Green reminded his constituency that by supporting the Twenty-First Amendment, Rhode Islanders showed a deep and abiding understanding and faith in the true meaning of the United States Constitution.[38]

Attorney General Homer S. Cummings responded to a need to replace Henry M. Boss, the Rhode Island district attorney, with a candidate more in line with President Roosevelt's New Deal. As rumors emerged stating that J. Howard McGrath would be appointed, the young Democratic state chairman replied that he had "not made up my mind as to whether I shall be a candidate for this position or not." He said that if he was officially offered the post, he would "think seriously about it."[39] As Democratic state chairman, McGrath oversaw the rise of the party, but he also presided over one of the most contentious periods in Rhode Island Democratic Party history.

The shift from state support of Al Smith to Franklin Delano Roosevelt coincided with the rise of Green over Gerry. For McGrath, this swing in the state's allegiance had profound repercussions for his political future. Strategically and skillfully moving from Smith to FDR, and from Gerry to Green, McGrath secured his path to success. Gerry's organization had served him well, but it was time to move on.

Never renouncing Senator Gerry publicly, McGrath eventually accepted Green's request to serve as his law partner. When in 1936, Green trounced his opponent, veteran Republican Jesse H. Metcalf, by a vote of 149,146 to 136,149 for a Senate seat, McGrath took on the role as landlord for their law office, managing the finances and working with Green's astute Executive Secretary Eddie Higgins to develop and strengthen financial and political ties while the senator was in Washington.[40]

As United States district attorney, McGrath would find himself taking a role in several high-profile decisions, including the Fall River Robbery in 1935, which implicated infamous gangster Carl Rettich and his gang; the fight over the Narragansett Race Track, which pitted Governor Robert Quinn against Walter O'Hara; and the wiretapping case, which cast aspersions upon the reputation of Republican governor William Henry Vanderbilt, contributing to McGrath's ticket to the top. Yet, as Green biographer Erwin Levine astutely observed, that "despite his Federal position as United States Attorney, [McGrath] continued to mastermind many of the Democratic moves in 1934."[41] Other than the legendary Bloodless Revolution, however, Levine was silent on the nature of McGrath's "Democratic moves."

4

Murder and Mayhem
in New England

On May 2, 1935, an article appeared in the *Boston Traveler* that compared the careers of two professionals: the first was James Howard McGrath, representative of moral certitude and industry, a model citizen by all outward appearances. Extolling the virtues of this industrious youth, the article described McGrath's brief, though impressive, career. Named his state's district attorney less than a year earlier, the "small, trim, quiet-spoken" young man was fast becoming a political phenomenon.[1] First elected city solicitor of ethnically diverse Central Falls in 1931, McGrath, according to the *Traveler,* had already proven himself an able attorney and politician.

Carl Emil Rettich, the second, was an archetypal felon "with the best of his life behind him." Unlike McGrath, Rettich had been drawn into a web of intrigue and murder when he, at the tender age of seventeen, overheard a plot to kill New York wholesale poultry dealer Barnet Baff in November 1914. Lured into the seamy "Jewish underworld," which dominated "some 80 percent of the live poultry moved to market" and 90 percent of the "supply chain" in the New York metropolitan area, Rettich earned the reputation as a crafty, though reliable, felon after he refused to reveal the identity of Baff's murderers.[2]

Implicated in the slaying of New Jersey bootlegger Frank D'Agostino in 1924, Rettich amassed a fortune in the trade of illegal liquor during the heyday of Prohibition. With the passage of the Twenty-First Ammendment in 1933, repealing the Eighteenth, Rettich continued to manufacture and sell home-grown spirits, and, with accomplices George and David Press, commanded a fleet of five trucks and four automobiles, which transported liquor throughout the Northeast.[3]

After appearing frequently in editions of the nation's leading newspapers from April to July 1935, Rettich would eventually spend the next fifteen years behind bars.

But the enigmatic Rettich, who captured the imagination of Rhode

Islanders, contributed greatly, albeit unwittingly, to the success of young J. Howard McGrath.

This chapter will chronicle McGrath's relentless pursuit of Carl Rettich and his accomplices following the robbery of the United States mail truck in Fall River, Massachusetts, in January 1935 and the murder of gang member Andino Merola that April. The case would link the New England and New York crime syndicates through the activities of New Jersey–born Rettich, whose foray into liquor trafficking had led him to Rhode Island to partner with the infamous bootlegger Danny "the Gentleman Farmer" Walsh. Rettich is presumed to have murdered Walsh in February 1933.[4]

McGrath was one of two federal prosecutors. The other was Francis Ford, who would later earn fame as prosecutor in *United States v. Dr. Spock* at the height of the Vietnam War. McGrath and Ford had as their goal to prove that (a) Carl Rettich carefully planned and executed the Fall River heist in January, (b) he ordered the murder of Andino Merola the following April, and (c) he was responsible for the slaying of Danny Walsh, and other unsolved murders, namely, the torture and killing of "Legs" Carella, found the previous year in an alley in Foxboro, Massachusetts, Ray Hacking, and John Capara, also discovered in 1934.[5]

Historians have attributed the rise in criminal activity in the 1920s and 1930s to the ratification of the Eighteenth Amendment to the United States Constitution on January 16, 1919. McGrath, in a speech a year later, would concur. In 1936, District Attorney McGrath blamed "the basis of the wake of crime and racketeering" on "the 18th Amendment and its accompanying Prohibition laws of the several states."[6]

The Eighteenth Amendment, and the subsequent Volstead Act,[7] the latter passed on October 28, 1919, hit the Northeast hard, especially Rhode Island, reputedly the "wettest" state in the Union. Coupled with a new, restless breed of criminal, who had returned from the First World War trained in the effective use of firearms, the aftermath of the amendment set off a crime revolution in New England.

Disregard for the law ran rampant in New England cities in the decade following the passage of Prohibition. With numerous accessible inlets on both the western and eastern shores of Narragansett Bay, Rhode Island offered bootleggers a natural setting to smuggle moonshine in and out of the state. For criminals like Carl Rettich, already on the run from authorities in his home base in New York, the move to Rhode Island was an ideal alternative to the fast-paced, competitive mid–Atlantic. In the smallest state of the union, Rettich could more easily become an undisputed underworld leader.

The blurred division between law enforcement and law breaker in Rhode Island at this time has already been noted in chapters 3 and 4; the failure of the police commission movement, the unwritten alliances among bootleggers, corruptible law enforcement agents, and elected officials, and the concurrent Prohibition repeal did little to discourage crime in the state. As rum and prostitution rings flourished during the Depression, Rhode Island developed an unsavory reputation that drew some nefarious characters to its borders. As McGrath observed in his 1936 address, "for years the criminal element took refuge in the fact that the criminal machinery of the Federal government was ineffective to cope with them."[8] Following the lead of other officials, McGrath demanded a more centralized, transparent machinery to confront society's indifference to law enforcement.

Less than a year after Roosevelt's appointment of McGrath as United States district attorney on January 24, 1934, and only a month before the mail truck robbery, Attorney General Homer Cummings held an important conference on crime in America. The conference opened on December 10, 1934, at Memorial Continental Hall in Washington, D.C. Former secretary of war Patrick J. Hurley, the Reception Committee chairman, set forth the "purpose" of the gathering: to establish "effective cooperation in the sphere of crime prevention and criminal law enforcement among the federal, state and local governments, as well as the effective assistance of all agencies, official and otherwise, which can participate in a sustained national movement to deal with the crime menace."[9]

The crime conference raised pressing issues. The first was how to streamline and centralize prosecution of criminal activity; the second was articulated by Secretary of State Henry Stimson, who warned that crime must be "strip[ped] ... of its false glamour"; and the third was that law enforcement agents must be prepared for the increasing sophistication of crime.[10]

No case was more representative of these points than the prosecution of Carl Rettich and his gang. Bringing together local, state, and federal officials, the case illustrated a successful merger of agencies at each level of the federal infrastructure. President Roosevelt reiterated these concerns, and in turn set forth the raison d'être for the gathering: to centralize the present haphazard organization of criminal prosecution and to educate the public on the need for a more streamlined system of administering the law.[11]

In calling the meeting, Cummings laid the groundwork for the expansion of federal control to counter the rampant criminal activity that had overtaken the country. The Rettich case was one of many examples of such lawlessness. Nonetheless, this case stands apart from others in that it precipitated the transformation of Rhode Island and Eastern Massachusetts from a decentralized, burgeoning crime lab, to a center of law enforcement.

In keeping with this sentiment, the federal crime package, proposed by President Franklin Delano Roosevelt, included laws to grant the federal government authority to capture fugitives from justice, to levy excise taxes on machine guns, sawed-off shotguns, and rifles, and, most importantly, to amend the so-called Lindbergh Law (the Federal Kidnapping Act of 1932), which made the transport of individuals across state lines a federal crime. This new bill would give the Federal Bureau of Investigation jurisdiction to intervene in kidnapping cases following a one-week waiting period. The penalty for such a crime was death.[12]

Underworld figures like "Baby Face" Nelson and John Dillinger rose to national prominence during this period and served to "excite atavistic emotions" among the country's more impressionable youth, who became fascinated with the exploits of these larger-than-life antiheroes. At the height of the Great Depression, American society, he observed, had "become sentimental over crime to a dangerous degree."[13]

Another rising star, John Edgar Hoover earned a solid reputation during Prohibition's heyday. Hoover, whose ambition dwarfed McGrath's, warned his audience, "We are no longer" confronted "with a low ignorant element … these criminals approach their work with studious care." He therefore urged the federal government to meet the new threat with careful study. "It must be remembered that the school systems of America are open to all, and that education is free and compulsory to a degree which a few generations ago was regarded as a high standard of learning." Hoover, who would become the director of the newly established Federal Bureau of Investigation in 1935, had convinced Attorney General Cummings that this separate unit was essential to confront the more sophisticated methods of lawlessness.[14]

Praising Cummings for his support of the Federal Bureau, he stated, "through his unremitting efforts before Congress," Cummings "made it possible for this Bureau to be backed by laws with strong teeth in them."[15] Several "G-men" from the embryonic agency, under Marshal William Gaucher, brother-in-law to vaudevillian Eddie Dowling, were instrumental in the capture of Rettich and his gang in Rhode Island.

McGrath proved to be a fitting representative of the new legal officer prototype: proactive, energetic, and relentless in the pursuit of justice as outlined in the celebrated Cummings conference. McGrath's appointment also illustrated the merger of machine politics and criminal prosecution, in this case, enhancing the reputation of the Democratic Party. For McGrath, good politicking and pandering to high profile superiors would be the ticket to fame and fortune.

As United States district attorney, McGrath set as his goal the successful closure of several unsolved criminal cases, including, but not limited to, the disappearance of Danny Walsh, the "Gentleman Bootlegger" of Charlestown, Rhode Island, in February 1933. Walsh, one of the notorious "Big Seven," the "bootleg syndicate" whose members included Johnny Torrio, head of the Chicago mob territory, vied for control of the entire Northeast.[16] In an assertion to the press on April 27, following Massachusetts and Rhode Island law enforcement officials' search of the Crime Castle, McGrath speculated,

> I wouldn't be at all surprised if that [the basement of the Crime Castle] was the place that Danny Walsh was killed.... He was an intimate friend of Carl Rettich.... Rettich was one of the last men to have been seen with him. I also believe that had this place been found soon after the disappearance of Walsh, the dragging of Green-wich Bay, which extends in front of the house might have revealed the body of Walsh.[17]

McGrath was not alone in his rush to judgment. Daily, area newspapers, namely, the *Boston Globe, Boston Traveler, Boston Herald, New York Times,* and *Providence Journal* issued hypotheses from other law enforcement agents linking Rettich or one of his gang members to the unsolved murders.[18]

Nonetheless, McGrath saw in this case a ticket to fame and fortune. His successful prosecution of Rettich would set him up to rise to national office. Federal and state officials, including Rhode Island governor Theodore Francis Green and McGrath as his able protégé, reasoned that McGrath's cooperation with state and local authorities and with the Federal Bureau of Investigation in prosecuting Rettich and his gang would only enhance his reputation, and elevate the political status of Green and by extension the Democratic party during a crucial period in Rhode Island politics. On the verge of a takeover in the General Assembly, the leading Democrats, most notably Green and Lieutenant Governor Robert Quinn, had in the works a plan to topple Repub-lican hegemony in the Rhode Island Senate.

In 1934, Carl Rettich, using the alias Charles Ryerson, moved into a twenty-room estate, formerly the summer residence of Providence Opera House proprietor Felix Wendelschaefer. Purchased by Rettich and business partner George Press in 1928, the mansion had been a prime port for liquor trafficking to and from Boston, New Jersey, and New York during Prohibi-tion.

According to local historian Donald D'Amato, the building was a testa-ment to a bygone era and was said to enhance the property values in the neighborhood. It would serve as a respectable hideout for the notorious Ret-tich/Ryerson, who had moved to the area to care for his elderly father.[19] Located on Greenwich Bay, in an area known as the Warwick Neck section of Rhode Island, the Wendelschaefer estate abutted the Warwick Country Club and stood a short distance from the private home of wealthy senator Peter Goelet Gerry.[20] The mansion's secret rooms would function as storage for contraband stolen during the infamous mail truck robbery of January 23, 1935.

Rettich relocated to Rhode Island at the invitation of "Gentleman" Danny Walsh and, along with his new business partner, brokered several lucrative connections in liquor trafficking along Narragansett Bay. Walsh, an accomplished horseman, owned a large estate on the water in Charlestown, where he maintained several stables. Affable and politically savvy, Walsh hosted high society gatherings and boasted friendships with entertainers, law enforcement agents, and other dignitaries; his popularity was due in part to his talent for quenching their insatiable thirst for illegal spirits.

The introduction of Rettich to the mix was Walsh's undoing. Rettich's arrival in Rhode Island set in motion a tale of intrigue, mayhem, and corruption that struck at the heart of federal and state law enforcement agencies. Rettich saw in Walsh's enterprise both an opportunity to escape his dubious circumstances in New York, where he was under suspicion for the unsolved murder of mobster Frank D'Agostino in 1924, and a chance to reap the benefits of the "Gentleman Farmer's" lucrative market, an enterprise that was the envy of all illicit traders in the Northeast.

Following Walsh's disappearance in 1933, authorities immediately suspected Rettich, who had much to gain from his partner's demise. With Walsh removed, the sly, unscrupulous Rettich could now assume full control of the enterprise. Walsh was seen dining at the Bank Café in East Greenwich in February 1933 with Rettich, two unidentified men in vehicles registered in New York, and another elusive figure, known simply as "Wireless." A ransom note issued shortly following Walsh's disappearance demanded $40,000 for his return. At the hearing that July, a waitress testified that Walsh and Rettich appeared in good spirits, but a second witness disagreed, claiming that the two were engaged in a heated exchange over unpaid bills totaling close to $30,000. According to later testimony, Rettich paid Walsh the $30,000, presumably to settle an outstanding business debt. Police Captain Alfred Stevens of Providence believed Rettich disposed of his gregarious partner to reclaim his money and gain full control of the business. The ledgers, presented to the grand jury by McGrath, revealed that both maintained independent records of each transaction, using initials or code names, indicating a growing unease in their partnership.[21]

As J. Edgar Hoover had observed that previous December in Washington, D.C., the criminal of the twentieth century was no simple outlaw. Rettich, the mastermind of the Fall River mail truck heist, was an example of Hoover's modern bandit: cold, calculating, and meticulous. In October 1934, Rettich ordered small-time bookmaker Andino Merola and pharmacist and gambler Joseph Fisher to chart the course of Herbert B. Reid, employee of Green Brother Trucking Company. They discovered that each morning at 7:45 a.m., Reid dutifully delivered parcels of bills and coin from the United States mail drop at the train station to the BMC Durfee Trust Company two blocks away on North Main Street in Fall River, Massachusetts.

Fisher and Merola secretly stalked Reid, plotting his route to and from the bank each morning. With scrupulous accuracy, they observed Reid's comings and goings, drew a detailed map of the route to the train station, and then returned to Warwick Crime Castle headquarters to report their findings to Rettich. Fisher, however, would soon commit a fatal error. He recruited Providence native and lifelong pal Herbert Hornstein, a 1932 Brown graduate and compulsive gambler, to perform the minutiae necessary for the success of the operation. Desperate for cash and employment, Hornstein convinced Fisher of his willingness to cooperate in the heist.[22]

Merola and Rettich were apprehensive, given the Brown graduate's flimsy criminal record. Hornstein's reputation paled in comparison to the more seasoned members of the gang. Each Rettich associate had proven their mettle; professional New York criminals John "Sonny" McGlone, Charles Harrigan, and "Irish Tommy" Dugan had committed robberies and murders throughout the country, and Providence entrepreneurs Fisher and Merola had stood up for Rettich in the past. In comparison, Hornstein had to his credit a number of unpaid debts and a brief stint in prison for a stolen microscope. Not a very impressive rap sheet for the high-level crime that was about to transpire.

Hornstein never met with Rettich directly, instead receiving his orders through Fisher and Merola. The three plotted a route for the mail truck from the railroad station to Oak Grove Cemetery, located in the exclusive section of Fall River known as The Hill, where they planned to dump the truck and transfer the cash to a stolen Plymouth sedan. The second leg of their journey would begin at the cemetery. Merola would drive the Plymouth to the waterfront, where they would board a boat in dry dock. On November 19, 1934, Fisher directed Hornstein to secure a registration for the Plymouth under the alias "Frederick Powers," license plate number #122823. In the meantime, Hornstein rented a room in the city, hid the stolen vehicle in a pre-appointed garage nearby, and purchased three burlap bags, a brown cap, and blue lumber jackets at small town establishments.[23]

When Fisher learned that Rettich postponed the heist from December 1934 to January 1935 after New York gunman Charles Harrigan had been delayed, he had Hornstein rent a different room at 51 North Main Street, Fall River, from proprietor Mrs. Ida Horovitz, and secured a new set of plates under the alias "Peter Dubois."[24] Fisher apprised Hornstein of the change in plan, which now called for a second "hide truck" to conceal the stolen cash instead of the boat, the owner of which had become suspicious.

With the details of the operation assured, Hornstein agreed to chauffeur Fisher and Merola to the Crime Castle in Warwick, Rhode Island, the headquarters of Carl Rettich, a few days before the heist. Although Hornstein never spoke to Rettich, he observed three New York "gunmen" sitting in Rettich's living room, Dugan, McGlone, and Harrigan, on January 22, the eve of the robbery.

The month of January 1935 experienced some of the coldest days on record in New England. On January 22, the National Weather Bureau warned of impending snow, which began to fall by 8:00 a.m. the following morning.[25] The dipping temperature and bleak conditions that followed, however, did not deter Carl Rettich and his gang of thugs from committing one of the largest crime capers of the decade. On the morning of January 23, 1935, Herbert B. Reid followed his usual course, arriving for work at his usual time and immediately proceeding to the garage where his truck was parked. Employed by the trucking company for the last two years, he had proven himself trustworthy and reliable. Driving to his typical pickup point at the train station, he patiently waited for the Boston and Newport trains, which arrived at 8:17 a.m. according to his later testimony, and, upon securing the five packages of bill and coin from railroad employee Henry F. H. Arnold, he distributed the bags evenly on the tailboard of his truck, and then drove to the front of the BMC Durfee Trust Company, a few blocks away.

Climbing from North Main Street up the incline, he spotted men, possibly four or five, in a black Plymouth sedan. The driver, later identified as Joseph Fisher, pulled up alongside Reid's truck, and swerved to prevent Reid's passage. Ordering Reid to stop, Fisher then directed two of the four robbers, Thomas "Irish Tommy" Dugan and John "Sonny" McGlone, to hijack Reid's vehicle, while he followed in the Plymouth.

When they reached Davol Street, near the waterfront, they forced Reid into the rear of the sedan, bound and gagged him, placed burlap over his head, and taped his eyes shut. They then abandoned the automobile with Reid still tied down, stole the packages of coin and bills, and drove to Somerset, Massachusetts, the next town over from Fall River. When he was confident that his assailants had left, Reid loosened the bandages around his hands, then carefully removed the tape from his eyes and bound feet. Running toward the main road, he discovered the two vehicles: a truck and a sedan. At 8:45 a.m., Reid flagged down motorist Sidney Ainsworth who volunteered to drive him to the North End Police Station.

Fall River police captain William O'Brien, a twenty-eight-year veteran of the force, interrogated Reid at 9:20 a.m., and then sent Reid to the exact location in Somerset where the robbers had left him bound and gagged. O'Brien later investigated the scene himself, and upon inspection of the sedan, discovered a fully loaded .38 caliber Colt revolver. He brought both the weapon and the vehicle to headquarters. He was able to trace the registration for the mail truck, but could not initially identify the Plymouth.

Following the robbery, print media exploded with headlines about the search for the notorious gang members who had boldly robbed the U.S. mail. As if to prove FBI Director Hoover's assertion, the newspapers emphasized the pervasiveness of lawlessness that had plagued the Northeast, stating that the more professional criminal had become more judicious, and the danger more insidious. Newspaper reporters highlighted Rettich and his gang's resourcefulness, describing in great detail Rettich's carefully laid plan, from his gang's painstaking efforts to plot Herbert Reid's steps from pickup to delivery to their success in securing stolen vehicles. Even more astounding and troubling was Carl Rettich's ability to conceal his identity from Warwick police and his unsuspecting neighbors while he conducted illicit activity at the mansion on the banks of East Greenwich Bay. The only clue that January that might possibly identify the thieves came from amateur robber Herbert Hornstein, posing as lodger, Peter Dubois.[26]

After tracing the stolen money to the Federal Reserve Bank in Boston, federal authorities issued an all-points bulletin for the assailants. The *Fall River Herald* reported the activity of acting inspector Joseph Jette, who closely examined the Plymouth sedan for possible clues, but the 11.7 inches of snow that fell between January 23 and 24 stymied the investigation as it buried much of the evidence.

Nonetheless, the *Herald* reported that inspectors, while failing to identify the thieves, were able to account for the Plymouth, which was registered to one "Peter Dubois" of Pawtucket, Rhode Island. They further determined that Dubois had rented a room from Mrs. Ida Horovitz ten days before the robbery. This information would eventually lead them to Herbert Hornstein.

Fisher gave Hornstein $20, and advised him to "take it on the lam." Hornstein complied, first hiding out at the Statler Hotel in Boston. Fisher then paid Hornstein $400, and ordered him to leave Boston.[27] He and Fisher agreed to communicate via Fisher's sister and brother-in-law, Helen and Morris Ruben, of Brighton, Massachusetts.[28] Here, both would commit a fatal error: Fisher, for issuing stolen cash to Hornstein, and Hornstein for carelessly spending the marked currency, as well as later boasting of his role in the robbery.

J. Howard McGrath, only recently appointed United States district attorney by President Franklin Delano Roosevelt, was engaged in pressing political matters that January. As Rettich and his gang prepared for the heist, Governor Theodore Francis Green, Lieutenant Governor Robert "Fighting Bob" Quinn, Mayor Thomas P. McCoy, and McGrath had wrested control of the Rhode Island General Assembly from the Republicans for the first time in the state's history. The historic coup enabled Lieutenant Governor Quinn to push through reform legislation that had been blocked after years of conservative domination.

McGrath was also engaged in other duties related to his role as United States district attorney. Assuming Andino Merola was slain, he and federal "G-men" were closing in on Merola, who had previously been implicated in an illegal gambling ring and burglary of an automobile, among other crimes. Their investigation took a decided turn in late April.[29]

On the morning of April 26, 1935, a break in the robbery finally occurred. As winter turned to spring, the Fall River heist had ceased to be front-page news, with attention instead focused on the opening of Narragansett Parkway in August 1934, which followed the law legalizing pari-mutuel betting. Governor Green's reform program, which brought welcome relief to thousands of Rhode Islanders suffering from the Depression, also interrupted discussion of New England's crime caper.

That April morning, however, the public was again reawakened to the crime, following engineer Otis Swett's discovery of Andino Merola's body slumped over the floor of a Chevrolet sedan parked on the banks of Lake Pearl in Wrentham, Massachusetts. A .38 caliber bullet was lodged in his left temple, and another had pierced his left side. Merola had been dead a few hours when Swett first noticed the parked car.[30]

Theories abounded as to why Merola was murdered. Federal officers speculated that Merola had been pressing Rettich for an equal share of the stolen cash; when none was forthcoming, he confessed his role in the bank robbery to the authorities, prompting Rettich to mark his partner for a gangland hit. The unnamed assailant drove Merola to an area roadhouse, plied him with alcohol, and then "rubbed him out" after they reached Lake Pearl, the ideal "secluded spot" to slay a possible stooge.[31]

The small-time racketeer and bootlegger Andino Merola, Providence, Rhode Island, resident, would accomplish more in death than in life. His corpse and a Chevrolet sedan would serve as clues that tied Merola to Rettich and his gang.[32] Merola's death and the testimony of several key witnesses eventually would implicate Carl Rettich and his gang in the burglary of the Fall River mail truck.

Swett's notification to Wrentham police chief Perlay Dexter set in motion a series of events that led to the capture and conviction of Rettich and his five accomplices in the robbery of the mail truck that previous January. The news media from across the country immediately latched on to the story, and, following interviews with several local, state, and federal officers, theorized that Merola was "the victim of a gangland ride."[33]

At the time of his murder, Merola had already been missing for twenty-four hours, as subsequent testimony from those who either spoke or met with him before his fateful demise revealed; in the few days prior to his death, Andino Merola had come to the dreadful conclusion that he was a marked man. He had appeared optimistic only a few days earlier, according to Providence law enforcement officers, who reported seeing Merola emerge clean-shaven and well manicured from a local barbershop. They also spotted Merola and Rettich in a Providence hotel the night before the murder. But Merola's affable demeanor had changed noticeably by the time he made a frantic call to his wife, just three hours before the shooting.

Following Swett's notification to the police, the body was transported to Foxboro Hospital where medical examiner Dr. Carl Richardson called in a noted specialist, Dr. Timothy Leary of Boston, Massachusetts. Leary concluded that the splattered blood on the front driver's seat, window, and door handles of the vehicle indicated that the body was moved to the rear floor of the automobile following the shooting. By the following week, medical examiners determined that Merola had been drugged with chloral hydrate, and also suffered the effects of advanced alcoholism.[34]

Since Merola and Rettich had been under surveillance for suspected crimes in the area, postal inspector John J. Breslin of Boston, United States district attorney J. Howard McGrath, fifty additional inspectors, Providence and Massachusetts police, and federal "G-men" were able to get a warrant to conduct a massive search at Crime Castle headquarters. Thanks to their combined efforts, especially the work of Lieutenant Ernest F. Stenhouse of the state police, who directed the Crime Castle search, their probe unearthed some startling finds.

After eight hours of tapping walls, and combing each floor carefully, the workers discovered four freshly whitewashed posts, which, when scraped of paint and rust, unearthed a large screw. Turning this screw revealed a stairway that led to a subterranean floor. Armed police combed each room and unearthed $6,000 worth of ammunition, a bulletproof vest, a bootlegging still, and traces of blood—the blood that McGrath falsely claimed to be Walsh's. A few days later, sixteen FERA workers discovered a five-gallon can of nickels and a fourteen-inch thick strong box filled with bills, bringing the grand total of stolen cash discovered to $20,096.85. Accompanied by armed guards, the strong box was taken to the federal building, where police would later match the serial numbers with those of the stolen Fall River currency.[35]

The most notorious gang member, however, was still missing. Rettich's sister and brother-in-law, Mr. and Mrs. Ira Steele, and Rettich's father, Emil, all residents of the Warwick mansion, stated that they had not seen "Carlie" for a few days.

District Attorney McGrath saw in this case an opportunity to earn a solid reputation among legal professionals. Following the initial inspection of the Crime Castle, he and police authorities placed an all-points bulletin for Carl Rettich and Joseph Fisher at noon on April 26. Previously incarcerated for complicity in a botched attempt to build an aerial bomb, which killed his brother in 1934, Fisher had recently been held again for a traffic violation, but upon his release, he was named as a direct assailant in the robbery.

In the meantime, on April 29, 1935, a rainy, somber Monday, former racketeer and human trafficker, thirty-two-year old Andino Merola was lowered to his final resting place at St. Ann's Cemetery in the west end of the state, following a solemn requiem mass, as a soloist, accompanied by a fifteen-piece band, sang "Nearer My Soul to Thee." Not one underworld figure was present at the service, but Providence police were stationed in the heart of Federal Hill as the procession drove from Providence to Cranston, Rhode Island, in order to direct traffic and stand watch for any sightings of known racketeers.[36]

Andino Merola's death was ruled a homicide as a result of a "pistol wound of head." None of the Massachusetts or Rhode Island authorities could verify the exact time and place of his demise, although they suspected Rettich had "put the finger" on him.[37] McGrath would later corroborate the story, and further revealed that the prime suspect in the murder, Carl Rettich, had fled Providence *en route* to New York, shortly after Merola was killed.[38]

The day after Merola's funeral, at 4:45 p.m., Carl Emil Rettich gave himself up, and Rettich's long-time legal counsel, Joseph Fitzpatrick, and J. Howard McGrath boarded a train to New York to retrieve him. Fitzpatrick, who convinced Rettich to give up, had formerly served as United States assistant district attorney for the state of New York. Upon his arrival in Rhode Island, Fitzpatrick fainted, but refused assistance when McGrath tried to call for an ambulance. Rettich, the tough mastermind of the robbery, was reduced to tears at the sight of his friend's collapse. During his initial interrogation, Rettich had to face McGrath without the aid of his fateful ally, a relentless examination that went on until well after midnight.[39] Fitzpatrick's spell inadvertently aided in McGrath's investigation, as Rettich, who presented a strong, cold-hearted public appearance, was now vulnerable before the young McGrath and his team of interrogators. Instead, Fitzpatrick, who was home recuperating, sent his associate Mortimer W. Newton to represent Rettich during the latter's arraignment.[40]

Rettich, telling reporters that he was "innocent of all these charges," coolly informed them that he was happy to return to Rhode Island after a pleasant trip to New York. Within three minutes, Rettich found himself being "grill[ed]" by District Attorney McGrath. Following intensive questioning of Rettich, McGrath contacted Chief Inspector John A. Sullivan of the New York City Police Department and called for the arrest of thirty-five-year-old Charles Harrigan and "Irish Tommy" Dugan, the latter a member of the deadly Dutch Schultz gang. Harrigan was laid up in Mount Sinai Hospital after a barroom brawl on April 12, but was subsequently transported to Rhode Island, along with Dugan, who was nabbed when he paid Harrigan a visit. Dugan, confident of his ability to elude the "coppers," claimed that his only knowledge of the "crime factory" was what he read in the newspapers. In addition to the Fall River robbery, Harrigan and Dugan were implicated in a host of other murders and robberies, including Harrigan's infamous theft of an American Railway Express vehicle in Perth Amboy in October 1934.[41] The well-dressed Dugan, whose rap sheet included eight previous arrests, responded to an interview by *Boston Globe* journalist, saying, "I don't know nothing about anything, see."[42] He denied knowledge of the Fall River robbery and claimed that he could not identify Merola's assailant. Nonetheless, federal officers had also associated Dugan as one of many "bad men" from Manhattan who were complicit in a Brooklyn heist that yielded over $420,000 from an armored car, but not one eyewitness came forward to identify him at the time.[43]

Officials justified the $125,000 bail, the highest to date by the state of Rhode Island, by the magnitude of the crime: "On January 23 Rettich put the life of Herbert B. Reid, driver of mail truck in jeopardy, by the use of loaded pistols, and during said assault did steal registered mail packages containing $129,000." The bail warrant was signed by United States Commissioner Edwin C. Jenney of Boston, and submitted to United States Attorney Francis J. W. Ford, who then expedited the document to prevent Rettich's release on bail and probable flight.

Meanwhile, Governor Theodore Francis Green took advantage of press coverage to cast a shadow on his nemesis, Republican Albert Reurat, by accusing the Warwick police of negligence in allowing rampant criminal activity to continue in the exclusive Warwick Neck cove of East Greenwich Bay. In response, the Warwick Board of Police Commissions met in closed session to determine the alleged complicity of its police department. City Solicitor Joseph W. Grimes represented the police officers.[44]

Ironically, a "police shake up" had occurred a few years earlier in February 1932, as the police chief at the time, Henry J. Ledoux, and the police commissioners spearheaded a campaign to purge the city of "countless speakeasies, dives, and dens of iniquity." The less than satisfactory results, however, precipitated this latest probe of the municipality's law enforcement infrastructure.[45]

Governor Green proposed the abolition of the Board of Police Commissioners and granted the mayor exclusive authority over the police force.[46] The plan was a continuation of the Democratic organization's move to centralize state and local government by eliminating city and town police commissions. The Rettich case provided Green with justification for this move.[47]

After the police "round[ed] up" the Rettich gang, Assistant United States Attorney Joseph J. Hurley of Boston stated that the federal government will arraign them for the alleged kidnapping and killing of Andino Merola, and the Fall River mail truck theft. By employing the Lindbergh Law, which states that assailants who kidnap and murder their victims and then cross state lines are subject to federal prosecution, U.S. District Attorneys Ford and McGrath were confident that they had amassed enough evidence to charge Rettich and his gang. Therefore, they began preparing for the subsequent trial, which took place in the Federal District Court in Boston, Massachusetts.[48]

Undoubtedly, McGrath also saw another ticket to fame as this case generated much media attention.

Impounded evidence included a diamond bracelet, appraised at $2,500, a wristwatch and a man's diamond ring, worth $600 and $400, respectively. Hidden in a strong box, the jewelry matched items sold at the Magnolia Branch of the Hodgson Kennard Company in Boston, Massachusetts, which was robbed on July 6, 1934.[49]

Before the trial commenced, Judge Hugh B. McLellan and the jury traveled to Fall River to retrace the steps of the crime.[50]

On the heels of Hornstein's detailed confession, Ira Steele's taut narrative, and Joseph Fisher's impassioned admission of guilt after his original plea of not guilty, Rettich's testimony seemed flimsy. Claiming that he was ignorant of the robbery until after the fact, he also maintained that he never saw the strong box filled with money whose serial numbers matched those stolen by the robbers, until District Attorney Ford, in his cross-examination, forced Rettich to recant and admit ownership of the box. When asked about his relationship with Merola, Rettich stated that he met with him "a number of times" in March and April, the last time "at the Biltmore in [his] room" at approximately 3:00 p.m. Later that same day, Joseph Fisher claimed that he "committed" the crime "by himself." Fisher also accused the driver of exaggerating the crime, stating that Herbert Reid "ma[de] it [the mail truck robbery] look like a real hold-up."[51]

District Attorney Ford prosecuted the case, detailing the part played by each assailant. Ira Steele, Rettich's brother-in-law and caretaker of the Crime Castle property, implicated the gang for the Fall River robbery, stating that he saw Merola, McGlone, Harrigan, Dugan, Rettich, and "two other men" at the Crime Castle the night before the heist.

According to Joseph Fisher, Merola received $30,000 of the $129,000, and the two allegedly hid the money on the grounds of Rettich's property in an attempt to unload the evidence. He also allegedly buried the can of nickels since "it was suspicious to have them on your person at that time."[52]

Counsel for the defense William Scharton attempted to appeal to the jury's emotions by directing their attention not to Rettich, Fisher, or the hitmen, but to Herbert Hornstein, the "rat." In an impassioned indictment, Scharton cried, "Christ had his Judas. The United States had its Benedict Arnold, and Fisher had his Hornstein."[53]

In the end, despite the histrionics exhibited by Fitzpatrick and Scharton on behalf of their clients, they were unable to secure a retrial, and Rettich, McGlone, Fisher, Dugan, and Harrigan were each sentenced to twenty-five years in a federal penitentiary. Rettich's hold over his public did not end with his confinement, however. While in East Cambridge, a prison guard was accused of spending "an unnecessarily long period of time" talking with Rettich.

This, coupled with rumors of a prison break, led the "G-men," Massachusetts state police, and United States deputy marshals to guard the jail particularly closely, but no break was attempted.

Rettich was transported to the Atlanta State Penitentiary on July 22 and moved to the newly constructed maximum-security prison at Alcatraz in October, where he remained until 1943, at which time he was transferred to Leavenworth, Kansas.

On July 11, the *News Tribune* extended its congratulations to the government for its "victory in the trial of Carl Rettich and his subordinate gangsters," singling out U.S. district attorney J. Howard McGrath, Postal Inspectors John J. Breslin, Thomas P. Cronin, and Benjamin G. Hadfield, the chiefs of police, and U.S. attorney Francis J. W. Ford, the latter who is said to have "directed the court-room climax with flawless skill." In the final analysis, they wrote, "a group of bad men [were] going to jail because they foolishly thought they could beat this tireless opposition."[54] Writing five years later, after McGrath announced his decision to resign as United States District Attorney, to campaign for Governor, Postal Inspector James Breslin commented, "I shall never forget your personal interest and hearty cooperation in the famous 'Rettich' Case.... I do feel that without that personal interest that you manifested and the cooperation which you extended, we might have failed in our efforts to bring to justice the criminals who were responsible for that heinous crime."[55]

The celebrated trial of Carl Emil Rettich and his accomplices did not directly affect the political scene in Rhode Island, but Rettich's incarceration was proof enough for Rhode Island that the Democratic Party would be successful in protecting them from the evils of gangland murder and robbery.

As for Rettich, he managed to convince his jailers of his transformation. Deemed thoroughly rehabilitated, he was released at 9:00 a.m. on May 1, 1950, nearly a decade earlier than his sentence mandated. Upon thorough evaluation, the warden judged Carl Emil Rettich physically and psychologically sound and no longer a threat to society.[56]

The "brains" of the Fall River mail heist, with an IQ of 85, lived with his wife in Tampa, Florida, until his death in 1973.[57]

J. Howard McGrath's promising career received a welcome boost from the Carl Rettich case, and he would time and again refer to Rhode Island's role in successfully capturing and convicting the notorious gangster. Still, criminal activity in Rhode Island did not end with Rettich's confinement. While McGrath, Ford, and the FBI investigators were able to prove that Rettich masterminded the Fall River robbery, they failed to implicate him in the murders of Merola, Walsh, Carrella, and the others. In fact, although recent evidence had provided hope to Rhode Island police that the unsolved murder of "Gentleman Farmer" Danny Walsh had been solved, to date, the identity of the murderer(s) has yet to be found.[58]

Additionally, illegal gambling flourished in the state, despite the celebrated and legal opening of the Narragansett Race Track in 1934. This second chapter in the uneasy alliance between legal and political interests would continue unabated; United States district attorney McGrath would play an important, though perhaps less public, role in the so-called "Race Track War" in 1937.

Fast Track vs. Race Track

Fresh from his success in prosecuting Carl Rettich and his gang for the Fall River post office heist in 1935, J. Howard McGrath found himself a secondary, though significant, character in another scandal-ridden chapter of Rhode Island history. Governor "Fighting Bob" Quinn, the feisty, pugnacious leader of the Pawtuxet Valley faction of the Democratic Party, and Walter E. O'Hara, the corrupt proprietor of the Narragansett Race Track, went toe-to-toe in a public stand-off throughout the better part of 1937 for control of the Blackstone Valley.

One year later, in response to the election in November 1938, Democratic National Chairman James Farley wrote the state organizations requesting an overall assessment of local conditions. Concerned about the party's situation in Rhode Island, Farley wondered whether Rhode Islanders had repudiated the New Deal. United States district attorney J. Howard McGrath assured Farley that his state was safely behind the president's economic plan, and instead blamed the Democrats' defeat almost exclusively on the Race Track War, despite Republican protestations to the contrary.[1]

Many contemporaries supported McGrath's appraisal of the Quinn-O'Hara fight; he had publicly stated to reporters of the *Providence Journal* what others had only privately admitted to Chairman Farley: the Democratic loss in Rhode Island was primarily due to Governor Quinn's extreme response to O'Hara. According to McGrath, this setback was temporary and would easily be rectified in the next election. As it turned out, McGrath was wrong in one instance. Governor Quinn would lose in his bid for reelection in November 1938.

A close analysis of events surrounding the Race Track War, however, reveals a slightly different interpretation of the dispute than the one offered by Green and McGrath. By focusing on the entertaining standoff between O'Hara and Quinn, scholars have inadvertently overlooked the other legal battles that ensued behind the scenes.[2] In the local arena, Quinn and O'Hara had forced leading business and political notables of the day to take a stand:

either support Governor Quinn in his campaign to rid Rhode Island of its gambling enterprise or rally behind O'Hara, whose controversial reputation and contentious behavior threatened the stability of the state. According to Green's report to Farley, Quinn's vendetta against O'Hara and his determination to close the track at all costs drew negative attention to the state, which exacerbated tensions among the Democratic factions and resulted in the calling of a grand jury, two Supreme Court trials, and a devastating defeat for the Democratic ticket in November 1938.[3]

Born in Middleborough, Massachusetts, in 1897 to a middle-class family, Walter E. O'Hara moved to New Bedford as an adult. There, he eventually amassed a small fortune in textiles. Relocating to Rhode Island in 1934 after purchasing the former "What Cheer Airport" property on Newport Avenue between East Providence and Pawtucket, O'Hara raised $1.2 million in a little over two months to build the Narragansett Race Track.[4] Wary of O'Hara's erratic management of the track and his public defiance of Racing Commissioner Francis J. "Red" Kiernan, Governor Quinn ordered the track closed, ultimately declaring martial law when O'Hara refused to comply.

However, McGrath's part in the story had more to do with another of O'Hara's business interests. By 1936, O'Hara had established the *Pawtucket Star*, funded primarily from the Track's profit, to rival the Republican-backed *Providence Journal*. Supporting his journalistic venture through profits earned from the racetrack, O'Hara then bought Peter Gerry's *News-Tribune* in March 1937 and combined the two papers, which reemerged as the *Star-Tribune* the following month.[5]

While O'Hara's paper nearly upset the plans of McGrath and Eddie "Rip" Higgins, Senator Green's executive secretary, to dominate the airwaves through Pawtucket station WFCI, his battle with the governor turned the public's attention from their private negotiations to the Quinn/O'Hara battle. As a result, McGrath and Higgins brokered a deal with the FCC through their ally, Frank Crook, Jr., to secure ownership of WFCI, Pawtucket. By systematically and meticulously wooing potential supporters, which included the owners of major department stores in Providence, they prepared for a major coup, the result of which would place McGrath in a position to run for governor in the near future.

Additionally, O'Hara's campaign against Providence Department Store owners for refusing to advertise in his *Star-Tribune* placed McGrath as district attorney in an untenable position, because he had represented the owners following a two-day strike in March 1937.[6]

In all, it will be shown that in four short years, O'Hara threatened to undo the work achieved by the Democratic Party during and since the Bloodless Revolution, while at the same time providing McGrath cover for his own dealings.

"And they're off"

In 1932 Rhode Island Democrats had finally achieved success in the state election; the winning slate of Theodore Francis Green and Lieutenant Governor "Fighting Bob" Quinn had served to unite the warring Pawtuxet Valley (Quinn) and Providence (Green) factions of the Democratic Party. Making hay with his timely campaign rhetoric of "humanity first," Green plunged into action. Three years into the Great Depression, nearly 30 percent of Rhode Island's workers were unemployed, owing in large part to the declining textile industry. Green's public support of President Franklin Delano Roosevelt meant that federal funding would funnel into the state, when the General Assembly passed a bill in 1933 authorized $6 million in relief funds to the 39 cities and towns.[7] Also as a result of President Roosevelt's New Deal, the state's Civilian Conservation Corps called upon young men to revitalize the state's camps and parklands, and the Public Works Administration employed 7,000 Rhode Islanders to beautify Point Judith.[8]

In the following year, however, a measure appeared on Governor Green's desk, which would transform Rhode Island's political and economic environment by potentially adding significant revenue to the state coffers. The bill was aimed at overturning a 1777 law, which had rendered gambling on horse racing illegal; it authorized pari-mutuel betting and established a three-man Racing Commission.

The concept of pari-mutuel betting was launched in 1865 by Parisian Pierre Oller, who was seeking to replace corrupt nineteenth-century gambling practices with a system whereby winnings would be divided equally among bettors. Oller's scheme captured the attention of Leonard Jerome, a New York businessman and the future vice president of the Saratoga Association for the Improvement of the Breed (SAIB), who was on a fact-finding tour in Europe.[9] Jerome imported Oller's concept and successfully adapted the process for U.S. markets. The results were phenomenal. Jerome Park, located in the Bronx, spearheaded a thoroughbred racing phenomenon when it opened its doors in September 1866.[10] It was not long before this cultural sensation expanded beyond New York, eventually reaching Rhode Island.

First, however, Rhode Island racetrack promoters had to overcome the state's most vocal moralists, especially the Rev. James V. Claypool of East Providence who despised all forms of gambling, pari-mutuel or otherwise, arguing that the practice promoted graft and corruption.[11] The future of betting on horse racing hinged on Governor Green's response to the measure legalizing this controversial practice. Initially Green supported the bill, but his close advisors urged him to poll his constituency before signing the measure into law. Green concurred and temporarily tabled the legislation, publicly declaring, "betting such as authorized by this act appeals largely to the very classes in the community who can least afford to lose money,"[12] and observing, "there is no large group of real lovers of running horses in Rhode Island to back this movement." He placed the onus for approval in the hands of the people, requiring a state referendum. Lured by the thrill of horse racing, Rhode Island's constituency voted overwhelmingly in favor of the measure, which became law on May 18, 1934.[13]

The union of high-stakes gambling and Rhode Island politics, however, proved lethal in the hands of the Narragansett Race Track's unstable proprietor, Walter E. O'Hara. According to historian Steven A. Reiss, horse racing in New York in the late nineteenth century had become "a key nexus between machine politicians and organized crime."[14] Legal pari-mutuel betting in Rhode Island was no different, as it encouraged illegal bookmaking and exacerbated the other forms of crime and corruption that had dogged the state throughout the 1920s and early 1930s. Moreover, critics questioned the efficacy of relying on gambling to lift Rhode Island from the depth of economic depression.

Governor Green's authorization of the bill in 1934 set in motion James E. "Judge" Dooley's ambition to bring thoroughbred racing to Rhode Island. A patron of several Rhode Island sports enterprises, including the Providence Grays Minor League baseball club and the Providence Reds Canadian-American Hockey League, Dooley saw his ambition transformed into reality when Walter O'Hara moved to Rhode Island and purchased the former "What Cheer Airport" on the border of Pawtucket and East Providence in the Blackstone Valley for the construction of a thoroughbred racetrack.

Beginning construction of the racetrack the following month, O'Hara's workers completed the project in just over six weeks, in time for opening day on August 1, 1935.[15] A phenomenal 37,281 people attended opening day, including Governor Quinn, Theodore Francis Green, and J. Howard McGrath. O'Hara spent $351,482 to build the racetrack, and by the conclusion of the racing period that first year, his track had yielded close to $30 million. Of that figure, he contributed almost $500,000 to the state's 39 cities and towns, which gave him undue influence in local politics. This influence increased after he began publication of the *Pawtucket Star* on April 29, 1936.[16]

Despite unemployment and economic decline in Rhode Island as a result of the Great Depression, the public returned to the track again and again, leaving its hard-earned money at its gates. At the same time, the track injected renewed vigor into Rhode Island's depressed economy by creating jobs and encouraging spending. Additionally, it gave the Democratic Party a new source of patronage since the track needed employees for its restaurant, concession stands, grounds, and ticket booths. Prominently featured in the first pages of Peter Gerry's *News-Tribune* featuring the opening day festivities were Lieutenant Colonel Peter Leo Cannon, Governor Green, Democratic

National Chairman James Farley, and Lieutenant Governor Quinn, standing with their host, Walter O'Hara and Cle, his second wife. By presenting the image of unity among legal, military, state, and elected officials, the *News-Tribune* editors lent authority to the track and by extension O'Hara.[17]

However, the seedier side of horse racing became increasingly apparent as more and more people flocked to the track. As a result, religious leaders, such as Episcopal minister James V. Claypool, stepped up their protests of state-supported gambling institutions, and their cries, though initially muffled by the greater appeal of easy money, soon bore fruit.

Meanwhile Green had stepped down as governor in order to challenge Republican Jesse H. Metcalf of Providence in the 1936 U.S. Senate race. Green and his lieutenants, including J. Howard McGrath, cast their considerable weight behind Lieutenant Governor Bob Quinn, who defeated Republican opponent Charles P. Sisson 160,776 to 137,369 in the ensuing gubernatorial race. Quinn's candidacy provoked bickering within party ranks, however, as Thomas P. McCoy of the Blackstone Valley faction of the party also coveted the seat. Initially rebuffed in his bid for the lieutenant governorship on the state ticket in 1932, McCoy was determined to finally earn his due. When Green and the state organization again overlooked McCoy in favor of Quinn, McCoy threw his lot into the Pawtucket mayoral race, where he roundly defeated his opponent in 1936.[18]

The newly elected Governor Quinn was noted for his feistiness, as evidenced by his handling of his Republican opponents on the floor of the General Assembly during the 1924 filibuster and his cunning maneuver during the 1935 Bloodless Revolution. Quinn had also proved himself to be a forthright proponent of Democratic ideals. For example, when President Roosevelt declared his famous "Bank Holiday," then–Lieutenant Governor Quinn, covering for Green, who was attending the inaugural in Washington, proclaimed, "the State of Rhode Island and Providence Plantations, do hereby order all banks and banking institutions to close and remain closed on Saturday, March 4, 1933."[19] The subsequent 11-day "holiday" enabled Rhode Island's leading bankers and industrialists to confer on the most equitable methods to ensure the state's economic solvency.[20]

Quinn's public deportment was in stark contrast to Green's outward gentility and intellectualism, which marked his hard-bitten dictatorial control over the state party. Quinn, who hailed from a working-class West Warwick family, confronted his adversaries head on; the results of which made for interesting copy in the *Providence Journal* during the 1920s and 1930s and earned him the nickname "Fighting Bob."

Governor Quinn took the oath of office in January 1937, and immediately called for the closing of the racetrack. O'Hara was in need of a strategic alliance and called upon Pawtucket mayor McCoy as his battle against Governor Quinn intensified. In 1934, McCoy, then Pawtucket city auditor, had threatened to shut off the track's water supply unless O'Hara promised the city's laborers sufficient employment, calmly explaining that they had "granted the permit [to build the track] with that understanding."[21] O'Hara, who realized the importance of McCoy's support to completing the project, acquiesced and promised favorable consideration for Pawtucket workers. From that point until their public split in 1938, McCoy and O'Hara enjoyed a brief, though significant, association. McCoy offered O'Hara a foothold into the Blackstone Valley's business community, while O'Hara's newspaper afforded McCoy a public podium on which to vent his frustration against Governor Quinn, Senator Green, and District Attorney J. Howard McGrath. O'Hara's Democratic newspaper published sentiments that could have been written by McCoy himself, denigrating and challenging Green and Gerry's control of the state organization.[22]

Compounding the issue, McCoy and McGrath had vied for political power throughout the 1930s, with McGrath often emerging victorious. Using O'Hara's newspaper and money, McCoy hoped to dethrone the Rhode Island kingpins: Peter Gerry, Theodore Francis Green, and J. Howard McGrath.

On the other hand, O'Hara could not afford to alienate Quinn entirely, since the governor's close ally, Francis "Red" Kiernan was commissioner of the Racing Division and had the sole authority to secure optimal racing dates.[23] O'Hara had become acquainted with Quinn in 1934, and in October 1937 Quinn commented that he initially found O'Hara to be respectable, despite rumors to the contrary. According to the governor,

> he wanted me to know that he was an honest man, etc. I told him that I always assumed that every man was honest and decent until I found out otherwise. During the years 1934 and 1935 I saw O'Hara, maybe three or four times, and upon each occasion he professed his friendship and admiration for me.[24]

Governor Quinn's opinion of the young entrepreneur, however, changed in the early months of 1936, when O'Hara began publication of the *Star-Tribune*, and the governor felt the sharp edge of the "honest and decent Irish lad's" poison pen.

In the meantime, the track netted financial and political rewards for both O'Hara and McCoy in 1936. Commenting on daily betting, revered legal contemporary Zechariah Chafee, Jr., observed, "Everything [at Narragansett Race Track] is standardized and mechanized and regularized," proving that the "Industrial Revolution, which began in manufacturing in the Eighteenth Century ... has now in the Twentieth Century reached horse-racing."[25] Attracting the most competitive thoroughbreds in the country, the track brought throngs of people to Rhode Island. The Narragansett Race Track rivaled New York's Saratoga Springs as the most popular racing establishment in the country, drawing all sorts, from the wealthy and prestigious, including Charlie Chaplin, Gloria Swanson, and Mickey Rooney, to the average laborer.

For Americans in the Depression, horse racing provided an exciting diversion from economic dislocation and despair. If only for a brief moment, the common man could rub elbows with the elite. As alcohol and money poured into the park, however, troubles emerged. Evidence of illegal betting surfaced. O'Hara was accused by Governor Quinn of "tip[ping] the elbow," beginning in the morning, and by midafternoon becoming fully inebriated, intransigent, and malicious. O'Hara publicly chastised Dooley, his original benefactor, and members of the *Providence Journal*, which resulted in messy legal battles.

The *Star-Tribune* under a more balanced director would have provided the Democrats with a platform to rival the Republican-backed *Providence Journal*. Instead, it heightened tensions among the various Democratic factions as O'Hara, fueled by his alliance with the disgruntled Tom McCoy, used the paper as a bully pulpit from which to level vituperations against anyone who challenged him, including Governor Quinn and Sevellon Brown, the managing editor of the *Providence Journal* and *Evening Bulletin*. O'Hara's malicious newspaper copy served to unite these two former adversaries in a campaign to remove O'Hara from Rhode Island before he defiled the good name of the state.

Alleging that the *Providence Journal* editor was out to destroy his newspaper, O'Hara became unduly suspicious of its reporters and photographers, who had begun to frequent the racetrack. In 1936, a Pawtucket clerk was arrested for destroying the camera of a *Providence Journal* reporter. Although later acquitted, the clerk set in motion an all-out war between the *Journal* and O'Hara, which climaxed in August when O'Hara's thugs physically barred the *Journal*'s sports writer Jack Aborn from taking a seat in the press box.[26]

In 1935, as a result of the Bloodless Revolution in January, Governor Green had appointed a three-man Narragansett Racing Commission to oversee the management of the track, rescinding the original 1934 law, which placed control of the track with the Department of Taxation and Regulation. Thus, the reorganization had now charged the Commission with "establishing the racing schedule, removing any employee or official of a licensed racetrack" for "just cause," and revoking the track or racing license "for any cause which the commission shall deem sufficient."[27] Commissioner "Red" Kiernan, clothed with additional power, gave his commission and its steward, James Doorley, the final say in contested races, and strengthened the Commission at O'Hara's expense. In retaliation, O'Hara flouted the authority of the commission at every opportunity, claiming that he alone held jurisdiction over horse racing. In angry protest over the Commission's findings of the September 5 and 6 races, O'Hara and his lieutenants marched into Doorley's office and verbally attacked him, using, according to Doorley, the most "vile" language he had ever heard uttered by a so-called professional businessman.[28]

As a result of O'Hara's behavior, Commissioner Kiernan and Governor Quinn determined that he must be removed as president and general manager of the Narragansett Race Track. His obstruction of Steward Doorley's authority, coupled with his refusal to admit *Providence Journal* sportswriter Jack Aborn into the press box,[29] constituted enough evidence for a hearing. Although the Racing Division found that O'Hara did not violate Rule 463 of the Racing Commission Ruling, which held that equitable treatment be conferred to "accredited" newspaper reporters who frequented the racetrack, they did rule that he did "unlawfully interfere with, threaten and intimidate James H. Doorley, a steward appointed by the Division of Horse Racing."[30] On that basis, the grand jury provided Governor Quinn and Commissioner Francis Kiernan with the necessary ammunition to remove "Walter E. O'Hara as an employe [*sic*] and official of said Narragansett Racing Association, Inc."[31] At that point, the grand jury subpoenaed his financial records, and the state budget director ordered an audit.

In an infamous headline, the *Star-Tribune* on September 8, 1937, lashed out: "Gov. Quinn Will Land in Butler's." However, O'Hara allegedly positioned the print to appear in such a way that, when folded for delivery, the copy read, "Quinn in Butler's." The state institution for emotional and psychological illness and addiction prompting the public to conclude that the Governor had suffered a nervous breakdown.

In the same edition, O'Hara charged "Colonel" Patrick Quinn with accepting bribe money to the tune of $50,000: $20,000 for legal fees, and the remaining $30,000 to quash an earlier version of the governor's inaugural message, which allegedly voiced opposition to horse racing. Quinn, who had represented the racing entrepreneur when he first arrived in the state, dismissed the charge, observing, "If I had known Mr. O'Hara then as I later knew him I would not have accepted employment by the Racing Association while he had anything to do with it."[32]

Allegations against both Quinn and O'Hara from the opposing camps intensified, growing more ludicrous as the fight continued. For his part, Governor Quinn saw the conflict as a fight between good and evil. Viewed from this perspective, his determination to banish the Race Track entrepreneur from the state at all costs becomes more comprehensible. He later explained, "It was impossible to permit an unscrupulous and ruthless individual to continue to operate under a license issued by this State."[33]

In a radio address in October 1937, the governor admitted, "maybe it's not good politics to get into this fight with Mr. O'Hara. Maybe it will hurt me politically. But what difference does that make?"[34] After the Rhode Island Supreme Court failed to uphold Commissioner Kiernan's ruling[35] removing

O'Hara as a racetrack official, Quinn retaliated by cancelling the fall schedule of races, alleging that the Narragansett Racing Association had not submitted a list of officers by the date required by law. Quinn thereby effectively shut out O'Hara, and by association Tom McCoy, from earning hundreds of thousands of dollars per day on average for approximately 20 racing meets.[36]

Then, on October 16, 1937, in a controversial move, the governor ordered the forced removal of O'Hara from his position as managing director of the Narragansett Race Track.[37] In a brief explanation, Governor Quinn responded to reporters, "We want proper racing.... I am convinced that ... cannot occur with Mr. O'Hara.... Mr. O'Hara is out." He then imposed martial law, cordoning off a one-mile radius around the track with three hundred troops led by Adjutant General Herbert R. Dean. Seventy-five soldiers patrolled each entrance to the track, ensuring that O'Hara, who was away on business in Maryland, would be barred from entrance.[38]

According to Governor Quinn, "This is not a fight against the Narragansett Association. There is nothing personal in this fight." But there was. While the governor believed that his cause in support of "the decent people of this state" was just, his rhetoric reveals an emotional, partisan response to O'Hara's antics. Staking his reputation and quite possibly his future in politics on this issue, the governor had embarked on a crusade to remove Walter E. O'Hara, a Tom McCoy ally, from Rhode Island.[39]

In his anger and frustration, Governor Quinn suffered a lapse in judgment and lost his perspective; his call to arms against O'Hara provided onlookers with an example of political folly at its best, arming critics with ammunition against the governor's forces and a lens through which to gauge Rhode Island's Democratic Party. The results of this folly would blacken the reputation of the party in the coming years.

A Lucky Strike: McGrath, the Providence Department Stores and Rhode Island Radio

For his part, McGrath had no strong personal feelings about the racetrack proprietor. Yes, O'Hara was unscrupulous, and, yes, he was a menace to the state, but, more importantly, he threatened to derail McGrath's behind-the-scenes business machinations with some very wealthy and powerful department-store owners. Up to this point, McGrath had wisely refrained from direct involvement in the Quinn/O'Hara altercation, but he now found himself drawn into the controversy when O'Hara lashed out against him because he would not intervene on O'Hara's behalf. Democratic store retailers, represented by some of the savviest industrialists in the state, owned, in addition to their garment interests, considerable stock in the area's burgeoning radio stations.

Mr. John Shepard, of Shepard Company, a fine retail outfit, and Joseph and Leon Samuels of the Outlet Company, which had opened their doors in 1880 and 1891, respectively, initially called on McGrath to represent the stores' interest in March 1937 after some 2,500 workers threatened to walk out in protest over poor wages and long hours. After negotiating for two days, McGrath, the store owners, and union representative Joseph Sylvia succeeded in working out a temporary compromise, which proved satisfactory to the store owners and the labor unions.[40]

Nonetheless, Joseph Sylvia, Rhode Island representative of the Committee of Industrial Organization (CIO), had been working behind the scenes to establish a chapter within Rhode Island's retail industry.[41] Later that summer, several department stores, including the Outlet Company, Cherry and Webb Company, the Boston Store, and the Shepard Company, collectively retained McGrath's services, at $3,250 per establishment, to negotiate a solution that would be mutually beneficial for owners and workers.[42]

When all was concluded, the owners acceded to some of the workers' demands: the stores would continue to grant workers paid holidays and agreed to raise the hourly rate: "on a 10, 7½, and 5 percent basis for salaries of $30 and under." Later, they conducted a "general study ... of wages paid," which resulted in the "equaliz[ation] of wages as between the several stores for similar types of service."[43] The proprietors also allowed employees of one year or more two weeks' paid vacation.

In the meantime, O'Hara initiated a public attack on McGrath. Briefly turning his attentions from Governor Quinn and Commissioner Kiernan, O'Hara alleged in 1937 that the proprietors of the leading department stores in Rhode Island, namely the Samuel brothers and John Shepard, had refused to allot funding for advertisement in his *Star-Tribune* because of O'Hara's support for the New Deal. Demanding equal consideration by the retail owners, O'Hara first enlisted the aid of McGrath to act as intermediary between the department store proprietors and Governor Quinn. Caught in the middle, McGrath stalled for time, prompting O'Hara's public outcry against McGrath and the department store owners.

Meanwhile, McGrath and Eddie Higgins, Theodore Francis Green's executive secretary, attempted to secure strategic alliances among business entrepreneurs and store owners, some of whom had vested interests in radio, to carve out a niche in the broadcasting industry. Through their association with a prominent Rhode Island businessman, Frank Crook, whose father earned a tidy profit as an automobile entrepreneur, they were able to obtain a stake in Pawtucket's burgeoning station, WFCI. Crook, who appeared before the Federal Communications Commission, received its authorization to purchase the Pawtucket Broadcasting Company (WFCI), thereby providing McGrath and Higgins with a public forum for McGrath's potential gubernatorial campaign.[44]

McGrath first became acquainted with Crook in March 1937. Impressed by Crook's wealth and influence, McGrath believed Crook and himself to be compatible business associates. In a very short time, Crook and McGrath forged a personal and professional partnership that spanned nearly 15 years, ending with Crook's untimely death in December 1950, the result of an automobile accident in nearby Attleboro, Massachusetts.[45]

However, O'Hara's connivances threatened to derail McGrath's negotiations with Crook and the FCC. By insisting that McGrath persuade store owners to advertise in his *Star-Tribune*, O'Hara placed McGrath in an untenable position. Serving both as legal representative for Shepard's Department Store and as United States district attorney for the state, McGrath's public support for O'Hara might have resulted in cries of conflict of interest.

McGrath could not allow O'Hara's erratic behavior to upset his plans or ruin his reputation. Only recently, scuttlebutt in and around the state had charged that McGrath used his federal office for private gain. One complainant, John H. Rooney, Esquire, of Providence, wrote the president of the United States, prompting the Department of Justice, through its representative Assistant Attorney General Joseph Keenan, to write McGrath:

> Criticism has reached the Department of alleged activities on your part in acting as private counsel in so-called labor difficulties involving certain department stores in Providence.... The Department has no doubt but that you have acted in a perfectly proper, circumspect and ethical manner, but it would appreciate information as to the facts.[46]

Within three days, McGrath responded to Keenan, a fellow Rhode Islander, with a detailed report of his actions over several months. Careful to include a notation on the "commendation of many outstanding leaders" on his performance during the department store strike, he commented, "I cannot conceive how, at any time during the course of this dispute ... there could be any possible conflict between my representation of my clients and my official duties."[47]

Satisfied by McGrath's response, Keenan wrote Rooney, "you are advised that the rules of the Department do not preclude United States Attorneys from handling matters of private interest, provided the business of the Government does not suffer thereby."[48]

Although McGrath believed the matter closed, it resurfaced again in August when O'Hara's *Star-Tribune* published an editorial charging McGrath with acting in violation of his duties as district attorney. In a tongue-in-cheek editorial, O'Hara charged McGrath with "coercion," particularly in representing the department stores, whose owners refused to advertise in his *News-Tribune*.[49]

O'Hara, furious with the department stores for refusing to advertise in his paper, sought and found a scapegoat in the stores' legal representative,

District Attorney McGrath. McGrath in turn voiced his frustration in a confidential letter to Higgins that August: "O'Hara has tried to bring me into this situation, but his stories are entirely without foundation.... I do not believe that I can afford, as a member of the Bar, to have him [O'Hara] or anyone else tell me that I can't represent my clients."[50]

Careful to protect his reputation with the Department of Justice, McGrath again wrote Assistant Attorney General Keenan, apprising him of the situation. Assuring Keenan that "since the settlement of the strike last April I have taken the position that it is embarrassing both to myself, and no doubt to the Department for me to be taking sides on these semi-political or social questions."[51]

McGrath acted cautiously and with propriety, but his conversation with Keenan also reveals both the state and federal government's hesitation and indecision in this area. With the expansion of federal authority since the onset of the Depression, the boundary between public and private concerns overlapped, often causing consternation and confusion. For McGrath, this issue would resurface again and again, finally reaching its peak in the postwar period, when he became attorney general.

The Indictments

In the midst of this brouhaha, O'Hara raised yet another issue that placed McGrath in an unenviable position. Accusing the state's Democratic state chairmen William Shawcross and former chairman Thomas Kennelly of accepting large sums from him in violation of the Federal Corrupt Practices Act of 1925, O'Hara forced McGrath to decide where his allegiance lay, with the law or the Democratic Party. Producing a check he had written to Kennelly in July 1935, for $2,500 and one for $5,000 on October 28, 1936, and then another three days later for $7,500, O'Hara, by inference, challenged McGrath, a former Democratic chairman, to call for a grand jury. To add fuel to the fire, O'Hara also published a check made payable to the governor's uncle, "colonel" Patrick Quinn for $20,000, and intimated that Quinn also accepted an additional $30,000, which was presumably shared with his nephew, the governor.[52]

In response to O'Hara's latest antics against the Democrats, "Fighting Bob" Quinn challenged O'Hara to publish the checks made payable to his adversaries as well, namely, Democrat Thomas P. McCoy, who allegedly received funds from O'Hara during his mayoral campaign, and Republican William Pelkey, the latter a major power broker within the ranks of his party and an occasional ally, albeit covertly, of J. Howard McGrath.[53]

In response, McGrath called for a federal grand jury, which handed down a report citing Walter O'Hara for his extensive contributions to both the Democratic and Republican parties in 1935 and 1936 just prior to the state's elections of federal offices. It also issued two counts against Chairman Shawcross and one count against former chairman Kennelly for allegedly violating the corrupt practices act.

After an eight-month hearing, the jury found that O'Hara had contributed nearly $60,000 to the Democrats and $230,000 to the Republicans, supposedly in violation of the Federal Corrupt Practices Act of 1925. His "donations" in turn would clothe O'Hara with the power to control or at least influence the General Assembly regarding the Race Track. But the defendants, especially Thomas Kennelly, argued that the language of the federal act was insufficient to convict state officials. In its final report, handed down in August 1938, the federal jury recommended the adoption of a state corrupt practices act to handle alleged campaign abuses, since they could not convict O'Hara based on existing statutes.[54]

Ultimately, the fate of this case and potentially the future of the state's Democratic Party rested with United States District Attorney J. Howard McGrath. In preparation, McGrath wrote the Department of Justice, requesting its official stand regarding political contributions. He explained, "The newspapers have been asking me for an opinion whether these contributions constitute a violation of the Federal Corrupt Practices Act." In doing so, McGrath provided the assistant attorneys general with a report on the Narragansett Park situation to-date as he interpreted it. His narrative emphasized his public support for Governor Quinn's position. "Certainly the charges preferred by the Governor and substantiated by the Commission were reasonable causes."[55] In the meantime, he and his two assistants, George F. Troy and Joseph Veneziale, had produced subpoenaed records and handed them to the jury. After studying Congressional deliberations prior to the passage of the Federal Corrupt Practices Act of 1925, McGrath ruled that O'Hara's donations to the Democratic and Republican parties were not explicitly prohibited by the aforementioned federal legislation.[56]

McGrath reasoned, "I am being guided by the well-accepted rule that it [the law] must be strictly construed" so while "it may be that corporations should not be allowed to contribute to State committees ... [I do] not feel at all warranted or justified in securing further indictments based upon a statute [The Federal Corrupt Practices Act of 1925] so obviously contradictory in its terms, particularly in a criminal statute."[57] On that basis, United States District Attorney McGrath pleaded *nolo contendere.*

By all appearances, O'Hara had won. The Supreme Court in a *per curiam* opinion had already upheld his dominion over the Narragansett Race Track, and now in one stroke McGrath's decision had crippled Governor Quinn's position, and ultimately the November election, since the governor's credibility in light of this decision had been compromised. Nonetheless, O'Hara's victory was Pyrrhic, since the Board of Trustees had severed his connection to the track nearly seven months earlier when they ousted him as managing director.[58]

McGrath's rather cautious reading of the law drew criticism from several sources. According to the highly subjective *Providence Journal*, the district attorney's decision not to pursue additional indictments sent a message to the track that it may "now use its money ... for campaign contributions to the State committees of the two political parties, without fear of prosecution and without fear of detection."[59]

As far as the Rhode Island public was concerned, the Race Track War had ended. Lieutenant Governor Raymond Jordan had by November 1937 ordered Adjutant General Dean to remove the troops from the track, and following the Racing Association's ouster of O'Hara in 1938, horse racing had returned to Rhode Island under the more prudent direction of James "Judge" Dooley. In many ways the rightful heir apparent to the Narragansett Race Track, Dooley presided over its heyday, as thoroughbreds Sea Biscuit and Whirlaway sprinted to victory in 1942.

As O'Hara's empire came crumbling down, several buyers expressed interest in purchasing his defunct newspaper, most notably David Stern of the *Philadelphia Reporter*. But the deal fell through, since Stern did not want to become embroiled in the Kiernan-Quinn/O'Hara fight.

> There is genuine regret throughout the State that you failed to get the paper. I fully agree with you.... *The Journal* is doing absolutely nothing with it. I understand the circulation has dropped to around 10,000, and there is every indication that it will fold up very soon. I am watching the situation very closely and will keep you advised.[60]

After deliberating for several months with McGrath, Eddie Higgins, and Senator Green, Stern dropped negotiations, explaining that the costs of digging the paper out of receivership far outweighed its benefits. Ultimately, the *Providence Journal* purchased the syndicate only to tear down the edifice, and with it the possibility of a rival for the Republican-backed *Journal*.[61]

Although Walter O'Hara escaped prosecution at the hands of the district court, his reputation was ruined. He was required by federal law to repay personal debts that he had incurred as director, including income tax. Forced to apologize to Governor Quinn for his injudicious statements, O'Hara in March 1938 admitted, "In various issues of my newspaper the *Star-Tribune* and over the radio, I made certain statements which reflected upon the character and integrity of you, your family and certain associates. Those statements were ... without foundation in fact.... For all those statements, I hereby publicly apologize to you."[62]

His plea to the governor for forgiveness, and his declaration that he never "made any gift or gratuity of any kind whatsoever to you, either as

Governor, as an attorney or as an individual," appeared half-hearted and hypocritical.[63] According to Higgins, O'Hara's public contrition was suspect and the whole business foolhardy.[64] After running against Governor Quinn in 1938, O'Hara eventually sought his fortune in various enterprises from Texas to Fall River. In the winter of 1941, O'Hara lost control of his sedan in the wee hours of the morning in Taunton, Massachusetts, and was killed. According to the public report, no sign of foul play or alcohol abuse was evident, despite O'Hara's history of public drunkenness.[65]

In the 1938 election, reform Republican candidate William Henry Vanderbilt defeated Robert E. Quinn in the gubernatorial race, 167,003 to 129,603. Attempting to recover from this upset, the leaders of the Democratic Party stepped back during the next two years to assess the damages in preparation for the 1940 gubernatorial election. Concerned with the state of affairs in Rhode Island, Democratic National Chairman James Farley polled leading Rhode Island Democrats, demanding to know what went wrong.[66]

As had been the case all along, petty jealousies and factionalism had played into the hands of the Green/McGrath coalition. More and more the Pawtuxet and Blackstone Valley leaders came to realize that the Green/Gerry/McGrath bloc was unbeatable.

Although temporarily derailed, the party infrastructure would realign behind J. Howard McGrath, as he and Eddie Higgins paved the way for a 1940 victory. With Theodore Francis Green headquartered in Washington most of the time, McGrath would emerge as his heir apparent to the state.

Again, McGrath's position as a legal officer would serve the political needs of his party. In 1938, newly elected reform governor William Henry Vanderbilt, another crusader, would vow to end political corruption by whatever means necessary. His campaign, which eventually revealed the use of wiretaps, would provide the Green/McGrath bloc with ammunition to discredit him, as jurisprudence would again take a back seat to political intrigue.

6

The Wiretapping Case
Is Nothing Sacred?

By 1938 McGrath had earned a reputation as a smart, savvy opportunist. Having built an impressive clientele in his private law practice with mentor Theodore Francis Green as partner, in December 1936 he also netted a respectable income as the president of Home Savings and Loan Corporation.

By age thirty, McGrath had held five public offices, including city solicitor of Central Falls and Democratic state chairman. Because of Green's support at a crucial time in Rhode Island's political history, McGrath had been able to secure a spot as district attorney, surpassing more seasoned state politicians. His role in bringing criminal Carl Rettich to justice and in negotiating a successful settlement between department store proprietors and union officials ensured his reappointment in 1938. District Attorney McGrath would now find himself battling reform Republican William Henry Vanderbilt, who assumed the governorship after Robert Quinn failed to win reelection in November 1938. This battle served as a turning point in McGrath's career, securing statewide recognition and paving the way for his run as governor in 1940.

This chapter provides a close analysis of a wiretapping incident that called into question the local, state, and federal interpretation of the 1934 Federal Communications Act, which barred a third party from tampering with messages from one party to another, unless authorized to do so by the "sender." This case underscores the precarious nature of Rhode Island politics at the time and highlights the changing role of the state in criminal procedure.[1] Since the federal law did not directly address the use of wiretapping devices, the subsequent trials and investigations became mired in overlapping jurisdictions and lengthy court proceedings.

Technological advances in the late nineteenth and early twentieth centuries prompted serious debate among Constitutionalists concerning the federal government's right to use and regulate telecommunications. Following the First World War and the passage of the Eighteenth Amendment in 1919, which banned intoxicating liquors, the public's attitude toward law enforcement shifted. Before the world war, they rarely questioned the methods by which the police or federal agents performed their duty, placing their trust for the most part in local officials to act honestly and efficiently. However, the carnage of war and the subsequent excesses of U.S. Attorney General A. Mitchell Palmer in 1919 prompted Americans to demand more accountability from their public officials. The consequent Supreme Court decision in *Olmstead* v. *U.S.*[2] served as a turning point in this debate. Responding to the growing controversy over the use of wiretapping as a means of capturing criminals and exposing alleged spy rings, the ruling provided a benchmark from which to judge the practice in the future.

Rhode Island contributed to this debate through its federal ruling in the 1939 wiretapping case, which pitted McGrath against Republican governor William H. Vanderbilt. The case raised the issues of the right to privacy and the legality of using evidence obtained through electronic surveillance. Additionally, the case exposed the heated rivalry between the old and new guard within the Republican Party, while simultaneously restoring harmony among competing forces within the Democratic Party. All in all, the case contributes to the discussion of wiretapping and the right to privacy in the public realm and provides historians with an example of how state and federal law enforcement officials came to regulate the use of this highly controversial tool.

Governor Vanderbilt vs. Mayor McCoy

William Henry Vanderbilt, a wealthy, liberal Republican, assumed the governorship armed with a determination to eradicate voter fraud and dual office holding. Pawtucket mayor and city boss Thomas P. McCoy was the first object of his crusade. Holding multiple positions simultaneously, McCoy had won the 1936 mayoral race by questionable means, which were exposed during the Narragansett Race Track War. Although the track's proprietor Walter O'Hara and McCoy dissolved their partnership in 1938, a grand jury probe revealed that O'Hara had funded McCoy's mayoral race with earnings from pari-mutuel betting.[3]

Sensing McCoy's vulnerability, Vanderbilt set out to corner the machine politician by whatever means were available to him. In a complicated and twisted set of circumstances, Vanderbilt authorized the hiring of a New York detective agency to investigate voter fraud, gambling, and municipal corruption in Pawtucket. Under the direction of Assistant Attorney General Matthew Goring, the Bielaski Seaboard Detective Agency, owned and operated by Frank B. Bielaski, placed listening devices on the home and office telephone services of Mayor McCoy and Rhode Island attorney general Louis Jackvony.

Accordingly, U.S. Attorney General Robert Jackson asked McGrath to determine whether Bielaski's use of electronic surveillance in Rhode Island fell within the jurisdiction of federal law. McGrath's critics, however, charged McGrath with using the case to discredit the Republican governor and build support for his own bid for the governor's seat in 1940. Although Vanderbilt's hiring of a detective agency and his subsequent authorization of wiretapping may be construed as an effort to discredit his political enemies, his campaign to eradicate voter fraud and other forms of corruption point to his more principled motives. Nevertheless, the liberal-minded, urban-based Vanderbilt had incurred the wrath of old-line rural Republicans, who felt threatened by the new governor's stand on corruption, rendering him and the party vulnerable to democratic attack.[4]

McGrath used the case as an opportunity to cast doubt in the minds of the voting public as to the true nature of Vanderbilt's motives. The case also served to unite warring Democratic factions, particularly the Green/McGrath bloc and their Blackstone Valley opponent Tom McCoy. Although critical of McGrath throughout the 1930s, McCoy contacted the young district attorney as soon as he suspected that his telephone wires had been compromised.

The state's economy had improved little since the election of Franklin Delano Roosevelt. Only 53 percent of employable laborers were in the workforce in Rhode Island, and in 1934, according to Rhode Island historian William McLoughlin, 17,000 mill workers were on relief rolls, seeking a just and secure income. Their only answer was to strike, which they did on September 1, 1934.[5]

So, when the Democrats, as represented by Robert E. Quinn, were defeated by William Henry Vanderbilt and the Republican slate in the November 1938 elections, Rhode Island Republicans interpreted the win as a repudiation of Roosevelt's New Deal and Governor Quinn's excesses during the Race Track War. Amidst the Republican sweep, however, was an unprecedented Democratic victory in Pawtucket for its mayoral candidate, Thomas P. McCoy. It did not take long for reports to begin to surface that McCoy had employed questionable methods to win the election.

McCoy fit the criteria of a New England machine boss. He was born on June 13, 1883, two years shy of his beloved Pawtucket's incorporation as a city, and his extensive political experience more than made up for his lack of formal education. Schooled in the backroom caucus meetings of Blackstone Valley's leading political strategists, McCoy had emerged as a leading figure in the region, and by the early 1930s could claim Pawtucket as his fiefdom.[6]

On the other hand, Vanderbilt, at the time of his election as governor in November 1938, was lauded throughout the state as a selfless idealist with a noble cause: to rid Rhode Island of corruption. The great-great-grandson of Commodore Cornelius Vanderbilt had realized early on that wealth and prestige did not guarantee a stable home life. At the tender age of seven, his parents, Alfred Gwynne Vanderbilt and the former Ellen Tuck French, divorced. Vanderbilt was uprooted from New York City, his birthplace, to Newport, Rhode Island, where his mother, having successfully secured a $10 million settlement from her ex-husband, embarked upon an independent life. His father remarried in 1911 and sired two additional sons, before perishing aboard the *Lusitania* in 1915.[7]

Vanderbilt launched his career in politics in 1928 as a liberal Republican state senator from the town of Portsmouth, but he incurred the wrath of old-line Republicans by supporting a number of reform measures, including a civil service bill aimed at toppling "dual office holding," a practice that struck at the very heart of democracy.[8]

As the chairman of the Committee on Finance, Vanderbilt refused to be manipulated by Republican power brokers, who retaliated by denying him the 1936 gubernatorial nomination. Two years later, however, the old guard was losing ground politically, thanks to the expansion of suffrage in the state and the consolidation of various boards and commissions, the result of the Bloodless Revolution of 1935. Capitalizing on the national backlash against the economic recession in the United States, Roosevelt's heavy-handed "court packing" scheme, and the outcry in Rhode Island against Governor Quinn's role in the Narragansett Race Track controversy, Vanderbilt captured his party's endorsement and ultimately the election, in part by promising to eliminate voter fraud in Pawtucket, Central Falls, and Providence.[9]

Vanderbilt, who defeated Quinn by a 38,846 plurality in 1938, interpreted his win as a mandate to embark upon a thorough house-cleaning in Rhode Island government. Nonetheless, many Republicans, who held the majority of seats in the General Assembly, refused to support his program, which included a mandate for civil service reform, because they felt threatened by the new governor's stand on corruption.[10] Machine politicians "Boss" William Pelkey and Pierce Brereton, to name a few, chafed under this wealthy, naïve industrialist's plan to implement, among other things, merit examinations under the Broomhead Civil Service Act.

This measure, introduced into the General Assembly in 1939, required state employees, regardless of their political affiliation, to sit for a qualifying examination. Factions within both parties charged that the bill alienated the average workers by placing merit above experience and party loyalty. Nevertheless, with public support from the *Providence Journal*, Vanderbilt secured the passage of Broomhead's measure on March 9, 1940.

Vanderbilt's first order of business had been to appoint his Republican attorney general Louis Jackvony, elected in 1938, to head the investigation of election fraud throughout the state.[11] Jackvony, like Vanderbilt, had a history of alienating influential Republicans. Jackvony had served as assistant attorney general from 1925 to 1930 under his ally Attorney General Charles P. Sisson. Upon Sisson's ouster in 1930, Jackvony accused powerful Republican state chairman William Pelkey and Finance Commissioner Frederick Peck of influencing the decision against Sisson. In response, Democratic floor leader and sometime ally of Jackvony, the then–Rhode Island assemblyman Thomas P. McCoy, introduced legislation calling for a committee to investigate these charges. Unfortunately, the House was still predominantly controlled by the old guard and tabled the bill.[12] This incident drew attention to Jackvony's unlikely friendship with McCoy, which would prove troublesome for the attorney general.[13]

The successful implementation by the Democrats in the late 1920s and early-to-mid–1930s of long sought-after reform bills, which included the repeal of the property qualifications for voting in city and town council elections, the redistricting of cities and towns to reflect more equitable representation at the polls, and other legislative changes made possible by the Bloodless Revolution of 1935, allowed them to restructure the state government. It had also placed at their disposal a number of political appointments to dole out to loyal patrons. McCoy's undisputed hegemony in the Blackstone Valley was one outcome of the coup. Controlling patronage in Pawtucket through his role as city auditor, McCoy's desire was to become governor in order to gain access to the state reserves.[14]

Vanderbilt challenged McCoy's dominance in the region by accusing him of tampering with the 1936 election returns in order to secure victory in Pawtucket. His almost obsessive campaign against the Pawtucket mayor would ultimately cloud his judgment, but Vanderbilt began his investigation by placing it in the hands of Jackvony, appointing him to head the Subcommittee on Election Fraud. On January 19, 1939, the General Assembly granted "special power" to Jackvony, who in turn named Amos L. Lachapelle and Matthew W. Goring assistant attorneys general. He also assured the legislature that a grand jury probe would be forthcoming.[15] Initially, the governor's campaign against corruption won him admiration in the press and among the more liberal-minded in his party.

Nevertheless, as time wore on, Vanderbilt grew uneasy at the slow pace of investigation, and by the spring of 1939, he had lost confidence in Jackvony's ability or desire to expose graft in Pawtucket. The relationship between Vanderbilt and Jackvony had been strained ever since governor-elect Vanderbilt replaced Jackvony-ally Pierce Brereton of Warwick with J. Thornton Sherman of Middletown as Republican state chairman. Jackvony had come to oppose Vanderbilt's civil service legislation, resenting Vanderbilt's alienation of his party.[16]

Special assistant Matthew Goring took advantage of Vanderbilt's suspicions by intimating that Jackvony secretly harbored gaming interests in Pawtucket and purposely stalled the investigation to protect officials with ties to racketeering. Apparently, a reporter for the *Providence Journal* had seen Jackvony in the company of McGrath and McCoy, and subsequent rumors abounded that the attorney general's friendship with these Democratic power brokers, coupled with his interests in Pawtucket gambling, would prevent an objective investigation of the Pawtucket mayor and his cronies.[17] These allegations eventually proved to be unfounded, but the rumors contributed to Vanderbilt's decision to hire an outside agency.

After an encouraging meeting with Vanderbilt in the spring of 1939, Goring approached Jackvony about hiring Bielaski's agents to expedite the investigation into municipal corruption in Pawtucket and elsewhere. Jackvony was less than enthusiastic, telling Goring that the fees quoted by the Agency ($3,000 to $4,000 a month) were too steep for Rhode Island's Department of Justice. Jackvony's budget allocated $3,300 total for the election fraud investigation and, with that in mind, he preferred to rely on the state police, maintaining that they were well-equipped both physically and financially to handle the operation.[18]

Although the General Assembly would eventually allocate an additional $35,000 for the investigation, the money was not available until April 1939. Jackvony's plan was thwarted, however, by state police superintendent Jonathan Harwood, who opposed employing his 70-man force for the investigation of voter fraud. Jackvony persuaded Harwood to name three men outside of his department for the investigation.[19]

Meanwhile, the grand jury probe authorized to investigate alleged gambling and corruption in Pawtucket declared that an "extensive picture of election fraud" existed in Pawtucket, Central Falls, and Providence. In their partial report issued on November 22, 1939, they concluded that antiquated state laws had failed to protect the voters, allowing flagrant abuses to continue without consequence. Additionally, of 101 Pawtucket officials slated to oversee voting in the city, nearly 75 percent were chosen by the Pawtucket Board of Canvassers.[20] This had resulted in significant tampering by election representatives of the new voting machines, which had been installed in each district by 1936.[21] In response to this evidence, the grand jury recommended that the probe be extended to delve deeper into corruption in the city. The jurors also wanted to examine Pawtucket's finances, especially after accusations surfaced that the mayor and his officers of diverted municipal funds to persons in private industry. A year later, the General Assembly complied and in July 1940 voted to extend the investigation, granting them an additional $50,000.[22] The jury found that laws must be established to ensure that qualified canvassers man the booths on voting day.[23]

Innocent Bystander: The Case of Edward L. Freeman

On Friday, November 24, 1939, Joseph M. Bennett, Jr., manager of the Pawtucket Branch of the New England Telephone and Telegraph Company, received a peculiar call from Mayor Thomas P. McCoy, who suspected that the telephone wires of his personal residence had been tapped. Bennett assigned one of his best workers, Walter Gillis, to investigate. Tracing lines to the residence of prominent Pawtucket businessman Edward L. Freeman, Gillis and his crew discovered wires strung from Freeman's second-story window to a telephone pole, which intersected East Avenue and Kenilworth Way, parallel to the McCoy residence.[24]

Charging Freeman with "aiding and abetting" in the "unlawful interruption of electric currents over electric wires," the police held him for allegedly violating Rhode Island General Law #608, Section #74.[25] Authorities brought him in for questioning at 11:15 p.m. on February 27, 1939, and he was grilled for over 12 hours. Freeman pled "not guilty" in the Tenth District Court, Pawtucket, and only then was he allowed to call his attorney, Edward T. Hogan.[26] Bail was posted at $2,000, and Freeman was released pending trial. Freeman returned to his family bewildered by the harsh treatment. He soon discovered, however, that his transient boarder, Lee Edward Barton, was an operative working undercover for Frank B. Bielaski's New York–like Seaboard Detective Agency. Barton had not returned to the Freeman home and was considered a fugitive from justice.[27]

The trial of Edward Freeman was often front-page news in Rhode Island from late December 1939 until its closing days one month later. According to family and friends, Mr. and Mrs. Freeman had believed Barton to be an insurance agent investigating fraud.[28]

Immediately after the raid on Freeman's home, an all-points bulletin was issued for Lee Edward Barton. By January 4, 1939, Pawtucket city solicitor William A. Needham posted an official warrant for Barton's arrest on conspiracy charges, but despite several "sightings," he remained at large for the next two years.[29]

In January 1940, Judge William M. Connell of the Tenth District Court found Freeman not guilty, since no evidence existed to implicate him for the tapping of Mayor McCoy's phone. In his ruling, the judge took the opportunity to condemn wiretapping by repeating the oft-quoted statement of Justice Oliver Wendell Holmes's dissenting opinion in *Olmstead* (1928): "writs of assistance, and general warrants are but puny instruments of tyranny and oppression when compared with wiretapping."[30] Relieved by the verdict, Freeman announced that he was "glad to live in the United States where truth and justice still prevail."[31]

Shortly after McCoy's complaint, the New England Telephone Company received a call from James Hart, Vanderbilt's executive secretary, who alleged that the governor's wires had also been compromised. A subsequent test indicated that those telephone lines were clear.[32]

Meanwhile, McCoy, discovering that his telephone conversations had been tampered with, enlisted the aid of McGrath. Throughout the 1930s as state chairman, McGrath had conspired to eliminate McCoy's control of Pawtucket. McCoy vehemently resented this encroachment into his "city," and was noticeably peeved when in 1932 McGrath opposed his legislation to implement city-owned public utilities.[33] Now, McGrath and McCoy united to defeat the Republicans. If McGrath in his role as district attorney could clear McCoy of allegations of voter fraud, then McCoy might line up behind McGrath's "program" to wrest the Democratic nomination for governor in 1940 from former governor Quinn, who was intent upon returning to office.[34]

Although U.S. Attorney General Robert Jackson required McGrath to submit all evidence to the grand jury, McGrath first informed Louis Jackvony that listening devices had been placed on his office and home phones as well.[35] McGrath subsequently confirmed that Barton had also established temporary headquarters across the street from Jackvony's home and adjacent to his office on the twelfth floor of the Turks Head Building in downtown Providence. After thoroughly searching Jackvony's office, Providence police confiscated a step-ladder, telephone wire and snake, picture hooks, a typewriter, and six loose-leaf memo books. They would later use these articles as proof of Barton's crimes.[36]

It was soon made public that approximately 60 lines in the Turks Head Building had been tampered with; cuts were made so that the copper wiring was exposed and the devices could be inserted. As Rhode Island's principal legal officer, Attorney General Louis Jackvony was dumbfounded by what the investigators discovered. He deferred to McGrath, who had jurisdiction as a federal officer, to conduct an investigation of this magnitude. At the same time, the grand jury probe into alleged corruption and misappropriation of funds in Pawtucket continued unabated.

Governor Vanderbilt had been vacationing at his retreat in Williamstown, Massachusetts, seemingly unaware of what had transpired in Rhode Island during his absence.[37] Upon his return in December 1939, he informed reporters that "the investigation is in the hands of the Attorney General, and I have full confidence in him."[38] The duplicity in the remark would become evident within a few months.

As a federal officer, McGrath had in the meantime obtained permission from his superior, United States Attorney General Robert Jackson, to travel to New York to secure logs from the telephone company and to question Bielaski about his connection with the wiretapping incident. McGrath was thus able to determine that Bielaski had stayed at the Crown, Narragansett, and Biltmore hotels in Providence. Telephone logs and testimony from hotel employees substantiated this evidence. More importantly, McGrath found that in late December the attorney general's special assistant, Matthew Goring, was in constant communication with Bielaski. Ledgers indicated that Goring had been in contact with Lee Barton throughout the latter half of September and all of October.[39]

In early December, Jackvony demanded that Goring state in writing the nature of his connection with Bielaski and his agents, Barton and Davenport. In a written memorandum to the attorney general, dated December 4, Goring admitted to meeting with the detectives, but claimed to be ignorant of the tapping of McCoy's or Jackvony's phones, explaining that his meeting with Bielaski was "purely social."[40]

Unaware of Goring's secret agreement with Bielaski, Jackvony, frustrated by his deputy's insubordination, publicly announced his decision to fire Goring on December 16, 1939.[41]

McGrath "obtained permission from the Department [of Justice] to proceed to New York again for an interview with the New York Telephone Company," in order to collect evidence that Bielaski or those working for him made several telephone calls to and from Rhode Island. He also ascertained that Bielaski called Goring frequently from the Biltmore hotel in Providence.[42]

The Chaffee Committee

In the interim, the General Assembly had authorized the creation of an ad hoc committee following Vanderbilt's request for a legislative probe. Established under the chairmanship of Republican senator Alfred G. Chaffee of Scituate, the Chaffee group was granted additional funds to uncover flagrant misuse of voter trust.[43]

What followed, however, was a politically damaging row between the governor and Chaffee over financial compensation for the ad hoc committee that resulted in an open breach, which nearly cost Vanderbilt the nomination in 1940. The nature of this argument not only revealed a pattern in the way the governor handled politically explosive situations, it also exposed Vanderbilt's disregard for compromise even within his own party.

Chaffee insisted that Vanderbilt had previously authorized a payment of $6,950 to the fourteen members of the Committee. In March, Vanderbilt replied that he was "extremely sorry for the unfortunate misunderstanding, but he was under the impression that each member would receive $1,500 for expenses incurred. Vanderbilt attempted to smooth over the disagreement by offering to pay each member "out of his own pocket."[44] This was a grave political mistake, which exposed his weakness, flaunted his wealth, and alienated a Republican of high political standing.

Not surprisingly, Chaffee shared this "misunderstanding" with the *Providence Journal,* claiming that he and the members of the Committee should not be expected to work eight months without payment, especially since their position as part-time legislators only paid them a mere five dollars a day for a sixty-day period.[45] He further presented the newspaper with an itemized list of tasks performed by the Committee, including the gathering of roll calls of voters of Central Falls and Pawtucket.[46]

In March 1940, the *Italo-American Tribune* reported that the debate over funding prompted Senator Chaffee and members of the Republican Senate to publicly chastise Vanderbilt for his "insincerity" in dealing with the commission, and, as a result, eleven of the fourteen members of the committee declared their opposition to his renomination for governor. According to the *Tribune,* the Republican senators had met secretly and criticized Vanderbilt's "cold feet" after promising the committee members a stipend for their services. In their version, Vanderbilt tried to minimize controversy by inquiring whether there was some "way we can sneak it through" the House Finance Committee.[47] This request for additional funding was rejected, causing an open rift between Vanderbilt and Chaffee.

Chaffee, under advisement from Attorney General Jackvony, refused to accept the governor's offer of private payment, arguing that "acceptance ... would violate Chapter 612 of the General Laws of 1938." According to Section 22 of the Chapter, "no person shall corruptly give or offer any gift or valuable consideration to any such agent, employee, servant, or public official as an inducement or reward for doing or forbearing to do ... any act in relation to the business of his principal, master or employer, or the state, city or town of which he is an official."[48] Vanderbilt recoiled at the insult, and in a written exchange demanded that Jackvony retract his statement for the public record. In heated correspondence with Chaffee, Vanderbilt bellowed, "Am I correct in understanding that you [Chaffee] and the Attorney General have charged me with having corruptly made an offer?"[49] Chaffee denied the accusation, but Jackvony refused to stand down, explaining that as a public official Vanderbilt was not authorized to finance a legislative committee with private funds.[50]

Nevertheless, the Chaffee Committee conducted their investigation with the utmost care and professionalism. The subsequent report confirmed the findings of the grand jury. The fourteen members ably canvassed 33,766 out of 41,597 eligible voters in Pawtucket and 9,766 out of 12,363 voters in Central Falls. After thorough investigation in the Blackstone Valley, the committee discovered discrepancies of 12.6 percent in Pawtucket, and 13 percent in Central Falls. The injustices reported by the committee, however, were more revealing than these figures indicate. As an example, in District 3,[51] Ward 6, a handy garage located across the street from the polls, served as a fitting room for floaters who hurriedly changed their outer garments and rushed to the side door with their bogus "identification cards," where policemen "in the know" ushered them in to place their multiple ballots, in some cases up to 20, for McCoy and his lieutenants. Meanwhile, legitimate voters were prevented from entering the polling place and forced to return to their homes, their civic rights violated.

Because voting machines had only recently been introduced for the 1936 elections, the government was ill-equipped to handle discrepancies caused by misuse of the machines. Consequently, according to the Chaffee Committee, "machines were jammed throughout the day; voters were prevented from voting; … Democratic election officials changed Republican votes to Democratic votes … [and] roving squads of policemen kept Republican workers away from polling places and prevented them from coming anywhere near the ward rooms."[52]

The complete report, submitted on January 23, 1940, recommended that a bipartisan election board be created to ensure that proper procedure be followed when conducting elections, and that a Financial Investigating Commission be instituted to hold Pawtucket officials accountable. Ironically, however, the Committee did not recommend prosecution for officers implicated in the report. Instead, the Committee maintained that although "elections in Pawtucket and Central Falls in November 1938 were clearly unfair," they could not remove any officials since they had no "definite proof … that fraud is what elected them." Although Chaffee later boasted that subsequent reform instituted in Rhode Island election procedures was due to the work of his Committee, the *Pawtucket Times* argued that their refusal to oust McCoy's cronies was a sham.[53]

The Chaffee report contributed to the return of 166 indictments by the grand jury in February 1940. Among those implicated were Public Works Commissioner Albert J. Lamarre, Probate Judge Lawrence A. Flynn, Director of Public Welfare William T. Flanagan, six members of the Pawtucket Police Force, and 75 city employees.[54]

In the meantime, McGrath and Eddie Higgins had been looking for Barton, the key to discovering who financed the detective agency. After months of investigation, McGrath, in conjunction with the Federal Bureau of Investigation, discovered that Vanderbilt had financed the Bielaski Agency with his private funds.[55]

According to a memorandum submitted to Judge Francis Biddle, acting attorney general, on March 27, 1940, Whiting Willauer and McGrath proposed the following: "Due to the high position held by the Governor he should be apprised of the nature of the information in the possession of the

Department of Justice before this information was presented to the Grand Jury."[56]

Granting the governor the respect due to his high office, McGrath and Willauer, special assistant to federal Attorney General Robert Jackson, paid a visit to Governor William Vanderbilt to confront him with the evidence, namely his personal $6,900 payment to Bielaski's Seaboard Agency. The Senate subcommittee hearing would later disclose that, according to McGrath's records, $15,500 had been paid in total to the agency, beginning on September 8, 1939, and ending with the last installment on November 25, 1939.[57]

As McGrath and Willauer entered the governor's chamber, reporters rushed to inquire about the nature of the meetings. McGrath refused to respond immediately, granting Vanderbilt the professional courtesy of responding to the accusations confidentially. In a closed-door session, Willauer and McGrath presented their evidence to the governor. Although Willauer had offered the governor time to confer with his lawyer, Vanderbilt, without hesitation, admitted that "the payments were not indirect." Anxious to tell his side of the story, he continued: "I determined that it was my duty as chief law enforcement officer of Rhode Island to get at the bottom of the allegations of election frauds, and that I further felt that where these frauds were so rampant they must be for the purpose of covering up other forms of corruption.... I, personally, paid for his services."[58] He acknowledged that a detective agency was not his first choice, but since "state law enforcement agencies" were not equipped to handle such widespread graft, he had no alternative.

According to Vanderbilt, Bielaski told him that the "people in Pawtucket" would "not be prosecuted on election frauds" because "Jackvony was connected with interests in Pawtucket," and that McCoy allies "had been successful in reaching members of the State Grand Jury that was then considering election fraud matters."[59] He also noted that he was unaware of Bielaski's methods of obtaining information and had not agreed to the use of wiretapping devices. He only discovered their use "sometime near the end of the investigation."

McGrath's confrontation with the governor was his last official duty in the wiretapping inquiry. On April 9, 1940, Attorney General Robert Jackson publicly stated that he was relieving the Rhode Island district attorney of his duty concerning the case because he did not feel that the "Department of Justice can in good conscience prosecute persons in Rhode Island for a practice which was at that time engaged in by the Department itself.... I wish to take this opportunity to commend U.S. Attorney McGrath for the efficient and tactful manner in which he has conducted this investigation."[60] McGrath then submitted his final report a few days later to Jackvony, who subsequently presented the information to the Grand Jury.[61]

On April 10, Governor Vanderbilt made his confession public, adding that wiretapping "has been a usual method of getting information and obtaining leads in investigations."[62] Nonetheless, Vanderbilt knew that he had been beaten before he embarked on his bid for reelection. Despite the courtesy that Willauer and McGrath displayed in their initial meeting with the governor, McGrath and his Democratic allies wasted no time in capitalizing on the governor's complicity in the wiretapping incident. The ensuing political volleying and finger pointing contributed to Vanderbilt's political defeat in the November 1940 election.

The governor, in turn, accused McGrath of whitewashing the election fraud case in Pawtucket in order to focus on the more politically beneficial wiretapping case. He decried, "Mr. McGrath has turned to the political side of the picture," and had thus cheapened his august role as United States district attorney. When he assumed the position of U.S. attorney general, McGrath would hear similar charges leveled against him.

McGrath responded to Vanderbilt's accusations by declaring, "it was my duty as U.S. attorney to conduct the investigation [of wiretapping], that I sincerely tried to avoid any act that justly could be charged as politically inspired."[63] McGrath further charged that Vanderbilt and his executive secretary James Hart deliberately tried to misdirect the investigation by claiming that the governor's two homes had been tapped. According to McGrath, "I feel that this request was a deliberate attempt to implant in my mind the impression that certainly the Governor knew nothing about wiretapping activities."[64]

The Senate Subcommittee Investigation

In addition to his thorough investigation of the Bielaski Agency and its operatives, McGrath was also the driving force behind Senator Green's motion to conduct a Senate investigation of the whole affair. The request was approved on March 19, 1940, after the subcommittee met with McGrath and Jackvony to hear the evidence.[65]

Since McGrath had researched the steps that led to a conviction involving wiretapping operations in eastern Massachusetts, Pennsylvania, New York, and Indiana, Green was able to support his proposal with persuasive evidence for a national hearing. Green contended, "the activities of a detective agency in New York State," which brought agents to Rhode Island to "tap the wires of elected public officials and private citizens holding responsible positions in the political and business world," was rampant throughout the United States.[66]

In a confidential exchange between a "Father Deery" and Green's executive secretary, Eddie Higgins, the latter corroborated the senator's statement by revealing, "I believe that those wire-tappers working out of the Bielaski Detective Agency in New York have tapped the wires of prominent persons in ten or eleven states." Higgins also disclosed, "the investigators and the G-men have discovered ... that all calls made from Cardinal [George William] Mundelein's home in Illinois to the White House ... have been recorded as a result of taps placed by agents of Bielaski." He added, "a Buffalo newspaper has stated that this wiretapping investigation will be as scandalous as the Teapot Dome of the Harding days."[67]

In his correspondence with McGrath, Higgins also divulged a petty mis-understanding that ensued between Senators Green and Wheeler, which could have "thrown" the whole national wiretapping investigation "out the window." Higgins contacted Tom Corcoran, a powerful FDR New Dealer and political lobbyist from Rhode Island, enabling Senator Green to secure friendly subcommittee members for the wiretapping subcommittee. However, the chairman of the Senate Committee, the powerful Burton K. Wheeler, nearly refused to authorize the formation of the subcommittee on Interstate Commerce for the Investigation of Wiretapping because of Green's off-hand comment that he "never had heard of Wheeler." Higgins told McGrath that he had secured a truce between the two senators by "arrang[ing] for Senator Green, early Wednesday morning to see Senator Wheeler and straighten the whole affair out," which they did.[68]

During this period, Senator Green underwent two separate operations (one for a hernia and another to remove his appendix). The Senate Subcom-mittee, however, met as scheduled with Senator Thomas Stewart presiding, and Sherman Minton serving as an alternate. Commencing on May 21, 1940, as mandated by S. Res. 224 of the 76th Congress, which "authoriz[ed] and direct[ed] an investigation[69] of alleged wiretapping and installation of listen-ing or recording devices."[70] In his opening remarks, Senator Wheeler stated that "the dangers to personal liberty that may result from unrestricted use of wiretapping and similar practices have long been a subject of political argu-ment and judicial controversy."[71]

Taking the stand one week later, Governor Vanderbilt testified that he had authorized the hiring of the firm that tapped the phones of McCoy and others because he had lost confidence in his attorney general. In this he was spurred on by Matthew Goring, who had criticized Jackvony's lethargic approach to the McCoy case.

Back in Rhode Island, an altercation between *Providence Journal* editor Sevellon Brown, and FBI Director J. Edgar Hoover threatened to spoil McGrath's bid for the governor's office in 1940. Brown accused "corruption-ists" of whitewashing the Pawtucket investigation in an effort to discredit the Republican governor. According to Brown's recollections, "the FBI has had an operator in Rhode Island named Hogdin, investigating charges of wiretapping. In several instances, Mr. Hodgin has used my name in making inquiries." Now, Brown charged, there are "various distorted versions of a report that the FBI has me under investigation for complicity in wiretapping."[72]

Hoover replied, "I am not cognizant of, nor have I at any time tolerated any procedure which may in any way implicate innocent persons in any offense." He, however, learned from "the Special Agent in charge of my Boston Office that a Special Agent interviewed you in connection with this matter on February 14, 1940."[73]

Brown was not satisfied, and remarked that he was "amazed at the evasiveness of your letter of February 15th." Charging that "a ring of political corruptionists has long controlled the cities of Pawtucket and Central Falls," he believed that a campaign was underway to discredit the investigation into corruption in Pawtucket and Central Falls, by instead focusing on wiretapping. He informed Hoover that despite their efforts, "seven office holders of Central Falls have been convicted and 169 in Pawtucket are under indictment," even though McCoy "and his political associates quite naturally endeavored to screen the investigation of their corruption under the news sensation of the tapping."[74]

Brown continued,

"All this time your agent never came in to see me. And now you have the temerity to put in your letter that he came in to see me on February 14th. He did after I had sent a reporter out to bring him in."[75] Hoover countered, "when information is received from any reputable source to the effect that any individual may have violated any Federal statute, an investigation is thereupon conducted and appropriate inquiries are made relative to the allegations."[76]

Hoover sent McGrath the entire exchange on April 6, four days before Vanderbilt admitted publicly that he had paid for the wiretapping of McCoy, and, with Senator Green, they worked behind the scenes to have Brown called in for questioning. Higgins advised Green, who was recovering from surgery, that when Subcommittee Chairman Tom Stewart paid him a hospital visit, "you insist that the correspondence between Brown and Hoover go in the Record and that Sevellon Brown be questioned as to his threat ... to Hoover relative to having the publishers' association go after the FBI."[77]

On Thursday, June 6, 1940, Sevellon Brown and Harold A. Kirby, the state editor of the *Providence Journal*, were called to Senate chambers. Charging that Senator Green "thwart[ed]" the *Journal*'s probe into alleged voter fraud in Pawtucket by calling for a Senate inquiry, Brown stated that "McCoy and his political associates tried to screen our investigation."[78]

Brown further revealed that Vanderbilt wanted the *Journal* to foot some of the bill for the tapping. He stated, "As a matter of fact, the Governor said his reason for telling me was that he was carrying the cost of the entire thing and he felt he could not continue to carry the cost, and he believed that such an investigation might turn up information that might be valuable to the newspaper."[79] Brown then brought the question to the publisher, Allison Stone, who declined.

Green also made clear that he did not direct the investigation in order to implicate "the Federal Bureau of Investigation or Mr. J. Edgar Hoover, its Director. I have the greatest feeling of regard for Mr. Hoover, for the splendid work that he has done in law enforcement, and for the efficient and excellent organization he has built up."[80]

Nonetheless, McCoy insisted until the day he died that Brown was the instigator in the wiretapping controversy, but no proof to that end ever surfaced. In the meantime, McGrath and the state organization moved to join forces with McCoy and the Blackstone Valley before his run for governor.

McGrath's Run for Governor

In August 1940, McGrath petitioned President Roosevelt and Attorney General Robert Jackson to accept his resignation, so that he could embark on a campaign for state office. In choosing to run, McGrath received many letters from personal and professional alliances that he had formed while in public office.

According to an FBI agent conducting a confidential probe on the situation, "much of the publicity [of the election] was released in such a manner as to make it appear that United States Attorney McGrath was directing personally the efforts of the Bureau's agents in this investigation." He continued, "Rumor has it that this case was political capital to him and it has been stated that it will be used as ammunition by the Democratic Party in the coming State elections which may result in the election of McGrath for Governor."[81] While the agent's revelation merely corroborates the scuttlebutt of a similar nature, it is striking that the FBI was drawn into McGrath and Vanderbilt's race for governor. In this instance, the agent's suspicions were born out, since McGrath did indeed capitalize on the information he obtained from the case to discredit Vanderbilt, weakening his bid for reelection.

McGrath and Eddie Higgins began gathering their forces to wrest the Democratic nomination from former governor Quinn in 1939, lining up support throughout the state. Yet McGrath dangled leading Democrats about in his bid for the gubernatorial nomination, refusing to commit initially.[82]

To the power brokers in the state, McGrath was the right man for the position: handsome, well dressed, and politically and financially successful. Thus, Higgins cajoled, maneuvered, and used every means at his disposal to secure the election for McGrath. By calling in past political debts, tapping into his national ties as the executive secretary to Senator Green, and securing financial backing, he proved to be an invaluable ally and political strategist for McGrath and the Democrats. Higgins would become the go-to person for both McGrath and Senator Green.

As a result, McGrath won the 1940 election handily, garnering 177,161 votes to Vanderbilt's 139,820. The Democrats carried the day in November, capturing 59 seats in the lower house to the Republicans' 41.[83] Although the wiretapping incident is directly linked to Vanderbilt's defeat, his alienation of his party, *laissez-faire* method of investigating, and insistence that political disagreements could be solved by his signature on a check also contributed to his undoing. Had he researched Bielaski's methods of investigation more thoroughly and played a more hands-on role in uncovering election fraud in Rhode Island, perhaps the tables would have turned against the Democrats. By the time Vanderbilt's hand in the incident was exposed, his justifications appeared paltry.

Upon McGrath's election that fall, he received a laudatory note from Director Hoover expressing his "heartiest congratulations over the vote of confidence you have received from your constituents."[84] Eventually, as attorney general, McGrath would ironically authorize the FBI's use of electronic surveillance devices in their investigations. At this point, however, the 37-year-old James Howard McGrath was ready to embark upon the next chapter in his eventful career.

Aftermath

As an interesting addendum, one month after McGrath was sworn in as governor of the State of Rhode Island, Lee Edward Barton, mysterious operative for Frank Bielaski's Seaboard Agency, reappeared. In a note to McGrath a year earlier, Eddie Higgins shed some light on the whereabouts of Lee Edward Barton and his connection to the wiretapping scandal. McGrath and Eddie Higgins had been looking for Barton, who was in hiding, throughout this ordeal. In response, Higgins wrote McGrath, "Strictly off the record Lieutenant Knox of the Naval Intelligence, gave me Barton's address in Memphis. I believe that Norton [Buddy, ally of Tom McCoy and *Journal* writer] has got something when he says that C. Oliver O'Donnell is in this wire-tapping picture.... He is the boy that collected plenty of money for the Vanderbilt campaign."[85] Barton now appeared willingly before a special session of the Senate subcommittee.[86] During the height of the scandal, this story would have been front-page news, but now the public tired of the case. Since New York courts had failed to implicate Bielaski for conspiracy, Providence officials believed that they could not hold its operative, Barton.

With McGrath at the helm, more pressing international problems took precedent.

Nevertheless, Rhode Island officials stood at the vanguard of state and national legislation on wiretapping. National attention was drawn to the widespread application of electronic surveillance after Green's petition for a Senate probe. Concurrent legislation was subsequently passed that narrowly defined the possible use and abuse of electronic surveillance. According to House Bill #2266, wiretapping would be authorized in cases of "sabotage, treason, seditious conspiracy" thereby overruling Section #605 that prohibited such practices.

President Franklin Delano Roosevelt, in a letter to Representative Thomas H. Eliot of Massachusetts, a member of the Committee on the Judiciary, averred that although "citizens of a democracy" must be "protected in their rights of privacy," he underscored the right of the federal government to employ this method against persons who "today are engaged in espionage or sabotage against the United States."[87]

Over fifteen years later in 1956, Title XI, Chapter 35, Section 12 of the General Laws of Rhode Island officially declared that wiretapping was a felony, which carried a penalty of up to five years in prison. Other states, such as Massachusetts, also barred the use of electronic devices unless approved by the Attorney General.[88]

As this chapter of his political life ended, J. Howard McGrath was to embark upon four successful years as governor of the State of Rhode Island. In the public eye, he was viewed as a diligent and objective civil servant who had brought to light the corruption in the Vanderbilt administration. In reality, however, he had been instrumental in sweeping under the rug the graft that existed in Pawtucket. In the final analysis, his political ambition far outweighed his contribution to good government.

7

McGrath and the Quonset Summer Colonists

Contributing to McGrath's successful three terms as governor was the acquisition of a naval-air base on the site of Quonset Point, which was situated on 1,192 acres of land on the southern shoreline of Narragansett Bay. Lobbying on behalf of their state, Republicans Governor William Henry Vanderbilt and Representative Harry Sandager, worked with Democratic Senator Theodore Francis Green, a member of the Naval Affairs Subcommittee, to secure Quonset Point as the Northeastern site for a base in the Atlantic, competing with Democratic senators David I. Walsh of Massachusetts and Robert Wagner of New York, who both argued forcefully in favor of locations in their states.[1] Although a highly respected senator, Walsh had been critical of Roosevelt's policies, especially his decisions to revamp the Supreme Court in 1937 and run for an unprecedented third term in 1940.[2]

As an unapologetic advocate of Roosevelt, Green was looked upon favorably by the administration, which boded well for the future of Quonset Point. With federal monies hanging in the balance, Green left no stone unturned when it came to funneling revenue into his state. Unlike some liberals who feared that the war would lead to excessive federal control of state expenditures, Green instead advocated collaboration between the national and state governments in order to provide Rhode Island with the financial support it needed for its shoreline defense.[3]

J. Howard McGrath would reap the benefits of Vanderbilt, Sandager, and Green's efforts, when, as governor, he presided over the economic boom precipitated by thousands of workers and servicemen and women who poured into Rhode Island to train following Quonset's commissioning on July 14, 1941. Quonset Point would enhance McGrath's reputation, as it forged a positive balance between the state and federal government.

The name "Quonset" was derived from the Native American word "Seconiquonset," meaning "a neck or strip of land, along the deep water, that sticks out where the bay runs to the sea."[4] Giovanni da Verrazzano originally explored in and around Quonset in 1524, in the name of the King of France, Francis I.[5]

Located in the outpost of Wickford in the town of North Kingstown, the Quonset site was officially established in 1637 by Richard Smith and Roger Williams. Smith, an engaging and mercenary fellow, lived in Taunton, in the Plymouth Colony but moved to Rhode Island to purchase the land as a trading post to barter with the Narragansett sachems.

Two hundred forty-four acres had been utilized as a training ground for the National Guard from the time of its purchase by the state in 1893. Six years later in 1898, during the Spanish-American War, the site served as a training ground for troops. By 1927 it became the landing point for famous aviator Charles Lindbergh, after much political volleying.[6] Its claim to fame, however, came when the land was purchased by the United States Navy for the site of a major naval air base in the North Atlantic. According to Sean Milligan, Quonset was one of four possible sites that could "support traditional seaplane operations and provide a landing field and other facilities for aircraft carrier-type planes."[7]

The state's victory, however, came at great cost to a number of summer residents who were forced to surrender their vacation homes in the name of national security. During the 1920s and 1930s, these "Quonset Colonists" had purchased individual plots of land with their hard-earned money in the hope of enjoying the beautiful shoreline of Narragansett Bay.

When hurricane-force winds engulfed Rhode Island in September 1938, however, several of these properties were severely damaged, diminishing the return on the investment of the colonists. Nonetheless, many of them would initially reject the $926,641.60 figure quoted by the U.S. Navy appraisers for their homes.

At the center of the maelstrom was J. Howard McGrath, who first encountered the site at Quonset Point, formerly known as the Quonset Point "Summer Colony," shortly before he resigned as United States district attorney to run for governor of the state. Called upon by the justice department to issue condemnation papers "in what is believed to be one of the most extensive land condemnation proceedings in the history of the State," McGrath appeared to represent both the citizens of Rhode Island and the federal government.[8] Balancing their needs with the national emergency, McGrath and his assistants worked to find an equitable solution that would satisfy the government and the nearly four hundred disgruntled citizens, who would soon be voting in the state's gubernatorial election.

War in Europe

Following Adolf Hitler's invasion of Poland in September 1939, President Roosevelt deemed it essential to rebuild the navy, which counted only 1,000 planes in its arsenal.[9] Nonetheless, the President would need to change America's attitudes, which at the time favored neutrality, in order to achieve his goal of a fully-manned naval force. In a confidential letter to President Roosevelt, future secretary of the navy Frank Knox feared "the lack of a public sense of crisis and imminent danger," that caused resistance to the president's program in building up the armed forces. Knox believed, however, that hostilities in Europe and Asia would cause a "change" in their thinking: "The continuing success of the German submarine and mine Blockade against England is a threat to Allied success of which the country is becoming more and more conscious.... It may easily be that if Russia throws in with Germany in a military sense, the growth of the feeling of alarm over here might be very swift."[10]

As he anticipated, Americans had begun to understand the imminent crisis. The targeting of Jews on November 10, 1938, known as Kristallnacht, had begun to alter America's thinking toward Germany's aggression. The torching of approximately 200 synagogues, the destruction of hundreds of private homes and businesses, along with the removal of tens of thousands of Jews to concentration camps, served to unify America in its antipathy toward Nazism, if not toward intervention.[11] The president warned his cabinet that the United States and its neighbors were at risk of invasion. In response, he sought to alter the neutrality legislation that had been enacted during the 1930s in order to allow America to sell to the belligerents, if war should break out. The result was "cash and carry," a compromise measure, which authorized the allied forces to pay for munitions upfront and transport them back to their home base.

In response, the adjutant general in Washington moved to modernize the nation's harbor defenses. Projects deemed obsolete were scrapped in favor of those designed to shore up security along the North Atlantic coastline.

Rhode Island, as a strategic location on Narragansett Bay, would prove vital in the protection of national security, and Quonset Point a project worthy of subsidizing. Following U.S. Congressional approval of monies to support air and naval strength in the spring of 1938, a five-man board under the direction of Admiral Arthur Hepburn was established by Secretary of the Navy Charles Edison, in order to investigate possible sites for an Atlantic base. After careful evaluation, the Board concluded, "the most favorable site was found at Quonsett [sic] Point, R.I." Theodore Francis Green explained to the Senate in March 1941, that the base was part of the overall plan for "improved defense of the Atlantic seaboard virtually from the Arctic Circle to the bulge of Brazil."[12]

The Role of William Henry Vanderbilt

On June 7, Congress, under the 1938 Naval Expansion Act, also known as the Walsh-Vinson Act, which earmarked $1,090,656,000 to build a two-ocean navy over a period of ten years,[13] authorized ailing Secretary of the Navy Claude A. Swanson to name a five-man committee, to be led by Rear Admiral Arthur J. Hepburn to investigate possible locations for the site. Acting Secretary Charles Edison moved to establish the Hepburn Board, which was imperative since, according to Admiral William D. Leahy, the chief of naval operations "Developments ashore have not kept pace with the increase in the forces afloat and in the air, and ... we have now reached the point where the efficiency of the striking forces afloat and in the air will soon be seriously impaired by the absence of shore facilities needed for the servicing of these forces."[14] According to the Hepburn report, "An adequate defense plan requires that the shore establishment be capable of supporting the whole fleet in either the Atlantic or Pacific ... it may be said that the need for additional shore-based facilities for aircraft far overshadows that for destroyers, submarines, or mines."[15]

After careful survey, the Committee officially recommended Quonset Point as a suitable location for a North Atlantic naval base, maintaining that it contained "sufficient depth of water for carrier anchorage" on its northern tip at Conanicut Island, which, after "suitable dredging and filling," would be transformed into a "major [naval] air base."[16] Its deep channel, which flowed into the ocean, impressed the naval engineers, who supported the Rhode Island site. On May 25, 1939, President Franklin Roosevelt signed a measure earmarking $1,000,000 for its construction. The official transference was filed with the attorney general via United States District Attorney J. Howard McGrath on December 20, 1939.[17]

Sandager suggested that the governor issue a "gentle" note to chairman of the Naval Affairs Committee Carl Vinson of Georgia, asking for a firm commitment on the possible location of the North Atlantic base. Though he was "evasive," owing, Sandager surmised, to his preference for a base in the South, Vinson would eventually support the enterprise. Funding, however, would not begin until the following year.[18] Thereafter, Vanderbilt lobbied persistently for the enactment of the Windsor Bill, which authorized the "donation" of the 244 acres of land (a former training facility known as Quonset "Summer Colony") to the federal government "for the express purpose" of the construction of "a naval air base," which included the "erection of hangars, buildings," and additional construction necessary for the smooth running of a base. Thereafter, Vanderbilt, along with fellow Republican Sandager, believed that the base could be secured if Rhode Island donated its state land to the federal government as a show of goodwill.

Although Rhode Island was the smallest of the forty-eight states, its position along the Atlantic seaboard was deemed vital to the defense of the country. Two-hundred-fifty miles from Canada with a direct line to Europe, the coastline of Narragansett Bay was considered by the Navy Department one of three naval air bases to be constructed along the Atlantic as part of President Roosevelt's campaign to expand naval resources.[19]

On Vanderbilt's advice, Green, as a member of the Naval Affairs Subcommittee of United States Senate Appropriations Committee, proposed an amendment to the Walsh-Vinson Naval Base Bill (Senate Bill 830), which shifted the classification of the Quonset base from "Category B" ("for later completion," as originally recommended by the Hepburn Committee) to "Category A" ("for earliest completion"), and called for an additional $1,000,000 to purchase of the 379 acres of private property from the "summer colonists."[20] By June 1940, Green had secured $24,204,000 for the base's initial construction, and by the time the project was completed, appropriations would be allocated four more times.

In order to expedite the process of transferring the additional land to the federal government, the Navy hired three appraisers at the insistence of McGrath and Eddie Higgins. The appraisers worked behind the scenes to secure the best estimates for the project: John B. Carpenter, Arthur W. Drew, and James Devine divided the property into three designated zones and were responsible for determining the "fair market value" of the acquired homes. The majority of the land that was "condemned" was situated along the Narragansett coastline, and reasoning that the shoreline, which had suffered severe damage after the devastating Hurricane of 1938, Naval officials assumed that the "needed private property at Quonset ... probably can be purchased for considerably less"[21] than the appraisers' estimation. This assumption was mistaken.

After the names of residents and the individual sums that would be offered for each property appeared in the *Providence Journal* on July 10, 1940, McGrath's office was barraged with complaints from 300 colonists who cried foul. He met with nearly 100 residents and managed to allay their "considerable resentment against the Government"[22] by maintaining that the "figures in the Government's petition for condemnation" should not be considered "exact" but were instead a "legal fiction" meant to save time. McGrath mollified the irate homeowners by clarifying that the total amount $926,041.60 credited to the U.S. District Court would in all probability be renegotiated.[23] He also emphasized that "every owner ... is entitled to receive from the United States Government just compensation under the law,"[24] and he reminded the colonists that those who agreed to the navy's appraisal would receive their portion of the money immediately, while those who contested the sum would be required to file a claim with the United States District Court.[25]

Despite McGrath's astute diplomacy, the disgruntled citizens banded together and took to the streets to voice their concerns to the press. The wife of Wallace Thornley, "second" vice president of the Quonset Community Association, complained to the *Providence Journal* that the "disgraceful" offer of $8,800 for her home that originally sold for $12,000 was proof that "Hitler has taken over Quonset Point."[26] Matthew T. Dunn, a vocal member of the association, impressed upon the enraged colonists the necessity of a united front in the face of adversity. The Rev. John L. Cooney, of St. Bernard's Catholic Church in the affluent Wickford section of North Kingstown, urged them to demand a "square deal" for their property.[27] Cooney emphasized to his parishioners that the land was "appraised at half" its "value," and argued that the government had abused its citizens most shamelessly.

The Quonset leaders appointed representatives to negotiate with McGrath. As an initial step, McGrath counseled all to file a claim with his office. These documents in turn would be sent to the federal government, which would run a title search against the figures quoted by the private owners. The district attorney cautioned the protesters to allow four-to-six weeks for the process.[28] By July 25, all residents of the Winfield Beach section (designated "Area D" by the government appraisers) of the Point had followed McGrath's advice, and by mid–August, nearly eighty percent had filed claims with the U.S. district attorney's office.[29]

Despite this progress, McGrath's patience was sorely tested by the time and energy expended on this project. In a letter to Assistant Attorney General Littell later that July, McGrath complained that since this case commenced, "it has been practically impossible to do any other work in the office."[30]

At this time, McGrath gradually began to remove himself from the controversy in anticipation of his run for state executive office. On July 30, he stated to Littell: "I desire to keep myself and my regular assistants in an impartial position to represent the Government in such cases as will arise in these proceedings," and, as a result, "all negotiations with owners from this point on could better be carried out under the direction of [his assistant] Mr. Smith."[31] Before McGrath's resignation as United States district attorney, however, he offered a viable solution to the problem of the "summer colonists" to Littell. Verifying the integrity of the three government appraisers, McGrath urged Littell to "enter" into "contract" with them "on a per diem basis" until all cases were resolved. McGrath claimed that he did not "know what factors were taken into consideration by the Navy Department in establishing the low appraisals as recorded in the Declaration of Taking"[32] arguing that the navy's "valuation as set forth in the Declaration of Taking is approximately $240,000 lower than the minimum appraisal as reported" by the three appraisers.[33]

He warned that "there will ... be certain cases where Mr. Smith [McGrath's assistant] will be recommending to the Department settlement figures in excess of the minimum set by any one of the Government appraisers."[34] Nevertheless, as the likely Democratic nominee for governor of the state, McGrath recognized the advantage of having the federal base in Rhode

Island and privately wrote to Littell in August 1940 that his office would attempt to reach a settlement based on the lowest value appraised, assuring him that all amounts paid to individuals would "not be entered until the Department has given expressed approval."[35]

On September 6, 1940, two days after President Roosevelt accepted McGrath's letter of resignation as United States district attorney, the navy enforced its dictate and ordered all property owners to leave posthaste. At the fifteenth and final meeting of the Quonset Community Association, newly elected president John W. Ward pledged to continue meeting at the Mount View Plat Community Hall, a building to the north of their present site. Fighting for back taxes against the town of North Kingstown, Ward hoped that the amount awarded to them would allocate funding for the additional levy in their final settlement. To that end, three commissioners, former mayor of Providence James E. Dunne, prominent lawyer Frederick W. O'Connell, and realtor Robert L. Walker, were sworn in by federal judge John P. Hartigan and charged with investigating the Quonset property claims.[36]

Meanwhile, construction commenced, and 200 workers were placed on roll call, with an anticipated 3,000 additional skilled and unskilled laborers to be hired before the project's completion. Commander R. V. Miller, USN, a native of St. Paul, Minnesota, was appointed to oversee the project, and George A. Fuller Company and Merritt-Chapman and Scott Corporation of New York were awarded contracts to erect the naval facility.

Working his crew from dawn until dusk, the Minnesota native took advantage of improved technology (tarpaulins and heaters)[37] that allowed his crew to continue throughout the year regardless of weather conditions. The contractors, George A. Fuller Company and Merritt-Chapman, out of New York, bid successfully on the project, loaning their best laborers to complete the task in half the projected time, and subcontracting with Rhode Island firms, including Gilbane and Company.[38] The result was a state-of-the-art facility, equipped with a hospital, movie theater, and ideal officers' quarters, which were situated along the Narragansett Bay coastline.[39]

Commander Miller, an extremely efficient taskmaster, completed the Quonset project in less than a year. Although he publicly stated that the colonists would receive "every consideration," he also reminded them that they must vacate the premises as soon as possible. Construction workers were instructed by site authorities to have the military police remove colonists who impeded the progress of the project.[40] Seventy of the Quonset residents were required to evacuate on August 14, while another 90 were given until the 19th. By September 6, nearly the entire population of summer colonists had evacuated their properties to make way for the "prefabricated" housing that was erected at Coddington Point, where usable concrete pavement already existed. Rental fees for the new homes were $15 to $20 a month, a reasonable rate for naval personnel, who began to move in gingerly, trying to avoid confrontation with the former summer colonists.[41]

By September 13 the federal government had condemned 225 additional acres for the purpose of laying rails along the Post Road from Quonset to New Haven, Connecticut. Attorney Smith promised a deadline of November 12, 1940, to those newly ordered to vacate.[42] He managed to elude controversy in spite of the emotionally charged atmosphere generated by the residents following their discovery that their land would be confiscated by the United States Navy. By this time, however, McGrath was free from any obligation to the additional colonists removed from their property by eminent domain, and concentrated on his gubernatorial campaign.

As the project was nearing completion, the newspapers began to focus on the benefits of the Quonset Point facility, noting the transformation that had occurred in such a short period of time. Quonset had become a "booming" naval city, with a police force, a fire department, shops, and a movie theater.[43] New tenants began to move into the Quonset neighborhood, coined "Little Norfolk," by the civilian laborers who now populated the colony. "Moving vans and furniture store trucks emptied a steady stream of furnishings into the homes.... Children were sent off to school early in the morning. Like all good neighbors, the first residents of the colony at the end of their day's work gathered in front yards in last evening's twilight to exchange pleasantries and introductions."[44] Approximately 56 families had relocated from Virginia City to Wickford, just outside of Quonset Point. Their inauguration to the Point was much more idyllic than the former colonists, who in many cases were forcibly removed from their homes.

Nonetheless, the project was truly a remarkable feat of engineering. In all, dredging and filling extended the landmass by nearly 300 acres, which would now be enjoyed by the new generation of Quonset colonists.[45]

The base proved a source of patronage for McGrath and his fellow Democrats. Able to "recommend" friends and supporters for employment at the base, the Democrats built a powerful coalition that expanded throughout the 1940s and 1950s.[46]

The speedy construction of Quonset Naval-Air Facility[47] commissioned in July 1941, and the addition of its sister site at Davisville in 1942, the latter an advance base depot, combined with the development of Newport Naval Base for torpedo production, brought thousands of sailors to the already densely populated state. Quonset Point, which cost the federal government a combined $30,000,000, became the largest naval air base in the country.[48] The presence of these bases proved fortuitous for Governor McGrath and Rhode Island, a fact he raised time and again in his public addresses.[49]

On July 12, 1941, a small commissioning ceremony inaugurated the opening of the Rhode Island naval station. Noted attendees included Assistant

Secretary of the Navy Ralph Bard, Senator Theodore Francis Green, and Governor J. Howard McGrath. Secretary of the Navy Henry Knox, who did not attend the ceremony, applauded the remarkable speed at which the base had been completed and concurred with Green that "Commander Miller and those under him are doing a splendid job."[50] Secretary Bard, like so many others during this period, failed to mention the sacrifice of those whose land was confiscated in the name of progress and defense.

The success of Quonset constituted one aspect of Rhode Island's contribution to the war. Following Japan's invasion of Pearl Harbor in December 1941, America readied its forces for a two-front war. Rhode Islanders, who had earlier been lukewarm or opposed to intervention, now defended President Roosevelt's call to arms. The sister site to Quonset, at Davisville Advance Base Depot, was commissioned on August 11, 1942. Sitting on the shore of Allen's Harbor, Camp Endicott at Davisville transported half a million tons of cargo per annum to allied bases overseas, and also constructed pontoon bridges, which proved instrumental in transporting cargo to dry land during the invasion of Sicily in 1943.[51]

As J. Howard McGrath entered the next phase of his life, he and the state would continue to reap the benefits of a thriving naval base, which would employ thousands of workers, and the town of North Kingstown, where the base was housed, expanded from 4,606 to 14,810 residents by the war's end.

Rhode Islanders viewed Quonset Point as a source of pride in achievement and ingenuity. McGrath informed his constituency that Rhode Island's position on the Atlantic made "the presence of naval establishments at Newport and the Northeastern Air Base at Quonset" the state's "greatest security."[52] Upon the base's official closing in June 1974, the *Providence Journal-Bulletin* quipped that "colonists would never know Quonset today." Accordingly, the commemorative piece echoed a familiar praise from Assistant Secretary of the Navy Ralph A. Bard: "We have here at Quonset an outstanding example of what the unrestrained giving of brains, time, sweat, and toil can accomplish."[53]

8

McGrath's Ticket to the Top

On the heels of his wiretapping success, J. Howard McGrath sent his formal resignation as United States district attorney, in order to seek his party's nomination for governor of Rhode Island. Newspapers throughout the state predicted his win, and they were not disappointed.[1] After a long and bitter campaign,[2] McGrath won with a plurality of 37,461 over the Republican incumbent William Henry Vanderbilt.

McGrath's campaign was based on a platform of bipartisanship and advancement of the needs of the state; he promised to "make every effort to co-operate with leaders of both parties to produce a constructive legislative program for the next two years."[3] In a statement released the September following his nomination, McGrath wrote: "It will be my purpose ... to work for party unity. The former Governor's [Quinn's] position substantially contributes to this end. When nominated and elected I will surely strive to maintain that *unity and I believe that the State itself will be the beneficiary of such accord* [material in italics handwritten]."[4] Working with Eddie Higgins, McGrath succeeded in lining up bipartisan support for his candidacy, including some of his most ardent critics, such as former opponents Thomas P. McCoy and Robert E. Quinn.

Through his campaign, he united the warring factions of his party. He secured the support of the Blackstone Valley bloc through his successful pursuit of the wiretappers and promised McCoy and former governor Quinn representation in the governor's cabinet. His well-coordinated legal and political team masterminded both Governor Vanderbilt's ouster and the dismissal of 167 indictments against many of Mayor Thomas McCoy's closest confidantes.

To solidify his position further, McGrath won over McCoy by granting him the opportunity to choose two members to serve in the administration. Armand Cote and Russell Handy, of the Blackstone Valley, served as secretary of state and general treasurer, respectively, and were instrumental in securing wartime legislation for the governor.

Robert Quinn proved more difficult to sway. Seeking another run for governor, Quinn eventually gave up the idea when his ally John Nolan of Newport pledged his support to McGrath. Years later, Quinn, who lost to McGrath in the drive for the 1940 nomination and later in the 1946 bid for the Senate, believed that he could have accomplished a great deal had he been given the opportunity.[5]

McGrath relied on his earlier training as part of the Gerry organization and called on his own political team to conduct a statistical analysis of voting patterns in each of the state's thirty-nine cities and towns, which revealed the strengths and weaknesses of the party in the 1938 election. In doing so, he received assistance from an unlikely source. Former Republican state chairman William Pelkey provided him with invaluable information regarding support for his 1940 run, commenting, "Ever since I became acquainted with you, and that was when we were rival state chairmen of our respective parties, always I have had a high regard for your character and ability, your honesty of purpose, your devotion to square-dealing and your firm belief in party organization in politics."[6]

He continued, "that is why I and countless other Republicans in all parts of the state with whom I have discussed the situation can consistently support you...." Expressing his disgust with Vanderbilt, he condemned the Republican governor's "strictly personal machine" and complained that "party committee members and legislators are no longer taken into confidence as to party policies and there has been a complete discounting of the character and ability of many of his former Republican friends...."[7]

Former governor Quinn unwittingly corroborated Pelkey's statistics by alerting McGrath to the geographic areas of the state most in need of attention. McGrath's close analysis of local wards and precincts, coupled with the strategic political alliances he forged while serving as United States district attorney, combined to assure his victory in November. Further, he worked from the ground up by bargaining with local machine bosses regardless of their past sins or defection. In securing the Blackstone Valley, for example, he not only promised his nemesis McCoy two seats in the state administration, he bartered with Central Falls politico Andrew Sherry to line up the city behind McGrath.

> This morning Andrew Sherry was in and had a long talk with me about conditions in Central Falls.... He asked me to try to help to bring the forces together.... He assured me that the boys out there would be all right for our program, and also that he has had several talks with Tom McCoy, and that Tom has given him the distinct impression that he and I can get along well together. Andrew seems to think that we will have little trouble in the Blackstone Valley.[8]

McGrath's candidacy also benefited from the impending war clouds threatening America's borders. By 1940 graver struggles awaited, and the

McGrath mends fences with Pawtucket mayor Thomas McCoy. Here they are shaking hands at the Sesquicentennial in Pawtucket, 1940 (courtesy Special and Archival Collections, Providence College).

Democrats had to unite or face ruin. Just over a year after the election, the country would be thrust into global conflagration. Vowing to protect the civil liberties of all Rhode Islanders, despite foreign and domestic threats, J. Howard McGrath appeared on major radio stations to deliver strategically timed speeches that emphasized the need for all citizens to prepare for possible enemy attack.

Professing his support for the New Deal, McGrath followed the lead of his mentor, Theodore Francis Green, in backing Franklin Roosevelt's run for an unprecedented third term while he prepared Rhode Island's extensive coastline for the undeclared war in the Atlantic. He would accept nothing less from Washington than a guarantee that his state would not be forgotten. In McGrath's mind, the federal government must ensure the equitable distribution of goods and services in order to facilitate the destruction of totalitarianism in Europe and Asia. Capitalizing on President Roosevelt's New Deal legislation, McGrath organized the government with an eye toward reform and an expansion of the state bureaucracy to meet wartime needs, careful not to extend the state's resources beyond its means. Nonetheless, this period in Rhode Island history is also notable for the expansion of the power of the chief executive.

Despite, or perhaps because of, his history as a political insider, Governor McGrath gave the impression that he had minimized political concerns, orchestrating an effective balancing act both before and shortly after Japan's strike on Pearl Harbor on December 7, 1941. Between his inauguration in January 1941 and the attack that December, he initiated two separate but complementary programs:

1. A reorganization of state government;
2. An operative mobilization of the state's manpower to meet the impending crisis.

An analysis of McGrath's transformation from partisan politician to wartime statesman illustrates his emerging stature as leader of his party. With Green in Washington and McGrath in Rhode Island, their relationship represented the standard for effective cooperation between state and national government. As a result, the Democratic Party enjoyed national, as well as local, support. This period is also instructive for understanding the man and his motivations. Throughout his career thus far, McGrath had focused on building his status within party ranks and in the business community. With his reputation as party leader intact, he now redirected his efforts toward achieving a reputation as spokesman for his state and his region. By maintaining an effective equilibrium between federal and state power, McGrath was able to win the confidence of his constituency and praise from Washington officials.

Despite this success, McGrath had incurred enemies in his race to the top. The controversy surrounding his dual role as public servant and private banker and investor,[9] which had an overall impact on the final outcome of the Narragansett Race Track War and the wiretapping incident had not been addressed satisfactorily, and his detractors maintained that McGrath's personal and business ties influenced his legal decisions. These charges would dog him throughout his political life and eventually contribute to his final undoing in 1952.

While the evidence for what truly led to his final undoing will be dealt with in a later chapter, one factor can be stated with conviction: McGrath's determination to advance from state to national office prevented him from appreciating fully the vital role he would play as governor of Rhode Island. Up to this point, McGrath had fought for and achieved a solid reputation in the state, but the deliberate pace that he maintained without fail had allowed him little time for introspection. Having relied first on his father to direct his future, and then on Senator Gerry and General Hamilton, he had throughout the latter part of the 1930s turned to Senator Green as his principal advisor. Green taught McGrath well as he emerged from the war as an up-and-coming Democrat in the nation. So, while the governorship would eventually serve as a stepping-stone to higher office, for now, J. Howard McGrath had a state to run.

The New Governor

As newly elected governor in November 1940, McGrath looked forward to the awesome task that he would confront. He had been groomed throughout his life, first by his father then by Hamilton, to assume this role. He now looked to Green, who had recently recovered from surgery,[10] especially. Above all others, McGrath would come to value Green's restraint and political acumen to transform him from an eager political lieutenant to a refined statesman. McGrath reaped the benefits of Green's political ties and legislative genius. In exchange, Green was able to channel his success on the national level to Rhode Island, such as securing federal support for a naval air station, which was housed at Quonset Point on the western shore of Narragansett Bay. The commissioning of Quonset Point in July 1941, bringing with it both federal funds and national recognition, almost assured McGrath's success as a governor. The alliance of Green and McGrath fostered a balance between state and federal control. Though not guaranteed, their personal and political connections elevated Rhode Island as a leader in wartime initiatives, the successful construction of Quonset Naval–Air base, a case in point.

In December 1940, McGrath promised the Auto Dealers Association of Rhode Island that he was "not going up to the State House to knock the foundation from under it, nor to blast the Independent Man [the state's proud symbol, which rests loftily atop the State House] from the dome," but instead to improve the reputation of Rhode Island, known nationwide as a "State for Sale."[11] McGrath promised to put aside petty squabbles and foster a united front to meet the challenges ahead. Judging from several newspaper reports, he generally succeeded in his goal of overcoming partisan opposition and publicly united Rhode Islanders behind many of his programs.

In his inaugural message, delivered on January 7, 1941, to both houses of the General Assembly and an array of local notables, McGrath opened with a passage from the Book of Judges: "If indeed you mean to make me king, come ye and rest under my shadow." Implying his deference to God and to the people of the state through this clever allusion, McGrath constructed his image as a disinterested public servant who humbly chose "to take this oath with hand resting upon the Holy Bible and upon these words which are found in the Old Testament."[12]

Throughout his political life, J. Howard McGrath relied on the sage advice of Theodore Francis Green. Here he is (left) with Green (right) and presidential hopeful Alfred E. Smith in Washington, D.C., on September 13, 1932 (courtesy Special and Archival Collections, Providence College).

McGrath's inaugural message set the tone for his administration. Keenly aware of the public's immediate concerns, he contended that the reorganization of the state bureaucracy and social welfare reform would work hand-in-hand with a clear and active program for civilian defense. In turn, he would be assured of the state's active role in facilitating war preparedness.

Following the covert advice of Republican, William Pelkey, McGrath fostered bipartisanship by first writing to both Democrats and Republicans, alerting them of his desire "to interfere as little as possible with the function of your respective bodies." He reminded them, however, that he could not "escape [his] responsibility to do everything possible to secure passage of the legislation promised by my party," and also to recommend "passage of legislation promised by the Republican party where conflict did not exist."[13]

Thus, he forwarded a copy of his reorganization plan to both Democrats, including Senator William G. Troy and House leader James H. Kiernan, and Republicans, including Senate leader Charles Algren, and Representative

Governor J. Howard McGrath with Mrs. McGrath (the couple at center) and Lieutenant Governor Louis Cappelli and Mrs. Cappelli at the Governor's Inaugural Ball, January 1942. Also pictured are Secretary of State Armand Cote and Mrs. Cote (courtesy Special and Archival Collections, Providence College).

Hugo A. Clason. McGrath employed his personal and political sense to promote goodwill with both parties and the press.

Following the pattern set by the Bloodless Revolution of 1935, which replaced 80 overlapping boards and commissions with 11 departments, and replaced all five Republican Supreme Court judges with Democrats, McGrath now sought further reorganization of the state bureaucracy.

McGrath considered his plan a "first step in the program of mutual cooperation." At the suggestion of former Republican state chairman William Pelkey, McGrath recommended that the basic rules of the General Assembly be altered "upon unanimous petition of the minority members of either House, any bill in committee that had previously passed one House and was in the other House awaiting concurrence would be placed upon the calendar for a vote." Citing similar legislation in the U.S. Congress, McGrath presented his proposal as a means to gain control of the General Assembly.

By consulting with both parties as suggested by Pelkey, McGrath shrewdly appeared to support bipartisan cooperation and honest government. Appealing to patriotic and parochial sentiments, McGrath suggested that "an orderly process at the State House would be the finest selling point that we could have to promote the good name of Rhode Island beyond the borders of the State."[14]

Yet McGrath did not entirely eschew opportunities to jab his opponents, including the amendment of the Republican-sponsored Broomhead Bill. The Broomhead Civil Service Bill, first enacted under Republican governor William Henry Vanderbilt, required all government employees regardless of political affiliation to sit for a merit examination. It had been enacted into law in 1940 after several heated debates between Republicans and Democrats.[15] Vanderbilt had heralded the Broomhead Bill as a revolutionary step toward eradicating corruption in the state, accusing the Democrats of using civil service legislation as a means to control patronage. To counter political cronyism, Vanderbilt recommended publicizing examination results so that no candidate, or candidate's supporter, would be tempted to alter their scores for political gain.[16]

Because Vanderbilt, however, was viewed by his party as an interloper, he failed to receive the necessary support from within the ranks to ensure the law's permanence. McGrath set to amending it as soon as he took office. As governor, McGrath publicly denounced segments of Vanderbilt's civil service legislation, but was careful not to criticize the plan wholesale, since portions of it, according to the civil service commissioner, writing to Senator Theodore Francis Green in 1939, were highly workable. Instead, McGrath pointed to particular features of the Republican version that were in need of improvement.[17] The first of these was the appeal process. McGrath explained that similar laws in many other states had provided more direct and effective appeals procedures to protect the rights of injured parties. Under the current law, he argued, civil service workers terminated or were otherwise denied basic civil rights had no mechanism to voice their concerns and no assurance "of a fair and impartial hearing before disinterested bodies."[18]

The second section that needed improvement was that which awarded civil jobs to the highest scorer on the examination. The winning applicant would then be officially appointed by the director of civil service, thereby completely bypassing the various department heads, who, according to McGrath, were the best judges of the needs of their respective agencies. Informed by executive assistant of the U.S. Civil Service Commission that this section of the bill was potentially unconstitutional, McGrath suggested an alternative based on proposals recommended to Senator Green by the U.S. Civil Service Commission. The new plan would grant the governor sole authority to name a three-member state Personnel Advisory Board whose primary function would be to choose a candidate from among the top three scorers on a merit-based civil service examination.

After months of debate between the two parties, the Broomhead Bill finally passed with several revisions on May 1, 1941.[19] Following the date of passage, the term of the sitting Civil Service Commission ended, and McGrath was granted authority to appoint a new body. The revised bill stipulated that those who had served the state for five years would be required to pass a "qualifying" examination based exclusively on job-related information, whereas those employed for ten years or more would be excused from taking a written test. However, the method of choosing the director as stipulated in the Broomhead Bill was kept intact.

Ironically, by widening the chief executive's power to distribute political patronage at will, the bill would potentially increase, not reduce, political nepotism. Thus, while the plan was hailed as a move toward progressive, nonpartisan government, it in reality replaced the sins of one party to make way for the sins of another.

McGrath's second major reorganization proposal came in the form of an omnibus bill, introduced into the House of Representatives on February 21, 1941. This Bill contained a number of provisions that would strengthen state control by expanding McGrath's role as governor and modify existing programs. Although some of the changes were editorial and mechanical, others were more substantive, granting the governor, for example, the authority to transfer jurisdiction of duties or offices from one department to another. The entire Reorganization Bill, at 182 pages, proved difficult to maneuver, and much of it died in the General Assembly, since many Republicans feared that it would ultimately grant the governor too much power. Nonetheless, important proposals in several areas of the Reorganization Bill passed.

Senate opposition to McGrath's reorganization plan, which strengthened the state executive and increased government spending for the development of wartime agencies, was based on the grounds that it was too costly. Many Republicans in the Upper Chamber became alarmed at the possibilities of postwar debt, an unwieldy infrastructure, and a dominant chief executive.[20] Capitalizing on the global crisis to play simultaneously upon the patriotic and parochial sentiments of the legislators, McGrath warned the assembly that a politically split legislative branch would stymie important, perhaps life-saving, measures vital for the state's defense. He argued that in the interest of all Rhode Islanders, the Reorganization Bill must be implemented to eliminate outdated, confusing procedures that had caused logjams in the government process. With the rise of global authoritarianism, he believed Rhode Island could ill-afford the luxury of bipartisan jealousies.[21] He underscored the urgency of streamlining existing programs and enacting new measures to ensure the state's readiness to confront threats from abroad. Thus, by presenting his program as the first line of defense against the enemy, he gave his measures a better chance for success in the General Assembly.

McGrath looked upon his limited successes as a victory and punctuated his first months as governor in a speech that underscored his efforts at bipartisanship: "Since my inauguration, I have never permitted myself to forget that ours is a government no less of Republicans than of Democrats. I believe that the events of today have been the justification of our two-party system, of progress by compromise."[22] In keeping with this sentiment, McGrath allayed Senate fears of financial insolvency by laying the foundation for a just, categorical fiscal plan for the future, which emphasized a balanced budget.

Addressing the Thirty-Third Annual Governors' Conference in Cambridge, Massachusetts, in July 1941, he proposed setting up a reserve fund in times of prosperity to meet the growing needs of the crisis and maintained that wartime spending would not inevitably result in economic insolvency. McGrath reminded his audience that "state governments ... have an important part to play because of home defense,"[23] suggesting that his fellow state governors postpone nonessential expenses, such as elaborate building programs, until the postwar period.

At this meeting, McGrath proposed the formation of a commission to prevent the overlapping of state and federal taxation. Since the First World War, he explained, the federal government had increased its demands on the public, while the states also continued to levy taxes based on the need to meet expenses and protect citizenry from threats overseas. To solve the potential crisis, McGrath recommended that this commission coordinate the outlay of federal and state taxes, warning his fellow governors not to rely too heavily on federal funds, saying, "If we do we may find when the war is over, that the cause of democracy will have suffered."[24] He believed that by surrendering its jurisdiction to the federal government now in the name of expediency, the states would inevitably suffer later when their power was diminished.

McGrath then called for the formation of a board to coordinate state and federal tax outlays, ensuring that neither the state nor federal governments would levy taxes (such as personal, inheritance, gasoline, and tobacco) beyond their respective jurisdictions.[25] Accordingly, he averred, "States can't sit and allow the encroachment of the Federal system of taxation upon the fields heretofore reserved to the States."[26] As a leader and outspoken proponent of his region, McGrath earned a reputation as a credible, fiscally cautious chief executive. Reminiscent of his mentor Peter Gerry, who also looked upon excessive federal controls suspiciously, McGrath, while recognizing the importance of a strong central government, fought on behalf of his state's independence.[27] His stand would come to represent an important breakthrough in the balance between federal/state jurisdiction in Rhode Island.

Capitalizing on President Roosevelt's New Deal legislation, McGrath organized Rhode Island's government with an eye toward reform and the expansion of the state bureaucracy to meet wartime needs. He sponsored social legislation, administering funds for reform measures, such as veterans' benefits, and a State Housing Authority for defense workers, which would work in tandem with the federal government to "assure the availability of safe and sanitary dwellings for persons engaged in national defense activities."[28] He also called for an updated old-age insurance bill in keeping with his mentor Theodore Francis Green's commitment to New Deal policies.

Internationally, war clouds loomed, and in response, President Roosevelt requested a $1.1 billion appropriation for military expenditures. As a result, he had to endure a mountain of abuse from the rising tide of American isolationism.[29] The passage of neutrality legislation in 1935 tied the president's hands, but by moving slowly and efficiently he was able to circumvent many of these restrictive laws. Stretching each measure to its constitutional limit, FDR slowly began to rearm America in preparation for a war he believed to be inevitable. When he proposed the passage of universal conscription through the Selective Training and Service Act of 1940, several vocal isolationists responded. Senator Gerald Nye of South Dakota insisted that the last war had been fought over munitions profits and claimed that a peacetime draft would violate the United States Constitution.

On December 18, 1941, following the Japanese attack on Pearl Harbor, Congress granted President Roosevelt extraordinary powers to regulate production by placing wartime agencies, including the War Production Board and the Office of Price Administration (OPA), directly under his control. The expansion of federal power was justified on the grounds that a centralized bureaucracy would facilitate a more seamless transition from peacetime to wartime. Charged with establishing price ceilings to prevent inflation, the OPA also facilitated the nation's rationing drive, which proved essential for winning the war. The OPA assumed unprecedented control over the economy.[30]

In Rhode Island, McGrath responded by outlining a seven-point plan on December 8, which included his directive for all Japanese "aliens" to register with local authorities. He further charged the new adjutant general Peter Leo Cannon[31] to call up the state guard's sixty-nine officers and nearly one thousand men to protect locations, such as the state airport and state armories, that were deemed vital to national defense. Rhode Island manpower responded post haste; recruiting offices were flooded with enlistments. According to McGrath, by December 16, 36 air-raid posts had become operational and 39 cities and towns (or 100 percent participation) had organized defense councils.[32]

McGrath conferred with Adjutant General Peter Leo Cannon to convert the state to a wartime "footing," coordinated effective local defense plans with city and town officials, and negotiated with the five other New England governors to ensure that the region was treated equitably by the federal government.

Almost immediately, additional National Guard units were stationed at waterfronts, oil tankers, and reservoirs to prevent possible sabotage, and patrols were posted along the coast to defend Narragansett Bay from possible enemy attack.[33] Mayor Dennis Roberts of Providence increased police presence at Fields Point,[34] and guards were posted at industrial and utility plants, such as Brown and Sharpe Manufacturing and the Narragansett Electric Company.[35]

Although only 22 percent of Rhode Island's population had supported intervention in May (just above the national average), the majority of the state's population backed the president by December. "Hundreds storm recruit stations," reported the *Providence Journal*. U.S. Representative Aime Forand, who had rejected Congress's repeal of neutrality just months before, now proclaimed that "there is no time for argument."[36]

America's entry into war also modified the state government's approach to foreign-born citizens. Although the state's Japanese population was small (50 Japanese in Providence) in comparison to the West Coast, McGrath ordered them to register with local police within 36 hours of the attack, as per federal directive. Police superintendent Edward J. Kelly is quoted as saying, "we now know where we can put our hands on them [the Japanese]."

Additionally, Rhode Island had a significant Italian and Italian American population, who, if considered an "alien" were also required to register with the Federal Bureau of Investigation in the Industrial Trust Building in downtown Providence. McGrath attempted to ameliorate the potential social crisis that could result from their suspicions. In Rhode Island, nearly 12,000 Italian Americans registered with local authorities as illegal aliens and those deemed by the FBI as "dangerous" were transferred to internment camps at Fort Meade, Maryland, Fort Missoula, Montana, and Fort McAlester, Oklahoma.[37]

Even before America's entry into the war, McGrath as governor had pledged support for those on "relief," including the 25 percent of the population categorized as "alien" and thus deemed ineligible for employment in defense plants. He and Department of Social Welfare director Clement France took steps to facilitate the naturalization of as many as possible, thus improving their employment status. The immigrant population still considered unemployable would receive training in order to improve their opportunities for future employment in other sectors.[38]

Cautious in his overall approach to social issues of the day, McGrath nevertheless was a pragmatist who refused to discard productive or potentially productive members of society simply because of their race, religion, or ethnicity. According to historian William L. O'Neill, "the integration of so many new ethnic groups into the mainstream of national life was the greatest American accomplishment of this era."[39]

As the son of an immigrant father, McGrath was sympathetic to those less fortunate, and was consistent before, during, and after the war in his support of marginalized groups. His efforts on behalf of the thousands of displaced persons during the Cold War period is another illustration of his overall support for racial, religious, and ethnic diversity.

Not unmindful of possible danger from internal threats, McGrath warned his constituency to be vigilant and cautious at all times. However, he never advocated indiscriminate incarceration of aliens living within Rhode Island's borders. This firm, yet temperate, response ensured the loyalty of a majority of Italian Americans, who in December 1941 pledged their support for the United States, which turned into a loyal following at the polls that previous November.

McGrath's response to the call for civilian workers was no less vigilant. A few days after the Japanese attack, McGrath proclaimed to the people of Rhode Island, "none shall be idle in the common service." Although the State Defense Council had already been established under his predecessor, McGrath facilitated the smooth coordination of local defense councils. In line with the Office of Price Mobilization director William Knudsen's support of the "Work or Fight Program," McGrath predicted that at least 10,000 in the state would be "engaged" in civilian defense.[40] Still, he issued a mild reproach to local leaders who failed to heed the call for the establishment of defense councils in each city and town. He explained later, "the danger then seemed so remote that our appeals in many cases met with apathy and indifference."[41]

McGrath's successes during this time rested on his ability to rally his constituency behind a national ideology. According to James J. Landis, "Modern warfare requires of us, as of all nations, a total effort. Our morale must be all-comprehensive."[42] A leader must be able to inspire, and a cause must be considered worthy in order for men and women to endure physical deprivation. "It is not a state of mind existing in one man alone, but in many."[43] The governor, acting as the commanding officer of his home army, must ready the people for battle on the home front. Like war on the battlefield, civilian defense, according to Landis, is "total."[44] In this regard, J. Howard McGrath was a notable success, accomplishing a near total mobilization of Rhode Island's manpower and resources due to his ability to inspire the state's citizens to join in the effort to combat totalitarianism.

Nonetheless, Rhode Island's civilian defense experienced setbacks. When a false alarm sounded at Mitchel Field in New York on December 9, miscommunications to New England municipalities, including those in Rhode Island, resulted in a haphazard, bungled performance by local civilian defense teams. Alerted to the need for a more uniform system of air-raid preparedness, Governor McGrath named Colonel Earl C. Webster, formerly commander of 243rd Artillery, director of civilian defense on December 16. McGrath then concurrently conferred with Adjutant General Peter Leo Cannon to convert the state to a wartime "footing."

Among the many duties of the Council of Civilian Defense was the assurance that all Rhode Islanders were prepared in the event of enemy attack. Thus, the governor and his council met in closed session, and as a result Rhode Island soon became an exemplar in establishing the authority between local and state defense.

Warning Rhode Islanders to be vigilant, the Rhode Island Council of Civilian Defense cautioned, "you may be fighting in this war tomorrow, or next week, or next month," so each citizen must "learn and remember what to do if enemy planes and bombs come."[45]

In all, lights must be extinguished. "Don't light matches. Don't smoke." Those away from home "in an automobile" must "pull over to the curb … shut off lights and ignition and seek shelter."[46] The directions were disconcerting and caused confusion, and in some cases, anger.

One citizen, lamenting the restrictions, provided a creative response to dimout restrictions imposed by the state government:

> Last night when I lay down to sleep,
> My mind was all at sea.
> The evening paper I'd just read
> Had not made sense to me …
> If "Dimout's" end is coming soon,
> As noted by the press,
> Why all this extra ballyhoo,
> I pass—it's now your guess
> [Published in "Warden New" East Providence Dist. 1., October 20, 1943].[47]

Despite grumblings, Rhode Island soon became a model of harmony between local and state defense. Authorizing the development of educational programs to teach potential air-raid wardens proper procedures for guiding air-raid drills, McGrath achieved his objective of having all posts operate at nearly 100 percent efficiency within a year. In April 1942, the General Assembly finally granted the governor broad and extraordinary powers to be utilized in defense of the state and its people," and the executive immediately ordered statewide blackouts, which proceeded without error in sixteen of the state's locales.[48]

By December 1942, Rhode Island's defense program had earned accolades nationally. McGrath reported that during that year, 350 women and 250 men worked a total of 25,000 and 16,000 hours, respectively, overseeing the Providence District Warning Center. With a combined total of 41,000 hours, Rhode Island citizens had worked to protect their state from enemy air raids. McGrath was quick to point out that this figure did not include the conscientious performance of the Newport District Warning Center volunteers.

He reported that 2,000 citizens had learned vital skills necessary in the event of attack through their enrollment in the 16 civilian defense schools established throughout the state. With the publication of manuals for auxiliary police and radio's sponsorship of various "classrooms" on the air delivered by employees and other experts on topics relating to civilian defense,[49] Rhode Island's citizenry appeared well manned and aptly prepared to confront the hardships commensurate with wartime.

As over 90,000 Rhode Islanders who would serve in the Second World War departed for basic training, many shipping to ports unknown in Europe or Asia, their families fought to maintain a normal, stable existence.[50] For the people of Rhode Island and throughout the United States, "security had been family, and bank deposits and life insurance and of a sudden it seemed to hinge on the spitting fire of bullets in the Solomons, on the speed and firepower of pursuit planes, or on the salvo of big guns at Midway."[51]

Civilian defense had become real for Rhode Islanders, as it had for all in the United States. It "created a system of protection and through that same organization more scrap could be found that would make bombers and ships and tanks that would fight, more rubber could be conserved that would keep wheels turning that otherwise might stop; more food might be saved that was as necessary to the defense of Stalingrad as ammunition."[52] In his final analysis, McGrath summarized the meaning of civilian defense for Americans. "The local defense council must be, in short, the war cabinet of the community."[53]

Reflecting on Rhode Island's achievements, McGrath in his 1943 inaugural address commended the armed services and the state's defense programs. Soon thereafter, he would exercise his authority under the Emergency War Powers Act by declaring Rhode Island in a state of emergency due to food and fuel shortages. Placing schools on a fixed schedule of four days a week, McGrath fought to maintain the state's independence while simultaneously seeking its compliance with federal regulations.[54]

As the *Pawtucket Times* noted in a 1942 editorial, "No citizen with wholehearted interest in the welfare of the state will wish to have the Governor's hands tied; he must be given the power of initiative in wartime in greater measure than in days of peace." However, the paper cautioned that "every piece of legislation designed to enlarge his authority must be debated with the greatest thoroughness."[55] The author, however, shared his faith in the governor's discretionary use of power. "We believe him fully when he says: 'I realize fully that only the bitter act of war could justify any Governor in asking for such extended authority.'"[56]

By the end of 1943, air raids continued to run monthly, and the director of the state's defense council Brigadier General Earl C. Webster cautioned local chapters to be sure to "forward to the Warning Centers" notification of "enemy action that has taken place" in each city or town. Webster's reproach evidenced a lack of full cooperation from each city and town and indicated a breakdown in the system despite accolades that had been bestowed upon the state for its efforts. According to one Davisville newsletter, 65 men failed to show for an important air-raid drill, which looked like "dollar day at Macy's Basement" since the gunners moved about haphazardly, seemingly unaware of their surroundings. Another writer sardonically replied, "If it had been the real McCoy, the enemy could have moved in, mowed the lawn, had a chicken dinner and a 2-hour nap before the defenders knew what the score was."[57]

Nonetheless, instructions to each command center were explicit:

To Receive Message:
  Answer telephone
  (a) Be seated in front of Warning District Phone ...
  (e) Speak in conversational tone.

Each signal was color coded, from the original "use of GREEN 1, GREEN 2, GREEN 3, and GREEN 4," to "YELLOW, BLUE, RED and WHITE for all actual "air raids and for air-raid drills" will be preceded by the word 'Practice.'"[58]

Rhode Island strove to achieve "uniformity and clarity" in its civilian defense exercises and to secure full participation. Accordingly, Webster directed, "voice is extremely important" for Control Center Telephone Operators. The original "Green 1" et. al, was established in order to avoid "confusion with regard to the type of test being given," since the Rhode Island Council had ordered four separate series of tests, including "Mobilization, Control Center, Communications, and Blackout Tests." Misreading signals may have resulted in a breach of security.[59]

Despite the drawbacks, Governor McGrath commended the armed services in his 1943 inaugural address, although he would warn all who were complicit in black market activities, that they would be punished. Exercising his powers under the Emergency War Powers Act, McGrath declared Rhode Island in a state of emergency due to food and fuel shortages. He also mandated that all Rhode Island schools adhere to a fixed schedule of four days per week, and that all public buildings remain closed on Mondays. Retail establishments not vital to the war effort were ordered closed on Saturdays.[60]

The Black Market in Rhode Island

As director of the local Office of Price Administration (OPA), Italian American Christopher Del Sesto mounted a vigilant campaign in October

1943 against the black market in fuel and the questionable use of ration coupons, which led to the capture of several possible conspirators. His call for an investigation eventually yielded positive results, since illegal usage declined by 7 percent, but not before he endured criticism from several sources.[61]

Although most Rhode Islanders observed federal regulations restricting the allotment of rationed goods, such as rubber, sugar, and scrap iron, Del Sesto uncovered a black-market ring operating out of the Blackstone Valley and other Rhode Island regions.

His campaign commenced after a woman referred to as Mrs. Frolich grew suspicious when she witnessed the removal and burning of ration coupons in her Pawtucket office. Thomas R. Kelley, associate investigator, secretly probed alleged violators in Central Falls and Pawtucket, Rhode Island, where illicit trafficking was most prevalent. Investigators discovered that gasoline coupons were either missing or destroyed, which provided an opportunity for certain individuals to receive greater allowance than the government mandated. Tracing the origin to chairman of the Ration Board Dr. Peter J. Savoy and Andrew Sherry, former bootlegger and then-current boss in Central Falls, Del Sesto issued stern warnings, but he found breaking local machine control over the local civil service difficult to overcome.

After a theft was discovered in the Woonsocket civil defense office on Montagu Street, McGrath gave his blessing to Del Sesto for the establishment of a new "black market special squad," whose first duty was to solve the mystery of the robbery.[62] Composed of one officer each from six local precincts, the squad, in cooperation with the city and town police departments, would eventually root out offenders.[63]

Del Sesto vowed to eradicate the practice, punishing "'known and ruthless criminals who have control of the black market in gasoline ration coupons" and urging prison sentences for violators. Uncovering 12 (twelve) gas station operators engaged in black market activities in violation of the War Powers Act, the OPA director declared war on them by calling for a grand jury probe. According to the *Providence Journal*, "the story of a black market in gasoline is so prosperous that its operators could afford to give a bonus of 10,000 gallons worth of coupons to one filling station." Albert A. Passerelli and Ralph Palumbo, the ring leaders of the Providence fuel racket, were both questioned by the police and held at $65,000 bail awaiting trial.[64]

In 1944, severe restrictions on tire and fuel use also proved inconvenient, and in some cases, detrimental to the state's economy. Even surplus reserves from the previous year was insufficient to meet the crisis.[65] Subsequently, Del Sesto and his fellow New England directors mounted an all-out campaign to stamp out violators by "strik[ing] at the heart of a vicious criminal group responsible for much of the multi-million-dollar ration racketeering in New England."[66] They determined that many black-market racketeers had extensive police records "dating from prohibition." An unnamed OPA representative predicted that "a large number of important arrests of known ring leaders will come at any time."[67]

In Rhode Island, Del Sesto instructed local boards to refuse to distribute fuel "where the intended recipient has at least a ten-day supply, except for public gas and electric utilities, and for domestic use."[68] He also mounted a campaign to root out counterfeiters, warning that "those found guilty of accepting them [counterfeits] will be severely punished."[69] For his efforts, he was lauded with a "Roger," an honor bestowed upon recipients for "outstanding community service."[70]

Despite setbacks caused by these violators, McGrath was able to ease the burden for many in the state. He called upon his political and administrative expertise to maneuver around the various roadblocks that he encountered in leading the smallest state through the war. His efforts produced a significant, though modified, civil service act, a revised tax structure, and a praiseworthy civilian defense. His timely negotiations had secured for Rhode Island a naval air base, and would succeed in overcoming Republican opposition to obtain notable social legislation.

9

McGrath and FDR's Second Bill of Rights

In the midst of World War II, President Franklin Delano Roosevelt delivered an emblematic State of the Union Message on January 11, 1944, intended to awaken the country to the needs of the postwar world. This speech has come to be referred to as the Second Bill of Rights. It grew out of the National Resources Planning Board's 1943 draft blueprint for postwar planning, Postwar Planning and Security, Work, and Relief Policies.[1] In this speech, Roosevelt called for health care reform, full employment, and federally funded housing, among other significant proposals, the seeds of which originated during the Second New Deal in 1935.

This address, however, became the defining point for a "new" New Deal, which equated the health care needs of individuals with the security of the country. Roosevelt built on the edicts originally outlined in his "Four Freedoms" speech in 1941. Now, in addition to freedom from fear, he further developed one to ensure a postwar America free from want, poverty, unemployment, and inadequate health care. In bold language, the president declared that the original Bill of Rights could not meet the needs of a population that had witnessed the heinous atrocities carried out by totalitarian regimes bent on world domination. In the president's estimation, "people who are hungry and out of a job are the stuff of which dictatorships are made."[2] The nation's prosperity would be compromised if its government failed to secure inherent rights for present and future generations. As a culmination of a plan advanced during the Great Depression, Roosevelt saw an active, though not unwieldy, federal government as a remedy to help secure the basic needs of all Americans. He sought the assistance of the New England state's governors to guide his program to its thoughtful conclusion.

By 1940, the president had chosen more conservative advisors, and in this 1944 State of the Union speech he refrained from wholesale blandishment of industry, instead working to attain a balance between the private and public sectors. He continued this progression, as he began to plan for a postwar economy, by equating full employment with security.[3] Thus, the Second Bill of Rights, according to Constitutional theorist Cass Sunstein, was the apogee of a decade-long trial that challenged and ultimately redefined the nation's traditional concept of rights.[4]

In Rhode Island, Democratic governor J. Howard McGrath worked to position himself as an advocate of the president's postwar policies.[5] He targeted several social reforms in his campaign to align himself with the president's Second Bill of Rights. McGrath realized that support for Roosevelt's program would benefit both the state and his career. Following the directive of his mentor, Theodore Francis Green, McGrath was careful to forge an independent path for his state, while at the same time expressing his support for the President's initiatives regarding the Second Bill of Rights.

McGrath's platform incorporated full employment and health care (cash sickness benefits, among others), as well as social reform for veterans (a hospital and other agencies to assist in the veterans' acclimation to civilian life) and families (notably, a juvenile court). But first McGrath had to overcome the resistance to his legislation from Republicans, beginning with their hesitation in granting him emergency war powers.[6]

While praising the president's wartime initiatives, McGrath argued that "neither government nor industry, nor labor, nor the vast accumulation of financial reserves" must assume unchecked power. In order for democracy to capitalize on its victory over totalitarianism, "all of these agencies and all of these resources must be brought together to work in a cooperative and unified effort."[7] Only then would the fruits of democracy prevail over the ravages of war.

With this in mind, he spearheaded legislation to promote disability benefits for Rhode Island workers and included in this initiative the support of cash sickness benefits and compulsory hospital insurance. In addition to his healthcare plan, McGrath campaigned for the implementation of a juvenile court. Recognizing that war had brought about the disruption of family life, McGrath called on the General Assembly to put aside its partisan misgivings and agree to sponsor a separate children's court to hear cases involving youngsters under the age of 18.[8]

In an address at the Biltmore Hotel in Providence on Wednesday, February 10, 1943, Governor McGrath outlined his program for the visit of Mr. Charles P. Taft, the assistant director of the Office of Defense, Health and Welfare Services: "I think it is particularly appropriate that Mr. Taft should come to Rhode Island at this time because our State is not so deeply concerned with the problems with which his office has been established to cope.... We know that defense is not just a matter of planes ... guns and tanks. We know that the defense of civilian health and social welfare play an important role."[9]

McGrath reiterated and streamlined his plan in a more detailed presentation on postwar planning at the National Governors' Conference in Pennsylvania in late May 1944. He reminded his fellow governors that each state possessed the requisite tools to direct its public works initiatives "without undue national direction," sounding the alarm against a postwar national behemoth and opting for industry to partner with each state to ensure the safety and security of all Americans.[10]

Accordingly, McGrath recognized that the emergency brought on by external threats called for America's citizens to be healthy, well educated, and employed to combat internal and external threats. "Recognizing that conflict abroad brings about 'many serious problems ... problems of care for the children of working mothers ... of juvenile delinquency ... of recreation ... of public health ... of social protection ... of justice to aliens ... and of family adjustments due to war time conditions.'"[11]

Insisting that the "morale of the people on the home front is important," McGrath established a "revolving fund" available for Rhode Island's citizenry to use during wartime, remarking that "a man fighting in the Solomons is dependent to some degree upon the fact that his pregnant wife is receiving satisfactory medical care."[12] The revolving fund would be utilized when "civilians" working in home defense needed help paying their medical bills. He insisted that the president's "Four Freedoms," especially the third freedom ("freedom from want") would be met by Rhode Island during the conflict. "We, in Rhode Island, believe that the cities and towns, and the State have some responsibility for making this freedom a reality now."[13]

At the same time, McGrath's proclamation invoked President Roosevelt's 1941 Inaugural Address by calling on all Rhode Islanders to uphold the Four Freedoms. According to the governor, "economic security by which we can claim to be both a free government and a democracy," to the "boys from Rhode Island and New England [who] are defending democracy with their lives."[14] He advanced the idea that in order to protect the economy, state government must work in tandem with industry to foster a strong, viable postwar world.

Given the changing political climate, legislation guaranteeing postwar reconversion in the United States took on new meaning. Democrats endeavored to follow Roosevelt's blueprint for reforming the economic infrastructure, but state governors had to balance their need for federal assistance with the need to retain their autonomy. McGrath's third inaugural address, delivered days before Roosevelt's Second Bill of Rights speech, anticipated the president's plan for the postwar country, while maintaining the integrity of his state, and by implication his power as governor.[15]

The governor explained, "A compulsory hospitalization insurance law would give to Rhode Island hospitals a measure of financial stability." He vowed to ensure "the right to adequate protection from the economic fears of old age, sickness, accident, and unemployment." He also promised to wait until "the time when such increased facilities would be available," and extended his concern to Rhode Island's veterans: "We, in Rhode Island, do not believe that the responsibility for the care and readjustment of the veteran to civilian life is the sole obligation of the Federal Government."[16]

This chapter will focus on McGrath's implementation of the principles in Roosevelt's initiative in the Second Bill of Rights as he prepared his state for the transformation from a fully mobilized war machine to a peacetime state. The world war had provided an opportunity for a new look at the role of the state and federal government in the lives of America's citizens. Eager to capitalize on this transformative attitude, McGrath latched on to the country's willingness to accept a more active federal government while emphasizing that his initiatives would be best controlled by the state. His cash sickness plan was an example of a program "operated better by the States where the details of the system could be integrated efficiently to the economy and the needs of local conditions."[17]

Cash Sickness Bill

On the issue of health care, McGrath stood at the vanguard of change. His cash sickness bill, passed by the General Assembly in 1942, became the standard for other states to emulate. The bill was introduced into the General Assembly by Pawtucket notable Ambrose P. McCoy, brother of the city's mayor, and signed into law by McGrath on April 28, 1942; recipients would begin receiving benefits on April 1, 1943, and could receive them for up to 20 weeks.[18] At that time, the fund had a reserve of $2,659,937.33, procured from the unemployment compensation account at a rate of 1 percent of the employee tax.[19]

Rhode Island provided an ideal setting for this bill, since cash sickness funds would be administered by the Unemployment Compensation Board (UCB), in place since 1936. The measure required both employees and employers to earmark money specifically for unemployment benefits. The governor believed that cash sickness was necessary since neither the unemployment nor workman's compensation plans would provide for loss of wages due to illness. According to *Providence Journal* reporter David Cameron, "the State will [after April 1] begin another lively experiment under its Cash Sickness Insurance program, the first State in the United States to undertake a plan by which the $22-a-week weaver or the shipfitter at Fields Point will be cushioned against part of the financial shock of sickness."[20] The program would eventually allocate monies for returning veterans.[21] Cameron further pointed out that the plan "is another step toward cradle-to-the-grave security."

If successful, Cameron predicted, "sickness insurance plans such as the one here in Rhode Island may be the common practice throughout both England and the United States."[22]

Chairman of the Public Health Committee of the Rhode Island Medical Society Dr. Herman C. Pitts echoed McGrath's fear that well-meaning senators or representatives might weaken the state's power over its health care benefits, saying, "the very laudable effort Rhode Island has made to maintain her independence in purely State affairs will be overshadowed by the greater power of the Federal Government."[23]

Despite the guidelines established by the Unemployment Compensation Board, the bill in its initial form proved too open-ended. The *Providence Journal* reported that in the first six months of operation, from April 1 to September 30, nearly two million dollars in benefits were distributed to 123,154 claimants, resulting in a deficit of $724,519.18. In November 1944, analysts reported that $3,335,044.20 had been distributed to claimants in an eight-month period, whereas only $3,881,162.07 was paid out in the entire previous fiscal year. Some physicians found themselves in a difficult position: "What am I to do—I am the family doctor—the patient asks me to sign the form so that he can collect benefits—I am not sure whether or not he comes within the Act, so I sign and let the Board decide."[24] The marked increase in outlays alarmed the governor and prompted critics to call for change. According to the *Providence Journal*, "At this rate disbursements during the current fiscal year will have increased approximately 50 percent by next March."[25] The *Journal* also reported that a sizable portion of the fund had been distributed to 4,309 pregnant women, some of whom suffered from "allied complications" following birth, while additional funds were allocated to workers who lost income due to "mental and nervous disorders and … heart ailments, arthritis, tuberculosis, cancer, neuritis, and asthma."[26] While the categories in and of themselves do not reveal cause for alarm, the overlapping outlay of benefits troubled the governor, who directed the UCB to conduct an investigation. The subsequent report revealed some interesting loopholes in the cash sickness law.[27]

According to the Ninth Annual Report of the State Unemployment Compensation Board, published in 1945, the cash sickness benefits were disbursed in excess of receipts over a 21-month period. They found twelve persons guilty of fraud after investigating 32,624 claims made in 1944.[28] In addition, many women still collected benefits during the year following their pregnancies, depending on the birth date of their child. The Board stated, "it is now possible for large numbers of women to collect from $300 to $500 for one pregnancy." In total, women constituted 15,094, or 56.4 percent, of the total 26,415 claims.[29]

The Board also discovered that funds had been distributed to 25.3 percent of claimants for both workmen's compensation and cash sickness, in excess of 100 percent of their regular weekly earnings. Finally, Board members criticized fund outlays to retirees, since, they stated, former workers no longer contributed to cash sickness. In all, by the end of 1944, the program "face[d] insolvency." The *Providence Journal* estimated that at the 1944 rate of distribution, the fund would confront a $600,000 deficit in the following year.[30] It recommended that since the program was "not run on a sound actuarial basis,"

1. one half of 1 percent of employee deductions should be transferred from unemployment compensation to cash sickness fund,
2. claimants should not receive both workmen's compensation and cash sickness benefits that would exceed the maximum figure allowed,
3. all information of claimants should remain confidential in administering of benefits,
4. restrictions should be imposed on benefits allocated for pregnant women [according to Mortimer W. Newton, chairman of the UCB in 1945, pregnant women were allowed to claim illness for up to eighteen weeks],[31] and
5. subsidies should be apportioned for the administration of both the state and federal programs.[32]

The Board's findings contributed to a reform of the cash sickness program, which was instituted over a three-year period, from 1943 to 1946. In April 1943, the act was amended to allow the governor the right to issue a state of emergency upon notification that the reserve fund would become insolvent. In addition, the General Assembly also approved an increase from 1 to 3 percent "in excess" of the yearly contributions for the administration of the fund.[33]

In this legislation, McGrath proposed the establishment of a five-man committee, "knowledgeable in financial matters," to oversee the management and allocation of monies, and demanded an immediate cessation of "double dipping," whereby claimants collected funds from both workmen's compensation and cash sickness.[34] According to the bill, the governor would appoint the board, with endorsement required from both houses of the General Assembly. The legislation stipulated that "whenever the directorate believes that a change of benefit rates would become necessary to protect the solvency of the fund," it may announce a state of emergency and act accordingly by withholding or decreasing benefits as necessary.[35]

Suspecting McGrath's desire for more control over the Board, the Republican Senate labeled the plan unconstitutional. Chairman of the Republican Steering Committee John G. Murphy criticized McGrath's call for this additional advisory body because it "is a too broad delegation of legislative power."[36]

An editorial in the *Providence Journal* challenged Republicans to consider legislation that they had supported in the past, namely the state unemployment compensation law. The author argued that the law would not "set a bad precedent," since the governor's bill was "identical in purpose and closely similar in language to a section of the State unemployment compensation law for which Republican members of the Assembly voted in 1937 and which has been a part of that law ever since."[37] Although the author was concerned about the measure's constitutionality, "we are informed by competent legal advisors that they are 'unable to find, either in Rhode Island or elsewhere any precedent which bears at all closely on the constitutionality of all provisions such as those' contained in the Governor's bill."[38]

By August, however, unemployment claims had increased alarmingly, and critics of the plan were overshadowed by the immediate needs of the state. Thus, Rhode Island disbursed $67,757.16 to 4,094 out-of-work laborers the week of August 11, with $58,222.37 granted to 3,507 workers the following week. Three hundred and fifty claimants were former employees of the U.S. Rubber Company in Warren, in the East Bay region, while in the Blackstone Valley, several Woonsocket textile mills closed their doors temporarily to convert to a peacetime economy.[39] Many of these workers had hoped to return to work when the conversion had been completed, but some plants, like the Goodyear Fabrics Corporation, closed their doors for good, leaving many workers without a job.[40]

These layoffs affected the cash sickness program, since outlays decreased during the period when unemployment compensation demands were highest. During the first week of September, 4,929 claimants received a total of $386,406.37 for the month of August, the lowest level since April. In their analysis, the Unemployment Compensation Board deduced that a reduction in hours improved the health of Rhode Island workers.[41] However, that explanation did not account for stress due to loss of wages and/or employment.[42] At the end of September, Brown and Sharpe Manufacturing announced the need for skilled laborers in their foundry, and jobs also became available in other manufacturing plants.[43]

McGrath continued to laud the cash sickness program, and it helped gain him notice. However, the plan was not foolproof. As he found during his tenure as governor, those reaping the benefit of sickness funds continued to receive benefits under workmen's compensation, causing the balance to shift dangerously as the war came to an end.

Under McGrath's successor, Governor John O. Pastore, the General Assembly paid heed to the Board's suggestions by requiring each person who claimed both cash sickness and workmen's compensation funds in excess of his/her income to register with the Unemployment Compensation Board.[44] This limited reform ensured the future of cash sickness. The new governor deferred to financial and medical analysts to determine the most "equitable" method of distributing funds, which discouraged abuse, and in the end this plan opened the door for government support of cash sickness. He maintained that in order to "safeguard" the fund, the General Assembly should "appoint a committee, or grant me the authority to appoint a commission," to "report ... on the proper changes to be made after a complete study."[45]

Compulsory Hospitalization

McGrath had less success with a bill establishing compulsory hospitalization, an idea that received media attention with Roosevelt's delivery of his Fourth Inaugural Address, namely his Second Bill of Rights speech in January 1944. National legislation was proposed in anticipation of the president's message, but it, like the Rhode Island version, suffered from its ambition. McGrath first mentioned compulsory hospitalization insurance in his 1944 Inaugural Address to the State, and in it expanded on the president's Second Bill of Rights. Realizing that cash sickness, while innovative and a step in the right direction, "only partially meets this threat [serious illness in a family, which would result in heavy hospital costs]." The governor explained that "a compulsory hospitalization insurance law would give to Rhode Island hospitals a measure of financial stability." His plan called for comprehensive hospital coverage at a total cost of 5 cents per day, paid for equally by the employer and employee on a quarterly basis. The insured would be entitled to meals, medical attention provided by qualified nursing staff, and medication deemed essential by physicians.[46]

Deferring to the medical profession, McGrath promised to wait until "the time when such increased facilities would be available.[47] By cautioning his constituency that "we must begin to think ahead of the Federal government with respect to future social security programs," McGrath in his 1944 inaugural address paved the way for state-led health care reform with an emphasis upon a secure role for private enterprise. He cautioned, however, "the events of the past year have demonstrated clearly the need for close cooperation between the State and Federal Governments if a happy solution of our common problems is to be reached." To that end, he recommended that the total contribution to this program should be five cents a day shared equally by employer and employee, thus further increasing the amount deducted from the paychecks of Rhode Island's citizens.

In concurrence with the Rhode Island Medical Board, McGrath proposed several guiding principles:

1. a reliance upon "existing facilities," rather than the construction of new ones,
2. a broad program to ensure that the maximum number of citizens could participate,
3. a program in which businesses and the state "share together financial responsibility for a program with a minimum State participation."[48]

Following his message, the *Providence Journal* applauded McGrath's plan as far superior to the two-hundred-page national bill drafted by Senators Robert F. Wagner of New York and James E. Murray of Montana, as well as Congressman John Dingell of Michigan, which called for national compulsory health insurance.[49] McGrath's program, however, was still too ambitious for Rhode Island legislators.

Still, McGrath was initially optimistic about compulsory hospitalization insurance, which he referred to as a "broadening" of the existing Blue Cross plan to insure that all workers received social security allotments. He continued, "Blue Cross has shown to me in my state that prepaid hospitalization represents a sound principle of society." Nevertheless, four months later, on May 12, 1944, in addressing the Tri-State Hospital Assembly, he advised, "we must have support of the medical profession if [these] programs will succeed."[50]

Just after his annual message in February 1944, McGrath named the president of the Rhode Island Medical Society, Dr. Michael H. Sullivan of Newport, and Dr. Elihu S. Wing as chairman and vice chairman, respectively, of the newly formed Health Council, which would also include members of the medical field, representatives of hospital administration, industry, labor, nurses, and others. Tasked with conducting a study on the viability of compulsory hospital insurance, they would report their findings to the governor upon completion.[51] Dr. Sullivan applauded McGrath's deliberate approach to the health care issue. The governor comprehended the enormity of the task that lay ahead for the committee and urged patience on the part of the public, cautioning, "it must also be borne in mind that the hospitals today have not the facilities to furnish all the services contemplated."[52]

In a *Providence Journal* editorial, the author, like Dr. Sullivan, praised McGrath's stand on Rhode Island's health care needs, and pointed out that the governor should not be hasty since "[additional hospital] facilities cannot be provided until after the war." Cautioning that "insurance for hospitalization alone raises numerous questions that cannot be answered overnight," the author reminded Rhode Island legislators and the governor that "the people would not be justified in approving the proposal unless they were convinced that it was a financially prudent one."[53]

McGrath set out to prove that it was. In concurrence, Dr. Sullivan proposed a thorough study on hospital insurance and other related health care plans. To facilitate the process, he recommended the establishment of several committees, including a technical committee, which would weigh the possibility of eliminating surgical care in a proposed hospitalization legislation calling for "a comprehensive plan of benefits which would meet the social objectives implied in a compulsory program."[54]

By his third inaugural address delivered on January 2, 1945, McGrath focused on the compulsory program, and also encouraged moderate federal intervention, urging the General Assembly to assume a "businesslike approach" to building projects and universal health care. He agreed with Dr. Sullivan and proposed a voluntary advisory council be formed to gauge the viability of compulsory hospital insurance and postwar planning, which would include the construction of additional hospitals, including a veterans hospital, and health care facilities without precipitating an economic crisis.[55] This council, led by Dr. Arthur H. Ruggles, superintendent of Butler Hospital in Providence, included representatives from the medical and business fields, who were privy to the latest data.[56] Further, the members of the council formed a subcommittee to research the needs of the state relating to compulsory hospital insurance and the construction of new hospitals and medical facilities.[57] In the meantime, as a result of the proposed plan, local hospitals embarked on expansion and fund-raising programs to improve their facilities; Rhode Island Hospital in Providence proposed a $5,000,000 modernization plan, while Memorial Hospital in Pawtucket sought $300,000 to construct a new building.[58]

Their subsequent report, published in February 1945, recommended that the compulsory hospitalization proposal be tabled for the time being, pending additional study. The advisory council reported that "hospital facilities are not now available for the number of patients that might be expected if compulsory hospitalization insurance were made effective immediately."[59] They also recommended that the technical committee investigate several insurance companies as possible options for funding the plan.

After polling a number of insurance firms, the committee found their rates prohibitive, and recommended a delay in implementing comprehensive hospitalization insurance. Although disappointed, Governor McGrath observed that "we are perhaps making as rapid progress under the present (voluntary) system as we could make under compulsory hospitalization."[60] Based on the committee's findings, then, Governor McGrath mandated that employers work in tandem with Blue Cross to provide reasonable health coverage under a voluntary system. He reasoned that the state had been working toward "100 percent coverage," and with additional encouragement would achieve positive results once the war had been won.[61]

Following the hospitalization study, a subcommittee of three representative governors, including McGrath, Democrat Herbert R. O'Conor from

Maryland, and Republican Raymond E. Baldwin of Connecticut, traveled to Washington in July 1945 to discuss possible solutions to the serious food shortage in the North. Drawn from a larger committee of 14 governors who had convened in New York on June 22, McGrath, O'Conor, and Baldwin gained national attention and wide coverage in the press. Traveling from Mackinac Island, Michigan, they expressed their views on unemployment compensation, the construction of additional hospitals, a constructive plan for the postwar country, and national health insurance. McGrath expressed his disapproval of plans funded entirely by the federal government, and instead supported the concept of federal/state grant-in-aid, where the state would only accept federal funds when it could no longer subsidize its program.[62]

Governor McGrath recognized that many governors were fearful of sweeping health care programs, commenting that "states' rights were bound to be a major question in a proposal of this magnitude."[63] He responded that federal monies would be available for the construction of state hospitals and other agencies and facilities as granted by the surgeon general of the United States. Yet, he pointed out, while the program will be administered on the federal level, local agencies will be established with authority to direct state and regional operations, including outlays to individual claimants for each respective program.[64]

At the conference, McGrath emphasized his support for the Wagner-Murray-Dingell Bill, especially its provisions for additional financial assistance to the states. He reminded his fellow governors that failure to enact the legislation would breed economic insecurity and in the long run provide socialists and communists with ammunition against democratic governments.[65]

The Wagner-Murray-Dingell Bill, first introduced in the Senate on May 24, 1943, then modified and reintroduced to the 79th Congress on May 24, 1945, embraced the concept of equitable health insurance. Senator Wagner and his co-sponsors capitalized on president Roosevelt's Economic Bill in backing an insurance plan for all Americans, which would add approximately 15 million laborers to the existing program.[66] In addition, the bill increased the benefit package from $5 to $30 per week (based on dependents and income) and supported six different programs, including liberal federal grants-in-aid to states to construct hospitals, public health facilities, welfare services for pregnant women, and compulsory hospital insurance[67]; it would prove to be one of the most controversial bills of the decade. The bill also included a clause extending temporary disability to between 26 and 52 weeks, based on the availability of funding, and included "Old Age and Survivors' Insurance" at $20 to $120 per month. The bill's directive to "centralize" and "nationalize" the economy terrified conservatives and state leaders alike. Wagner "pooh-poohed" detractors by stating, "We cannot win the peace with forty-eight separate economic programs."[68] In endorsing the Wagner-Murray-Dingell Bill with the stipulations above, McGrath adapted Roosevelt's Second Bill of Rights to the needs of his state.

The national response to the Wagner-Murray-Dingell Bill presaged the fate of similar legislation in Rhode Island. Senator Robert F. Wagner, a liberal reform advocate, would die without realizing his goal for national health care. According to his biographer, J. Joseph Huthmacher, Senator Wagner's measure, "nearly two hundred pages," foreshadowed the "emerging welfare state." He further observed that although Congress supported liberal treatment for veterans as espoused in the GI Bill,[69] they would not loosen the barrier against nationalized health care or unemployment insurance for war laborers on the home front. Thus, this plan went down in defeat both in the country as a whole and in Rhode Island.

Like the cash sickness plan, the fight for compulsory hospital insurance would continue under his successor, John O. Pastore. Pastore, in his annual message as the new governor of Rhode Island, paid "tribute to [his] predecessor, J. Howard McGrath, the Solicitor General of the United States," for the "splendid manner in which they conducted the State's business during the war emergency."[70]

In his address, Governor Pastore noted the "great job of production that was accomplished here at home and in which Rhode Island played such an important part." The conversion and development of Rhode Island businesses and naval bases, such as Brown & Sharpe Manufacturing (Walsh-Kaiser), Textron, Inc., Quonset Point and Davisville-Naval Air Station, and the Newport Navy Base, resulted in the production of liberty ships, parachutes, Quonset huts, uniforms, and torpedoes.

Pastore emphasized the number "of those who served will return bearing the scars of battle." As Governor Pastore recognized, "we cannot fully repay our debt to them ... [but] we are determined ... to do everything that a grateful state can do to see that our disabled veterans are properly cared for, hospitalized and rehabilitated."[71]

The Rhode Island Juvenile Court

During the war, Rhode Island, like other states in the Union, wrestled with the rise of juvenile delinquency. Democrats wanted to have the young people treated as juveniles rather than adults in the criminal court system, but the state had to overcome several political impediments to this reform effort.

On June 15, 1898, a year before the very first national juvenile court bill passed in Cook County, Illinois, the Rhode Island legislature passed Chapter 581 of the Public Laws: "An Act Relating to Juvenile Offenders," which designated that a minor "under the age of sixteen years charged with any crime or misdemeanor" would be tried "separate and apart from the arraignment and trial of other cases." Seventeen years later, in 1915, the General Assembly built upon this legislation by recognizing juveniles as a distinct class under the law.[72] Governor Quinn attempted to pass further legislation on behalf of these children in 1937, but it took groups like the League of Women Voters and the Junior League of Rhode Island, along with the political guidance of Governor McGrath, to finally bring the campaign to its successful conclusion in 1944.

In his first inaugural address, McGrath called for the "establishment of a juvenile court system" and authorized his attorney general to gather all data available on the situation in the state.[73] Following the Japanese attack on Pearl Harbor, McGrath called for the state to act as a community parent, while ensuring the preservation of the nuclear family. By all measures, the juvenile court bill would be a positive step toward fulfilling that role.[74]

Anticipating an uphill battle, McGrath named Dr. John E. Donley, former state director of social welfare, to lead a group of Rhode Island representatives from the American Federation of Labor, the Rhode Island Bar Association, the Consumer League, and the Parents and Teachers Association, plus the chiefs of police and the state's chief information officer in creating a report on the feasibility of a separate children's court for the state.[75]

The committee prepared legislation to submit to the General Assembly in 1941, which they believed would respond positively and equitably to the epidemic of delinquency. The bill emphasized a need for a separate children's court designed to handle the sensitive nature of juvenile infractions. They argued that with America at war, President Roosevelt's cry for America to become the "arsenal of democracy" required the combined efforts of men and women to transform the country's industrial infrastructure into a war machine. This meant that an increasing number of mothers found work in automobile and aircraft factories and shipyards and were away from the home, possibly exposing the country's children to demoralizing influences.[76]

Statistics compiled in the Providence District Court supported McGrath's concern with the juvenile justice system.[77] It was during the war years that the state's capital experienced the greatest number of juvenile infractions. Providence Sixth District Court judge Luigi DePasquale noted a 22 percent jump in the number of delinquent boys and girls from 1942 to 1943. Further, a newly formed Youth Service Committee, organized to determine the causes of increasing delinquency, concluded that rehabilitation of the child must emphasize the role of parents as the primary caregivers.[78]

Despite growing support for the movement, McGrath still had to overcome one of the greatest obstacles: the Rhode Island General Assembly, especially Senate Republicans who balked at the bill's provision to grant the governor the sole power of appointment. The core Republican opposition had organized itself into three main camps: first, conservatives who preferred to retain juvenile matters in the 12 district courts; second, those who supported a children's court housed within the Superior Court infrastructure; and finally a more liberal faction, which advocated a separate court but recommended that "during the formative period" the body should function as an appendage of the Sixth (i.e., Providence) District Court, under the auspices of Justice Luigi DePasquale, the judge most familiar with juvenile problems.[79]

The *Providence Visitor*, a newspaper that was read devoutly by Rhode Island's Catholic population,[80] took particular exception to the bill's premise that parents should "surrender to law [their] Christian duty ... to cultivate their children."[81] In the end, however, political and social considerations outweighed religious ones, for the governor had strong support on many fronts, and despite the *Visitor's* reservations, many of his Catholic friends supported a juvenile court bill. By 1944, he had succeeded in getting the measure through the Senate. Addressing his constituency on April 6, 1944, after he signed the amended Broomhead-Shunney Juvenile Court Bill into law, Governor McGrath announced, "I think this will mark a great step forward that no one will be sorry for."[82]

What made the Rhode Island law unique was its insistence that each officer of the court be "a member of the Rhode Island Bar in good standing." According to Richard John Maiman, "portions of the Juvenile Court Act are remarkably legally-oriented considering the character of juvenile courts elsewhere."[83] The bill also offered three distinct classifications of "children" as concerns of the criminal justice system.

(a) "Delinquent children: those under 18 who have "violated city or town ordinance."
(b) "Wayward" children: those who "deserted home without good cause," or those who "habitually associate[d] with dissolute, vicious, or immoral persons."
(c) "Neglected" children: those whose parents "neglect or refuse, when able to do so, to provide such support ... necessary for the health, morals or well-being."[84]

Finally, the bill provided families unable to afford legal counsel with public defender services. Although adolescents were granted the right of appeal to the superior court, the law did not establish their rights to trial by jury, an omission that would eventually prove troublesome.[85]

Representatives from the League of Women Voters celebrated the bill's passage, writing the single word "Success" in their "Voters' Log" for April 1944.[86] They commended Governor McGrath on his guidance throughout the process.

Despite the bill's carefully worded passages, House Republicans still opposed McGrath's sole power of appointment. Furthermore, they viewed the selection of his close ally, Providence Democrat Francis J. McCabe, as chief judge to be a vindication of their fears. Even the appointment of Republican James B. Littlefield as associate judge did not silence their opposition. But the Republican-dominated Senate, pressured by vocal and prominent supporters of the bill, eventually approved the candidacy of both.[87]

While juvenile court advocates hailed the legislation as being of epic proportions, the initial operations were delayed until July 1944, and a report of July 1944 through July 1945 revealed that the number of wayward and delinquent youths was still substantial. A total of 1,381 juveniles were brought before the court; 1,183 of whom were boys, while 198 were girls. According to the report's statistics, 14- and-15-year-old boys committed most of the infractions, while the majority of girls brought in for various offenses were aged 15. Judges McCabe and Littlefield reported that in all cases fair-minded judicial officers handled the young miscreants with care.[88] A report in the *Providence Journal* substantiated this, concluding that after close observations of approximately 40 cases "in at least ninety percent" of children brought before the court, "the defendants and their families left feeling obviously a lot better than they did when they came in." Commending the judges' approach to justice, the reporter was confident that "the proceedings" were "on the level of the social clinic and seminar."[89]

McGrath and the Veterans' Hospital

In addition to Rhode Island's youth, McGrath also paid particular attention to veterans returning home. Treading gently where veterans were concerned, McGrath wanted to ensure that legislators and citizens did not overwhelm soldiers with well-meaning but impractical legislation designed to force their readjustment to peacetime. In his Inaugural Address delivered on January 2, 1945, McGrath cautioned the General Assembly that "none of us knows exactly what the veterans collectively would have us do for them," but Rhode Islanders could "keep our State financially strong so that when they [the veterans] do come back we can offer them an acceptable token of that gratitude."[90] To that end, he facilitated the establishment of various agencies designed to help veterans transition to domestic life.

The governor was able to secure $20,000 specifically to insure veterans. Reminding Rhode Islanders that the veterans represent the "taxpayers of tomorrow," he believed that the country owed returning soldiers proper benefits to meet their needs. He also conferred with General Frank T. Hines, who reported that from January to November 1943 more than $8,443,000 was issued to widows and other dependents of men killed in the line of duty, and over 222,000 pension applications were filed with the local Veterans' Administration.

Nationally, President Roosevelt had set up legislation to ensure that the country would be ready to meet the needs of its fighting men. According to the manual issued to soldiers and sailors upon their return,

> most men who have already received a discharge have found out that when you go home you don't just go out of Army or Navy life; you go into another new life. With considerable surprise you get home and find that civilians live in a different world. They speak a different language. They don't know what you have been through.[91]

In his Second Bill of Rights, Roosevelt tried to anticipate the physical needs of the returning men. According to the provisions of the GI Bill, a modified version of the Second Bill of Rights, Congress was authorized to appropriate $500,000 to build hospitals and other facilities deemed essential to the overall health and livelihood of the veterans. In the following year, the new president Harry Truman, in keeping with Roosevelt's initiatives, approved legislation calling for the construction of a state hospital for veterans in 1945. This factor prompted Rhode Island senator Green, who was instrumental in the drafting of the original plan, to lobby with Rhode Island representative Aime Forand, for federal funding.

The campaign for a veterans' facility in Rhode Island began after the First World War. Republican Jesse Metcalf had first proposed a hospital for returning soldiers in 1937, pointing out that the state's fighting men had sacrificed for the country and were now in need of proper care.[92] Green in the Senate and Forand in the House of Representatives took up the banner in the mid–1930s, but, unlike Metcalf, the federal authorities believed the hospital unnecessary since Rhode Island's hospital in Newport would be sufficient to meet the demands of the interwar years.

Unfortunately, the Second World War brought more casualties, both physical and emotional, which revealed the state's limitations in dealing with the needs of servicemen and women. As one of three states (with New Hampshire and Delaware) that did not have a fully functioning veterans' hospital, Rhode Island, argued Green, suffered undue hardship, since its wounded veterans would have to travel great distances to receive proper medical care.[93]

Confronted with a recalcitrant Veterans Bureau chief and a Congress leery of the expense, Senator Green finally won his point by campaigning on behalf of the "number of disabled veterans from World War No. 2 added to those of previous wars." In his estimation, Rhode Island with "the huge expanse of Narragansett Bay," has supported "a large part of the American Fleet" and should be guaranteed ample facilities for its disabled soldiers (and sailors).[94]

In Rhode Island, Republican senator George Beaucage led the way by drafting a bill, which he introduced into the General Assembly; at the same time, Governor McGrath was campaigning vigorously for a state veterans' hospital. Senator Green and Representative Forand introduced new legislation in the Senate and the House, respectively. Appealing for a 200-bed hospital and an allocation of $1,300,000, they finally claimed victory, when President Roosevelt lent his support for their plan. The president's Serviceman's Readjustment Act, or GI Bill of Rights, was an outgrowth of Roosevelt's Second Bill of Rights and would provide the necessary funding for construction of the new hospitals.

In February 1944, the senator told Rhode Islanders that the state "is practically assured" of a veterans' hospital. President Roosevelt, who was "sympathetic" to Green's proposal, arranged for him to meet with General Frank Hines, who assured Green that he would propose to the Federal Board of Hospitalization the construction of a new hospital for Rhode Island veterans.[95]

In June 1944, Green finally convinced the Veterans Administration to build a VA hospital in Rhode Island. He had a welcome ally in Dr. Arthur H. Ruggles, superintendent of Butler Hospital, who understood, at least in part, the ramifications of soldiers returning home from war. Ruggles warned that the medical personnel and facilities in Rhode Island were inadequate to care for these returning soldiers, some 45 percent of whom would be suffering from the effects of "neuro-psychosis."[96] The inauguration of the Charles V. Chapin Psychiatric Clinic, which opened its doors in Providence on April 30, 1945, was a start, but not enough to handle the onslaught of discharged soldiers returning from overseas.

A fully functional veterans' hospital was essential for the economic and social health of the state, Ruggles argued. He, along with many medical professionals, supported a "business as usual" response, focusing on postwar planning for a viable economy to employ the soldiers coming home from war. Most of the literature of the period advised soldiers to return to life as it was before the war began, and Ruggles suggested that employment would be "one of the best treatments"[97] for a distraught postwar veteran. However, he argued, this did not obviate the need for a veterans' hospital; instead the two should work together.

McGrath supported the need for added facilities, including a hospital on the one hand and economic recovery on behalf of the veterans returning to the state on the other. He sponsored a veterans' center, to "provide assistance to the 80,000-odd Rhode Islanders in the armed forces as they return to face the difficult problems of rehabilitation and readjustment to civil life."[98]

The bill (H 624), which permitted Governor McGrath to "convey State property to the United States Government for the purpose of erecting a Veterans' Hospital," passed the General Assembly on February 10, 1944. The law stipulated that if the land proved inadequate, the governor "was authorized to use up to $50,000,000" to seek out an optimal location "within Rhode Island" to erect the hospital.[99] However, it took an additional thirteen months for the state legislature to agree on Davis Park in Providence as the site for the new facility.[100]

Following the bill's passage, the VA sent their leading design coordinator, Roy E. Guard, to investigate possible locations for the hospital. Guard recommended the Comstock property in the western part of Rhode Island over other sites that had been suggested, including the Vanderbilt Estate in Portsmouth, the Colt Estate in Bristol, the Dexter Asylum in Providence, and the Warwick city farm. The Comstock land's 145 acres was composed of ten acres lined with oak trees to the west, 74 acres of woodlands to the south, and a readily accessible clubhouse, estimated to be between 150 and 200 years old, situated to the north, with easy access to major roads into Providence. This provided an ideal location to house a 500-bed hospital, according to Guard.[101]

Nonetheless, Theodore Francis Green had originally targeted the soldiers' home in Bristol as a possible site to begin construction. However, he and the proponents of the legislation were stymied when Bristol senator Daniel G. Coggeshall, appearing to represent a number of older veterans who lived in the home, voiced opposition to the transfer of current residents of the Bristol facility to a new location. He stated that he "believe[d] the present arrangement for such maintenance and care should not be changed" to make way for a veterans' hospital, noting the unnecessary upheaval that the move would have on these older soldiers. Eventually, Coggeshall's wishes were granted, since he successfully blocked legislation permitting construction of the facility, and alternate locations were then considered more closely.[102]

In the meantime, local leaders in Cranston (Comstock), Cumberland, Warwick, and Smithfield continued to campaign for their respective city or town, but Senator Green's options were limited by the parameters set by the director of Veterans' Affairs, General Frank T. Hines, and the federal delegation who had been tasked with investigating the Green-Forand proposal for a veterans' hospital in Rhode Island.

The Veterans Administration Hospital finally opened on June 6, 1949. Operated by the federal government, 21 medical practitioners were hired to treat veterans of all conflicts. Able to care for nearly 400 patients, the hospital was not scheduled for "full activation" until May 1950.[103]

All told, then, by January 1, 1946, or shortly thereafter the State's Veterans Administration was able to offer the veteran a wide choice of services for physical and emotional illness. In addition to several Veterans Administration offices throughout the state, health care professionals provided medical and psychiatric screening to "determine [the] type of therapy" recommended for

each patient.[104] From outpatient treatment offered in "neuropsychiatric clinics" located at the Charles V. Chapin and Butler Hospitals, both in Providence,
to "fee-based" private consultation with physicians and psychiatrists throughout the state, the veteran was given a broad base from which to choose.
Nonetheless, the hand of the Veterans Administration guided and supervised
all referrals, and maintained a strict regimen for both patient and doctor.[105]

McGrath's Final Bid for Governor

At an open forum of the Women's State Democratic Committee, J.
Howard McGrath announced his decision to run for a third term as Rhode
Island's governor. After nearly four very successful years as the state's leader,
McGrath maintained that "Rhode Island owes me no further honor, 'for to
have served as the Governor during these trying days of war.'"[106]

His approach to office, by his own account, had been to encourage rather
than resist reform.[107] Now, his task would be to guarantee a healthy postwar
economy for returning veterans and those fighting the war on the home front.

Like President Roosevelt, McGrath realized that "unless there is security
here at home there cannot be lasting peace in the world."[108] According to Cass
Sunstein, the "most concrete result of the second bill of rights proposal was
the GI bill of rights."[109] As the nation prepared for America's returning veterans, governors throughout the nation took advantage of the funding, the
result of the President's Second Bill of Rights, to offer their constituencies a
variety of services ranging from public works, education, and health care.
McGrath was no different.

He had already authorized the establishment of a reserve fund to prevent
postwar deflation, and anticipated that Rhode Island would require approximately one million dollars per year for internal improvements. To speed the
process, he appointed a coordinator and executive committee under the
Rhode Island State Planning Board, which was created in December 1943.[110]
The General Assembly approved his request for a reserve fund earmarked
for the committee.[111]

Rhode Island's economy had been sustained by a number of industries,
recently converted to meet wartime needs. Brown & Sharpe Manufacturing,
which produced "an array of metal machine tools and precision instruments,"
Imperial Knife, which designed "blades and bayonets," and U.S. Rubber,
which crafted manufactured goods for the war effort, proved essential for
winning the war and for employing Rhode Islanders. Finally, McGrath's close
friend, Austrian-born Antoine Gazda patented the 20-millimeter Oerlikon-
Gazda antiaircraft gun, which proved most useful against Hitler's navy.[112]

In addition to existing facilities, McGrath oversaw the construction of
new industries, built to keep abreast of the needs of the war effort. Originally

housed at Fields Point, in Providence, the Rheem Shipyard proved challenging for engineers, who compensated for poor conditions by transporting soil, known as "fill" to the location.[113]

Representatives of the Walsh-Kaiser Plant, following the directive outlined in the Merchant Marine Act of 1936, which authorized production of modern vessels, journeyed to Providence to consider possible sites for a shipyard. They deemed Field's Point an ideal location. The commissioners then recommended that a six-way shipyard be built to support the construction of 32 Liberty Ships.[114] Rheems Manufacturing, noted for its water heaters and cartridges, had originally commenced operations at Field's Point in Providence in May 1942, but found the shipbuilding project too burdensome, so on February 28, 1943, the Walsh-Kaiser Company of California was commissioned to complete the job, and operated until July 1945.[115] Thus, McGrath had the good fortune of serving as governor during the oversight of the construction of Quonset Naval-Air Base, Davisville-Depot, and, now, the Walsh-Kaiser plant.

Economic difficulties at some of these facilities, most notably at Walsh-Kaiser, however, left the governor vulnerable to attack by the opposition. Although the political playing field was relatively calm in comparison to the interwar years, 1944 and 1945 would be trying for Governor McGrath. In seeking to ensure that Rhode Island would meet the demands of a wartime economy, while simultaneously preparing for peacetime, he would encounter some opposition from his Republican opponent Norman D. MacLeod, who challenged McGrath's bid for a third term as governor.

MacLeod questioned the record of the popular governor. Assailing him for his tentative approach to a labor strike at the Walsh-Kaiser plant in Providence in September 1944, MacLeod charged that the governor would prefer to let production lag rather than "hurt" his political supporters. He further blamed McGrath for the serious disruption in assembling cargo-combat ships at Walsh-Kaiser, essential to the Allied war machine in the Pacific Theater, and was quick to point out that this devastating stoppage "had a direct relation to our casualty lists and to the length of the war."[116]

In seeking to oust the Democratic incumbent, MacLeod exposed McGrath's penchant for avoidance when the political stakes were high. "You don't entertain [McGrath had most recently hosted the Duke and Duchess of Windsor] when your house is afire," pointing out that "it takes strength of character and selflessness to tackle such a problem. It might hurt a political future to put the State's machinery into action and bring about a prompt settlement."[117] The implications targeting the governor and the Democratic Party were painfully obvious.

While McGrath publicly dismissed the criticism as campaign rhetoric, he immediately responded by conferring with Walsh-Kaiser union leaders to facilitate increased production. He then planned several meetings in order to reconcile the demands of workers to the exigency of war.[118] A month earlier, in August, the Walsh-Kaiser Boilermakers' Union had walked out, protesting low pay and less than ideal working conditions. Lambasting strikers for their response to wartime controls, McGrath remarked that their behavior was "indefensible" in light of international conditions. He continued the strike had "marked and blackened" labor's history. In doing so, McGrath would cite the work of his father, James J. McGrath, who had led his knitters' union through many trials. McGrath stated that his father inculcated a certain work ethic in his children, and "at my father's supper table" the family had been steeped in the culture of labor unions. Identifying with labor, McGrath cautioned its leaders that "we (labor) are a minority, but that minority is supposed to raise the standard for everybody."[119]

Concluding with a very effective campaign strategy, he remarked,

> Don't vote for me if you feel that what I say is harmful to the cause. Don't vote for me if you feel I am inspired by any other motive than to raise the labor movement to a still higher level. Don't vote for me unless you can say, "My God, we have faith and trust in our State which can give us justice."[120]

His impassioned speech struck the voters, and by November 1944 he had easily trounced Norman MacLeod. Nonetheless, he could not dismiss the very real criticisms that were heaped upon him by MacLeod and the Republican hierarchy in the state.[121] Similar attacks would be lobbed at him when he entered the national scene. At this point, however, McGrath was viewed as a successful and proactive governor, and this attracted the attention of those in Washington, such as Vice President Harry Truman. McGrath began to harbor aspirations that would take him beyond Rhode Island's borders; nonetheless, he still hoped to leave the state in good working order for civilians and servicemen.

McGrath's Final Term

Thus, in his attempt to follow the prescribed blueprint outlined by President Roosevelt in his Second Bill of Rights, James Howard McGrath would commence his final term as governor by proposing a strategy for economic postwar planning to the Providence Chamber of Commerce. The plan had three main components for a federal and state strategy, which would determine how private industry can assist postwar efforts toward:

1. full employment,
2. demobilization, and
3. reconversion.

Although McGrath originally discouraged federal intervention, he came to believe that certain state government needs could only be realized with federal support. The Second Bill of Rights, no doubt, provided him with the impetus needed to secure federal-state funding. Nonetheless, he reiterated his oft-quoted warning not to "repeat the cardinal sin of joyously heaping their burdens on a central government and then complaining when Federal controls become irksome." McGrath cautioned private business not to become so mired in the exigencies of war that they overlooked the inevitable transition to peacetime when "we shall merely be catching up with a repressed demand and entering the era of a balanced and self-supporting economy."[122]

He supported a coordination of government and private industry to facilitate a seamless reconversion to peacetime. As early as 1942, McGrath began to address the anticipated postwar needs.

While profit losses both for business and government would be the casualty of the postwar period, and "none of us shall escape some of the hurts of post war adjustment," he aptly warned that "the war shall have been [fought] in vain if we sabotage the advances we have spelled into this spirit we call Americanism."[123]

With that in mind, McGrath embarked on a program to facilitate Rhode Island's transition from wartime to peacetime. Following President Franklin Delano Roosevelt's call for a Federal Retraining and Reemployment Committee under the aegis of the War Mobilization Board, Governor McGrath designed a plan aimed at ensuring the safe and productive return of its "sons and daughters to Rhode Island" at the end of the war. Subsequently, the Rhode Island General Assembly passed a law creating the Veterans' Retraining and Reemployment Committee in January 1945. Gathering one hundred citizens of the state from all walks of life to study the "rehabilitation problems" of returning veterans, the governor facilitated the establishment of various veterans' information service centers throughout Rhode Island to inform the veterans of "where and how [they] may obtain medical care which might improve [their] general health."[124] McGrath had already appointed 30 to an executive committee established to facilitate postwar planning for the servicemen and women.[125] Thus, the state in conjunction with the federal government was keenly aware of potential issues that could result from the decommissioning of its veterans, especially those with mental and physical disabilities.

In turn, Rhode Island officials promised that employment for former state workers now serving overseas would be guaranteed when they returned to the states. Already in late August 1945, 70 veterans resumed their old positions. The Department of Civil Service recorded 471 military personnel who had formerly held state jobs.[126]

McGrath, like President Roosevelt, pledged full employment for the state's soldiers, vowing "the fullest cooperation of the state government and all agencies which have been established to aid in this work, calling on the Veterans' Reemployment and Rehabilitation Committee to advise him on veteran affairs. Rhode Island became the first state to launch centers to train its counselors in the specific needs of returning military personnel."[127]

McGrath offered as a solution the establishment of a federally-run public works fund, which would act as a "lending agency" for the state loan applications to facilitate the development of public works' projects.

McGrath Resigns as Governor

Upon the death of President Franklin Delano Roosevelt on April 12, 1945, Rhode Islanders bowed their heads in reverence for the leader who had guided them through the Great Depression, the attack on Pearl Harbor, and the Normandy invasion. Though Roosevelt did not live to see the end of hostilities, Americans would still credit him with saving them from the evils of foreign aggression. Now, they looked to President Harry Truman to lead the country to the war's fateful conclusion.

When word of Japan's surrender reached Rhode Island in August, Governor McGrath cautioned his constituency to refrain from celebration until the official end to hostilities was confirmed from the president of the United States. He reminded Rhode Islanders that "the example of Japanese treachery" should "prompt us to be extremely cautious" in our actions. When President Truman officially proclaimed victory on August 15, McGrath followed suit by declaring "a period of thanksgiving for total victory," and requested that all "our people in their rightful jubilation" should "conduct themselves with dignity and decorum and a fitting sense of the majesty of great events" that led "to this day."[128]

Yet McGrath was going to have to count on others to see his vision through to reality. On September 29, 1945, he announced his decision to accept the post of United states solicitor general under new president Harry S Truman.[129]

McGrath was at the height of his power during this period. Dominating the state's airwaves and print media, he was nearly guaranteed a positive reception for his programs, despite Republican grumblings to the contrary. Demonstrating an active, yet balanced leadership style, as governor he had proven that he could successfully guide his constituency through the arduous demands of war rationing and the constant reminder of the conflict in the Pacific and Europe. As the world war drew to a close, the governor reminded Rhode Islanders that "none of us" will "escape all the hurts of postwar adjustment. That is as impossible as the thought that we can escape all of the bitterness of war." To his credit, his leadership combined the appropriate level of compassion and candor to gain the respect of the people and calm their fears.

10

A Vote for the Veterans

Before McGrath embarked on his national career, he needed to make certain that his final goal of ensuring that soldiers fighting overseas or training in camps throughout the United States would be able to cast their ballots in the 1944 election. Dedicating his annual address to the veteran, J. Howard McGrath promised to "build a better social and economic civil State to which in the glory of victory, they may one day, return."[1]

Over a year later, in March 1944, Governor McGrath affixed his signature to Rhode Island's Soldier Vote Bill. Flanked by the National Legionnaires, McGrath emphasized the historic significance of the event.[2] And indeed it was.

J. Howard McGrath's quest for the establishment of an absentee ballot for soldiers depended, in large measure, on the political environment between the Republicans and Democrats. Historian Donald Inbody comments in his recent study on the soldier vote that "it [the story of absentee voting] is a story about politics."[3] Yet, its impact represented so much more. It forced state and federal officials to determine whether they would surrender control of the ballot to those outside their jurisdiction. This fight pitted Northerners against Southerners, Democrats against Republicans, and states' rights advocates against those who supported federal control of absentee balloting. In many cases, these arguments intersected and overlapped causing a delay in the democratic process.

In Rhode Island, print media emphasized the bipartisan nature of the effort, where both Republicans and Democrats joined forces to guarantee civil rights "to those who are most entitled to it." According to McGrath, "this privilege should be theirs wherever their post of danger may be." Referencing the national campaign for a federal absentee ballot spearheaded by Senators Scott Lucas of Illinois and Theodore Francis Green of Rhode Island, the governor reminded his Republican opponents in the General Assembly, "No conclusions reached in Washington can possibly remove the barriers to a free exercise of the franchise by Rhode Island military personnel without cooperative legislative action on your part."[4]

Nonetheless, though Rhode Island's quest appeared noble and free from partisan jealousies, the evidence behind the scenes suggests otherwise. An astute public figure, Governor McGrath was not free from political intrigue. His covert wrangling with Republicans and Democrats to ensure that Democrats rather than Republicans received the credit for the bill's passage showcased his political acumen rather than his quest for patriotic bipartisanship. Only when he was assured the necessary votes did he publicly equate passage of the bill with patriotism.

On the other hand, the symbolic importance of securing the soldier vote, perhaps at first unbeknownst to McGrath and others who sought its passage, also represented a unique and tangential facet of civilian defense. It sent a message to the soldiers and the enemy forces that they so steadfastly sought to defeat that democracy would transcend national boundaries, and would ultimately showcase the resilience of federalism, as outlined in Article IV of the United States Constitution. Assuring Rhode Islanders that the United States would protect the inalienable rights of the boys fighting on the frontlines, McGrath pledged to men and women at home and abroad that totalitarianism would not interfere with their exercise of the vote.

After giving a brief background outlining the national effort to secure an absentee ballot, this chapter will focus on the steps that Governor McGrath took to guide this bill to its successful conclusion. In working to ensure that the Democrats, most particularly his administration, would be credited with the passage of the bill, McGrath, in guiding this important measure to its passage emphasized his role in guaranteeing the vote for the state's absentee military personnel. As with other legislation, namely, cash sickness and the juvenile court bills, McGrath's ability to galvanize the public in support of social causes contributed extensively to the successful passage in the General Assembly of the Soldier Vote Bill. Coupled with a carefully worded media campaign, which played upon the patriotic sentiments of the public, McGrath cornered his Republican opponents, who had no choice but to pass the bill or else appear unsympathetic to the needs of the fighting servicemen and women. The partnership between Senator Theodore Francis Green and McGrath, while political in nature, also served as a guarantor that the federal and state government would work in tandem to protect democratic institutions.

Background

Although the history of absentee voting rights for soldiers and sailors in America began when its nascent colonial governments declared their independence from England in 1776, serious debate over this issue did not commence until the outbreak of the American Civil War. Colonial and early national political intellectuals rejected the notion that voting privileges should be universal, since, as John Adams articulated, it was a mistake to open the franchise to "those men who are wholly destitute of property." Accordingly, he believed, they could not possibly hold a stake in the political health of the nation.[5] Thus, the necessity for an absentee ballot was not a priority for most government officials in the eighteenth century, and in fact, many believed that separate voting requirements for soldiers or other absentee citizens would inevitably lead to fraud and mismanagement.

Even more prevalent among critics of the absentee ballot, throughout its history, was the fear that the federal government would overstep its boundaries by venturing into the realm of state law. All considered, then, Rhode Island had not established absentee voting rights for its soldiers until the adoption of Article IV of the Rhode Island Constitution in August 1864, which mandated,

> Electors of this state who, in time of war, are absent from the state, in the actual military service of the United States, being otherwise qualified, shall have a right to vote in all elections in the state for electors of president and vice-president of the United States, representatives in congress, and general offices of the state.[6]

The amendment charged the General Assembly with the enactment of this legislation, and provided for the delivery of a "written or printed ballot, with the names of the persons voted for thereon, and his christian [*sic*] and surname, and his voting residence in the state."[7] The amendment was allowed to lapse until Rhode Island sent volunteers to fight overseas in the Spanish-American War. At this point, a makeshift provision was adopted, which allowed the military to vote in absentia. By 1924, however, Rhode Island had become one of three states that held the dubious distinction of failing to enact permanent, binding laws permitting its soldiers voting privileges.

The Second World War

The onset of the Second World War spearheaded a national movement to secure a federal mandate for absentee balloting for the country's military. However, passage of the bill was in no way guaranteed, since its advocates had to overcome serious obstacles before victory would be won. Most states, Rhode Island being no exception, instructed all citizens to register in person prior to election day, which proved unworkable after Congress enacted the Selective Service Act in September 1940, raising the number of personnel drafted into the armed forces to 335,000. After the Japanese attacked Pearl Harbor, the figures reached nearly two million. Included in these statistics were draftees from all ethnic and racial backgrounds, and although the military remained segregated, Southern states rejected a federal law authorizing absentee balloting, predicting that passage would bring the cause of African American civil rights to the forefront. Southern congressmen refused, therefore, to support any bill that would weaken the power of individual states to determine the requirements for voting and the time and place of elections. Opposing the federal government's infringement on segregation and other Jim Crow laws, Southern congressmen refused all efforts to nationalize the absentee balloting procedure. For them, this jurisdiction belonged to individual states.

On the other hand, President Franklin Delano Roosevelt soon realized that a national service vote could be a key factor to success at the polls in 1944. Although the date of Roosevelt's final decision to seek an unprecedented fourth term is open to question, evidence supports his desire to see the nation through to the war's end. With the brutal breakout following the amphibious landing at Normandy in June 1944, and the protracted struggle in the Philippines, the Marianas, and the China-Burma-India Theater, the Allies were in for a long road before peace could be realized.

Thus, advocates of a federal Soldier Voting Bill believed that it would garner the necessary encouragement for the president's fourth and final term. Public opinion polls, still in their infancy, corroborated their assumption by reporting that the majority of servicemen and women favored the incumbent president and a Democratic Congress.[8] A Gallup poll administered in December 1943 reported that over 60 percent of recruits supported the reelection of President Roosevelt.[9]

Successful passage of absentee ballot legislation for servicemen and women, then, would provide the Democrats with a lynchpin to victory and signal an important step in securing civil rights for America's military. More importantly, the measure would link the rights of the fighting men and women to the Democratic Party. According to historian J. Morton Blum, "the Democratic party would have to get out the vote … particularly [among] labor and servicemen." He continued, "the soldiers had to be enfranchised, the South appeased, the city machines rewarded, and the various ethnic constituencies recognized."[10] As part of his postwar program, which included public works projects, expansion of public transportation, improved housing, and an interstate highway system, Roosevelt also asked Congress to approve a plan for social security and educational provisions for returning soldiers. His call for a Second Bill of Rights for the veteran met with success in both houses of Congress by June 1944, and it was left to the American public to secure for the soldier his inalienable right to vote that November.

First proposed by West Virginia Democrat Robert L. Ramsay in the House, and Senator Theodore Francis Green in the Senate, the measure permitted the secretaries of war and the navy to deliver postcards to the various military bases throughout the United States. Then, the secretary of each state would submit a ballot listing all federal officers. Upon the state's approval, its candidates would be included as well. Soldiers would complete their ballots and mail them to their respective states. The bill, however, did not include a provision for servicemen and women stationed overseas, and made no attempt to alter Jim Crow laws in the south.[11]

Careful to protect states' rights in "naming the time and place of respective elections," Ramsey announced that this bill would only be invoked in areas where local laws were not already in place. Nonetheless, the Senate found the bill costly and unworkable, objecting that it would interfere with essential training in the field.[12]

Although Green, as chairman of the Subcommittee on Privileges and Elections, was disappointed with the final bill, he urged its passage since election day was drawing near. Finally signed September 16, 1942, the Soldier Voting Act only provided for absentee voting in the United States. Weakened by Southerners, who, even with Russell's revisions, feared that federal control of the ballot would frustrate their ability to secure Jim Crow restrictions on voting, the final legislation had only a minor impact on the national election. With only two months left until its passage and November, only one half of one percent, or 28,000 of the five million soldiers in the field were able to take advantage of the absentee privilege.[13]

While agreeing to the passage of the 1942 bill, Republicans nevertheless assumed that the service vote would favor the Democrats both nationally and statewide, and would thus impact significantly the 1944 national election.

Recognizing the importance of the soldiers to the election, the Democrats pressed more stridently for stronger absentee ballot legislation. Subcommittee Chairman Theodore Francis Green and Scott W. Lucas, Democrat from Illinois, sought to quicken the pace of election returns by introducing a new measure to streamline the process. The Green-Lucas bill stated that while military personnel would continue to use the postcard ballot as outlined in the Ramsay bill, they would issue ballots weeks earlier in order to allow for more timely voting procedures. Thus, the ballots would be submitted to the unit commanders, who would then choose an official election day for its military personnel. Green and Lucas later included a War Ballot Commission to oversee the process. Still opposed to a federal ballot, Southern congressmen rejected the notion, and by the time the measure passed, all controversial provisions, including nearly all "Federal controls" from the bill were omitted, much to the disgust of President Roosevelt.[14] While disappointing to advocates of a federal Soldiers' Vote Bill, the campaign did serve to quicken the pace of several states to confront this issue. Rhode Island, under the guiding hand of J. Howard McGrath, took hold of the reins to urge successful passage in the state.

Pursuant to the law establishing the federal war ballot legislation, a commission was established under section 301 (a) of Public Law 277 during the 78th Congress. Made up of the administrator of the War Shipping Administration, the secretary of war, and the secretary of the navy, the commission invited both the Democratic and Republican national chairmen to name a "qualified individual" to represent the voice of the respective political parties.[15]

The Rhode Island Soldier Voting Bill

The national trajectory regarding this legislation was not lost on Rhode Island's governor, who would use the bill to strengthen his appeal with the voters, and finally amend the state's constitution. Political issues played into the passage of this bill in Rhode Island as well, but for different reasons than in the South. The cumbersome nature of the state's constitution after its ratification in 1843, rather than race relations, impeded legislative progress. Only proposed 14 times in the state's history, amending the constitution was an arduous, convoluted procedure, and derailed a good many reformers throughout the latter half of the nineteenth and first half of the twentieth centuries.

Nearly impossible to achieve given the state's political makeup during the industrial age and beyond, the constitution thus retained its conservative provisions, including outmoded property requirements, an unrepresentative assembly, and inadequate provisions for ensuring suffrage rights for absentee soldiers and sailors unable to register to vote as required by law.

First promoting the concept of absentee voting in his 1942 annual message, McGrath informed his constituency that Rhode Island laws were "inadequate to preserve the franchise for our soldiers and sailors."[16] Approximately 75,000 soldiers would have become eligible for the franchise in 1944. Secretary of State Armand Cote reported in mid–October that only 265 men and women of the 988 absentee ballots received were members of the armed forces. At that time,

> any legally qualified elector of Rhode Island, whose name appears upon the official voting list of the City of Providence, expecting to be absent from the State on Election Day, November 3, 1942, and desiring to vote for National and State Officials ... MAY APPLY TO THE SECRETARY OF STATE, STATE HOUSE, PROVIDENCE, RHODE ISLAND IN PERSON OR IN WRITING OR AN AFFIDAVIT FORM SETTING FORTH HIS APPLICATION FOR AN ABSENTEE VOTERS' BALLOT.[17]

In addition, the existing law in the state only allowed absentees to cast their ballot for national office (i.e., members of the United States Congress), thus effectively silencing their voice in local elections. Finally, Cote predicted that many more military personnel would essentially be denied the vote because their applications would arrive too late for them to participate in the national election.[18]

In addressing the needs of the state and the party, Governor McGrath outlined the following steps needed to ensure that absentee soldiers and sailors would be permitted to vote in the next election:

1. The governor would call for a special election between June 15–November 15, 1943, whereby Rhode Islanders would respond to the following query: "Shall a Constitutional Convention be held for the purpose of providing that special provisions be made for qualifications of and voting by members of the armed forces?"
2. Upon approval, the convention would convene between November 15–May 15, 1944 to prepare an amendment to the Rhode Island state constitution, which would waive the registration requirement for absentee military personnel.
3. Finally, the amendment would be presented to the Rhode Island constituency for final ratification, the time and place of this special election determined by the members of the constitutional convention.[19]

Fearing that this legislation would result in the further disintegration of their party, while simultaneously elevating the reputation of J. Howard McGrath, a popular and powerful governor, Republicans at first resisted the change, clinging tenaciously to their narrow lead in the Senate. In the end, however, they realized that rejection of this proposal would ultimately hurt rather than protect their party, so they agreed to support the bill.

McGrath leveraged both his popularity and the dangers posed by totalitarianism abroad to secure passage of legislation that would ensure civil rights for soldiers and sailors fighting overseas, and at the same time, enhance the reputation of his party.

In his annual message before the General Assembly, Governor McGrath proposed granting the Assembly the right to hold a convention for the purpose of amending the constitution in order to waive the registration requirement for absentee servicemen and women. In summary, the governor proposed the calling of a special election between June 15 and November 15 to determine whether

a limited convention [should] be held for the sole purpose of amending the constitution of this State in order to provide substantially as follows: that every citizen of the United States of the age of 21 years, who in time of war is absent from the State in the actual military service of the United States, who had his residence and home in this State for two years ... shall have a right to vote in all elections in the State for electors of president and vice president of the United States, senators and representatives in Congress, general officers of the State, city or town officers and also to approve or reject any proposition or amendment to the constitution.[20]

McGrath also included a provision that would allow military personnel to cast their ballot for their party rather than for individual candidates, thus simplifying the process. If the Assembly supported McGrath's proposal, the measure would go before the people for ratification at a "time and in a manner prescribed by the convention."[21]

In an interview with the *Providence Journal*, McGrath explained that the respective ballot would state, "I vote for all candidates of the Democratic or Republican party." He advised that should the United States Congress approve a federal service ballot then it too should include a similar provision. He emphasized that no soldier or sailor should return to Rhode Island and find that "in his absence the government had failed to retain or obtain for him his voting privileges."[22]

Republicans suspected that McGrath's motives were primarily political, which the governor shrewdly addressed. Careful to ensure bipartisan support, he reminded his constituency that the process need not be "complicated ... in view of the high purpose it is meant to serve." He suggested that military personnel oversee the collection and distribution of ballots, and he warned, "it should go without saying that anyone who sought to use such a convention to gain a political end other than that purpose which we have in mind would certainly bring disgrace upon himself and receive the rebuke of our people at the ratifying election."[23]

Behind the scenes, however, former Republican chairman William Pelkey, informed the governor that Republican Representative, 2nd District Harry "Sandager has in mind to have the Republicans make a play to the soldiers on duty outside the State by making it possible for them to register though outside the State." Thus, Pelkey, who as aforementioned, had begun his defection from the Republican Party during former Governor Vanderbilt's term, exacted his revenge by advancing the career of J. Howard McGrath. At times heavy-handed, Pelkey proved to be an asset to McGrath during his three gubernatorial campaigns. Sensing the obvious advantage of supporting absentee voting, Pelkey advised McGrath to

> get the jump on them [the Republicans] by making some statement as to your already having taken steps to have either a special act prepared for entry into the Assembly in January, else an amendment to Sec. 16 of Chapter 312 of the General Laws, providing for an Absentee Registry form permitting those in the service, stationed outside the State to register by mailing a prepared affidavit blank, duly aknowledged [*sic*] to the respective town clerks or Board of Canvassers, at least 15 days prior to the close of the next registration period, namely June 30.[24]

McGrath's response has not been registered, but his subsequent actions indicate that he followed Pelkey's advice.

Additionally, Joseph A. McMahon, a veteran stationed in New Guinea, wrote McGrath's executive secretary Fred Kilguss to send the necessary "papers before November to use the *McGrath way* [italics mine] … just prepare the blanks and I will see that you get them and properly *fixed your way* … we don't need any machine just this little pen." In response, Kilguss assured him that the apparatus would be put in place to allow "for you and the other members in the Armed Forces to cast your ballots in the November election."[25]

On March 28, 1944, a limited constitutional convention met and approved an amendment to the state constitution by a unanimous vote of 189 to 0. Presided over by Governor McGrath, the convention set April 11 aside as the day to hold the special election to ratify the amendment, which granted the General Assembly the power to waive registration requirements for absentee military personnel, both at home and abroad, for the duration of their service, "and for two years thereafter," and also fixed the time, location, and procedure for voting. The *Providence Journal* celebrated the achievement, calling it "unmatched in historic significance in the last 102 years of Rhode Island history." Stating that the amendment was "the first … proposed since the present Constitution was adopted in 1842," it hailed the convention as a wonderful example of "bi-partisan co-operation," whose "work was completed in less than three hours. Throughout, Republican and Democrats shared convention offices."[26]

Sanctioned by National Selective Service Director Major General Lewis B. Hershey, who praised Rhode Island for its Herculean effort to ensure that its "fighting sons and daughters" enjoy their most precious right to vote,[27] the measure proved to be a remarkable achievement and a perfectly crafted media event. The governor, standing at the rostrum accompanied by Secretary of State Armand H. Cote and Mayor Ernest E. Dupre of Woonsocket, who commenced the singing of the "Star Spangled Banner." Laying aside past grievances, two assemblymen, chairman George Greenhalgh of the Republican State Committee and John Mullen of the Democratic State Committee, joined in solidarity to show support for the fighting men and women overseas. According to Chairman Greenhalgh, "In joining with Mr. Mullen I would like to say that we have worked on this resolution with one thought of getting together the proper amendment to the Constitution to do the particular job that must be done if men and women of Rhode Island are to be allowed their vote in November."[28]

Accordingly, Chapter 1390 of the Public Laws 1944 was ratified, and hereby established as Article XXII of the Rhode Island Constitution, which

"authorized and empowered" the General Assembly "to enact legislation to exempt from the registration requirements of Article XX of the amendments to the constitution members of the armed forces and the Merchant Marine of the United States in active service" during the war and two years hence, "and also to exempt from such requirements during a like period persons absent from the State in the performance of services."[29]

As former governor Quinn, who had in the past been lukewarm to McGrath, would remark, "The significant thing about this convention is the fact that in the midst of a great conflagration of total war, the processes of democracy can still function, and the people of Rhode Island can unite on a program for the benefit of the armed forces."[30] For J. Howard McGrath, he had the good fortune to preside over a period of bipartisan support amidst the conflagration, and to lead the state toward its peaceful conclusion.

When the votes were tallied that November 5, McGrath easily trounced his opponent, Norman D. MacLeod, by 54,344 votes, the largest plurality to date in Rhode Island's history.[31] The Democratic Party handily won both state and national offices, and while the Republicans held on to the upper house of the General Assembly, it was by a mere one-point lead. The service ballot count commenced on December 5, and by December 14, the *Journal* reported that 14,255 out of 21,540 of the state's absentee voters cast their ballots for President Roosevelt. Of the 1300 federal ballots, the president garnered 936, to Republican Thomas Dewey's 364. Governor McGrath sustained a higher percentage than the president, winning a total of 29 precincts/wards/areas even before the absentee ballots were returned to the election committee. Nonetheless, McGrath's "landslide" victory "by the greatest plurality ever given a candidate for governor" obfuscated the argument that he supported the absentee ballot merely for political gain. The absentee ballot count that December confirmed McGrath's victory, but did not change the election's outcome.

On the other hand, the absentee vote "pushed Gov. J. Howard McGrath's election plurality to a record of 62,731 votes." In addition, Representative John E. Fogarty received a 33,969 plurality, and President Roosevelt's plurality in the state increased to 50,914 votes.[32] It also influenced the outcome of the General Assembly. In the final analysis, democracy had been preserved, the Rhode Island Constitution amended, and the reputation of the Rhode Island governor as a solid New Deal Democrat secured. The governor would continue to capture the attention of Washington officials for his administrative ability and his firm support of democratic ideals.

Equally important, state control had been preserved under McGrath's direction. By strengthening state power, he had taken a step toward ensuring that America's transition to peacetime in the postwar would be shared equally by the state and federal government.

11

The Quest to
Place the Displaced

British journalist George Rendel observed,

> the biggest human problem with which we shall be faced in re-ordering the world
> after the end of the war will probably be that of re-establishing the peoples who have
> been displaced from their homes or localities for one reason or another. The magni-
> tude of the problem is such as to cause the heart to sink.

The United Nations Relief and Rehabilitation Administration (UNRRA),
established in 1943 to confront the crisis and assisted by the United States
military, set out to prepare for the postwar world, unsure of how to approach
this vexing and potentially explosive issue.[1]

As a United States senator, elected in 1946, J. Howard McGrath would
become intimately involved with bringing several hundred thousand displaced persons into this country. His journey and the journeys of hundreds
of thousands of refugees have until recently been nearly forgotten in the historical record, despite the extensive United Nations reports published during
the crisis. Only since the 1980s have historians taken up the postwar displaced
persons problem and its role in fueling the antagonism between the United
States and the Soviet Union during the Truman administration.

James Howard McGrath's contribution to the displaced persons crisis
helped define America's legacy during the Cold War. Like so many others of
his generation, he treated the problem as another opportunity to combat
Communism. In his mind, failure to meet the crisis would ultimately result
in the homeless refugees disappearing under the umbrella of the Soviet Union.

McGrath's role in the crisis is an example of (1) the growing influence
of America in the world and (2) the conflation in America of humanitarian-
ism and the growth of the postwar security state. Men like McGrath, while
eager and bright, had been elected to public office because of their political
acumen; few had the requisite experience or predilection needed to confront
the monumental global issues that awaited them. Caught between an altruistic

desire to aid peoples in need and the growing fear of admitting Communist subversives from foreign lands, McGrath and others, including President Truman, acted with caution, recognizing the high price they would pay for making the wrong decision.

In October 1945 McGrath assumed the important legal position as United States solicitor general. Thrust into the national spotlight, he found himself competing among a wider pool of equally ambitious and talented young men who vied for the attention of the new president, Harry Truman. McGrath now had to work harder to build his following. The press complicated the picture by constructing an idealized image of the Rhode Islander and a mythic relationship between McGrath and Truman unsupported by the historical record.

The New Solicitor General Meets Washington Society

Introducing the "debonair, soft spoken" Rhode Islander J. Howard McGrath to Washington society, the press noted his fine taste in clothing, his steely blue eyes and affable, but guarded, demeanor, and his political and financial expertise. Representative of the upwardly mobile modern business-man, James Howard McGrath had it all: a precocious, adopted son, David, who respectfully greeted political and religious luminaries, and a lovely wife, Estelle, who carefully chose her husband's wardrobe and prepared him for success while quietly remaining behind the scenes. Highlighting his work ethic and religious faith, the press initially considered James Howard McGrath the quintessential everyman. Noting that the family attended mass often, whether before important events or meetings, and McGrath's fondness for collecting timepieces and fishing with friends, the journalists portrayed him as a happily married, driven politician.[2]

The family moved to the Chevy Chase section of the national district, where they enjoyed a panoramic view of Washington.[3] During a pleasant interview with Mrs. McGrath, *Washington Post* reporter Kay Stokey also took note of the McGraths' waterfront property off Old Point Judith Road in Narragansett, Rhode Island, and the stables where young David kept his horses. Father and son, out for a day of fly fishing, had left Mrs. McGrath at home. Their black-and-white fox terrier, Scarlett, frolicked in the yard, while Mrs. McGrath entertained the reporter. According to Ms. Stokey, "For, in Washington or back in Rhode Island no one has to argue with Mrs. McGrath about woman's place being in the home."[4]

His idyllic initial encounter with the nation's capital and its rapacious paparazzi obscured its seamier, unforgiving side, which propped up celebrity,

McGrath's work left little time for family, but his wife Estelle and adopted son David adapted seamlessly to their changing environment, circa 1950 (Harry S Truman Library).

only to tear it down with abandon. While J. Howard McGrath's educational and legal background trained him for the role of United States solicitor general, it in no way prepared him for this aspect of Washington society with its gossip-mongering press moguls such as Drew Pearson and Westbrook Pegler, as well as the distinguished *New York Times* journalist Arthur Krock. The McGraths were quickly included in the string of cocktail parties given by the likes of Mrs. J. Averell Harriman and Mrs. Perl Mesta. In a tongue-in-cheek observation of the Washington social scene, Milburn P. Akers of the *Chicago Sun* quipped, "Ordinarily, no cocktail parties are scheduled in this town during the breakfast hour. That's the lull between the ones you've just been to and the ones you're still scheduled to attend."[5]

According to newspaper accounts, President Truman appointed McGrath in a "surprise move," although negotiations behind the scenes indicate otherwise. Green's advocacy of McGrath had ensured that the lawyer/politician would ascend to national office. Preceded by a number of distinguished legal minds such as William Howard Taft, Charles Evans Hughes, and Nicholas Biddle, McGrath, according to the *Springfield Daily Republican*, "steps into a position in which he will be measured by somewhat exacting standards and subjected to inevitably severe comparisons," but "if he makes good as solicitor general, he will be conspicuously available material either for elevation to full cabinet rank, in the department of justice or some other."[6]

Others observed, "those who know Governor McGrath well believe that he will acquit himself admirably and may go further in national affairs as result of holding it."[7] The message was clear; the position of solicitor general would serve as a stepping-stone to higher office. Citing parallels with William Howard Taft, who served as solicitor general and then went on to the presidency and the Supreme Court, journalists noted that, while McGrath may never be president of the United States or a Supreme Court justice, his future appeared bright and the ease with which he was confirmed in the Senate supported that contention.[8]

Upon his accession to office, his immediate predecessor, Charles Fahy, who went on to serve as legal counsel in Germany, sent McGrath a congratulatory note, commenting "it is a great office you have entered, and you have my most sincere good wishes."[9] The office of solicitor general served an important legal function, as it was the second highest legal officer in the country, subordinate only to the United States attorney general and the president. Serving as the official lawyer for the United States government, the solicitor general in many ways assumed a more active legal role than even the attorney general.

The Federal Bureau of Investigation also weighed in on the McGrath appointment. In a secret memorandum, Federal Agent A. Rosen furnished director J. Edgar Hoover with background information on the former governor. Rosen found that although McGrath "had no criminal or credit record in Rhode Island," a 1944 crime survey report intimated that the governor had allegedly offered a number of "bookies" protection. Efforts to substantiate the claim proved fruitless and the charge was dropped, but not before it was revealed that a rather unscrupulous individual, the name blocked by the Freedom of Information Act, funded "some of McGrath's political expenses."[10] These damning allegations did not prevent the Rhode Islander's unanimous confirmation by the Senate, or the praise that was heaped upon him by the national press.

After eleven months as U.S. solicitor general, J. Howard McGrath earned praise from several legal and political luminaries for his role in prosecuting Japanese war criminal General Yamashita Tomoyuki and the Tidelands Oil Controversy.[11] However, inserted among lavish tribute from news sources throughout the country, the *Providence Journal* highlighted a particularly telling incident, which dampened this otherwise model Horatio Alger–like story. Reminiscent of his outburst fifteen years earlier, when as a young Rhode Island state chairman in 1930 he accused six seasoned Democrats of selling out to Republicans after they had allegedly bowed out of an important redistricting vote in the General Assembly, McGrath chastised the *Providence Journal* for reporting on his secret meeting with high-ranking state Democrats.

Attending this meeting were Lieutenant Governor John O. Pastore, Mayor Dennis Roberts, and Chairman of the Democratic State Committee John Mullen. At one point during their conference, local Democrats telephoned Senator Green and Eddie Higgins in Washington, and the two groups deliberated for 30 minutes by phone regarding McGrath's decision to leave Rhode Island. Prominent in their discussion was the possibility that the aging Peter Gerry might not choose to run for reelection in 1946. Conspicuously absent from the conference was Senator Gerry, who had yet to announce his future political intentions. McGrath and his conferees considered his retirement a given and had already lined up the presumptive Democratic slate for November: McGrath as senator, Pastore as governor. When the *Journal* published the contents of the discussion in the paper the following day, McGrath and Green found themselves in an awkward position since Gerry had no knowledge of his former protégé's decision to accept Truman's offer.[12]

Demanding that the paper expose its source, McGrath threatened a lawsuit unless the *Journal* cooperated. When its editor failed to reveal the informant, McGrath accused the paper of planting wiretapping devices in order to cause a rift between Senators Gerry and Green.[13]

Although no evidence has surfaced that either notes Senator Gerry's response or corroborates McGrath's fear of wiretaps, a close study of correspondence between Gerry and McGrath points to their cordial, but distant relationship. Senator Gerry's public response upon his decision, whether forced or voluntary, mirrored his stoic demeanor, and, more importantly, his opposition to Roosevelt's New Deal. "I have been looking forward to getting out of politics." Tired of the game, he commented to the *Providence Journal* reporter, "the only thing I am interested in now is taking a rest.... I hope it [the Democratic Party] gets away from the New Deal theory of government centralization."[14]

McGrath saw this act on the part of the *Journal* as a racial slur against Irish Catholics, writing:

> The day has gone by when any American citizen is going to be dominated by pressure, by hatred, by bigotry, by narrowness. The day has gone by, thank God, in Rhode Island when ... anyone, because he comes from a particular racial group, must bow his head to those who would be his master.[15]

He later made similar accusations against other real or perceived enemies of his "racial group." Positioning himself as the champion of Irish Catholics, he boasted that his "glorious record" would benefit the country and prepare him for higher office.[16] The statement reveals McGrath's growing insularity and his inability to temper his reaction when directly challenged. By lashing out at outside forces, he exposed his vulnerability and failed to consider the consequences of his actions.

This episode is also indicative of McGrath's rocky transition from local to national prominence, and signals his growing suspicion of forces outside his control, which included the Republican-backed *Providence Journal*, Communist subversives, and xenophobic Yankees (who had been targeting Irish Catholics since the nineteenth century). Whether real or imagined, McGrath feared that these enemies threatened his future.

The incident also sharpened the differences between Senators Gerry and Green. Their disagreement served as a microcosm of the growing division between liberal Democrats in Congress. On the one hand was Gerry's faction who were fearful of the "burden of Federal taxation on our industries and citizens," and who had opposed Roosevelt's election in 1932, his "Court Packing scheme" in 1937, and his reelection in 1940. The second group, represented by Theodore Francis Green, were ardent New Dealers who welcomed Roosevelt's economic platform and publicly defended the president's decision to pack the court in 1937 and run for an unprecedented third term in 1940. Green, as a "progressive Democrat … [who] reoriented [his] political rhetoric and congressional activity away from themes of economic equality as the Cold War got underway."[17]

By supporting Green, McGrath chose the more politically viable course, irrespective of personal loyalties or political ideology. Though, in the end, he would come to find a balance between Theodore Francis Green's New Deal liberalism and Peter Gerry's more cautious model of a Democratic state.[18]

This time period exemplifies that paradox of McGrath's political persona: Although a bright new star on the horizon, he was plagued by his failure to carve a theoretical niche for himself and sought the most idyllic set of circumstances for political fame and fortune. McGrath's transition from state to national leader can be seen as a parallel to America's emergence as a world power.

By the end of the war, America had become subsumed in its prosperity. It had emerged triumphant against the forces of totalitarianism, and would now assume its place as leader of the free world. Its young men had fought for their country, many risking their lives aboard PT boats chartered for the South Pacific, others marching along the historic Norman coastline to meet the German enemy in June 1944 amidst a barrage of enemy fire. These veterans returned home eager to reap the benefits of victory. Realizing the American Dream became synonymous with earning vast riches and power. Washington society served as the brass ring for upwardly mobile young men and women eager to take advantage of the new prosperity, which made their sacrifices in battle somewhat more palatable.

Although J. Howard McGrath did not serve in the field, he led his state through war by securing resources, maintaining order, and spearheading reform. McGrath's juvenile court and cash sickness legislation was in keeping with President Roosevelt's Second Bill of Rights, which furthered the post–New Deal concept of "rights-based liberalism."[19]

On the other hand, McGrath was known to support extensive business interests at the expense of labor. His legal representation of and friendship with noted industrialists Royal Little of Textron, Frank Crook of Crook Motors, and John Shepard of Shepard's Department Store, to name but a few, speak to his valuable business ties.

J. Howard McGrath's view of the world is best exemplified by his response to the problem of displaced persons, an issue that plagued the country during the first years of the Cold War. This issue generated much debate, and served as an early test for McGrath on the national stage.

McGrath as Senator and the Displaced Persons Act

Although he earned some respect as solicitor general, McGrath contributed more deliberately to the postwar political atmosphere when he returned to Rhode Island to accept the nomination as United States senator upon the retirement of Peter Gerry, his long-time mentor.

The president, in accepting McGrath's resignation in October 1946, praised him for "the superior character of" his "work," which, entitled him "to take rank among the most eminent of" his "predecessors ... in the legal profession."[20] Honored along with recently appointed U.S. District Judge for the Eastern District of Pennsylvania James P. McGranery, McGrath was lauded by Attorney General Tom Clark as a man who would contribute a "wealth of experience" to the upper house.[21] McGrath would later follow Clark as attorney general in 1949.

Washington officials, including the president, worked diligently on behalf of McGrath's Senate campaign, since his victory in Rhode Island would offset Democratic losses in Congress. Future executive director of the Democratic National Committee and fellow Rhode Islander, Gael Sullivan, then the second assistant to Postmaster General Robert Hannegan, visited Rhode Island and campaigned actively for McGrath. In eloquent prose, Sullivan reminded his audience, "Washington needs McGrath.... We can be grateful that men like Howard McGrath and Governor Pastore and Mayor Roberts are the human engineers helping to build a better Rhode Island."[22]

A close reading of election statistics reveals, however, that although McGrath was successful in his bid against Republican W. Gurnee Dyer of Portsmouth, his plurality, 27,968, reflected a considerable loss in the Democratic column from Senator Gerry's bid for the same seat six years earlier. Dyer, a descendant of four governors and at that time a chairman of the Advisory Council on Agriculture and Conservation (appointed by Governor McGrath), was a prominent, well-respected businessman. His popularity was evidenced by his plurality in 25 cities and towns, although his total of 122,780 to McGrath's 150,748 was insufficient to capture the election. While McGrath won the densely populated urban communities of Providence and Pawtucket, Dyer was able to secure the Pawtuxet Valley and Kent County, which included Warwick and Coventry.[23]

Voters had begun to question the efficacy of wartime price controls, state planning, and other forms of New Deal liberalism. Truman and his party would have to work harder to secure the confidence of the people for the next presidential run in 1948, carving out a new postwar liberalism, which linked industrial development with rights-based reform. This reform would emphasize full employment, an expansion of medical care, and unemployment compensation.

On the international scene, the new liberals sought to strengthen America's presence abroad to counteract Soviet expansionism. Men like McGrath, while eager and bright, had been elected to public office because of their political acumen; few had the requisite experience needed to confront the monumental global issues that awaited them.

While the United States had existing legislation to deal with immigration, its performance in the area of refugees and displaced persons had been haphazard. During the Second World War, President Roosevelt secured two changes that proved instrumental in the postwar discussion on displaced persons. First, he succeeded in transferring control of issues dealing with immigration from the legislature to the executive branch, which strengthened the role of the latter. Second, he transferred the Division of Immigration from the Department of Labor to the Department of Justice in 1940, and in the Alien Registration Act of the same year, all aliens were instructed to register with the federal government. Those deemed dangerous by the president were either deported or refused entry into the country.[24]

In Europe, Germany emerged from the Second World War a mere shell of its former glory. The country would be forced to rebuild according to a zonal postwar occupation governed primarily by the United States, France, England, and the Soviet Union. Wandering among the ruins were hundreds of thousands of displaced persons, among them, refugees from Germany, Austria, Poland, and the Baltic states. Some feared political or racial persecution from the Nazis, while others had escaped from forced labor camps. Jews, whose fate at the hands of national socialism was by that time well known, found themselves adrift in their home countries. Finally, the *volksdeutsche*, the German elite of the Third Reich, fled to escape punishment from the liberating Allied forces.[25]

Wide-ranging in scope and consequence, the United States found itself in the role of helping to determine the future of these refugees who had been driven from their homes and forced to remain in detention camps throughout Europe.

While attempts by President Roosevelt had been made to deal with the problem of refugees during the war, no substantive legislation was forthcoming until Harry Truman assumed the presidency. He proved decisive in meeting the crisis. Seven months after the official end of hostilities in Europe, on December 22, 1945, the president ordered Secretary of State James Byrnes to issue visas to displaced persons, and as a result, 42,000 refugees had immigrated to the United States by 1948.[26]

According to Mark Wyman, writing in 1989, "the displaced persons of the post–World War II years were caught up inextricably in politics" globally and nationally. In the United States, the issue became entangled in the anti–Communist movement that heated up during the Cold War. Fearing that an open-door policy would increase America's vulnerability to Marxist ideology, conservatives in Congress, especially Patrick McCarran of Nevada and William Chapman Revercomb of West Virginia, rejected unlimited entry. In addition, factions within the American Legion, the Veterans of Foreign Wars, and the Daughters of the American Revolution opposed unrestricted visas for displaced persons. At the urging of Senator McCarran and other conservatives from both parties, a careful screening process was instituted and severe restrictions were established to ensure that unwanted refugees would be barred from entering American ports. Overall, however, more groups supported the expansion of immigration legislation than opposed it.[27]

Under the auspices of the newly established United Nations, the International Refugee Organization (IRO) was organized in 1946 to replace United Nations Relief and Rehabilitation Administration (UNRRA) in the governance of the camps.[28] Composed of Slovenians, Slovaks, Germans, Poles, Italians Rumanians, Frenchmen, and Jews, the population known as "displaced persons" had abandoned ruined farms and bombed homes. Fifty-eight thousand of the six million Jews held in concentration camps like Bergen-Belsen, in northern Germany, were liberated by the British army; of these 14,000 would perish from malnutrition. The refurbished Belsen became the largest of these detention camps, a stark reminder of former Nazi atrocities, and a current example of the inhumanity forced upon unsuspecting peoples who found that their suffering did not end with the destruction of Nazi Germany. Forced to sleep alongside their SS *Waffen* captors, Jews from Belorussia, Poland, the Ukraine, and Russia resided in detention camps, unfit even for enemy prisoners. Given gruel and coffee, these unfortunate souls were in need of a permanent home.[29]

When President Truman appointed Dean Earl G. Harrison, of the University of Pennsylvania Law School, to draft a report on the situation, he was horrified by the findings. According to historian Leonard Dinnerstein, "the Harrison report hit the leaders at the highest level in Washington like a bombshell."[30] Harrison and Dr. Joseph J. Schwartz of the American Jewish Joint Distribution Committee (JDC), Patrick M. Malin, vice director of the Intergovernmental Committee on Refugees (IGC), and others found that "as matters now stand, we appear to be treating the Jews as the Nazis treated them except we do not exterminate them."[31]

Harrison had advocated four possible solutions to ensure that displaced persons would be allowed to evacuate with dignity:

1. Repatriation
2. Migration to Palestine
3. Entrance into the United States
4. Removal to improved camps

Harrison supported the migration of Jewish refugees to Palestine, the admittance of a "reasonable" number of displaced persons to the United States, and for those who refused repatriation, the resettlement "outside of camps or moved to better camps or sanitaria."[32]

Truman valued Harrison's advice, so after he read the report, he acted immediately, requesting legislation in 1946 to ease the suffering of the displaced.

In the meantime, the United States 80th Congress passed Senate Resolution 137 in 1947, which established a subcommittee of the Judiciary Committee to conduct "a full and complete investigation of our entire immigration system." This included a probe into America's strategy on refugees and immigration, including its "immigration and deportation laws, and practices, thereunder," the state of affairs concerning displaced persons, and "the extent, if any, to which aliens have entered the United States in violation of circumvention of such laws."[33] A subsequent amendment stipulated "that the committee shall report its findings and recommendations in a separate report with respect to the displaced persons on or before January 10, 1948."[34]

Following the November 1946 election, junior senator J. Howard McGrath was assigned to membership on the Subcommittee on Displaced Persons. The small bipartisan Senate group included its chairman, Republican W. Chapman Revercomb, Republican Forrest C. Donnell of Missouri, Democrat Pat McCarran of Nevada, and Republican John Sherman Cooper of Kentucky. They were tasked with reviewing the European detention camps. In compliance, Senator Revercomb concluded:

> I think it is always best for those who have to decide to see the evidence first hand. But as to who will be sent and how the hearings shall be conducted, that is a question for the committee to determine. We shall have hearings. Evidence will be produced by the Army and by those who have had contact with these people.... Then of course, the visual evidence will be very helpful.[35]

Nonetheless, resistant legislators, Revercomb being one of three special subcommittee members who placed a bar on unlimited entry, prevented positive action until Representative William G. Stratton of Illinois sponsored a bill (H.R. 2910), drafted by the Citizens Committee under the auspices of Harrison, the following April 1947 calling for the admittance of 400,000 persons into the country over a four-year period. By that point close to one million resided in Germany, Austria, and Italy, while 600,000 were placed under camps controlled by the United States.[36] The Stratton legislation required a strict vetting process, which stipulated that refugees entering the country must be sponsored by American citizens, corporations, or military personnel.[37] Accordingly, the measure should "attest to the persistence and vitality of our democratic heritage by excluding no person because of his race, nationality, religious belief, or occupation," and should secure all means to ensure that the "family unit" is preserved.[38] Further, it "authoriz[ed] the United States during an emergency period to undertake its fair share in the resettlement of displaced persons in Germany, Austria, and Italy."[39]

Stratton's support helped to further the movement toward the integration of displaced persons into the United States since he was a Midwestern conservative Republican.

While the decision to repatriate was under the jurisdiction of UNRRA and not the United States, Americans, according to the American Institute of Public Opinion Poll, supported refugee immigration to Palestine, but frowned upon increasing immigration to their own borders.[40] Senate opposition echoed these findings, and conservative members, including Pat McCarran of Nevada, Alexander Wiley of Wisconsin, and Chapman Revercomb of West Virginia,[41] were adamant in their refusal to accept Stratton's bill. Thus, Stratton's legislation, watered down by Revercomb, Wiley, and McCarran, was still locked in subcommittee when Congress recessed for the summer.[42]

Revercomb's position stood in sharp contrast to Harrison's report, which came out in April 1947. While Harrison believed that immigration to the United States would ease the problem, Revercomb instead advocated a solution that would place the onus on Europe rather than America.[43] Essentially, restrictionists like Revercomb, McCarran, and Donnell feared that European immigration would endanger the American security state by allowing potential Communists or other subversives entrance into the country. Their position would dominate this debate, and frustrated the plans of the more open-minded senators of the sub-committee, like Cooper and McGrath, the latter especially keen on immigration since it had contributed to his success during his three gubernatorial runs.

The select Senate subcommittee left in October 1947 for Europe and interviewed consuls in Paris, Frankfort, Stuttgart, Berlin, Munich, Vienna, and Rome on the consequences that would arise from placing the displaced. They questioned military officers in Germany and Austria, as well as those of the Preparatory Commission of the International Refugee Organization (PCIRO) located in Geneva, which was tasked with the repatriation, the identification, registration and classification; the care, and assistance; the legal and political protection; the transport; and the resettlement and reestablishment, in countries able and willing to receive [the displaced], of persons who are the concern of the Organization.[44]

In addition to McGrath's tour of detention camps and bombed sites, he also held an audience with the pope. In a letter to the Rev. Edward J. Killion, the Field Representative of the Vatican Migration Bureau, McGrath stated that he "was able to obtain a rather comprehensive picture of the problem."

At the Hanau Lithuanian Camp, several wrote McGrath thanking him "cordially for taking notices of our troubles and sorrows." In a detailed account, the group of expatriates recounted their tale of religious and political persecution at the hands of the "bolshevists," which prompted many Lithuanians to "emigrate to the USA (about 900,000)." Despite oppression, the "Lithuanian nation remained alive and kept its catholic faith only because of its endurance." No doubt this plea touched McGrath, who was sensitive to the needs of his fellow Catholics who resisted both Fascist and Communist domination.[45]

When the delegation finally returned to Washington from Germany at midnight on October 25, it was with a heavy heart but with renewed vigor for active legislation on behalf of the refugees.[46]

Before the trip, McGrath's comments on displaced persons were general and inconclusive. Stating that he "feel[s] this country should admit a number of displaced persons," he said he would draft more specific legislation upon his return. By the following month, he remarked, "employable DPs and their families" should be allowed entrance into the United States.[47] Senator Revercomb was more conservative in his public rhetoric, noting that approximately 800,000 refugees populated the camps housed in the American zone of occupation.

McGrath's public discourse reflected his exposure to a postwar Europe devastated by the harsh realities of global war. In a three-hour interview with French Prime Minister Paul Ramadier, McGrath expressed his confidence that "the French people are working very hard under very trying conditions." Accordingly, he noted that Ramadier maintained that the French would never succumb to Communism as long as they were given "half a chance" to realize full economic revitalization.[48]

Concerning the 900,000 displaced persons, McGrath recommended that the United States should grant them every opportunity to enter this country provided they would support and contribute to America's way of life. He stated that "many of these people offered heroic resistance to the aggressors in their own countries" and that Americans had a "high moral obligation" to help them.[49]

Upon his return to the United States, McGrath recommended that the

United States offer its immigration quotas, which had not reached capacity since the Second World War, to the displaced. He also proposed that a United States commission be established to determine which refugees would be "best able to contribute to American life."[50]

In an article published two months after McGrath and the Senate group returned from Europe, *Providence Journal* reporter Leonard O. Warner revealed that the then-solicitor general McGrath and Senator Theodore Francis Green were instrumental in rescuing 14 Russian monks during their impending eviction from their refuge in Switzerland.[51]

Escaping from Czechoslovakia in 1944, the 14 monks carried with them sacred relics encased in wooden boxes. The Soviet government demanded that the religious group return to Russia to face authorities for "stealing" these sacred objects.

Their real crime, however, was their rejection of Soviet Communism. Serafim Ivanoff, Bishop of the Russian Orthodox Church, continued to practice his faith, despite threats from government officials. Hiding out in Switzerland, the monks were ousted by the Swiss government, who feared repercussions from the Soviet Union for aiding and abetting the fugitives.

Rhode Island State College professor Nicholas Alexander appealed to Senators McGrath and Green on behalf of the monks. In response, the two Rhode Island senators pressured the Swiss authorities for travel visas, which finally arrived on November 7, 1946, after months of delay.[52] Safely tucked away at a monastery outside of Utica, New York, the monks expressed "their deep appreciation" to the Rhode Island senators for fighting on their behalf.[53]

Thus, McGrath's commitment to the plight of the refugee was well known; in this instance, he harbored sympathy for the underprivileged who roamed the European countryside in fear. His fight for a liberal law to allow the necessary number of displaced persons was testimony to his commitment.

Patrick McCarran, who eventually replaced Revercomb as chairman of the Judiciary Committee, had a different reaction. Unlike McGrath, who embraced the campaign to free the DPs, McCarran wanted the problem to disappear. Realizing that he must support some kind of measure or risk political suicide, he finally succumbed to a grudging acceptance of a limited bill, but wanted assurance that he would control the number of DPs allowed entrance into the United States. McCarran, a rabid anti–Communist and anti–Semite, drafted a major portion of the original displaced persons bill (known as the Wiley-Revercomb Bill of 1948), in order to bar the Jewish population from its benefits, as well as any refugee who supported socialism. Providing for the entrance of 100,000 displaced persons who had lived in refugee camps prior to December 22, 1945, the bill ignored most Jews, who only migrated into German detention camps after their liberation from concentration camps or their escape from deadly pogroms in Poland, Russia, and Eastern Europe.[54]

McGrath did not reveal his displeasure. Instead, he sent a cordial note to McCarran upon the latter's request for a meeting. Departing from Nevada, his home state, McCarran wrote McGrath that he was "grately [*sic*] interested in form and text of proposed bill to amend Displaced Persons Act. Respectfully request you withhold approval final form of this bill until I can have opportunity to confer with you." He closed his letter with a veiled salutation, "Kindest personal regards and I hope to be able to say Merry Christmas in person."

McGrath responded, "Will make no commitments pending your arrival and opportunity to talk with you. I hope that you and yours have a very happy Christmas."[55]

According to its critics in the Senate and House, the problem with the Wiley-Revercomb Bill, which was largely written by McCarran, was its limitation on the number of persons who would be allowed entrance into the country. The bill (S2242) said

> 200,000 displaced persons who meet stated eligibility requirements, 2,000 persons who fled from Czechoslovakia ... 3,000 orphans [under] 16 years of age ... 15,000 aliens [currently] in the U.S. [may] remain, ... before April 1948 ... DP's must have entered the German or Austrian occupation zones before December 22, 1945 ... 40 per cent must come from areas which have been annexed by foreign powers. At least 3 percent must be trained farmers.[56]

In Cohen's estimation, the plight of the displaced persons "was the first direct confrontation over political dissidents between the two emerging superpowers: human rights politics did not only hasten the end of the Cold War ... but also led to its outbreak."[57]

In response to the reactionary measure, Senators McGrath and Democrat Carl Hatch of New Mexico introduced an amendment on the Senate floor on July 28, 1948, a month after the president signed the Wiley-Revercomb Bill. Roundly criticized by Senators Scott Lucas and Kenneth Wherry for acting without the consent of the Judiciary Committee, of which McGrath was a member, McGrath responded by pointing out "the purpose of offering the amendment in the nature of a substitute is to have before the Senate a constructive proposal dealing with the problem as a whole."[58]

The McGrath-Hatch Bill was written with the express purpose of moving the date from December 1945 to

> on or before April 21, 1947 ... and [allowing the displaced] who on January 1, 1948, w[ere] in Italy or the American sector, the British sector, or the French sector of either Berlin or Vienna or the American zone, the British zone, or the French zone of either Germany or Austria, or a person who ... resided in Germany or Austria.[59]

McGrath stated that the Wiley-Revercomb Bill purposely "prohibited Jews from taking part in this program." He further challenged the Conference Committee, which voted the bill out: "The Committee may deny it had that deliberate intent, but I want the Record to show that the Committee had full knowledge that such would be the effect, whatever the intention of the Committee may have been."[60]

Although President Truman signed the Wiley-Revercomb Bill into law on June 25, he believed it a poor substitute for his original intention. Reflective of conservative suasion, the measure, according to the president, supported "a pattern of discrimination and intolerance wholly inconsistent with the American sense of justice."[61] Purposely omitting entrance of Jews and many Catholics, the bill, according to Truman, was an affront to "Americans of all religious faiths and political beliefs." He further contended that the displaced "will find it hard to understand, as I do, why the Congress delayed action on this subject until the end of the session."[62]

Its provisions stipulated that 205,000 displaced persons would be allowed entry into the United States after July 1, 1948, as long as they "entered the German or Austrian occupation zones before December 22, 1945," and "at least 40 per cent must come from areas which have been annexed by foreign powers."[63] Finally, "at least 30 percent must be trained farmers who plan to work on U.S. farms."[64] According to Emanuel Celler, who penned a more inclusive bill in 1949, the 1948 measure was "at best, a small gesture aimed to satisfy the pressure of public opinion."[65]

As historian Mark Wyman noted, "in 1948 the original U.S. Displaced Persons Act regarded refugees as objects of political concern, not simply as suffering humanity, for it focused on them as anti–Communist migrants. Ideology set the limits." The act would be enforced beginning on July 1, 1948, and favored peoples from the Baltic regions, especially farmers. By June 30, 1949, over 40,000 displaced persons had immigrated to the United States, an increase of nearly 38,000 in a six-month period.[66]

The liberal Citizens Committee on Displaced Persons, chaired by Dean Earl G. Harrison, which had proposed the Stratton bill, agreed with the president. Regretting America's poor response to the problem thus far, Harrison complained that the country had

> done virtually nothing to fulfill our responsibility to the almost one million men, women and children who survive in European Displaced Persons enclosures ... in the first six months of operation of our 1948 Displaced Persons Act, only 2,500 displaced persons were admitted ... out of 100,000 admissions authorized during the first year.[67]

The Citizens Committee was hopeful that

> Senator J. Howard McGrath (D., R.I.), in association with other Senators of both the Democratic and Republican parties, will introduce amendatory legislation in the

Senate and Representative Emanuel Celler (D., N.Y.) and other Representatives will introduce similar legislation in the House.[68]

Celler, a passionate advocate of displaced persons, had a personal stake in the legislation. His grandparents were Jews who had escaped from Germany in 1948 and settled in Brooklyn, and on the basis of their harrowing experience, and the plight of his constituents in New York, he sympathized with the Zionists in their support for a Jewish homeland.

Celler's bill increased the allotted quota of displaced persons from 205,000 over two years to 339,000 within three years, moving the eligibility date from December 22, 1945, to January 1, 1949. The former date was put in place primarily to eliminate Jews and those Catholics who had not entered the camps until 1946 or 1947.

As the new Democratic national chairman, McGrath voiced his opposition to the Wiley-Revercomb Bill by pointing out that "we have approached this problem from the point of view of seeing what we could do to prevent displaced persons from coming to the United States, rather than how to bring them here" and "questioned whether even the authorized maximum under the bill could enter the U.S. in view of the employment and housing prerequisites." Taking issue with the favoritism granted to agricultural workers, McGrath advocated the entrance of "employable DP's and their families" from the American zone in Germany.[69]

At the same time, the Soviets fought for the reentry of dislocated peoples within its umbrella: the Ukraine, Belorussia, Poland, and Yugoslavia, seeking to ensure safe passage home for those who fled or were evacuated from behind the Iron Curtain during the occupation of Axis forces. Just a few years before in 1946, a deadly pogrom had targeted Jews in Kielce, forcing several thousand to flee Poland in search of refuge. Their plight encouraged the Zionists to pressure the United States and all of Western Europe to support the establishment of Israel.[70]

America's shoddy response to the displaced persons crisis was in large part due to the resistance of Congress's Nevada chairman of the Senate Judiciary Committee, the powerful Senator Pat McCarran, who, according to frustrated Senate Majority Leader Scott Lucas, tasked with bringing the displaced persons' legislation to the floor of the Senate, "doesn't give a damn about DPs or the party pledges. He wants to kill the bill. He's conducting a two-bit Un-American activities committee hearing, dragging his heels, and trying to beat the DP bill every way possible."[71]

Preferring to admit "specific persons, such as a constituent's relative who overstayed a visa," McCarran was more inclined to support the entry of "250 Basque sheepherders into the country" than "mass immigration into the United States," regardless of conditions in Europe.[72]

Determined to block any legislation that would amend the 1948 bill,

Chairman McCarran employed underhanded tactics to delay the introduction of any such measure liberalizing DP legislation. Timing a three-week European tour of his own in order to stall the vote on the legislation, McCarran commented that he wished to observe the European situation before he would support any revision of the original bill. That was in September. He returned eleven weeks later on December 2, after a visitation with the pope, a leisurely excursion to County Cork, where his beloved mother was born, and a stop over to the residence of Fascist General Francisco Franco in Spain, whom he counted among his good friends.[73] Fixated on barring indiscriminate immigration, McCarran appeared unmoved by the fate of the wandering Europeans, forced from their homes during the war. Securing a promise from a reluctant Scott Lucas, Senate majority leader, that the introduction of an amended DP bill would be delayed until his return, McCarran kept the Senate Judiciary Committee from acting on any new legislation.

When Congress opened for its 1949 session, McGrath had already announced that he would be the administration's spokesperson on behalf of displaced persons, and would introduce more liberal legislation. His status as Democratic national chairman made his views doubly important for the party, especially given Truman's surprise victory in November.

According to Oliver Pilat of the *Washington Post*, "McGrath will have increased prestige in the new Congress," which should bode well for the future of displaced persons, since he will "certainly be in a position to exert some quiet influence on the selection of new members to the Senate Judiciary Committee, which handles all immigration matters."[74]

McCarran biographer Michael Ybarra, however, believed otherwise. Despite McGrath's prestige, his voice was drowned out by the powerful chairman of the Judiciary Committee. Although McGrath had opposed the original bill because it emphasized "agriculturalists" at the expense of industrial workers, he was hesitant to confront McCarran directly. While voicing his opposition to the existing bill, noting that he "would prefer that the bill provide for the admission of a maximum of 100,000 persons per year,"[75] he did not take advantage of the opportunity presented by the public's growing interest in the plight of the displaced. Although it was customary to show the bill to McCarran, the chairman of the Judiciary Committee, he bypassed him and went straight to the Senate with legislation that he and freshman senator Matthew Neely, who had replaced Revercomb of West Virginia on January 3, 1949, drew up in response to the half-hearted 1948 resolution. The McGrath-Neely bill (S.311), formally introduced to the 81st Congress in June 1949, would amend the Displaced Persons Act of 1948 (Public Law 774, 80th Congress) by increasing the number of displaced persons from 200,000 to 400,000 over a four-year period, and would move up the "cut-off date" from December 22, 1945, to April 21, 1947, in order to include Jewish refugees.[76]

Nonetheless, McGrath saw what happened to his earlier attempts at amending the bill, so by bypassing McCarran, he hoped to secure a better fate for his more recent measure. His strategy, however, backfired. Appointing a group of conservative senators to serve on a subcommittee tasked with reviewing the bill, McCarran set out to ensure that any amendment emerging from the Senate floor would be more reactionary than the original measure.

Supportive senators and representatives expressed their frustration at McCarran's delaying tactics meant to block any positive amendment to the Wiley-Revercomb Bill; the Celler legislation (H.R. 1344) continued to be "bottled up in the House subcommittee," and the McGrath-Neely bill fell by the wayside in the Senate.[77] Since McGrath had failed to present his bill in proper order (by first showing it to McCarran, as head of the Judiciary Committee), and then to the Senate body, the cunning McCarran used his powers to stall legislation until just before the outbreak of the Korean War in June 1950.

Nonetheless, Ybarra's criticism of McGrath fails to take into account the formidable opposition and inscrutable delaying tactics employed by McCarran, who outsmarted veteran senators along with the freshman senator from Rhode Island. After two years of debate largely spearheaded by McCarran, the Senate finally secured an amended bill more in line with McGrath's vision, but not before McCarran had his way with Congress.

According to Emanuel Celler, who introduced a similar amendment in the House, the final amendment to the original bill passed both houses of Congress, but not without serious consequences. "Friendships were broken; enmities incurred. Antagonisms flourished." Astounded by the virulence of the opposition, Celler commented that "the opponents of the bill had thrown themselves into battle with the ferocity of a mother protecting her young."[78]

The president was able to use Senate resistance as leverage during the 1948 campaign, despite the Democrats like McCarran, who numbered among the severest restrictionists. Following President Truman's State of the Union Address on January 4, 1950, a bill finally emerged from the Judiciary Committee after months of debate and delay.

By June 1950, over two years after the passage of the original bill, an amendment (H.R.4567) changed the cutoff date from December 22, 1945, to January 1, 1949, in Western Europe, after much deliberation. It authorized the entrance of 415,744 displaced persons over a four-year period, including those of German extraction driven from their home to escape Nazi persecution. Additional refugees allowed admission were Poles, Greeks, and the displaced from Venezia Giulia in Italy (in the postwar section of Yugoslavia). It also abandoned the provision which mandated that 30 percent be farmers and 40 percent come from the Baltic region.[79]

By the time McGrath had left the Senate to head the Justice Department in 1949, his public stand on immigration and the displaced had shifted somewhat, in keeping with the virulent anti–Communism that dominated the country. In October 1950, Attorney General McGrath wrote Secretary of State Dean G. Acheson "clarifying" the Department of Justice's "views as to the administration of the immigration features of the Internal [McCarran] Security Act of 1950." He stipulated that

> the Attorney General has exercised his discretionary authority under the ninth proviso of section 3 of the Immigration Act of February 5, 1917 (8 U.S.C. 136 (q)), to grant temporary admission to aliens in category 2 where the *only* ground of exclusion is the alien's *nominal* membership ... in either the Nazi, Fascist, Falangist, or other totalitarian party or organization, and ... the alien has a good and legitimate reason which would justify such temporary admission.[80]

In establishing the Department of Justice's policy, McGrath authorized a makeshift solution to the problem, granting "temporary relief" to immigrants who sought asylum in the United States "prior to the enactment of the Internal Security Act of 1950" and would consider "those who have not yet departed for the United States" only if the Department of State concurred. Thereafter, he announced that Congress would need to "consider appropriate amendments to furnish a permanent solution."[81]

In the end, McGrath was able to balance the views of the president with those of the legislature, all the while presenting himself as a staunch anti–Communist crusader. McGrath's marginal acceptance of McCarran's Security Act, which passed over the president's veto in 1950, was evident in the above communiqué.

Thus, the political volleying between restrictionists like Revercomb, Wiley, and McCarran, and advocates of a more lenient displaced persons bill like McGrath and Emanuel Celler occurred at the expense of the displaced in Europe. Buried within the humanitarian impulse from the more liberal legislators like McGrath, and the more repressive motives of the restrictionists like Revercomb, Wiley, and McCarran, was their mutual desire to root out Communism.

Also, underscoring their argument, was America's changing role during the postwar period. While some, like McCarran and Revercomb, sought a return to the past, where nativism was a publicly acceptable response to immigration, an ideology more commensurate with the nineteenth and early twentieth centuries, rather than post–World War II America, reformers like President Truman and Emanuel Celler saw their country as a leader on the global stage. Their outlook was exemplified in the battle on behalf of displaced persons.

For McGrath, his performance as Senate spokesperson for the displaced persons legislation was mixed. While he advocated entrance for the displaced of Europe, he failed to overcome the formidable power of Senators Pat McCarran and Chapman Revercomb. He opposed McCarran and Revercomb, but his common hatred of Communism tied his hands in the battle to provide these embattled refugees safe haven.

Time would determine whether he could ably meet the challenge as Democratic national chairperson in electing President Harry Truman in his own right. As opposition mounted from all fronts, the task would prove daunting, and required a steady hand. Would J. Howard McGrath from Rhode Island be up for the task?

12

He's Just "wild about Harry"[1]

The iconic image of a beaming President Harry S Truman showcasing the *Chicago Tribune's* erroneous statement "Dewey Defeats Truman" symbolizes the imprudent nature of the press reporting on the 1948 election. Yet, the photograph does not tell the whole story.

While historians have chronicled the roles of several advisors who contributed to the president's 1948 victory, few have emphasized the impact made by Democratic National Chairman James Howard McGrath, especially his behind-the-scenes fundraising and vote-getting to ensure the Republican defeat that November. As a product of a divisive Democratic machine in Rhode Island, McGrath possessed the requisite tools to meet adversity, but at the time it was unknown whether his experience on the local level would prepare him to confront a national party on the verge of dismemberment.

Although the Rhode Islander was not Truman's first choice for Democratic national chairman, McGrath demonstrated to the president that he could rebuild the party by ably balancing inter- and intra-party feuds.[2] In assessing the Democratic Party's relationship with the new president, political scientist Sean Savage, in *Truman and the Democratic Party*, contended that McGrath's job was the most difficult of all Truman's Democratic chairmen.[3] His duty was to elect a president during one of the most volatile periods in the history of the Democratic Party. Yet, this role suited McGrath, who would prove to the self-assured political pundits, smug pollsters, and sneering Republicans and Democrats that Harry Truman could, and in fact would, be reelected.

The Rhode Island senator faced mounting obstacles from several potential challengers, both Democrat and Republican. Among the more insistent in the president's own party was Secretary of Commerce Henry Wallace, who resigned in 1946 after a showdown with the administration over foreign policy; Governor Strom Thurmond of South Carolina, who convinced Southern segregationists to bolt the party and establish the Dixiecrats; and California's Democratic state chairman James Roosevelt, Jr., who spearheaded his own campaign to nominate Dwight David Eisenhower for the Democratic ticket. Balancing and counteracting these disparate forces would prove formidable for Chairman McGrath, but he met each obstacle efficiently and effectively. By preparing teams of canvassers to comb the local precincts and court city mayors and councilmen, he also proved that a traditional approach could still win elections—despite the increasing role of the media in politics.

This chapter will consider McGrath's oft-overlooked role as Democratic national chairman by assessing (a) his strengths and weaknesses measured against the burgeoning concept of the modern presidency, (b) his growing alienation from party ranks, especially after the Democratic National Convention in July, and (c) the long-term effects of the 1948 election for the future of the party.

The Role of the Democratic National Chairman

McGrath's tenure as chairman was pivotal; one of the last of the Northeastern machine politicians to assume the role, he would adapt his most successful regional strategies to the national campaign. In addition, he ably transitioned, and in fact contributed, to the nascent infrastructure of the Democratic committee. The 1948 election was, according to political analyst Zachary Karabell, the last in which a "an entire spectrum of ideologies was represented [on the air or in print]."[4]

The essence of the Democratic National Committee had changed markedly since Franklin Delano Roosevelt was first elected in 1932. At that time, Roosevelt had controlled the Democratic Party organization, including its national committee.

Former chairman and postmaster general Robert Hannegan, who assumed the position in January 1944, attempted to mold Truman in the image of Roosevelt.[5] This strategy failed, since Roosevelt's image as a Groton-educated aristocrat from the north contrasted markedly with Harry Truman's Midwestern background, with his education as a farmer, reputation as a haberdasher, and finally his work as a county judge under the direction of Thomas Pendergast, a notoriously corrupt Kansas machine politician.

The off-term defeat for the Democrats in Congress in 1946 was at least in part due to this misguided strategy.[6] Future publicity director Jack Redding, advising then–Democratic chairman Bob Hannegan and his second-in-command Gael Sullivan on the best approach to sell the new president Robert Hannegan, noted, "The difficulty is that you're … expecting the impossible. [Truman] isn't FDR. He isn't anything like him.… Harry Truman is a Midwestern farmer."[7]

Thus, when Hannegan resigned the following year, the president sought a loyal and successful Democrat with a proven record and enough political savvy and experience to confront the formidable obstacles in the upcoming national election. The president decided on McGrath, especially after the latter defeated his opponent in the 1946 Senate race. Accepting the nomination as his party's candidate for the Senate only after he was assured that his former mentor, Peter Gerry, was stepping down, McGrath had stymied the plans of prominent local Democrats Robert E. Quinn and Dennis Roberts, who also sought the seat. McGrath agreed to serve as Democratic national chairman in 1947, opting out of a salary in exchange for the retention of his senate seat. Unlike Roosevelt's chairmen, Postmasters General James Farley and Hannegan, McGrath, as a member of Congress, would, strategists hoped, lay the foundation for a more congenial relationship between the executive and legislative branches.[8] According to McGrath, "His dual role as Senator should contribute toward that result. To what extent, only time will tell. However, my job is to organize the party, not the Congress."[9]

McGrath's appointment ushered in a change in policy for the Democrats in other ways as well. Supporting the groundwork laid by Publicity Director Jack Redding, McGrath emphasized President Truman's unique qualifications to lead the country during the volatile Cold War era. For McGrath, Truman's presidency, even more than Roosevelt's, would define the postwar world. McGrath urged the president to highlight his practical, no-nonsense approach to the threats confronting Americans both at home and abroad as more daunting "than that which has confronted any previous President."[10]

McGrath's unstinting support of Truman's policies complemented the tactics employed by the publicity director, Jack Redding, also a consummate tactician. The two became fast friends, and with Redding's astute eye and skills, McGrath was assured a solid foundation for a successful campaign.

The one loose cannon in the organization, however, was McGrath's childhood classmate, Rhode Islander Gael Sullivan. Protégé of former Democratic chairman Bob Hannegan, Sullivan had often stepped in as acting chairman during Hannegan's last few months in office. However, Sullivan made several blunders that ultimately prevented his elevation to the chairmanship. Like McGrath, Sullivan had graduated from LaSalle Academy and Providence College. However, as McGrath forged solid ties with the powerful Democratic machine in Rhode Island, Sullivan moved from Rhode Island to Chicago, Illinois. After earning a Masters' degree from Thomas Aquinas University in River Forest, Sullivan accepted a professorship of Economics and Public Administration at DePaul University. His induction into politics came when he apprenticed under the tutelage of Chicago Democratic mayor Edward Kelly.[11]

Although his future initially appeared bright, Sullivan was prone to rash

Democratic National Chairman Robert Hannegan hands over the official gavel to new chairman J. Howard McGrath, October 29, 1947 (copyright unknown).

decision-making, as evidenced by his actions prior to Hannegan's resignation. Writing Republican chairman B. Carroll Reece in 1947, Sullivan suggested that both parties sign a petition pledging support for the administration's containment policy in Greece and Turkey. While on the surface this strategy was harmless enough, it sent ripples through the Democratic and Republican parties, as both interpreted Sullivan's move as an attempt to politicize a precedent-setting foreign policy initiative. Republican senator Arthur Vandenberg of Michigan, a proponent of bipartisanship, was shocked by Sullivan's actions, which, he charged, had reduced the Truman Doctrine to a political ploy to win votes. Vandenberg astutely observed that Sullivan's strategy could potentially signal the end to interparty cooperation.[12]

In another misstep, Sullivan practically read wavering Democrats Senator Claude Pepper of Florida and former vice president Henry Wallace out of the party, following their critical appraisal of its infrastructure.[13] Vice President Alben Barkley of Kentucky believed Sullivan exceeded his authority and ordered him to apologize to Senator Pepper, which Sullivan reluctantly did. These acts, coupled with his arrest in Rhode Island in 1947, allegedly for drunk driving, nearly ruined Sullivan's career.[14]

Sullivan's lapses in judgment benefited McGrath. To President Truman, McGrath appeared as the less volatile and more circumspect of the two New England contenders.[15] McGrath had a 99 percent voting record in support of the president; in addition, he was a Roman Catholic from an ethnically diverse New England state and was one of the few Democrats who emerged a winner in the 1946 nationwide Congressional elections. While Sullivan, the intellectually astute idealist, believed the Democratic chairman should formulate policy, McGrath, the pragmatist, saw the chairman as a political arm of the president, an interpretation more closely aligned with Truman's own.

Even so, McGrath was not Truman's first choice. Clinton Anderson, Secretary of Agriculture, appeared on the president's short list for the chairmanship, as did a few other notables. In fact, President Truman's secretary Matthew Connelly intimated that a few top strategists supported McGrath only on the condition that Eddie Higgins, the mastermind behind Theodore Francis Green's winning Senate campaigns, join McGrath at the Ring Street headquarters of the Democratic National Committee. In a private conversation, Green persuaded the president that McGrath alone could win the 1948 election, allowing Higgins to remain a Green lieutenant until Green's death in 1966.[16]

Thus, McGrath won the position of Democratic national chairman, and President Truman, at the urging of Jack Redding, agreed to retain Gael Sullivan as executive secretary of the party.[17] Before he left, Hannegan had convinced the president that, despite Sullivan's ill-timed remarks, he would prove a distinct asset to the campaign. Sullivan's creativity, experience, and, most importantly, ties to the liberal wing of the party would balance McGrath's more conservative, dogmatic approach. Truman acquiesced, and with some misgivings, Sullivan agreed to remain in the Democratic organization, as evidenced by his remark to Hannegan. "I am staying on at the committee. The President put it in such a way that there was no answer but yes to his request. It was an historic meeting—one that I shall always treasure and I am back in the front lines—eager for battle."[18] As a result, the two Rhode Islanders, J. Howard McGrath and Gael Sullivan, former childhood pals from the Fox Point section of Providence, would form a team that was united, at least publicly, in their support for Harry S Truman.

According to political historian Zachary Karabell, the Democratic infrastructure had built "the first modern campaign team that systematically obtained, analyzed, and collated information on the total spectrum of issues and personalities."[19] While Karabell deemed this development encouraging, it also presaged a growing and potentially cumbersome bureaucracy within the party.

As the national Democratic leader during the postwar period, McGrath presided at a time of growing influence of television as a news source. Introduced at the New York World's Fair in 1939, television had led to a revolution in political reporting.[20] At the time, television's auto-coaxial signal, which was based in New York, could broadcast no farther than Philadelphia, conveniently the setting for both the Democratic and Republican conventions. Thus in 1948, a candidate's public image was essential in disseminating the party's national platform. McGrath was not intimidated by the new medium, despite the fact that he appears uncomfortable in front of television cameras, images from which are preserved at the Truman Presidential Library.[21]

In fact, McGrath became one of the most watched figures of the period. He was practically guaranteed a positive reception in Rhode Island, since he had systematically gained control of the airwaves several years earlier. In his numerous speeches and appearances during the war, McGrath had attempted to assure voters of his commitment to Rhode Island, his vast experience, and his numerous accomplishments in office.

As he entered the national scene, however, McGrath's polished figure became somewhat tarnished. Political columnists began to question the origin of his alleged fortune. Reporters had much to say about the taut, well-groomed Rhode Islander, who they observed had scored major financial coups in his career as a politician. Leading Republicans, such as Governor Harold Stassen of Minnesota, claimed that McGrath had earned his vast wealth while ostensibly serving the public. Journalists estimated that his assets reached $8 million, which included his entangling trusteeship of Rhode Island Charities Trust, as well as lucrative interests in Rhode Island's Lincoln Downs Race Track, Yellow Cab Company, J. J. McGrath and Sons Insurance and Real Estate Company, and Metro Goldwyn Mayer, among others. Reporters took aim and casually lobbed barbs at McGrath; the more shocking the accusation, the higher the subscription rate. In response, McGrath argued his holdings were equivalent to little more than $100,000, and certainly not more than $200,000. *Saturday Evening Post* reporter Milton MacKaye graciously concurred, and alluded to McGrath's simple tastes: "The McGraths live well and certainly not frugally, but their possessions do not suggest vast riches."[22]

Highlighting McGrath's loyalty to Truman, the reporter maintained, however, that the success of the president in the election would rest with "faraway Czechoslovakia [a Communist coup that deposed the democratically-based government that February], faraway Palestine [the partitioning of Palestine between Arabs and Jews in order to carve out a Jewish state], [and] faraway Russia," which "may do more to determine the result of America's presidential election than baby-kissing and gift cigars."[23]

As governor, McGrath led his state successfully through the Second

World War. As a party chairman, his responsibilities were different. Learning to balance contending forces had been difficult enough in Rhode Island, where territorial allegiances and political corruption dominated, but pundits wondered whether McGrath was ready for the Herculean task that he would have to undertake to balance these forces at a national level.

According to political scientist Marie Chatham, the new chairman must neither challenge, at least not publicly, presidential decisions, nor invent issues, but instead must carry through the president's policies without fail.[24] Political scientist V.O. Key further maintained that a party chairman must serve as "a technician, a specialist in campaign management and machine tending, *who exercises his power only so long as he enjoys the confidence of the presidential nominee* [italics mine]."[25] This last phrase is significant, since it points out that the job inherently carried certain limitations.[26]

One significant challenge arose from within the president's administration. The urbane, sophisticated Clark Clifford, one of the president's closest advisors, wielded primary control over the president's choices in staffing the White House. McGrath, interested primarily in uniting all factions of the party, found himself unable to influence these appointments.[27]

For his part, Clifford had complained that the Democratic Committee

The new Democratic national chairman J. Howard McGrath meets with President Harry S Truman to plot strategy for the 1948 campaign, 1947 (copyright unknown).

"pours out reams of publicity" at the expense of "rebuild[ing] the Party organization from the ground up." Eager to direct Democratic strategy, Clifford
remarked, "The DNC is not all that important." In his estimation, analysis
of interest groups, such as labor, women, and minorities, comprised the
future of modern electioneering, and while McGrath saw merit in this
approach, he also believed that the big city bosses still held the key in many
municipalities.[28] The political infrastructure of the late nineteenth and early
twentieth centuries was, Clifford contended, fading into obscurity, but, as
McGrath would prove, machine politicians still held power at the grassroots.
Thus, the 1948 election represented the end of the traditional McGrath
approach and the growth of the more quantitative methods as advocated by
Clifford.[29]

   Despite these drawbacks, the new Democratic national chairman made
the most of his position by ably manipulating the media to the president's
advantage; television, radio, and print sources became fertile ground for him
to exploit for the sake of the party's future. The 1948 election proved a turning
point in the party's history for other reasons, as well. For one, the more liberal
Democratic advisors, known as the "Wardman Park Group" (the brainchild
of George Elsey and Clifford), of which McGrath was a frequent and, according to Truman biographer Gary A. Donaldson, important contributor,[30] persuaded the president to add a Research Division to the Democratic National
Committee. With a $50,000 budget paid for by the DNC, the Division, headed
by William Batt of Philadelphia, was responsible for gathering important
information on political opponents. Despite the DNC's financial support,
Clifford and the White House controlled this group, completely bypassing
McGrath. Both McGrath and Redding found this arrangement less than satisfactory.[31]

   At McGrath's suggestion, the president had approved Redding as director
of publicity for the Democratic committee. His division was tasked with
securing news coverage and "radio spots" for the party. The advent of this
media meant that presidential candidates were now required to allocate a
sizable portion of their party's treasury for radio time to broadcast their message into American homes.[32]

   By obtaining support from his personal and professional backers,
McGrath gathered a formidable coalition. As state chairman in 1930, he had
learned that effective electioneering began at the grassroots level, and money
and power could make or break a candidate.

   According to Stephen White of the *New York Herald Tribune*, "the means
by which the national chairman of a political party achieves his ends may
often be devious and subtle," but his success must be judged solely on the
final election tally. At the core of this process was his ability to raise money
for his party. With these criteria in mind, White concluded, "the Democratic

party could hardly have made a better choice for its national chairman than J. Howard McGrath."[33]

However, McGrath's strengths lay in practical politics, not in political ideology. Relegating the party's foundational debate against racial and religious oppression to others, he instead focused on uniting his party, securing votes, and organizing fundraising activities. In his *Power to the People,* published during the campaign, McGrath characterized his role succinctly: "At present, I am the Chairman of the Democratic National Committee. That does not mean that I am the most important man in the Party organization. I am not." Referring to the "precinct and county leaders of the Democratic Party," he continued, "there are at least 180,000 members of the organization who are more important than I am."[34] McGrath would serve, then, as the president's representative in matters concerning the campaign. For McGrath, his primary responsibility was to guarantee that Harry S Truman became president in his own right, and in this ultimate objective, he was successful.

Civil Rights

Despite the fact that McGrath played only a tangential role in public policy, he found himself at the epicenter of one of the most heated debates in modern history: civil rights.

For the first time in American history, a president raised the volatile topic of civil rights for African Americans to the forefront of a national election. Harry Truman, who as the son of Confederate sympathizers from the border state of Missouri had been known to drop racial slurs, chose to risk his political future for the advancement of basic civil rights by convening a committee in 1946 to investigate violence against African Americans in the South. The president's Civil Rights Commission, established by executive order that December, authorized the appointment of several leading activists. Charles E. Wilson, the president of General Electric Corporation, chaired the commission and was assisted in carrying out the president's mandate by a diverse group that included Sadie T. M. Alexander, an African American lawyer from Philadelphia and a vocal member of the American Civil Liberties Union; African American Channing Tobias of Georgia, Director of the Phelps-Stokes Fund; and Franklin D. Roosevelt, Jr., son of the deceased president. In its pioneering report, the committee revealed the level of injustice that had held court in the South for centuries. Whether motivated fully or in part by politics, Truman's action was groundbreaking and promised to generate immediate reaction from the segregated South. When the report, aptly titled *To Secure These Rights,* was published in October 1947, a vocal media highlighted its conclusions, which, according to political historian Zachary Karabell, were "stark, unsparing, and a bitter pill to southern Democrats."[35]

The president's final election platform regarding this controversial issue was supported by an oft-quoted document composed in September 1947 by former Roosevelt advisor James Rowe, Jr., and Clark Clifford, Truman's special counsel. In it, they outlined a plan for the president, which included a federally mandated program to protect African Americans.[36] Clifford and Rowe pointed out that the party was an amalgam of otherwise disparate groups: Southern conservatives, Western reformers, and urban labor.[37] Although this diversity would present a challenge, it would not be an insurmountable one, since his ticket to victory would rest upon his ability to lure a substantial number of each group to his camp. In order to realize this goal, they advised the president to do three specific things. (1) Court the liberals and/or African Americans to prevent their defection to either the Republican camp or to the recently ousted Secretary of Commerce Henry Wallace, who they predicted would run as a third-party candidate. (2) "Successfully concentrate on the traditional Democratic alliance between the South and West," which if properly carried out would assure 216 electoral of the total 266 votes needed to win.[38] Under this scenario, Truman could forfeit New York, Pennsylvania, Illinois, New Jersey, Ohio, and Massachusetts and still claim victory. (3) Court American labor through its chief representatives George Meany, leader of the New York Chapter of the American Federation of Labor, and William Green, who had praised the president's veto of the Taft-Hartley bill. They argued that Truman should diffuse any controversies that developed and derail Republican governor Thomas E. Dewey (whom they predicted would be the Republican nominee) attempt to lure labor to his camp. Clifford and Rowe also urged the president to reach out to Philip Murphy, head of the more radical Congress of Industrial Organizations (CIO), which was itself engaged in an internal struggle between right and left, suggesting that Truman's overtures would help the group choose a more moderate path.[39]

Equally significant, they advised the president to break the hold the Republican Party had held over African Americans in New York, Illinois, Pennsylvania, Ohio, and Michigan. Deeming 1948 to be a pivotal year for Democrats in the area of civil rights, Clifford and Rowe characterized Republican leadership as vulnerable. The front-runner, Governor Thomas E. Dewey of New York, had a proven reputation as a spokesman for civil rights, but Walter White, the executive secretary of the National Association for the Advancement of Colored People (NAACP), described him lukewarmly as an affable, though colorless and "coolly efficient," candidate.[40] Democrats might be able to lure key civil rights leaders from the Republican roll call with a dynamic initiative that would call for the end of segregation, lynching, and the onerous Jim Crow laws in the South.

As many historians of the Truman era have observed, the memorandum is remarkable for its prescience, depth, and analysis, but Clifford and Rowe failed in one important respect: they did not predict the secession of states' rights Southern Dixiecrats from the party in response to the civil rights mandate, since they had not accurately gauged the depth of Southern racism. The authors believed that although the South would protest, they would ultimately rally behind the Democratic Party. At the same time, they reassured the president that he would be elected if "the administration [would] successfully concentrate on the traditional Democratic alliance between the South and West."[41] This misjudgment quite possibly accounted for the president and party chairman's steadfastness in the face of the virulent Southern reaction, and it ultimately influenced Truman's response to civil rights. Nonetheless, the Democratic National Committee, under McGrath's leadership, followed the guidelines set by these two strategists and achieved victory.

Extracting the essence of his platform from the committee's findings, the president, in a public address on February 2, 1948, mandated an expanded federal civil rights division within the Department of Justice, an anti-lynching law, abolition of the poll tax, a permanent Fair Employment Practices Committee (FEPC), and additional far-reaching provisions to ensure swift repercussions for those who practiced discrimination based on race. Truman's proposal ignited a bomb that rippled throughout the South, in part because it ascribed legislation that had heretofore been conducted by state legislatures to the federal government. For states rights' Southern governors, such as Strom Thurmond of South Carolina and Fielding Wright of Mississippi, advocacy of expansive federal control undermined individual liberty as guaranteed by the United States Constitution. Almost immediately, Southern leaders began seeking ways to prevent the nomination of Harry Truman.

Five days after Truman's February 2 civil rights speech, the Southern governors met at Wakulla Springs, Florida, to formulate a policy targeting the president's proposed Democratic platform. Suggestions by the more radical members of the group included Mississippi's Fielding Wright's proposal for immediate Southern secession from the party, and James E. Folsom of Alabama's advice to his compatriots to take their debate to the floor of the Democratic National Convention that July. However, Strom Thurmond of South Carolina encouraged a more circumspect approach. Using his immense power of persuasion, Thurmond convinced the five governors to adopt a "forty-day cooling-off period" in order to allow them to draft a reasonable manifesto, which would ultimately "regain some of our important privileges."[42] McGrath applauded Governor Thurmond's restraint and assured him that the president would support the civil rights platform as it had been articulated in the 1944 Democratic plank, but the Southerners were not placated.

McGrath had earned the wrath of leading Southerners the previous August by desegregating the Democratic National Committee. The Southern delegation, composed of several notable senators and representatives and their wives, responded by refusing to attend the traditional Jefferson-Jackson Day Dinner held in Washington in February. At $100 a ticket, the gala attracted leading benefactors of the party and was a major fundraising event. The Southerners had reserved a table directly across from the dais where President Truman was to speak, but the vice-chairperson of the event, Mrs. Olin D. Johnston, wife of South Carolina's congressman and former governor, abruptly canceled their reservation after McGrath informed the delegation that of the 2,900 attendees about 12 were African American. Johnston stated as a reason for her cancellation that she "might be seated next to a Negro." Further proclaiming that the "whole dinner seating issue is symbolic of party leaders' efforts to get minority votes through civil rights proposals that led to threats of a Southern bolt,"[43] she argued that their attendance would be bowing to the will of the Northern majority. Exasperated, she further noted, "Senator McGrath has made it impossible for us to go. He would not give an inch."[44] In the end, the Democratic organization had to refund approximately $4,000 to the resistant Southerners. McGrath, realizing that the white Southerners would not back down, prepared for battle.

Soon thereafter, the Southern governors, believing they held the power, organized a meeting with McGrath to outline their policy. Forcing McGrath to rearrange his plans in order to accommodate them, they chose February 23 as the date for their historic meeting. The gathering generated heavy press coverage and revealed the cavernous divisions that existed between the North and South that had been masked for the last 12 years, by the Depression, the Second World War, and the charismatic presence of Franklin Delano Roosevelt.

The five Southern governors projected an image of solidarity, but privately there were profound differences that would prove helpful to McGrath down the road. Representing the middle ground, Strom Thurmond of South Carolina, who led the Southern delegation, cut a dashing figure. Less than a year older than McGrath, Thurmond was born in South Carolina, the son of J. William Thurmond, the campaign manager for ardent racist Ben "Pitchfork" Tillman. Known for employing any means possible to purge the South of all African Americans, Tillman came to embody the deafening battle cry of the deep South: "We stuffed ballot boxes. We shot them. We are not ashamed of it."[45] His message touched the heart of Will Thurmond's six-year-old son Strom, who upon meeting the Southern legend, declared, "I want to shake your hand." Tillman is said to have replied, "You said you wanted to shake. Why the hell don't you shake?"[46] Nevertheless, Thurmond, Arkansas's Benjamin Laney, Texas's Beauford H. Jester, and North Carolina's R. Gregg Cherry were willing to work through their differences from within Democratic Party ranks. The more rabid Fielding Wright called for immediate Southern secession from the party.

To Thurmond and the four governors, "the methods recommended [in the President's Civil Rights Platform] will irrevocably change our form of government, and may well sound the death knell of local self-government through the sovereignty of the several states."[47] The governors presented McGrath with a typed list of carefully crafted questions, and Thurmond, who remained stoic and recalcitrant throughout the meeting, cautioned him: "Your answers, as the operating head of the Democratic party, will affect substantially our report and recommendations to the Southern Governors Conference."[48] Thurmond clearly hoped to force McGrath to back down, but McGrath was not intimidated. He had developed his debating skills while an undergraduate and his abilities had improved with age.

A partial transcript of the meeting reads

> THURMOND: Will you, as Chairman of the Democratic National Committee, deny that the proposed anti-poll tax law, the proposed anti-lynching law, the proposed FEPC law, and the Federal law dealing with the separation of races, and each of them, would be unconstitutional invasions of the field of government belonging to the states under the Bill of Rights in the Constitution of the United States?
>
> McGRATH: You speak of proposed laws and I have not seen specific laws so that I am answering your questions thus—by proposed laws you mean any law that would attempt to deal with these subjects on the Congressional level ...
>
> THURMOND: Will you, as Chairman of the Democratic National Committee, oppose the enactment of Federal legislation or the adoption of Federal regulation which:
>
> (a) Will provide for Federal control or supervision of the employment, promotion, or discharge of employees of private business and industries?
>
> (b) Will interfere with the separation of races or attempt to override existing state and local laws on that subject?
>
> (c) Will force upon any state, or upon the District of Columbia, which is the common concern of all States, the mixing of races in the public schools?
>
> (d) Will prohibit separation of the races in the use of transportation facilities where equal accommodations are provided?
>
> McGRATH: No.
>
> THURMOND: Will you, as Chairman of the Democratic National Committee, oppose the establishment of a special Federal police agency such as the proposed Division of Civil Rights in the Department of Justice?
>
> McGRATH: No.[49]

In one of the most controversial requests, Thurmond asked McGrath whether he would support a ruling that would necessitate a two-thirds vote (of the 1,234 votes in the Democratic National Convention) in the selection of a Democratic candidate for president and vice president, a practice that had been outlawed at the behest of President Roosevelt in 1936 in favor of a simple majority. The requirement of a two-thirds majority would arm the Southerners with an effective tool to dominate the convention in July.[50]

McGrath refused, commenting that it would be "a step backward" for the Democrats. The meeting continued in this fashion, with McGrath holding his ground, while reiterating the policy of his chief. His public stand earned praise from African American leaders, as well as from other Democrats.

Thurmond and his delegation saw the determination of the Democratic Chairman to prevent "the highly controversial civil rights legislation" from being removed from the Democratic platform. Frustrated and angry, they stormed out.

As far as McGrath was concerned, "What is going to happen will happen to them [the Southerners], not to us. President Truman will be nominated. And he will be elected, elected without the solid South and without New York [a Wallace candidate had recently won a significant victory in New York City]."[51] McGrath's performance had solidified his role as Truman's unflinching promoter in a time of turmoil within the ranks of the Democratic Party. As McGrath would wryly note to Publicity Director Redding, in a momentary lapse, "This was hopeless. These people don't realize the change in the times."[52] Commenting on their meeting with McGrath, North Carolina's R. Gregg Cherry observed, "McGrath handled himself pretty well."[53] Texas governor Beauford H. Jester, on the other hand, complained to reporters, "If there has been any divergence, they [the Northern Democrats] have gone off and left us." Of the meeting with McGrath, he said, "I didn't ask a question." Reaching into his pocket and removing a "crumpled cigar wrapper," he noted, "That was what we got from McGrath." One of McGrath's supporters observed, "The court jester [Governor Beauford H.] is no friend of yours."[54] It was the Democratic Chairman's finest hour, and he explained to an audience of Rhode Islanders, "If we are not forced to compromise, we will succeed."[55] "A few days later, on February 27, Finance Director of the Democratic Party, George B. Hamilton resigned because ... I cannot in any way agree with the civil rights program promulgated by the President and indorsed [sic] by you officially as chairman. I believe that this program will effectuate untold damage to equitable solutions to the racial relations that should and must be ultimately arrived at."[56]

Two weeks after their tumultuous meeting with McGrath, the governors published the following statement: "We feel we are expressing the firm conviction of our people when we say that the present leadership of the Democratic party has deserted the principles of government upon which the Democratic party was founded."[57] The governors, especially Thurmond, endured considerable pressure from segregationists at home. In response, Thurmond howled, "These big city bosses and their puppets in office ... should once and for all realize that on the question of social intermingling of the races our people draw the line."[58] In a radio address to the people of South Carolina, Thurmond denied President Truman's authority to demand these laws, saying, the Federal Government can do only what the Constitution grants it the power to do. All other powers are reserved to the States of the Union, or to the people.... Another law recommended is an anti-lynching law. The Federal Government does not have the Constitutional right to deal with crimes occurring within the States.[59]

Following the rally, Southern confederates in a symbolic move, promised to regroup in Birmingham, Alabama, after the Democratic National Convention. Fearing the "death knell of local self-government through the sovereignty of the several states," they promised to do all in their power to prevent the election of Harry Truman as president of the United States.[60]

Southerners had warned the president that their region was not "in the bag" for the Democratic Convention that July, and the Clifford/Rowe gamble that the South would eventually comply, proved flawed; they lost the South.

It is important to note that although the South's states' rights plank was egregious in its implications, the Southerners were reacting strongly out of fear that the national government had robbed them of their autonomy. Much of the postwar South suffered in squalor. The "American Dream" not only failed to reach African Americans; it never touched the Deep South. Thurmond of South Carolina and Big Jim Folsom of Alabama spoke to constituencies suffering in ways not entirely understood by the national candidates. By seeking to impose federal legislation to promote the African American cause, President Truman was, according to the segregationists, threatening to overturn their way of life.

Although McGrath was not the architect of national policy, his strong stand against mounting pressure from the Southern governors afforded him a voice regarding civil rights. Anticipating the political defection, which might cost the president the nomination, McGrath urged Truman to announce his candidacy in early March, thereby explicitly stating his intentions to the rank and file of his party. The president agreed and called on McGrath to issue a statement.[61]

McGrath reported,

The first thing I have to tell you is that in response to numerous requests from Democratic leaders throughout the country, I asked the President if I might state what his intentions are with respect to the coming convention. The President has authorized me to say that if nominated by the Democratic National Convention, he will accept and run.[62]

Following his initial row with the Southerners, McGrath attempted to mollify them while at the same time balancing the needs of the African American community. He reminded the Southerners that they had "much to gain in playing along with the party and in fighting our battles out within the Congress," but his words fell on deaf ears.[63]

A month after McGrath's meeting with the governors, representatives from eleven Southern states, including five governors and eleven congressmen, headed by William M. Colmer of Mississippi, pledged their solid support for the governors' call to overturn civil rights legislation.[64] Joining Mississippi were Georgia, Florida, Alabama, Tennessee, Mississippi, Arkansas, Texas, Louisiana, North Carolina, South Carolina, and Virginia. At the end of his "40-day cooling-off period," Thurmond told reporters that the group would probably have "some new plan" for Chairman McGrath.[65]

The responses from African American leaders, like those of the Southerners, were split. Many blacks were heartened by the president's stand on civil rights, and some commended McGrath personally. Mary McLeod Bethune, president of the National Council of Negro Women, wrote to Chairman McGrath in March 1948:

> It has been my desire to meet you and have you know me, and to have the pleasure of knowing you. I do want to express a deep and sincere appreciation for the statesmanlike defense you gave to the President's Civil Rights Report. The response you took has greatly deepened our confidence in your leadership and our belief in your sense of justice.[66]

Others were more skeptical, as evidenced by a *New York Post* piece, which praised the president, but cautioned African Americans that "what remains [of President Truman's Civil Rights package] is performance to back up the promise."[67] Many civil rights leaders, like Walter White, secretary of the NAACP, voiced similar concerns, warning that a "mere political gesture" would not placate the African American who was fed up with empty assurances that never added up to tangible goals. While White did not support either Wallace or Dewey, he demanded a call to action from the administration and would not be satisfied with the inconclusive, watered-down 1944 Democratic platform.[68] The patience of the African American leadership was growing thin.

In the meantime, Rick Dawson, secretary of the Tolerance Club of Dallas, Texas, sent McGrath a threatening letter which begins,

> You are too handsome a man to put crooks into your features by your "close communion" with Harry Truman ... they [the "Negroes"] would loot and riot, and rape and bludgeon, and laugh, and say, "Harry Truman and Howard McGrath say we can. Already your face is turning a little blacker, and your nose looks slightly flatter.... Maybe we will get a Negro President next."[69]

As the civil rights issue stirred, opposition to Truman arose from other camps. Only days before the altercation with the Southern governors, Senator Glen Taylor of Idaho had bolted from the Democratic Party to accept Henry Wallace's invitation to serve as his vice-presidential candidate. Wallace, who had resigned from Truman's cabinet in 1946 after his public disavowal of the president's foreign policy, chose to mount a third-party campaign to prevent the election of his former boss. When a Wallace supporter, Leo Isacson, defeated the Democratic candidate Karl J. Propper in a special election in the Twenty-Fourth Congressional District in New York in February, the floodgates opened to additional agitation from within the ranks.[70]

The usually buoyant McGrath expressed concern about Wallace's candidacy; in fact, at one point, he offered Wallace an opportunity to rejoin the party following Isacson's victory in New York.[71] When asked by a *Providence Journal* reporter whether the former secretary of commerce might successfully take New York, Pennsylvania, Illinois, and California, McGrath replied perhaps hopefully, "Certainly that sort of thing is possible, but is not likely."[72] McGrath warned that casting a vote for Wallace would ensure a Republican victory and assured Redding that Wallace would get no more than a million votes.

Following the urging of Clifford and Rowe that the administration concentrate on issues important to the Western states, including land reclamation, flood control, and farming, McGrath embarked on a trip to Montana, Oregon, California, and Washington in April. His goal was to circumvent possible Democratic defectors. With Redding, he settled on an itinerary that included Portland, Oregon, a Republican stronghold, as their point of origin. Informing his Western audiences of the merits of a Truman presidency, McGrath underscored the importance of supporting a known quantity in the face of threats from abroad. In Spokane, Washington, he reminded his audience that "all civilization looks to the United States to decide the way the rest of the nations shall follow. This responsibility is on President Truman and it is our responsibility to uphold him in meeting this terrific challenge."[73] He met with students, labor leaders, and local party representatives, and the tour was hailed as an overall success. Supporting projects to further the development of the Western states, McGrath promoted the expansion of conservation and irrigation programs "that will widen the scope of the nation's participation in world affairs."[74]

In addition to the usual political rhetoric, McGrath also made some important statements that foreshadowed the Democratic National Convention in July. Contending that Wallace's candidacy actually helped the party, since he "cleansed us of undesirable Communistic influences," McGrath used one of the most volatile topics of the Cold War against his rival.[75] Equating Henry Wallace with Earl Browder, leader of the Communist Party, McGrath highlighted the ideological gulf between Wallace and Truman, thereby fulfilling one of the objectives of the Clifford/Rowe memorandum. Wallace, he argued, "talks the same words, with the same reasoning" as Earl Browder, while President Truman "has supplied the kind of patriotic, sane leadership that is necessary in this day of fearsome decisions."[76] McGrath thus reduced a rather complex choice into a battle between good versus evil: either vote for a Communist or for a patriot. For most Americans in the postwar era, the decision when placed in that light was easy. On the other hand, this strategy also heightened fear of the Soviet Union and nuclear holocaust, which hung over the convention as eerily as the civil rights issue.

There were other potential nominees, in addition to Wallace: the Americans for Democratic Action (ADA) organized a campaign to nominate General Dwight D. Eisenhower or Supreme Court Justice William O. Douglas[77] for the presidency. A sizable liberal clique, which included former Roosevelt bureaucrat Leon Henderson and Franklin Delano Roosevelt's sons James and Elliott Roosevelt, spearheaded a "Dump Truman" campaign.[78] The support of James Roosevelt, California state chairman, was essential, not only because of his famous name, but also because of the 25 electoral votes that he could bring to the Democratic camp. Roosevelt's vocal promotion of an Eisenhower candidacy troubled the president, who, at one point, poked him, shouting, "Your father asked me to take this job. I didn't want it. I was happy in the Senate.... And if your father knew what you are doing to me, he would turn over in his grave."[79] A few of the Southern notables, including South Carolina senator Olin D. Johnston and Alabama's lieutenant governor Leven Handy Ellis, also expressed their support for an Eisenhower ticket.[80] Ostensibly, Johnston proposed that McGrath persuade the president to step down in favor of Eisenhower.

Meanwhile, Alabama denied President Truman its 11 electoral votes. McGrath, however, cautioned the Southerners that their decision to bolt would cost them in future elections. According to the party rules at the time, the 1948 convention permitted eight "bonus" delegates for states that had pledged support to the 1944 Democratic nominee for president and vice president. Each special delegate was allowed a half vote. Alabama's defection from the Democratic camp would cost the state its eight bonus votes in the 1952 election.[81]

Despite the mounting challenges, McGrath publicly maintained an aura of confidence and buoyancy, which, according to Chicago reporter Paul R. Leach, was "imperturbable." Insisting that Eisenhower would not accept the Democratic nomination, that the Republican platform was too bland to attract the voter, that the necessary number of Southerners would support the main ticket despite the Dixiecrat battle cry, and that Wallace would not steal the African American vote, McGrath worked systematically to ensure that his predictions would be fulfilled.[82]

A month before the Convention, Clifford and the Wardman Park Group supported Truman's campaign trip to the Western states. With five official appearances in Chicago, Omaha, Seattle, Los Angeles, and Berkeley, and 71 impromptu speeches from the rear of his train, the Truman entourage clocked 9,505 miles.

Before the president departed for New York, he boasted that "from north to south; from east to west, we are getting reports of imminent victory for the people's crusade. All of you know where I stand on the major issues.... But do you know where my Republican opponent stands on these things? If you do, you are better than I, because I cannot find out."[83] McGrath did not officially participate in the president's train travel in June, nor in the more famous "Whistle Stop" campaign that commenced in September. However, McGrath, appearing "worried," was in plain view when the president warmly greeted a crowd of 20,000 people in Providence, Rhode Island.

Democratic Research Division chief Batt's contributions, however, were immeasurable. With the addition of seven new recruits to the Research Division, his analysis of the president's speeches and the public's reaction to them aided Clifford and his team of speechwriters in tailoring the president's speeches to complement his demeanor.

Just three days before the Democratic National Convention opened at noon on Monday, July 12, Eisenhower gave his "final and complete" no to running against Truman,[84] although it did not stop the liberals from attempting to find another substitute. The ghost of the Republican Convention, held three weeks earlier in the same location, hung over that first day, but the keynote speech delivered by 70-year-old Kentuckian Alben Barkley, broke the trance with its stirring eloquence.

For vice-president, Truman had his heart set on Supreme Court Justice William O. Douglas, but after weighing his options, Douglas had decided to remain on the bench. Barkley's rousing speech assured him the spot on the vice-presidential ticket.

Despite McGrath's attempt to defuse the civil rights time bomb, the issue took on a life of its own during the Convention. Amidst the fury and anxiety of the Convention, two rival camps emerged: on one hand the ADA (Americans for Democratic Action) liberals, including former senator Andrew J. Biemiller of Wisconsin, Joseph L. Rauh, leader of the ADA, and young Hubert Humphrey, who was running for the Senate seat of Minnesota; on the other the Southern delegations who feared that the Democratic Convention delegates would approve a civil rights platform.

The middle-of-the road platform committee (favored by the president and Chairman McGrath) voted 70 to 30 in favor of the 1944 civil rights platform, which called for general equality and civil rights. However, the vocal Biemiller group supported a stronger position, which was similar to the president's Ten Point Plan put forth in February. McGrath's ally, Maurice Tobin from Massachusetts, also spoke out in favor of the stronger civil rights agenda.[85] Hubert Humphrey, a relative unknown, delivered one of the most memorable and inspiring speeches, shaking the Convention delegates from their lassitude and urging them to "get out of the shadow of states' rights and walk forthrightly into the bright sunshine of human rights." Humphrey challenged them all to break free from racial prejudice to honor the principles on which America was founded.[86]

In his welcoming speech to the Democratic National Committee, McGrath had tried to deflect attention from civil rights and focus on the president's resolute stand against Joseph Stalin, who had recently imposed a blockade preventing travel from East to West Berlin. McGrath played upon the emotions of his audience:

> Our pride in our accomplishments is tempered by the grim realization that the bomber, the submarine, the tank, the rocket and the atom bomb are also the ugly concomitants of our advanced skills ... the same modern technologies that have put at man's disposal the greatest potential mechanisms for increasing human welfare, hold a deadly effectiveness for collective human suicide when utilized to fashion the instruments of war.[87]

His efforts were in vain. The civil rights issue had taken on a life of its own, and the tide was turning toward a more radical approach to combat segregation in the South. Although President Truman and McGrath favored a moderate civil rights platform, the Biemiller amendment was adopted by a vote of 651½ to 582½, while the Southern plank, the Moody Report, named after Governor Daniel Moody of Texas, went down in defeat, 3 to 1. Immediately, all of the Mississippi delegates and half of the Alabama delegates (35 in all) abandoned the Convention. The NAACP was ecstatic over the South's decision to bolt from the party. Clifford and Rowe's predictions, however, had failed in this regard; now, the president had to win New York, Pennsylvania, Illinois, New Jersey, Ohio, and Massachusetts to make up for the solid South.[88]

Truman came to the platform at 2:00 p.m. He was officially nominated with 948 votes 12 hours later, at 2:00 a.m. on July 15, with Senator Alben Barkley easily receiving the requisite number of votes to be the vice-presidential nominee.

As the president approached the stage for his victory speech, a guard let loose a flock of white pigeons, which had been caged in the base of a flower stand located on the platform where the president was to deliver his speech. The gift of a Pennsylvania senator's well-meaning sister, the "doves" were meant to serve as a symbol of peace. They did not, unfortunately, serve this purpose: overheated and eager to escape, they dove headlong into the balcony and one bird, disoriented by the heat and lights, nearly flew into the blades of a fan, which Redding ordered to be shut down so that no other bird might impale itself.[89]

The president, ignoring the chaos, addressed the audience in clear, emphatic statements, delivering one of the most memorable speeches of his career. Pledging to call Congress into special session in order to enact several controversial measures, he said:

I'm going to call that Congress back and I'm going to ask them to pass laws halting rising prices, and to meet the housing crisis which the Republicans say they are for in their platform. At the same time I shall ask them to act upon other vital measures such as aid to education ... a national health program, civil rights legislation ... an increase in the minimum wage.[90]

In what has been labeled Truman's July 26 "Turnip Day" session, the president recalled Congress to a special session and dared the Republicans to honor their campaign speeches by passing legislation on civil rights, Social Security, and health care. With a cunning political ploy, the president had backed the Republican opposition into a corner. Republican leaders realized that "if we do as he asks, he'll claim all the credit.... If we don't ... he'll blame ... us for blocking his efforts."[91] By the conclusion of the session, the Republicans had only released two of the president's "executive orders," one desegregating the military and civil service and the other authorizing a permanent Fair Employment Practice Committee (FEPC). In protest, the president labeled the 80th Congress the "do-nothing" Congress, and the moniker stuck. It proved to be an excellent rallying point against the Republicans during the campaign.[92]

Two days after the Convention ended, Strom Thurmond was nominated as the states' rights candidate in Birmingham, Alabama, with Fielding Wright of Mississippi as his vice-president. On July 23, the Progressive Party in Philadelphia chose Henry Wallace and Senator Glen Taylor from Idaho as president and vice presidential nominees, respectively.

McGrath drafted a memorandum of political analysis in September 1948, and submitted it to the president. Compared to the Clifford/Rowe document written the previous August, however, McGrath's was weak. Praising the president's efforts and cautioning him to "measure" his accomplishments "in the light" of "the magnitude of the task [he has] had—more involved and difficult perhaps ... than that which had confronted any previous President,"[93] McGrath's narrative reads like a congratulatory note, rather than a political analysis. He urged Truman to authorize the *de jure* recognition of Israel and warned that the administration needed to "emphasize its strong opposition to Communism" to allay any doubt that the president may be "shielding them [Communist sympathizers]." Notably, McGrath omitted the significant civil rights issue. Aware of Dixiecrat strength in the South, he refused to bring attention to this volatile topic. Shortly thereafter, in an attempt to mollify the South, McGrath explained, "many implications ascribed to the President's message are exaggerated."

According to historian John Frederick Martin, Truman, unlike McGrath and Barkley, was not personally opposed to the liberal civil rights' platform. This contention is dubious, however, since the president on July 14 referred in his diary to Biemiller as a "crackpot."[94] While the president supported civil rights from a humanitarian perspective, his liberalism was, as historian Alan Brinkley contended, much more guarded.[95] McGrath's main concern continued to be party unity, for which he was willing to soften the civil rights issue, even after the Southerners bolted.

Following the Convention, McGrath returned to the West three times, all the while "counteract[ing] the feeling that 'it was impossible for us to win.'"[96] Especially important was the trip to California to address the so-called "California problem."[97] According to McGrath, "Jimmie Roosevelt has been building organization in the South [Southern part of the state].... There's never been anything like that before."[98] McGrath and Redding were expected to attend several meetings in which Roosevelt was the center of attention. Although Roosevelt's opponent, Edwin Pauley, was a Truman confidant, McGrath believed that "the only organization out here is Roosevelt's. It makes sense to go with him. He offers the only chance to win votes."[99] McGrath then had to work his magic with Pauley, who put it bluntly, asking, "What

The new chairman often found himself the subject of political lampoons. Here, political cartoonist Clifford Berryman shows McGrath with a shotgun promising President Truman that he would "run those Dixiecrats out of here" in 1948 (Harry S Truman Library).

you want is, for me to drop out at National Committeeman in favor of Roosevelt?" When McGrath answered in the affirmative, Pauley warned, "You'll regret it. Roosevelt will let you down. He's not interested in Truman, only in Roosevelt." Even so, Pauley stepped aside graciously to allow Roosevelt to assume center stage in California.[100]

California was not the only troubling state. A majority of columnists predicted a Dewey victory. Newspapers throughout the country, including the *New York Sun, Boston Herald, Kansas City Star, New York Herald-Tribune, New York Times,* and scores of others, saw Truman's defeat as a "foregone conclusion." For example, major columnist Drew Pearson predicted that Governor Dewey of New York would be elected president: "Harry Truman has put up a courageous and magnificent fight…. But, thanks to the combination of Dixiecrats and Wallaceites, he cannot possibly win this election. He will roll up a bigger popular vote than previously expected, which will be good. For it is always bad for one party to be too cocksure and over-confident."[101]

Pearson's rival, Westbrook Pegler of the Scripps-Howard group, predicted that Harry Truman would be defeated even before the Convention, writing in March 1948: "It is a foregone conclusion that the Democratic candidate will be defeated next November. It is even possible that President Truman will be rejected by his own party, but, in any case, the Republican nominee will be the next President."[102]

Several months later, on election day, these journalists were proven wrong. Truman received 303 electoral votes, 37 more than the 266 needed. Governor Dewey received 169, and Governor Thurmond 38. The president had secured California, Colorado, Illinois, Idaho, Nevada, Ohio, Washington, and Wyoming.

In thanking McGrath, President Truman was most gracious: "I don't think I've ever sent you a personal message of appreciation for the contribution which you made to that election…. I hope everything goes well with you in the Senate and every other way."[103]

Despite McGrath's success in returning President Truman to the White House, his worries about party unity did not abate. Seeking to mend party rifts following President Truman's victory, McGrath rejected all efforts to punish the South. On this he pitted himself against the grand dame of the party, Eleanor Roosevelt, who supported a "Dixiecrat purge from the Democratic organization." In her estimation, "there are really only two major political factions in the United States—liberals and conservatives." Roosevelt supported a "final break" with opponents of liberalism, particularly targeting the South. McGrath, more practically, extended an olive branch to the majority of states' rights advocates. Agreeing that high ranking Dixiecrats like Thurmond and Wright should be denied choice assignments in the Democratic Party, he nevertheless believed that by silencing the vast majority of

Southerners, an important voice in Congress, would further fragment the party and ensure a Republican victory in 1950.[104]

Given that 42 of 96 senators were Republican, any rash move against this bloc would probably cause Southern Democrats to seek aid and comfort from their former opponents and vote with the opposition.[105] McGrath's behind-the-scenes wrangling enabled the promotion of some former Confederate secessionists, such as Senator John L. McClellan of Arkansas, to prestigious chairmanships.[106]

As expected, the Southern Democrats joined forces with Republicans in the Senate to block any passage of the president's civil rights provisions in early 1949. Due to a Republican filibuster from February 28 to March 17, President Truman's forces failed to pass Senate Resolution 15 (S15), which prevented any attempt to "gag" Senate debate on any issue. The resolution would have amended the so-called cloture rule, which allowed for a two-thirds vote of the Senate (or 64 senators) to limit discussion on all legislation to a single hour.[107]

Walter White, enraged by what he viewed as an abandonment of civil rights by the Democratic organization, sent a scathing note to Senators McGrath and Scott Lucas, accusing them of hypocrisy for retreating in the face of Southern defection. Describing a shouting match with White near Senate Secretary Les Biffle's office in March 1949, McGrath admitted, "I used some language on him that a good Holy Name Society man can't repeat."[108] The immediate reason for their argument was a letter written by White on February 21, 1949, to his branch president, which claimed that the Democratic chairman "turn[ed] tail" to the Southerners. White charged, "Democratic Senators from outside the South gave up and sold the civil rights program down the river." He continued, "McGrath is not 'right' on the question of Negro rights. He is a trader.… Since the election last November he has ducked and dodged every discussion of the civil rights program.… McGrath forgets he is a victorious national chairman today … because of the support his party got from Negroes on the civil rights issues."[109] In response, McGrath stated, "I feel we have done our best in this fight and been faithful to our civil rights pledges to the detriment of other interests of the party."[110] Since the Democratic chairman had "done all he could" for race relations, he believed that White and the NAACP should be grateful rather than combative. The *DC Star* agreed, and categorized White's reaction as "a form of blindness" that "takes possession of some men whose whole lives are wrapped up in single causes."[111]

Yet by merely justifying his position, McGrath failed to grasp the root of White's anger. White's charge that McGrath "listens sympathetically to the Dixiecrats … [but] ducked and dodged every discussion of the civil rights program" reveals a fatal flaw in McGrath's approach to adversity. Choosing to promise each contending group small tokens, he had "never laid a card on the table." Eventually, White and other critics grew weary of McGrath's approach and sought other avenues to achieve their goals. In the meantime, McGrath was becoming more expendable.

Nonetheless, White wrote McGrath immediately after their row, ascribing the "unfortunate incident in Mr. Biffle's office late last night to fatigue and the strain under which you have worked these last few days." He continued, "I regret all the more the misunderstanding in view of the unequivocal fight which you made in the caucus against acceptance of the 'compromises' which you accurately termed as 'worse than the present rule.'"[112]

White, while diplomatic in his response, sought to remind McGrath not to accept "'compromises'" in the face of the "unequivocal fight" for civil rights. It was a masterful letter, respectful of McGrath's position and labor on behalf of African Americans, while at the same time forceful in its intent.

Post-Election Blues

Following the election, McGrath began to feel himself an outsider. A rift between the administration and McGrath developed, centering on patronage and finances. According to several reports, the White House passed over McGrath's choices for certain key posts. McGrath looked upon his ability to influence political positions as essential to encouraging party unity,[113] and he began to voice his displeasure with what he viewed as a slight from the administration.[114]

As an example, even before the election, in January 1948 the president demoted Marriner S. Eccles, Democrat and New Dealer, from chairman to vice-chairman of the Federal Reserve Board because he believed his decision to precipitate a "minor recession" in order to save the economy from major collapse in the near future was foolhardy.[115] Truman replaced Eccles with Republican Thomas B. McCabe, who McGrath believed would further distance liberal Democrats and Southerners from the party. McGrath had suggested a Southerner to replace Eccles, but his opinion was dismissed by the White House.[116]

Robert S. Allen, one of the most acerbic chroniclers of the period, predicted that an "oust McGrath" campaign would ensue, since the Rhode Islander's alleged failure to seek advice from former Democratic national chairmen Robert Hannegan, Frank Walker, and Edward Flynn had apparently produced ill will. Allen also raised the possibility that the inner circle was unhappy with McGrath's failure to raise enough funds during the campaign.[117]

McGrath did encounter, through no fault of his own, difficulty generating funds. According to one political satirist, "folks who contribute to political campaigns are seldom pure altruists. They desire something for themselves in return." In this case, no one was betting on Harry Truman's return to the White House. Following the resignation of George B. Hamilton as director of finance on February 28, the job of Democratic Party treasurer was vacant, with few offering to step up to the post.[118] When the Democratic Committee finally found a willing candidate in the cantankerous Louis Johnson, not one Democrat, according to Jack Redding, would raise a hand in protest, since no one else desired the position.[119] And Johnson was able to coral enough support to save the day.[120]

In October, the Democratic National Committee revealed that it had failed to balance its budget and suffered a $47,981 shortage-to-date; in comparison, the Republican deficit amounted to $123,771. The statement also disclosed that the Republicans had received $1,883,516 in contributions, $200,323 more than the Democrats. So, while the Republicans received more funding and spent more money than their Democratic counterparts, they still lost the election.[121]

Promising a "$1,000,000 war chest" for the 1950 and 1952 campaigns, McGrath and his executive vice chairman William M. Boyle, Jr., were successful in replacing Gael Sullivan, who had finally stepped down in 1948. In this estimate, they anticipated that the Jefferson-Jackson Day dinner celebrations should bring in $280,000 and $300,000, respectively.[122]

Although McGrath had been reelected to the chairmanship in July, rumors circulated that the president or some other high-ranking Democrat would oust him to make room for a Democratic head more in concert with the president's line of thinking.[123] In addition, while the correspondence between McGrath and Truman's personal secretary Matthew Connelly indicates a distancing between the two men, the reasons for this break remain unclear.

According to Drew Pearson, "a determined drive" was "under way by the White House palace guard to fire hard-working Senator McGrath."[124] As anticipated, McGrath was replaced as Democratic chairman in 1949 by his former aide, William Boyle. McGrath himself was transferred to the Department of Justice as attorney general. Sympathetic reporter Doris Fleeson wrote that "the McGrath policy of conciliation toward all but rampant Dixiecrats will be continued at headquarters."[125] She went on to write that "the retiring chairman leaves the party victorious, well heeled and speaking civilly to one another. The fact seems to be that McGrath, who will enter the Cabinet as Attorney General, always leaves his stepping stones in good order and with good will."[126]

Before he left his post, however, McGrath established a foundation for the 1950 election. While Republicans aimed their program at eastern, middle, and Midwestern states, including Ohio, Indiana, Iowa, Massachusetts, Illinois, New York, and Pennsylvania, McGrath explained to reporters that "the victory must be won at the precinct level."[127] He, therefore, counted on "strong local candidates, plus a good organization" to spell victory. He continued, "a party is as good as its local candidates and its precinct workers."[128]

In conclusion, J. Howard McGrath excelled against formidable odds to represent the president in the best possible light. As McGrath would later state to Jack Redding in the foreword of *Inside the Democratic Party*, his performance as chairperson was "his finest hour." He argued that the Democratic National Committee, including its research and publicity departments, coupled with the president's unfailing energy, had won against daunting odds.

Nevertheless, his role in the civil rights campaign, after opening on a high note, retreated in an effort to secure unity. While McGrath's efforts on behalf of the president were notable, he failed to capitalize on the link between civil rights in America and human rights globally. Because the United States was a major power, America needed to present itself as a place where all its citizens, regardless of race, enjoyed the fruits of democracy. Instead, Chairman McGrath had to confront a disillusioned civil rights leadership on the one hand and Southern reactionaries determined to maintain the status quo on the other. African American leaders feared that the president and his administration would rest on the laurels of the February 2 speech without moving on actual legislation.[129] However, with the momentum begun with President Truman's February speech, McGrath's stand-off against Southern governors, and Hubert Humphrey's rousing convention speech that summer, civil rights took on a life of its own.

The record supports the conclusion that Democratic National Chairman McGrath, while leading a successful campaign overall, chose the easier route when it came to civil rights; by marginalizing the wrongs of Jim Crow, he attempted to mollify the South, hoping to capture the remaining Southerners at the expense of the cause of freedom for blacks in America.

13

"He'll sink or swim with Harry"[1]

In 1948, seven-year-old Alex Ray was the object of a prank perpetrated by Senator J. Howard McGrath, "one of the most powerful [Democrats] in the nation in the late '40s and a close friend of President Harry Truman."[2] McGrath's majestic property on Salt Pond in Point Judith, southwest of Narragansett Bay, bordered the homestead of Ray's aunt and uncle, and Ray and his cousin would stroll along the beach, often stopping at the McGrath home for refreshments. Ray knew nothing of politics and did not realize that the friendly, neighborly gentleman who often entertained at his Point Judith estate had been instrumental in procuring the election of President Harry Truman in 1948. "After playing out in the summer sun," Ray recalled, "I came onto the porch where the adults were gathered and politely asked for a ginger ale." Handing him a glass full of clear liquid, McGrath urged the boy to "try this one." Ray swallowed its contents, immediately regurgitating them in disgust. Amused, McGrath informed him that all young men must learn to hold their liquor if they want to succeed in politics. Not at all pleased by McGrath's poor judgment, his father grabbed Ray's hand and stormed off the premises, never to return.[3] Ray himself would eventually serve as a backroom broker for the Republican Party in Vermont.

Since his introduction to politics in the 1920s, McGrath had demonstrated a "get along, go along attitude,"[4] as a man who tried to be all things to all men. Now, as he neared middle age, the façade was beginning to exert its toll, and it showed in poor choices like his prank on Ray. In addition, the once youthful, handsome Irishman's ruddy face had begun to exhibit signs of alcohol abuse. After he assumed the post of attorney general, his personal flaws were magnified as challenges surfaced. As historian Robert Ferrell would remark in 1994, McGrath was "a charming Irishman, [who had grown] a little bibulous and lazy" and "[would soon be] incapable of carrying presidential sins into the wilderness." Ferrell may have reached this conclusion, at least in part, by reading historian Robert Donovan, who used similar language to describe the Rhode Island Senator in 1982. Donovan added, however, that although "McGrath was never known to have been tainted with corruption himself," he "drank too much and neglected his responsibilities."[5]

Equally important, McGrath is said to have ranked "Communists and 'subversive activities,' above other pressing "business before him."[6] His questionable ties to business leaders compromised his public duties as a servant of the people and as a judicial officer for President Truman, and his inability to face the corruption within the Bureau of Internal Revenue and the Justice Department weakened his authority and, more importantly, led to a decline in the office itself.

McGrath as Attorney General: Accession to Office

Notwithstanding the success of the 1948 election, McGrath found himself vilified by critics in its aftermath. Some complained that he had pandered to Southern Dixiecrats by calling for unity within the party despite the secession of Strom Thurmond and his delegation at the Convention in July. Others faulted him for the party's financial difficulties, despite McGrath's unfaltering canvassing of city and town organizations to solicit donations and his success in securing future secretary of defense Louis Johnson as financial director of the Democratic National Committee when no one else would accept the position.[7] Rumors that President Truman wished to replace him with his Kansas City pal, Bill Boyle, circulated, although the president repeatedly denied them.

Then events took a fortuitous turn, enabling the president to replace McGrath in the DNC without either man losing face. The death of Supreme Court Associate Justice Frank Murphy in 1949 provided Truman with the opportunity to appoint Attorney General Thomas C. Clark to the Supreme Court and name McGrath to lead the Justice Department. Surprised by the turn of events, given speculation on the home front that Truman would offer McGrath the associate justiceship, he was publicly circumspect about the offer, and privately disappointed. According to the *Providence Journal*, "McGrath ... had been mentioned as a possibility for appointment as associate justice of the Supreme Court to succeed Justice Frank Murphy." Nonetheless, McGrath kept the bitterness of the blow well shielded from the public eye, telling reporters: "I am highly gratified at the President's confidence in me in making the offer."[8]

The press had assumed that the president would replace the Catholic Murphy with another man of the same faith, someone like McGrath or Senator Joseph O'Mahoney of Wyoming, instead of Clark, a Presbyterian from

Texas. Truman publicly defended his choice, responding that religion was not a litmus test for entrance into the Court,[9] but he quieted his critics by naming McGrath to the Justice Department. In a 1972 interview with archivist Jerry N. Hess, Clark recalled his conversation with the president, who said to Clark,

> "I am thinking of a package job and wished to know what you thought about it." So, the President said he wanted Howard McGrath.... He said, "Do you remember ... why I told you to get somebody that you thought would be a good man to succeed you ... I don't think that it's good to have the chairman of the Committee to be in an official position.... I want you to go and talk to Howard, and you all let me know." So, I talked to Howard, and of course, Howard was pleased and I was pleased.[10]

When he returned to Rhode Island on July 29 after a conference with Truman, McGrath directed State Chairman Stephen A. Fanning to summon Rhode Island's leading Democrats to his summer home on Salt Pond for a discussion on the future of the party should he accept Truman's offer. As he had with the solicitor generalship four years earlier, McGrath sought validation from leading Democrats, this time including Dennis Roberts, Governor Pastore, and his able mentor, Theodore Francis Green. Recognizing this decision as a life-altering event, McGrath proceeded gingerly, accepting the post only after receiving a nod from party leaders.[11]

McGrath's decision to step down left a vacancy in the Rhode Island Senate, as he would now be giving up his Senate seat. This resurrected old factionalism, dormant since the 1930s because the McGrath/Green bloc had held a virtual monopoly in state offices. Green's longevity in the Senate and McGrath's control of patronage and the local press had tied the hands of some up-and-coming Democrats. With McGrath out of the picture, there was an opening for new blood in the upper house. *The Providence Journal* speculated that "John O. Pastore, the man who would hold the power of appointment over a successor, would not manipulate the situation to put himself in the Senate now."[12]

The Rhode Island paper predicted that "McGrath's resignation would start a series of events which probably would find Pastore running for the Senate in the 1950 election and Mayor Dennis J. Roberts of Providence as the Democratic candidate for governor."[13] Although a Pastore supporter, McGrath feared that his move might sever the infrastructure that he had built for himself in the state, which explains in part his reluctance to accept the president's offer. When he left Rhode Island in 1945 to accept the post of solicitor general, some believed McGrath had abandoned his home base for a better offer. His return the following year and successful Senate race had quelled those comments, but if he accepted a national position now he faced the real possibility of a permanent break with the state's Democratic organization.

On the national front, the response to the president's appointments was mixed, although many political analysts were willing to give McGrath the benefit of the doubt. Former secretary of the interior Harold L. Ickes commented wryly, "it is a comfort to think of Sen. J. Howard McGrath as Attorney General in place of the misplaced Clark. Sen. McGrath cannot possibly perform as badly as has his immediate predecessor." Adding, "he has the character and inherent dignity that one who occupies such a high office ought to have."[14]

A journalist at the *Washington Post* questioned not so much the president's specific choices but his insistence upon rewarding the politically loyal with high judicial posts. On Truman's selection of McGrath, the paper prophesied that the "impropriety of designating the chairman of the Democratic National Committee to head the prosecuting arm of the Government" will levy "a high price indeed."[15] On Clark, the *Post* concluded, "He [the President] has treated a great coordinate branch of the Government [the Supreme Court] as if it were an institution for the reward of his personal favorites. The fact that this keeps the courts overweighted with former executive officials, leaves it politically lopsided."[16]

Formal portrait of J. Howard McGrath, 1948 (courtesy Special and Archival Collections, Providence College).

The *Providence Journal* contributed to the discussion by observing that "the American people generally, we believe, would have been happier if Mr. Truman could have found some other cabinet place for his deserving lieutenant from Rhode Island." Since the position "is a quasi-judicial post with peculiar responsibilities, it is not well suited to be used as a political prize."[17]

However, neither McGrath nor Clark was the first political appointee to be named to the Justice Department or the Supreme Court. According to legal historian Nancy Baker, many attorneys general in the twentieth century had served their respective presidents as party chairmen, managers, or campaigners. Others, including Harlan Stone, Robert Jackson, and the deceased Justice Murphy, had risen to the bench from the Justice

Department because of their political ranking within their party.[18] The condemnation in the press of the McGrath/Clark trade can thus be seen as predominantly a response to the continuation of this practice, rather than a protest against the candidates themselves.

Viewed in this light, McGrath's political background alone would not necessarily have barred him from carrying out his official duties as attorney general, but as senator his 99 percent approval rating of Truman policies cast him as an "advocate," causing some to fear that McGrath would serve as a mere mouthpiece of the president. Former advocate attorneys general, such as Eisenhower's head of Justice Herbert Brownell, had on occasion disagreed with the oval office,[19] but McGrath was seen as passive, as inclined to follow the lead of the president, rather than advise him on legal matters.[20]

A Constitutional issue also factored into whether McGrath could accept Truman's offer. On the legislative docket was a measure calling for a $10,000 pay raise for members of the president's cabinet. In the case of the attorney general position, McGrath, who earned $12,500 as a senator with a $2500 expense account, would earn $15,000 per year as head of the Justice Department. If the measure passed, however, his salary would increase to $25,000. According to the U.S. Constitution, no "senator or representative" may "be appointed to any civil office" during which time an "emolument whereof shall have been increased." McGrath avoided this pitfall by surrendering his Senate seat before accepting the post as attorney general.[21] McGrath resigned as Democratic national chairman and senator on August 24, 1949, and assumed the cabinet position immediately thereafter.[22] McGrath was confirmed unanimously, and Clark was endorsed "by 9–2 vote" in senate Judiciary Committee.[23] According to U.S. News and World Report, McGrath believed the position to be a "way station on the journey to the high bench."[24]

Appointed by the executive branch and subject to legislative approval and regulation, the attorney general was the ranking legal officer in the executive branch, answerable only to the president. Established in 1870, the Department of Justice was charged with overseeing the following subdivisions: the Office of Alien Property, the Criminal Division, the Anti-Trust Division, the Claims Division, the Lands Division, the Tax Division, Immigration and Naturalization, the Customs Division, and the Bureau of Prisons. The attorney general, tasked with ensuring the efficient administration of these disparate areas, would of necessity have to rely on his assistants to carry out the day-to-day duties of each sector.

In taking the position, McGrath would face tremendous obstacles, as the Department of Justice and the Internal Revenue Bureau had grown unwieldy in the years since the Great Depression. As governor of Rhode Island nearly a decade earlier, McGrath had warned of an overactive federal government, as it had expanded exponentially during the Second World War. Now he was in the position of having to control the results of this overexpansion in a department tasked with regulating the expanded federal sphere.

Thus, this chapter will address central questions for historians of the Truman era about (1) the evolving role of the state and its jurisdiction into the private lives of individuals and (2) the public's changing perception of its officials. The trial that followed the investigation of the Internal Revenue Bureau and the Department of Justice set the standard for how we in the United States judge our government officials today. What Americans expect from the men and women we elect to high office in the twenty-first century was thrashed about publicly in the twentieth as Assistant Attorney General of Tax Division T. Lamar Caudle, former Attorney General Tom Clark, J. Howard McGrath, and ultimately Harry Truman were judged in regard to whether they were fit to hold office.

Cold War Attorney General: McGrath and the Rise of the National Security State

According to Daniel S. Cheever and H. Field Haviland, Jr., writing in 1952, the problem with America's system of checks and balances "is that the United States sometimes speaks with more than one voice in world affairs."[25] The Cold War represents an excellent example of this phenomenon, which emerged with nearly tragic results as the executive and legislative branches and their subordinate departments and committees prioritized rooting out the Soviet menace in the name of internal security. In doing so, however, leading spokesmen of both branches compromised the individual rights of United States citizens.

A conflict between the president and Congress contributed to the development of the "national security state," a phrase coined by Daniel Yergin in analyzing postwar America. By evaluating attitudes, policies, and organizational infrastructures, Yergin found that the security state "brought about fundamental changes in American life," not to mention "a permanent military readiness in what passed for peacetime."[26]

As a representative of the Department of Justice, housed in the Executive Branch, McGrath actively participated in the tug-of-war between the executive and legislative branches. Forced to confront a divided America, an America that had never dealt well with the real or imagined Communist threat, McGrath for the most part supported his president's efforts, as he had during his three years in the upper house. Nonetheless, McGrath and his predecessor Tom Clark at times carried out an agenda independent of the president—at great cost to individual liberty. Despite his protestations to the contrary, McGrath employed anti–Communist rhetoric to gain the upper hand politically. During his term as Democratic national chairman and attorney general, he had encouraged a heightened fear of internal subversion. In an oft quoted speech, McGrath warned, "There are today many Communists in America. They are everywhere—in factories, offices, butcher stores, on street corners, in private businesses. And each carries in himself the germ of death for society."[27]

In three short sentences, McGrath encapsulated America's fear of the Red Menace. Communism, many believed, was pervasive. Neighbor must not trust neighbor, friend must be wary of friend, and all must be vigilant against agents of the Soviet Union at home and abroad. McGrath's speeches supported the president's rhetoric on internal threats from agents of Communist countries, especially the Soviet Union. Whether he advocated anti–Communist ideology as fervently as he let on or adopted it as a political maneuver is up for debate. Nonetheless, the fact that Pope Pius XII had labeled Communism an atheistic menace helped solidify McGrath's invective against Russia. McGrath's emphasis on the evils of Communism showed him to be a devout Catholic, as well as a staunch supporter of President Truman.[28] A testament to McGrath's devotion, the Catholic Church conferred its highest honor for a layman, the Legion of St. Mary, on him. Thereafter, he received the even more prestigious Equestrian Order of the Holy Sepulchre, a title also granted by the pope.

The crisis mentality during the period prevented an honest appraisal of American foreign policy. In their propaganda and hyperbole, McGrath and other anti–Communist warriors failed to distinguish between real and imagined dangers, both at home and overseas. For those like McGrath, who feared that Communism threatened democracy, there was no middle ground: Marxist-Leninism must be wiped off the face of the globe.

A small, but vocal Communist Party had been established during the Wilson presidency. In February 1919, this group instigated a wave of workers' strikes, including one in Lawrence, Massachusetts, another in Butte, Montana, and a third in Seattle, Washington. All told, 3,600 strikes threatened American industry. While some laborers took to the streets on behalf of wages, others fought their capitalist oppressors with radical ideology.[29]

In 1919, Attorney General A. Mitchell Palmer and his lieutenants, among them a young J. Edgar Hoover, set an important precedent for the method by which future attorneys general in the twentieth century would confront the so-called Communist menace. Hoover was largely responsible for a series of raids aimed at rooting out Communist and Socialist infiltration on the home front, which he believed would end the post–World War I intrusion of radical ideology onto America's shores. These raids, and the real and imagined threat of Bolshevism, formed the foundation of Hoover's argument for a separate police force to confront internal subversion (the future FBI). In addition,

Palmer's disregard for the rights of individuals as expressed in the United States Constitution paved the way for future breaches of the freedoms outlined in the Bill of Rights. This unfettered pursuit of Bolshevism ultimately diminished the taboo associated with raiding homes of private citizens in the name of national security. These actions set the precedent for the abuses that would follow when Hoover became Director of the FBI, with the tacit approval of the Department of Justice. Although American popular opinion shifted following Hitler's invasion of the Soviet Union in June 1941, virulent anti–Communism gradually returned during the postwar period.

Believing that the growth of Fascism and Communism on the world stage threatened America's security, the House Un-American Activities Committee, known as HUAC, led by Martin Dies, endeavored to root out dangers from the left and right. Accusing President Roosevelt of encouraging Communist ideology, Dies eventually charged that 1,121 government employees either harbored Communist sympathies or were double agents.[30] At first ad hoc, HUAC was made permanent during the 79th Congress, and Republican J. Parnell Thomas of New Jersey, who replaced Dies as the chairperson of the HUAC following the 1946 elections, pursued actual or alleged Communists with equal rigor.[31]

The executive branch, especially the Department of Justice and its subdivision, the Federal Bureau of Investigation (FBI), followed suit by vowing to combat internal and external subversion. Harry Truman became its main spokesman, and his attorneys general, Tom Clark and J. Howard McGrath, gave salient speeches on the evils of Marxist-Leninist ideology.[32] It was a volatile period: both Democrats and Republicans renounced any attempt at compromise with the Russians. In fact, Harry Truman was chosen as FDR's running mate primarily because former vice president Henry Wallace was perceived as being soft on Communism. In a representative speech in Boston on October 27, 1948, during his Whistle Stop Campaign, Truman told audiences, "I resent the contemptible Republican slur that charges me with being 'soft' where Communist tyranny is concerned.... The Communists would like to bring about my defeat and elect a Republican President."[33]

Unable or unwilling to deconstruct the actual from the perceived emergency, the Department of Justice under Clark and McGrath fostered a climate that hindered the possibility of peaceful coexistence with the Soviet Union in the postwar world. Although not the only factor, they contributed to the president's hard line against Communist aggression.

On November 25, 1946, President Truman established the President's Employee Loyalty Program and the Temporary Commission on Employee Loyalty (Executive Order 9835), led by Assistant Attorney General A. Devitt "Gus" Vanech. The legislation built on the Hatch Act, which had barred individuals from "holding membership in any political party or organization advocating the overthrow of the government."[34] It also set out to determine whether the executive, under existing law, possessed the proper authority to protect the nation from "disloyal or subversive persons." The subsequent Federal Employee Loyalty Program of 1947, which authorized the attorney general to draw up a list of organizations with ties to Communist groups, indicated that neither the Commission nor the president believed the tools in place were adequate to deal with the postwar threat of Communist subversion.[35]

Under the law, each department established a loyalty board to hear testimony from federal workers suspected of engaging in espionage. The board then determined whether grounds existed to dismiss the workers for their membership in subversive organizations.

The attorney general's "List of Subversive Organizations" intensified America's fears of the Soviet Union, especially as the 1940s drew to a close. The Soviet Union had continued its aggressive expansion on the continent of Europe. In 1948 Joseph Stalin closed off all traffic between East and West Berlin, prompting American forces to airlift supplies to West Berlin. At the same time, Russian forces overran Czechoslovakia and Hungary. According to historian Athan Theoharis, "the program [Employee Loyalty] rested on the premise that disloyalty and subversive tendencies must be determined in advance [of treasonous activity] to preclude a threat to national security."[36] This proved to be a risky distinction, as the motivation for prying into the lives of alleged Communist sympathizers was based on the investigator or investigating body's interpretation of who might threaten the United States.

The Program was problematic in other ways, as well. It decentralized bureaucratic channels, causing unnecessary delay and overlap. At the same time, it added a layer of bureaucracy to the federal government, which was focused on future rather than present danger.

The discovery of a web of undercover agents of the Soviet Union operating within the United States illustrated the limitations of the federal government to deal with real threats. In 1945, American Elizabeth Bentley confessed to her relationship with two highly placed Soviet spy cells in the United States to the FBI. Three years later, she testified before the HUAC in a well-publicized session, listing the names and whereabouts of the Silvermaster and Perlo groups. Her confession rocked the Bureau and contributed to the heightened paranoia that dominated the public rhetoric during the Cold War, as each branch of the federal government attempted to justify why it had failed to contain Communism within its own borders.[37]

Elizabeth Bentley had earned a degree from Vassar in 1930, then entered post-baccalaureate study in Italy. Upon her return, she became a member of the American Communist Party solely to fight the Fascist ideology she witnessed firsthand in Italy. Through her lover, Jacob Golos,[38] a Soviet agent, she was assigned to the largest Communist cell in America: the Silvermaster group, led by economist Nathan Gregory Silvermaster. Golos, whose credibility was unquestioned by Soviet NKVD (secret police) officers, died in 1943, and Bentley was reassigned to the Perlo group, another of the five major Soviet spy rings in America. Gradually, however, the group distanced itself, so that by 1944 she had no connection to Soviet agents. According to her later statement to HUAC, she defected from the party once her lover died. However, her movements following his death show that she attempted to establish an independent identity within the Soviet ranks, but grew frustrated when the Soviets rebuffed her efforts. Fearing that she was being followed by the FBI (unfounded), she turned herself in, exposing the party's top operatives to the FBI. The FBI, in turn, informed the president that "a number of persons employed by the Government of the United States have been furnishing data and information to persons outside the Federal Government, who are in turn transmitting this information to espionage agents of the Soviet Government."[39]

Tom Clark, attorney general at the time, allowed Bentley to appear as a friendly witness before HUAC in July 1948, and she named 100 Communists, many current or former employees of the federal government.[40] The FBI, however, botched the investigation by using extralegal means to gain entry into the homes and offices of the alleged Communist operatives, including reading mail and tapping phone lines without a warrant. Thus, all evidence obtained was dismissed by the grand jury on the grounds that it was gathered illegally.

Although the FBI failed to charge anyone with espionage, Bentley did expose many "Fellow Travelers" who subsequently either left government service or admitted their connection to the Communist Party. Her testimony, then, indirectly influenced the future direction of the Department of Justice.[41]

Only within the last 20 years has the government been able to substantiate her accusations. Following the fall of the Soviet Union, in July 1995, American archivists released the secret VENONA files, which included approximately 3,000 intercepted missives between Soviet agents in the United States and Moscow.[42]

Beginning in February 1943, American cryptanalysts set out to prove that a network of Communist agents had been stationed throughout the United States, most importantly in the inner reaches of the federal government. Code-named VENONA, the mission of this covert operation was to decipher messages intercepted between Soviet-American operatives and their handlers in the Soviet Union. By 1949, VENONA analysts had deciphered enough material to blow the cover of four NKVD cells, or *Rezidenturas*. Famously, the damning cablegrams implicated Ethel and Julius Rosenberg and David Greenglass in their plot to steal vital information for the Soviets on the atomic bomb mission at Los Alamos.[43]

McGrath accomplished two important objectives in his campaign against the "Reds" by employing his talent for oratory. First, he articulated and expanded on the administration's concerns, conflating the goals of the administration with those of the Catholic Church. This was fortuitous because the Catholic vote was essential for a Democratic victory in 1950 and 1952. Second, he legitimized the president's foreign policy against Communist threats overseas, especially in China and North Korea.

McGrath believed that problems, both domestic and foreign, could be solved primarily through political means. In his estimation, maneuvering, cajoling, and negotiating with the opposition at home and abroad was the only way to ensure the safety of the United States. His response to Communist aggression was, at least in part, an attempt to provide the Democrats with ammunition to fire at their opponents.

Viewed through this lens, McGrath had no choice but to denounce the anti–Communist investigations spearheaded by the legislature. No longer a senator, McGrath owed no allegiance to Capitol Hill; President Truman was the ticket to a possible Supreme Court appointment. On April 15, 1950, McGrath outlined his position for the Subcommittee on the Investigation of Loyalty of State Department Employees. This committee, chaired by Maryland senator Millard Tydings, had been established in February 1950 to root out possible subversives in the State Department. As chairman, Tydings requested that certain employee files from his office be submitted for the Senate investigation. After conferring with President Truman, who feared that such action would open the door to further infringement on executive hegemony, McGrath refused, citing examples of former presidents who denied Congress the right of access to official files "where a disclosure would injure the public." McGrath explained that in drawing up Executive Order #9835, which created the Employee Loyalty Program, President Truman had maintained that "reports, records, and files relative to the program be preserved in strict confidence."[44]

McGrath had always exhibited a certain reticence that reflected his personality and his training from his political mentors. He deemed it essential to withhold information from the public in order to preserve his reputation, seeking to protect his political and financial machinations from public scrutiny. His decision to withhold documents from the Senate committee, although a presidential directive, was in keeping with this approach to public and private matters. It also reflected his and the president's position that anti–Communist inquiries of government officials should be carried out by the executive and not the legislative branch.

Faulting the legislature's efforts to expose "Fellow Travelers," McGrath appeared in Los Angeles in 1950 to campaign for liberal Senate candidate Helen Gahagan Douglas. He declared,

My father was a Democrat, and worked for a living. In those days, when I was a boy, the sense of wealthy families who lived on the other side of the tracks, used to come over on our side once in a while and call us Socialists because we were Democrats … I don't think any intelligent person believes that I am a Communist and I don't think they believe that Helen Gahagan Douglas is a Communist.[45]

McGrath's speech was a response to ranking Republican representative Richard Nixon's (her opponent) charge that Douglas was a leftist "Pink lady" because of her opposition to HUAC. The not-so-subtle condemnation of Republicans ("I don't think any intelligent person believes that I am a Communist") is characteristic of McGrath's rhetorical style. McGrath, by implication, also took issue with the Internal Security Act of 1950, popularly labeled the McCarran Act, and with the authority of HUAC.

Nixon was critical of McGrath's speech, commenting that he was using the election to "play[ing] party politics instead of attending to his official duties." Nixon shrewdly noted that McGrath was acting as spokesman for his party rather than tending to the needs of the Justice Department. Nixon would successfully build on his membership in HUAC and his virulent anti–Communism to defeat Ms. Gahagan Douglas that November.[46]

McGrath claimed (dubiously) that the Justice Department alone had exposed Alger Hiss as a subversive, rather than Richard Nixon and his fellow "red baiting" legislators, but it was Richard Nixon who gained exposure through his pursuit of Alger Hiss, a State Department official who allegedly sold secrets to the Soviets. On the word of *Time* editor Whittaker Chambers, HUAC Chairman Thomas called Hiss to appear in 1948. He initially passed the examination, but Nixon browbeat Hiss until the latter was forced to admit that he knew Chambers under the pseudonym George Crossley. The committee failed to implicate Hiss for espionage, because the statute of limitations had expired, but it cast enough doubt in the minds of the American public to injure Hiss's reputation. Eventually, a New York grand jury convicted him on perjury charges.[47]

At times appearing inconsistent in his approach to anti–Communism, McGrath, in reality, was asserting his claim that the executive infrastructure, or the Justice Department, was better able to confront internal subversion than Congressional investigators. Charging that the HUAC slapped "the Communist label on everyone who has a liberal thought," McGrath declared that "Red hunting" should be conducted by the FBI alone, with the authority of the Department of Justice. His solution, however, did not eliminate the national security state; it just shifted its base from the legislature to the executive branch. Boasting that "there are 50,000 Communists in America and you can be sure we have the names, addresses and all the dope on all of them," he assured his audience that "we can handle them and we do not need to neglect sound procedures" to achieve the desired results.[48] McGrath's message was clear; the directive against subversive activity should rest in the hands of the president and his deputies, who would be no less vigilant and no less repressive. Thus, McGrath's attention to the anti–Communist campaign appeared in the short term to be good politics, and revealed his self-imposed subordination to the fastidious J. Edgar Hoover, director of the FBI.

The Attorney General and the Director of the FBI

The relationship of J. Howard McGrath with J. Edgar Hoover would come to determine the Department of Justice's response to actual and alleged internal security threats. Many sources insist that the two got along famously. However, their correspondence reveals a veiled mistrust of one another, which for McGrath translated into complete deference to the director.

In 1935, the Federal Bureau of Investigation, formerly the Bureau of Investigation, was housed as a subunit within the Crime Division of the Department of Justice. As a crime wave swept the country during the Depression, it became increasingly important, and in 1941, before the invasion of Pearl Harbor, President Roosevelt widened the Bureau's role to include a foreign division called the Special Intelligence Service (SIS).[49]

Roosevelt then placed the FBI in charge of censorship, which resulted in its continued incorporation of controversial methods to obtain information. After learning the art of chamfering, a select group of agents began intercepting letters from the main post office, bringing them to their laboratory where the content was photographed, and then returning them—the postal employees none the wiser. That practice, coupled with an increasing number of break-ins was justified as protecting America from enemy sabotage and other subversive activities, set a dangerous precedent for bypassing civil liberties. This would have major repercussions in the years to come. The practice that garnered the most attention, however, was the FBI's use of electronic surveillance or wiretaps.

The power of the Bureau had expanded by the time J. Howard McGrath became attorney general. President Roosevelt had allowed his attorney general, Robert Jackson, wide latitude when it came to its usage, but he inserted a clause warning that wiretapping must not be utilized haphazardly and should be "limit[ed] … insofar as possible to aliens."[50]

Under McGrath and Truman, Hoover assumed nearly dictatorial powers. In addition to the director's penchant for publicity, he had an insatiable desire to prey on the weakness of others. Maintaining secret files on just about everyone who captured the public's attention, from Hollywood notables to government officials, Hoover gave himself the upper hand in his relationship with the federal government. In fact, it was his knowledge of Hoover's

J. Howard McGrath and J. Edgar Hoover appear before the Senate subcommittee investigating wiretapping, circa 1951 (Harry S Truman Library).

probing eye that forced McGrath's hand in the long run. Hoover biographer Curt Gentry quoted one FBI assistant, "If he [Hoover] didn't like you, he destroyed you."[51]

The deference of the Justice Department to Hoover's machinations allowed him to employ wiretapping devices on anyone he deemed to be a threat to national security. Complicating an already untenable situation, the Federal Communications Act of 1934, which established the Federal Communications Commission (FCC) to monitor the use of radios and telephones, was vague on the subject of wiretapping. In *Nardone v. the United States* (1937), the United States Supreme Court ruled that evidence gained through the use of wiretaps would be inadmissible in court, and in the second Nardone case, this definition was broadened to include "the use of knowledge gained from such conversations."[52]

In the meantime, the FBI had been covertly assisting Congress with its anti–Communist campaign. In May and June 1947, the chairman of the House Un-American Activities Committee (HUAC), J. Parnell Thomas, had initiated a probe into alleged Communist subversive activities. Initially targeting Hollywood, the Committee then investigated the existence of possible Soviet agents in the federal government. Reinforced by Whittaker Chambers' revelation that State Department officer Alger Hiss was a Communist, the House Un-American Activities Committee gained wide exposure, which ultimately shook the executive branch to its roots and forced President Truman to take seriously the charges that were leveled against the State Department. The FBI also assisted the Senate Internal Security Subcommittee (SISS), established by Senate Judiciary chairman Nevada Democrat Patrick McCarran to uncover spies.

McGrath and Hoover joined forces on March 27, 1950, in response to accusations by Wisconsin Republican senator Joseph McCarthy, who on February 9 delivered a speech before the Ohio County Women's Republican Club, declaring that Communists had infiltrated the State Department and were "shaping [foreign] policy."[53]

As a result, Senator Scott Lucas introduced S. Resolution 231, which established a subcommittee of the Foreign Relations Committee to investigate McCarthy's charges. Led by Millard Tydings, a Democrat from Maryland, its members heard testimony from a variety of sources, including McGrath and Hoover, who testified on March 27 in the Senate caucus room, which was filled to capacity with reporters, television cameras, and other bystanders.

Just before their appearance, however, McGrath wrote the president advancing his objections to allowing the Senate full access to Department of Justice files. In response, President Truman noted that "I think you are correct," but "the situation ... is a peculiar one, and I may have to take some steps in it that otherwise would not be taken."[54]

Nevertheless, citing several instances in history where executives had refused to grant Congress unlimited access to executive files, Attorney General McGrath responded in the negative to the subcommittee's request to view executive department loyalty files. While appearing to stand pat against violations of individual rights, McGrath, in refusing Congressional access, had asserted the power of the executive over the legislature to conduct investigations against internal and external threats to security.

He prefaced his statement with the following:

Having had the privilege of serving in the Senate, as well as in the Executive Branch, I am fully aware and indeed extremely sensible of the degree of cooperation that must exist between the legislative and Executive branches of the Government if we are to make our tripartite system work.[55]

Therefore, McGrath stated, we must

reserve the confidential character and sources of information furnished, and [two] to protect Government personnel against the dissemination of unfounded or disproved allegations ... all reports, records, and files relative to the loyalty of employees or prospective employees ... shall be maintained in confidence.[56]

Both Hoover and McGrath believed that a release of all files would compromise the work of the Loyalty Board (as established under former attorney general Tom Clark). President Truman concurred. He would eventually compromise, making 81 files available to the Tydings subcommittee.[57]

These legislative actions led to the Internal Security Act, which passed over President Truman's veto in September 1950. It was more commonly known as the McCarran Act, named after Democratic senator Patrick McCarran of Nevada, who drafted the bill. A revision of the Mundt-Nixon bill that failed to pass both houses, the McCarran Internal Security Act authorized the president to establish a Subversive Activities Control Board and required those seeking employment in government agencies to list membership in the American Communist Party and other subversive groups. Also, it authorized the removal of all potential security risks from federal employment. The law resulted in the establishment of an extensive vetting process, threatening livelihoods, careers, and reputations.

President Truman declared in his veto on September 22, 1950: "We can and we will prevent espionage, sabotage, or other actions endangering our national security." McGrath, who found the bill unworkable, also expressed his opposition. As a result, he had to endure a litany of criticism and, in at least one letter, postmarked Christmas Day 1950, threats:

> How much longer do you expect to live? There is no doubt in my mind that your days are numbered unless you start enforcing the McCarran Act according to the wishes of the people and Congress.... I warn you, sir, that my patience is at an end, and that I can and will do more than threaten you in letter as our Mr. Harry S Truman does.[58]

In response, McGrath suggested to Hoover, "Perhaps you would want to check on this individual," and Hoover immediately assigned his boys to dust the envelope for fingerprints. The agents discovered that the author had been attempting to obtain a position with the National Park Service of the Department of the Interior and was not a threat to McGrath's safety.

According to Athan Theohars, "McGrath's deference to FBI Director Hoover, was not an exceptional practice of President Truman's various attorneys general."[59] On the other hand, McGrath's decision to "delegate complete responsibility to the Director to do whatever the Director felt should be done" went above and beyond what previous Justice officials had allowed.

McGrath's support of Hoover protected him from the director's probing eye while contributing to the growth of the Bureau. As Athan Theoharis reports, from 1936 to 1952 "FBI appropriations increased by more than 1,800 percent (from $5,000,000 to $90,665,000)," and the Bureau was allowed to "employ such investigative techniques as wiretaps, bugs, break-ins, ... and mail intercepts."[60] The director argued that these tools would serve to protect rather than compromise American democracy. Apparently, McGrath agreed.

The language of the president, his attorney general, and of Congress spoke of peace and the preservation of American principles, but their actions encouraged suppression and fear, and in the end, did little to protect the country from external and internal dangers.

McGrath would have better served his country and his president by focusing on eradicating the mounting corruption that existed in several of the federal agencies either directly or indirectly under his charge. The Department needed major reorganization and required the hand of a vigorous opponent of graft. McGrath, on the contrary, assumed a devil-may-care attitude that ultimately enraged the American public and caused his downfall. According to Robert J. Donovan, while the Justice Department was "weak when McGrath took it over," it suffered further neglect when McGrath assumed the position.[61] Donovan concluded that "McGrath seems not to have been aware of much that was going on around him."[62]

The Justice Department under McGrath was confronted with a number of important issues that had been delayed or exacerbated by the world war: anti-trust suits, internal security, and government corruption, the latter euphemistically referred to as "the mess in Washington." These difficulties had existed before McGrath was named to the post, but McGrath's inattention to detail and his alleged cover-up of serious inequities in his department and in the Bureau of Internal Revenue aggravated the problems. While on paper McGrath appeared qualified for the position, a look into his political past reveals some thorny situations, including his dealings with Boston-born entrepreneur Royal Little, that would compromise McGrath's ability to deal forthrightly with the problems he faced in the Justice Department. Before he was even named to the post, stories had surfaced about McGrath's reputation that should have given the president and his advisers pause.

McGrath, Royal Little, and the Rhode Island Charities Trust

McGrath's own questionable financial dealings prior to his appointment to the Department of Justice had been brought to light when he became Democratic Committee chairman in 1947, but the criticism intensified when he assumed the leadership role at the Department of Justice. The most sensational example concerned his involvement, while serving as governor of Rhode Island, with Royal Little, a Massachusetts-born entrepreneur whose innovative company Textron manufactured "textile products made from synthetics."[63]

Royal Little was the quintessential New England industrialist: frugal and enterprising, fastidious in his personal habits, and relentless in his pursuit of industrial growth. Intent on revolutionizing the textile industry, and on turning a profit in the process, Little transformed New England by closing, then buying up, old mills, refining business practices, and updating or scraping shopworn machinery.

In his quest to diversify his New England business interests, Little crossed paths with then-governor McGrath, another ambitious and industrious financier. Following Little's appointment of McGrath, banker Benjamin R. Sturges, and Godfrey B. Simonds in August 1945 to the board of the Rhode Island Charitable Trust, he was charged with using these men as "dummy" investors to hide profits from the Internal Revenue Bureau. According to critics, McGrath also compromised the integrity of his office by enabling Little to divert formerly taxable income into the tax exempt Rhode Island Charities Trust.[64]

Royal Little had established Yarns, Incorporated, in 1923, with little more than a $10,000 loan and a labor force of ten. In its first year of operation, Yarns Inc. realized a $75,000 profit. Five years later, in 1928, Little purchased stock (and thus a controlling ownership) of Providence Franklin Rayon Corporation, which held copyright on a new, more-efficient method of cotton dye for textile manufacturing. Little's new acquisition, renamed the Atlantic Rayon Corporation, brought him to Providence from Boston.

He locked in the loans using the Rhode Island Charitable Trust, which he had established in 1937, purportedly for the benefit of the Providence Community Fund. Little then liquidated several mills in 1944 and promptly leased the buildings and equipment, converting formerly fixed assets into readily available cash. In turn, the Rhode Island Charitable Trust used this liquid income to repay the First National Bank.[65] The Charitable Trust also purchased Manville-Jenckes Company, Suncook Mills, the Apponaug Company, and the sizable inventory of the Rhode Island Tool Company. Following the purchase of these textile firms, the Charitable Trust in turn sold them to Textron.[66]

Then-governor McGrath was named as one of three members of the board of directors when Little stepped down as the Charitable Trust's sole representative on September 16, 1945, because of "pressure of other business." Providence investment banker Godfrey B. Simonds and banker Benjamin R. Sturges joined McGrath as trustees.[67] Then in his third term as governor, McGrath had, in addition to his political interests, already invested in a number of business ventures, including, but not limited to, the Rhode Island Building and Trust (1937).

Immediate statements by McGrath and Simonds corroborated Little's explanation, ensuring Rhode Islanders that "we realize that our designation to the trusteeship was made by Mr. Little with the approval and the consent of the Rhode Island Hospital Trust Company, trustee of the Rhode Island Foundation, and the Providence National Bank," which acted as "depositories of the trust assets and the Providence Community Fund." They also assured all concerned that "Mr. Little has never personally profited by the business transactions through which he has built this trust to its present sizable amount."[68] Nevertheless, incited by the media and subsequent investigations, the public remained suspicious of Little's motivation for establishing the Charitable Trust.

Although critics questioned Little's methods, he did not come under intense scrutiny until Massachusetts resident and Textron shareholder Eva R. Levenson brought a derivative suit against Textron in the New York federal courts, claiming among other charges that McGrath, and to a lesser extent Sturges and Simonds, had submitted to the "wishes and will" of Royal Little in order to syphon the profits from the Charitable Trust into their personal accounts.[69]

Levenson's charges, coupled with plant closings in Esmond, Rhode Island, and Nashua, New Hampshire (in September 1948), which threatened to put 5,000 employees out of work, set in motion a public Senate investigation. Following the high-profile Nashua closing, local representative of the Congress of Industrial Organizations (CIO) Lawrence Daoust asked how "the system of charitable trusts woven into Textron's "fabric" was able to "extend subsidies and other inducements to Textron" and "how and why government units in Puerto Rico [where five plant openings were being considered], have extended subsidies and other inducements to Textron" for the sole purpose of launching subdivisions "in U.S. possessions"?[70] According to Daoust, Textron had scrapped the Nashua plant in order to "prop up a vast and complicated corporate structure," and he appealed for a Senate investigation to determine the consequences of Little's action.[71]

On the basis of Daoust's request, the subcommittee of the Committee on Interstate and Foreign Commerce, chaired by liberal Republican senator Charles Tobey of New Hampshire, convened on September 22, 1948, to investigate Textron and its subsidiary companies. Tobey demanded justice on behalf of the laborers in his state, vowing to "get to the bottom" of the plant closings and bring to bear all the powers at his disposal to bring the modern-day robber baron to justice. As former president and sole owner of F.M. Hoyt Shoe Company, Tobey believed that he understood the proper balance between industrial and labor interests.[72] The hysteria generated by Tobey's first hearing prompted the transfer of the rest of the hearings from New Hampshire to Boston to ensure more objective deliberations.[73] President Truman was silent, however, on Tobey's investigation into Textron, Incorporated, and the Rhode Island Charitable Trust.

At the time Little liquidated the Nashua, New Hampshire, plant, McGrath was serving as the junior senator from Rhode Island and the Democratic national chairman and was engaged in a determined battle to reelect President Truman. Informing fellow trustee Benjamin Sturges that he would not appear before Tobey's committee unless required to do so, he cautioned Sturges in 1948 to "maintain his equilibrium" before the committee. McGrath and the trustees were determined to downplay the hearings, but Tobey, who had a penchant for publicity, latched onto this crusade in an effort to improve his state's economy and his own chances for reelection in 1950.

In order to preserve his reputation, however, McGrath did not respond to CIO union leader Daoust's charge that Royal Little was personally responsible for the unemployment of some 10,000 New England mill workers. In August 1948, a month before the calling of the Tobey subcommittee, McGrath and fellow Rhode Islanders Governor John O. Pastore and Representative John E. Fogarty began their own investigation into the plant closings in New England, including those initiated by Textron, Incorporated. Both McGrath and Pastore found this strategy to be less than foolproof. In a *Providence Journal-Bulletin* editorial, the author charged Pastore and the Democrats with creating a smoke screen to deflect the investigators from the government's alleged complicity in the Little controversy. Republican Albert Ruerat of the Pawtuxet Valley offered a stinging indictment: "You ask yourself … why Royal Little, a shrewd and cold-blooded manipulator, picked out J. Howard McGrath to be a trustee of his charitable trust—the tax-exempt trust which hasn't distributed any charity yet, so far as anyone knows, except to its trustees." In damning rhetoric, Ruerat charged that Governor Pastore was a "helpless" dupe, unable to "unshackle himself from a chain of circumstances with which he is held prisoner. He is simply stuck with Sen. J. Howard McGrath, Democratic national poobah and right-hand man of Mr. Royal Little in Rhode Island."[74]

State Senator Raoul Archambault, Jr., who had recently submitted his name as the unendorsed Republican candidate for governor, also leveled a scathing denunciation of McGrath. "It [the Democratic state administration] dares do nothing itself because the state administration is tied hand and foot by its bonds to J. Howard McGrath, U.S. senator and Democratic national chairman, who is a director of the trust headed by Royal Little, the major offender."[75]

Appearing in Boston in mid to late November 1948, McGrath denied complicity in the venture. He explained that he assumed "existing committees of Congress" might "look into the thing. I'm not sure, but I would think the Senate small business committee might be the one to do it if there were an investigation." He dismissively added, "The whole thing makes no difference to me one way or another."[76]

When asked by the *Journal*'s Washington Bureau reporter whether he directed Textron business interests, McGrath vehemently denied the claim: "I'm not concerned with Textron in any way. I have been mistakenly reported as being a director of Textron, but I am not. My only connection is with the Rhode Island Charitable Trust, and that has no connection with Textron." In his testimony, McGrath defended his business activities, stating that he sought to ensure "the reorganization of" the small business, "with the idea of keeping it as a going concern."[77]

McGrath's response paralleled his reactions to similar accusations relating to his personal and professional finances. When cornered by political enemies or probing critics, McGrath would become defensive, denying culpability and rejecting any charge that his behavior had been improper. He was also at the time engaged in what he deemed to be more pressing matters. As Democratic national chairman, he had been working day and night to unite the warring factions of his party. Pressures had been mounting as journalists and pollsters throughout the country were nearly unanimous in their prediction of a Truman defeat. Yet try as he might, McGrath could not ignore the investigation. His recent attempt to do so had only served to expose his vulnerability before his political enemies.

In September 1948, Senator Tobey outlined the reasons for calling the Committee. Armed with allegations originating with Mr. Charles Rieve, union shop steward, Tobey accused Little of

1. "speculat[ing] in mill properties," rather than developing honest business manufacturing in the region, which caused undue hardship on the community,
2. establishing several charities trusts for the sole purpose of "tax avoidance and providing risk capital to Textron," and
3. compromising America's economy by "lur[ing] our industries to that territory [Puerto Rico] by promises of cheap labor and a 12-year moratorium on all property and income taxes."

Tobey hoped through these charges to discredit Little and restore employment to New Hampshire's sagging economy.[78]

Little's defense of his financial practices was more pointed and ultimately more effective. Appearing before the Committee in October 1948, Little engaged in heated debate with Tobey, denying the allegations leveled against him. He declared, "Mr. Rieve [union shop leader] has made serious and completely unfounded charges against me. These charges are false and the inferences drawn from them are false. It is my duty to set the records straight."[79] Denying that he "has personally profited at the expense of Textron," Little held up his "books, records and tax returns" for the committee to scrutinize as evidence of his innocence.[80]

Citing the shoddy work ethic of New England employees and exorbitant tax rates, he explained that in order for Textron to realize a profit, he had no choice but to liquidate the Nashua, Manville, Esmond, and Taunton mills. Explaining that the Manville plant "had the distinction of being the country's highest cost cotton mill," he reminded the Committee that the buildings were "in very bad condition," citing the estimated $250,000 price tag to restore the roof alone as evidence that cost far outweighed the benefits of maintaining these outmoded factories. The operating costs of the Manville plant amounted to $151,000 as compared to $60,000 for a comparable mill in the South.[81]

The same held true for the tax levies, which, according to Little, stood at 62 cents for each spindle at the Manville, Rhode Island, plant, while a comparable establishment in the South incurred between 38 to 58 cents a spindle in taxes. He concluded his testimony by explaining that his attempt to transfer workers from Manville to the Lonsdale mill ended miserably, as only 47 of the 2,000 employees took advantage of the opportunity. He added, "1,250 Manville workers refused to consider transfer, and [instead] applied for and received Unemployment Compensation."[82] Warning the 70,000 current textile workers that they "can no longer demand and receive a premium over other areas for their services unless their productivity and skill justify it," he predicted that the region would suffer economically unless laborers and textile owners adapted to new trends.[83]

In responding to the charge that he buried taxable income in tax exempt charitable trusts, Little faltered. After informing the Committee that his increased profit margin as a result of the establishment of these trusts placed him in a higher tax bracket, he dodged the initial charge. His legal representative, Eugene A. King, admitted that charitable trusts may engage in speculation, "if the indenture permits it," but that he and Little would encourage the charitable trusts to "submit a report periodically so the public or the world would know what is going on."[84] In essence, the testimony revealed some inconsistencies in Little's argument.

Nonetheless, Little was ultimately exonerated, since Tobey could find little evidence to support the committee's claim that the trusts were used for the purpose of tax avoidance. No "comprehensive [or general] information concerning the extent" of tax evasion was available. Tobey and his committee, however, were able to discern that the Rhode Island Charitable Trust accrued a profit of $500,000 in September 1945, and from September 1945 to September 1948, the trust earned $4,500,000, none of which was deemed taxable income.[85] Charging that hard-working employees carried the tax burden for this multimillion dollar plant, Tobey maintained that Little sheltered profits in charitable trusts, including the Rhode Island Charitable Trust.

While Tobey granted Senator McGrath absolution by not singling him out in his report, his committee was able to determine that a clandestine meeting took place in Senator McGrath's office of several trustees of Little's charitable trusts, including Little, Bayard Ewing, trustee of the Rayon Foundation Trust, Benjamin Sturges of the Rhode Island Charitable Trust, and MIT Trustee Andrew N. Winslow. The meeting concerned a Bureau of Revenue charge that some of the charitable trusts should not assume tax exempt status. According to Winslow, the trustees convened to discuss their next move.[86]

In an interview at the time with the *Providence Journal*, McGrath, who was busily tending to his duties in Washington as Democratic chairman, explained, "We had to know what its [RI Charities] assets and liabilities were and I asked them [the BIR] to adjudicate so we … would know what our liabilities were. That's as far as it went." Denying emphatically that he exerted any influence on the agency, he declared, "They can search 'till Doomsday and they'll never find anything like that. I never used any influence or asked any favor."[87]

When finally called to the stand in late November 1948, just days after the national election, McGrath confirmed the meeting of trustees held in his office the previous September, as he had with the *Journal*. However, he corrected many misconceptions about the meeting, one of which being that a letter from Bureau of Internal Revenue commissioner George J. Schoeneman, a Newport, Rhode Island, native, denying the Rhode Island Charitable Trust tax exempt status was sent directly to him on September 8, 1947. In fact, the correspondence was addressed to the Rhode Island Charitable Trust, and Mr. Sturges, "the most active trustee," was the first to read it. Sturges then informed McGrath, who promised that they would meet when McGrath returned to Providence.

The scheduled location for the conference was the law library of a prominent Providence law firm, Edwards & Angell, but the elevator was found to be inoperable, so McGrath suggested that as a time-saving measure they should all meet in his office across the street. He was careful to note that newspaper men were present in the lobby, and no participant attempted to conceal the content of the gathering from the press.

Tobey boasted that "as long as I am a senator I am not going to stop until I get to the very bottom of this mess, no matter who it hits."[88] However, in his final report, he omitted any mention of McGrath, although the gap in the report's narrative was obvious and McGrath's role in Little's business venture was clear. The findings revealed that each of the three trustees earned $15,000 per year, and the Providence National Bank was paid $7,500 to manage the assets. McGrath stepped down from his position as trustee when he became attorney general.[89]

Based on the evidence, Tobey concluded that the commissioner of Bureau of Internal Revenue should "take immediate steps to effect collection of these [back] taxes," from each of Little's subsidiary trusts, including Rhode Island Charitable Trust. Tobey also recommended that trustees submit financial records to the Bureau of Internal Revenue in order to determine to what extent they avoided paying taxes.

In total, it was found that the Rhode Island Charitable Trustees collected

$14,442,871 from a number of companies, including Flightex Fabrics, 44,186 shares purchased in June 1944; Lonsdale Company, shares totaling $7,000,000 on December 4, 1944; and the Hampton Company, 84,835 shares on September 27, 1945. According to the Internal Revenue Code, Section 101, foundations that exist for the sole purpose of "charitable, educational, and other designated purposes" are deemed tax exempt, while Section 162 of the said code maintained that

    (a) trusts [may deduct] ... any part of the gross income, without limitation, which pursuant to the terms of the will or deed creating the trust, is during the taxable year paid or permanently set aside for ... or is to be used exclusively for religious, charitable, scientific, literary, or educational purposes [and]

    (b) There shall be allowed as an additional deduction in computing the net income of the estate or trust the amount of the income of the estate or trust for its taxable year which is to be distributed currently by the fiduciary to the legatees, heirs or beneficiaries...[90]

Refuting the senator's contention that the Rhode Island Charitable Trust owed back taxes, McGrath argued that Tobey used faulty logic in his conclusions, since the latter "presupposes that taxes are due. That is not so far as the trust I'm connected with is concerned."[91] This, he argued, was based "upon false assumptions," since the commissioner erroneously believed the trust fell under section 101 of the Internal Revenue Code, when in fact it operated under section 162.[92]

Tobey recommended measures specifically defining the limitations of charitable trusts, advocating the publication of all financial transactions, advising that each trust register with federal authorities, and supporting the institution of federal regulations mandating a specific percentage derived from income earned to be earmarked for charitable purposes. These were attempts to close loopholes that would allow conglomerates to shelter their funds in these tax-exempt trusts. Royal Little was forced to compromise, and according to his semi-autobiographical account, published years later, his acquiescence cost Textron dearly. By promising to maintain sheeting operations of the Nashua mills until at least January 1950, he was able to retain some goodwill. He also issued advice on the newly formed Nashua-New Hampshire Foundation, which, like the Rhode Island Charitable Trust, was established as a "non-profit charitable organization ... with an agreement from Textron ... to lease ... about half of the mill property for 10 years."[93] According to Tobey's report, this compromise resulted in 1,200 positions for New Hampshire workers.[94]

McGrath had escaped with his professional reputation tarnished but not ruined. While thus far eluding conviction of any wrongdoing, his financial dealings had nevertheless been held up for public scrutiny. At this point, this maturing public figure had agreed to head the Department of Justice, which, among its many duties, had the oversight of the Anti–Trust Division. The irony in this choice appeared obvious to many.[95] The incident would resurface amidst allegations from Senator Harold Stassen that he became a millionaire while serving the public.

J. Howard McGrath and the "Mess in Washington"

In choosing McGrath to lead the department during its unprecedented expansion, Truman had opted for a stopgap solution that was doomed to fail. Forced to confront the widespread corruption evident in both the Bureau of Internal Revenue and the Department of Justice, McGrath chose to rely too heavily on his subordinates. Ineffective in his new role, and geographically and personally distant from Truman, McGrath had one final role to play: scapegoat for the "mess in Washington."[96]

Corruption

The last time the public had been subjected to corruption at the level seen in the 1950s was during the Teapot Dome Scandal that rocked the Harding administration in the 1920s. However, the rise of newspaper and magazine publication by the mid-twentieth century, not to mention the advent of television, meant that the public outcry against Harding cronies Harry Daugherty, Albert Fall, and the other wheeler dealers of the roaring twenties was nothing compared to that faced by Harry Truman and his cabinet officers in the 1950s.

Following the Second World War, Americans had enjoyed unprecedented prosperity, despite the threat of recession and unemployment as industrial plants laid off workers during the country's reconversion to a peacetime economy. This affluence, however, led to extravagance and corruption.

Tempted by the lure of luxury items, expensive vacations, and other windfalls, a number of public officials had succumbed to bribery and engaged in influence peddling, ushering in a new era of skepticism among the American people who were coming to demand more of the men and women they elected to public office. As Bert Cochran would observe in 1973, "Americans expect crookedness in their politicians but get indignant when their expectations are realized."[97]

Many of the muckrakers, political pundits, and legislative cronies of the New Deal were initially willing to give their commander in chief the benefit of the doubt, generally applauding the new president's determination in bringing the war to a close. But as President Truman's honeymoon ended, the public increasingly demanded to know why their leader was tolerating inefficiency and graft in the government infrastructure. Republicans and conservative Democrats, critical of the New Deal from its inception, had been waiting 12 long years to bury it once and for all. They found in Truman a more vulnerable target than in his predecessor and were only too happy to exploit his weaknesses.

The beginning of the end came in December 1947 when freshman senator John Williams stumbled upon a cover-up in the Bureau of Internal Revenue. The former Delaware chicken farmer became suspicious when he received an invoice from the Bureau for an outstanding debt on an income tax bill "he'd already paid." His methodical, persistent investigation revealed that Wilmington tax cashier Maurice A. Flynn had been issuing duplicate bills to Delaware taxpayers, amassing $30,000 over a seven-year period. Even more disturbing, Flynn's superior, collector Norman Collison, had convinced Bureau officials in Washington to turn a blind eye to the theft and subsequently buried the proof that would have implicated Flynn. Although Flynn was eventually jailed, Collison did not retire until forced to do so in October 1950.

Williams' dogged determination not only exposed the crime that sent Flynn to jail but revealed that Flynn was a mere cog in a much wider conspiracy to rob the federal government of millions of dollars. When he uncovered similar graft in New York City, Williams not only implicated its collector but called into question the judgment of Commissioner of Internal Revenue George J. Schoeneman, who had refused to fire the bureau official in question, stating that "the collector in charge of the district lacked the administrative experience to get the job done."[98]

Part of the difficulty emanated from the rapid growth of the department. Following the passage of the Sixteenth Amendment in 1913, which established the federal income tax and the requisite Bureau of Internal Revenue, only one reorganization had taken place (in 1917) while the volume of income tax returns processed had skyrocketed. When a new tax code was implemented in 1939, the first of its kind since 1874, all previous changes to internal revenue were gathered in a single document in an effort to streamline the work of the Bureau.[99]

The Bureau of Internal Revenue infrastructure, however, had not kept pace with the changes and growth in its responsibilities. According to statistics quoted by President Truman in 1952, the number of taxpayers jumped from 19 million in 1940 to 82 million in 1951, but the structure of the Bureau remained untouched; it retained its original 64 districts across the United States.[100] The over-burdened collectors were often underpaid, and therefore the office rarely attracted men of merit. The resulting abuse of power was not surprising.[101]

Williams's clarion call sparked a public campaign, led by the legislature. In March 1951, a subcommittee of the House Ways and Means Committee, chaired by Cecil King of California, met to determine why so many internal revenue cases had escaped prosecution at the national level. Federal Judge George H. Moore, who had convened a grand jury on March 1, 1951, to investigate alleged tax fraud in Missouri, complained to the attorney general that the indictment for Missouri collector James P. Finnegan had been "dammed up and blocked up" at the Department of Justice, of which the Tax Division was an important component.[102] McGrath, who was under pressure to act following these allegations, sent his assistant Ellis Slack to confront the issue. Judge Moore later testified before the King subcommittee that Missouri "is the worst district in the United States to have anything break out, because this is the President's home state."[103]

The subcommittee's investigation uncovered fraud in leading cities all over the country, including New York, Boston, San Francisco, and St. Louis, and brought down major officials in the Bureau and in the Department of Justice within the year. Many of these high-profile tax collectors, according to historian Andrew Dunar, had "slipped into virtual control of Democratic political machines operating within their districts."[104] Part of the difficulty, according to Dunar, lay with former commissioner of internal revenue Robert E. Hannegan, who had served as chairman of the Democratic National Committee in 1944 and was a Truman ally. Serving as commissioner from October 1943 to April 1944, Hannegan had populated the Bureau with political cronies, who were products of state political machines. This practice laid the foundation for the corruption and mismanagement that continued long after he left the Department.[105]

Because the King subcommittee at first focused on the Treasury Department, its secretary, John Snyder set in motion a secret probe to determine whether the rumors of iniquities among the several collectors' offices were true. He began a national investigation of "present internal revenue personnel" by

1. conducting intensive examinations of their income tax returns for the last three years;
2. requiring the ... submission of comprehensive ... net worth, income, and expenditures;
3. investigating thoroughly every lead from every source ... [and]
4. investigating ... the background ... of all persons proposed to be appointed to positions in the Internal Revenue Service...[106]

Snyder, with the willing aid of the new commissioner of Internal Revenue, John B. Dunlap, succeeded in exonerating himself and his department by his willingness to cooperate with authorities. The subsequent report, issued in several volumes, also stated that the "Bureau [would] open its files and records to the King Subcommittee of the Ways and Means Committee in order to benefit from any information that the Subcommittee might develop."[107] Thus, Snyder's transparency saved him, and he was allowed to both retain his position and be shielded within the Internal Revenue Department from the intense scrutiny of the legislature. The Treasury Department did, however, submit to probing by Dunlap, who replaced the beleaguered George Shoeneman when he resigned because of "ill health" in June 1951. Dunlap revealed to *U.S. News and World Report* that the Internal Revenue Inspection Service, established under Dunlap's watch, had conducted over 1,000 investigations resulting in "154 removals, 202 forced resignations, 308 disciplinary actions, and 189 acquittals."[108] Dunlap also required the department to complete "financial questionnaires" and ordered the "audit of all tax returns of enforcement and other key personnel."[109]

When asked about the six collectors who had been charged with wrongdoing, the commissioner reassured the *U.S. News* reporter that "decisive action in each case was taken as soon as the Bureau could develop the facts." He further revealed that the case against the Boston collector had commenced on March 30, 1951, that the "preliminary report" was issued on June 26, and that he was fired on July 16, 1951. In addition, a grand jury indicted James P. Finnegan of St. Louis on April 14, 1951, for burying $103,000 of his personal taxes, and other complicit collectors either resigned, were removed from office, or faced criminal charges.[110]

Unfortunately, the Justice Department suffered a worse fate, which began with the activities of T. Lamar Caudle, a seemingly innocent lawyer from North Carolina, who served as assistant attorney general of the Tax Division with direct oversight over the Bureau of Internal Revenue. The King investigators soon uncovered that T. Lamar Caudle, who had been slowly ingratiating himself with major players in the Truman White House, had been accepting favors from high-profile clients in exchange for clemency. Caudle's testimony called into question the actions of his superiors: former attorney general Tom Clark and current attorney general J. Howard McGrath.

T. Lamar Caudle was born in Wadesboro, North Carolina, on July 22, 1904, and earned a law degree from Wake Forest College in 1926. He practiced law at his father's firm until 1940, when President Roosevelt appointed him attorney for the Western District of North Carolina. An up-and-coming star, Caudle became assistant attorney general of the Criminal Division in charge of tax frauds, replacing Tom Clark when the latter was named attorney general.[111] By 1947, Clark had persuaded Truman to appoint Caudle head of the Tax Division, a subdivision of the Department of Justice, despite the fact that the Caudle, according to Time Magazine, had "no tax law experience and was up against the top legal tax specialists in the U.S."[112]

Clark and Caudle shared a curious relationship. Clark appreciated Caudle's ambition and effusive, pleasing manner. According to Caudle's later testimony, Clark had initially placed him in charge of a Kansas City voter fraud case involving Enos Axtell, President Truman's choice for Missouri's Fifth Congressional District. The Kansas City primary election in 1945 had come under scrutiny after charges of voter fraud, and the questionable ballots were placed in a safe at the Kansas City Courthouse, pending investigation. When a mysterious explosion resulted in the disappearance of the ballots, Clark publicly announced the commencement of a thorough probe into the affair. Clark then abruptly removed Caudle from the case and recommended his transfer to the Justice Department's Tax Division. The reasons for Clark's decision have never been adequately answered, but the Chelf subcommittee, formed in February 1952, would subsequently allege that Clark either removed Caudle because of the latter's incompetence, or because he wanted to prevent the enthusiastic investigator from discovering the cover-up, and in turn exposing Clark's hand in it. Regardless, Axtell lost the November election to Representative Albert L. Reeves, and Clark escaped further retribution because of his elevation to the Supreme Court.

Caudle's poor political judgment and penchant for high living proved unfortunate for the Bureau of Internal Revenue, for the president, and for J. Howard McGrath, Caudle's immediate superior. Caudle became the center of the Bureau of Internal Revenue scandals in the press, which exaggerated his every affectation. Caudle appeared to be a witless dupe in high-level organizational abuse. His testimony before the King subcommittee revealed his indiscretions: paid vacations to Florida and Italy and the purchase of a mink coat for his wife at a discount due to his promise not to prosecute certain high-level clients. Caudle refused to accept that his actions compromised the integrity of his department, but his testimony prompted the creation of the Chelf subcommittee.

Caudle's testimony before the King subcommittee in November 1951 revealed the inefficiency of McGrath's leadership, and members of Congress, especially Republican representative Thomas B. Curtis from Missouri, insisted upon his dismissal.[113] Following the revelation that McGrath authorized the receipt of a $5,000 commission rewarding Caudle for the sale of a Lockheed Lodestar, they began to question McGrath's ability to lead any department, let alone one with 31,000 employees.[114]

According to *U.S. News and World Report*, "few can afford to be blind to the power Mr. McGrath wields." And it had become evident that McGrath did not use his power wisely. In his description to Chairman King in December 1951, McGrath saw himself as the "administrative officer who has to concern himself with the financial affairs of the Department, with the overall general policies."[115] He, therefore, held the deputy attorney general responsible for the "day-to-day contact with each head of a division."[116] As allegations of corruption in the Bureau of Internal Revenue mounted, McGrath privately distanced himself more and more from the duties of his office. At that same time, McGrath rebuffed Chairman King's request for all the Justice Department's files on tax fraud cases, stating that it would infringe upon the work of his subordinates.[117]

Although McGrath argued in Caudle's defense, he could not convince the president to retain the assistant attorney general. By November 1951, Truman dismissed the assistant attorney general for behavior "incompatible" with his position.[118] Appearing before the Chelf subcommittee nearly a year after the incident, McGrath remarked that "if firing was going to be the order of the day there were plenty of places to start besides Caudle."[119] The subcommittee agreed, but in doing so, they placed most of the blame for Caudle's indiscretion on Attorneys General Clark and McGrath.

However, Chairman King refused to subpoena Clark because he did not want "to set the precedent of calling a justice of the United States Supreme Court" to appear before a subcommittee.[120] As for Caudle, the majority of the Chelf subcommittee would later take pity on him, concluding in March 1953 that he was under immense pressure from congressmen and other notables to dispose of their respective cases favorably. "Lamar Caudle, in enduring the personal tribulations of 1952, was serving his country as faithfully as he ever had in public office in prior better years. Every member of the subcommittee ... who observed Caudle and listened to his testimony ... shares in the opinion that he is an honorably motivated man."[121]

Although the report makes the bold statement that "every member of the subcommittee and its staff ... shares in the opinion that he is an honorably-motivated man," Colorado Democrat Byron G. Rogers, a representative and a vocal member of the Chelf subcommittee, took exception to the ruling, stating, "This praise is unwarranted by a man who has violated a public trust. He received a mink coat and $5,000 from persons interested in cases before him. How 'honorably-motivated' can one man get?"[122]

On December 5, just weeks after Caudle's dismissal, the president received a letter of resignation from Caudle-ally Charles Oliphant, chief counsel for the Bureau of Internal Revenue, after the King committee revealed that he had accepted "gifts" from high-profile clients under investigation for tax fraud.[123] In his resignation to the president, Oliphant blamed his exit on the baseless "attacks, vilification, rumor and innuendo" that were "beyond the point of human endurance."[124]

In the meantime, the walls began to close in on Attorney General McGrath, and he did not respond well to the pressure. Despite the public outcry to clean up the Justice Department, McGrath refused to turn over the files to the King subcommittee, defending his organization as "clean as a hound's tooth."[125] Expressing faith in his officers, he exclaimed, "I want to stay at the Department of Justice as long as it is feasible and practical for me to stay there."[126] On the other side, the press maintained that McGrath's dereliction of duty eroded the already "rotting" department, and that the organization was anything but "clean."[127]

Much of the controversy centered on the failure of the department to prosecute anti-trust suits. According to Chelf's report as paraphrased in *The St. Louis Post Dispatch*, "the Justice Department did very little to recover money for the Government or to prosecute for fraud contactors who did business with the Government."[128]

Especially scathing was the claim that "in the case of antitrust violations charged to the liquor industry, the subcommittee found the Department's investigative responsibilities to have been indifferently discharged, with possible favoritism toward the industry."[129] On criminal cases, Chelf's committee was equally unfavorable: "Delays of years in the criminal division have been followed by delays of years in United States Attorney offices to which the cases were sent."[130]

For McGrath, the realization that his job as attorney general would not lead to a Supreme Court appointment hit him hard.[131] Rumors began to circulate in Washington about McGrath's over-reliance on his assistants and his excessive drinking. His deputy attorney general, Peyton Ford, who had attempted to build his own private empire in Washington,[132] appeared more responsive to the nation's crime and corruption than McGrath. Meanwhile, the president was inundated with mail from a disgruntled public, which called for McGrath's resignation.

Truman's own frustration with his attorney general was evidenced by his correspondence, which became more pointed and distant. Beset by low approval ratings (23 percent), Truman decided to take additional action. Upon the advice of recently appointed Democratic National Chairman Frank McKinney, Truman set in motion a campaign to appoint an independent commission as part of an overall plan to purge his administration of scandal before the presidential election of 1952.[133] He remarked to the press in mid–December that "wrongdoers have no house with me no matter who they are or how big they are."[134] In mid–December 1951, he approached Judge Thomas F. Murphy about heading such a body.[135] At first, Murphy, who had commanded notice as the prosecutor of Alger Hiss, agreed. But complications arose with the other members of the commission, and the judge eventually removed his name from consideration.[136]

After the failed attempts to replace McGrath and establish the commission, the president laid the investigation of the Department of Justice at his feet, a regrettable and curious decision, probably made under pressure or at the suggestion McGrath ally, Theodore Francis Green. Although McGrath had seriously considered resigning in January, he changed his mind after a lengthy conference with Green, the contents of which remain a mystery. Instead, Green, with the help of Cardinal Francis Spellman and Truman's special assistant Charles Murphy, persuaded the president to retain McGrath.[137] When McGrath emerged from his subsequent conference with President Truman on January 4, he revealed little to the press, but did say that "no change in my status is contemplated."[138] The president ordered the beleaguered attorney general to seek out an independent agent to investigate corruption in the government. As many historians and contemporaries have pointed out, the president's decision was ill-conceived. According to the *Providence Journal*, one of many naysayers stated, "McGrath's selection drew immediate fire from Republican members of Congress."[139] That same day, a *Providence Journal* editorial warned, "The President has blundered.... The best Mr. McGrath can do to save the President from his own mistake would be to impanel a federal blue ribbon grand jury in the District of Columbia, appoint a man from outside the administration.... If Mr. McGrath will not do this, then the penalty will surely be exacted by the American people next November."[140]

McGrath consulted an old friend, Judge Billings Learned Hand, who recommended his own son-in-law, New York reform lawyer Newbold Morris,[141] for the position of special independent prosecutor. McGrath had never met Morris, but time was of the essence, so he hastily supported Morris's appointment as special assistant to the attorney general. McGrath told Morris that the investigation should take no more than "several months" and would be a "short-run operation." Morris was formerly named by Truman on February 1, 1952. His initial meeting with the president on February 11 was encouraging; the president appeared supportive and reassured the special assistant that he need only ask and the president would grant his wishes. In fact, the president told news reporters that Morris should be empowered to grant immunity to his witnesses. On February 20, the president directed all government heads to cooperate with Morris.[142]

In the meantime, President Truman delivered a prepared statement to the press:

> I am directing all departments and agencies of the Government to cooperate fully with Mr. Morris in the performance of his duties, and to give him any information and assistance he may require, and to give the highest priority to any requests made by him … and they will be given separate office space outside the Department of Justice.[143]

Nonetheless, Morris's position was tenuous. As outlined in Executive Order 10327, his duties were limited to an examination of each department, with no authority to prosecute any employee.[144] Doomed from the start, Morris failed to secure from Congress the power of the subpoena, a tool he deemed essential for a successful probe. Additionally, the Republicans were suspicious of his appointment, especially after the permanent committee on investigations uncovered his involvement in a so-called "Tanker Deal."[145]

Morris, as the president of China International, a petroleum company supervised by the Chinese Nationalist government, purchased three wartime tankers for the sole purpose of transporting oil from the Persian Gulf to oil refineries in Taiwan. According to the Merchant Ship Sales Act of 1946, however, in order to sail under an American flag, he was first required to prove citizenship. In compliance, Morris and his partner, Houston H. Wasson, "organize[d] a corporation [China International] to serve as 'citizen' in order to apply for surplus tankers should they "become available." In *Let the Chips Fall*, Morris claimed that the "use of tankers [was for the sole] purpose of aiding in the rehabilitation of China" and that he only agreed to proceed after the assurance from the chairman of the Maritime Commission and the State Department that he was "in accordance with government policy."[146]

It soon became evident to J. Howard McGrath and those around him that his personal and political empire was beginning to crumble. After Senator Williams's Bureau of Internal Revenue probe traced the origin of the tax corruption scandal to the Department of Justice, he appointed Stephen A. Mitchell as chief counsel for the House Judiciary Committee on February 1, 1952. Mitchell was given the daunting task of uncovering iniquities in the Justice Department. Aware of the resistance that Attorney General McGrath had given previous investigations, he relied on his confidence in the sincerity of the committee, which sustained him through the grueling months that would follow.[147]

As the press and the Chelf subcommittee relentlessly criticized McGrath's performance, Morris proposed the use of a questionnaire to gather information relating to the income and background of executive department employees. According to Morris's recollection, the president heartily agreed with the plan, but McGrath seemed to express no interest in uncovering the root of criminal activity in his department.[148] As Morris's appointed adviser Harold Seidman of the Bureau of the Budget warned him, "You've been had." According to Seidman, "It's perfectly obvious what McGrath will do. He'll have you sit in your office for six months or a year then announce that Newbold Morris was unable to find any corruption in Washington, which will be perfectly true, because you never really had an opportunity to look. He is playing you for a patsy."[149]

Appearing on *Meet the Press* in early March, Morris explained that, since the president had cooperated with his investigation thus far, he expected Truman to approve the use of the questionnaire. In response to queries about the purpose of his appointment, Morris explained that his job was to "pick up loose ends" left by ongoing legislative subcommittees.[150] Morris then boasted to the press that he would issue the first questionnaire to Attorney General McGrath.[151]

Just before his final showdown with Truman, McGrath spoke before various chapters of the Sons and Daughters of Eire in Rhode Island on March 16, 1952. During the previous month, McGrath had been under intense scrutiny concerning his personal finances, especially from Republican presidential nominee Harold Stassen, who stated that he "received persistent confidential reports that [McGrath] had become a millionaire during the years of [his] public office holding."[152] Now, before an audience of well-wishers from Rhode Island, McGrath warned his fellow Irishmen and women that "our faith and our race are at stake." He then, perhaps under the influence of alcohol,[153] stated dramatically that "when the clouds have passed, I will have something to say that will shake this country as it never has been before."[154] According to Truman biographer Robert Ferrell, McGrath never revealed what he was going to announce, but Ferrell surmised that McGrath quite possibly meant to expose alleged government ties to Communism as per a document sent to him by J. Edgar Hoover's office.[155]

When McGrath returned to Washington, he failed to distribute the questionnaire to his department,[156] stating that the questions violated his Constitutional right to privacy. McGrath then met with Truman and the cabinet and claimed that Truman supported him in his refusal to cooperate with Morris.[157] Appearing before the Chelf subcommittee at the end of March, McGrath stated that he could not in good conscience deliver the questionnaire. Further, he remarked that given another chance, he would not have appointed Morris to his position.[158]

Although Truman liked McGrath personally, the president's cabinet, especially Press Secretary Joseph Short and special assistant Roger Tubby, strongly recommended that the president fire McGrath. In a tragic drama, McGrath emerged from the White House after a meeting with Truman on the morning of April 2, tight-lipped and noncommittal before press queries. Later that day, the cabinet gathered at the Washington airport to greet Queen Juliana of the Netherlands. Allegedly, McGrath, the president, and later the president's press secretary Joseph Short engaged in heated debate out of earshot of the press. Presumably, Short told McGrath to resign to save the president additional embarrassment. McGrath again repeated his half-hearted threat, "If I go—I'll really blow the lid off."[159]

McGrath followed his statement the next day with a terse note to Morris: "your appointment as Special Assistant to the Attorney General is hereby terminated, and your services as an employee of the Department of Justice shall cease at the close of business today." Realizing his position, President Truman telephoned McGrath with a similar message: "I think I ought to announce your resignation."[160]

Three years later, McGrath confided to Truman archivist that "He [Joseph Short] came over, and my God, no sooner were the words out of my mouth than the son-of-a-bitch exploded, 'What has the President got to do with this? You brought Morris down here.' Well, I was dumbfounded. I said, 'I brought him here with the President's approval and consent, and you took him over. You gave him his independence. Are you mad?' With this the President is smart; he walks away. The press gets the story that a disagreement is going on in a public place, and I said, 'Look, Joe, let's not argue it here. I'll meet you at the White House.'"[161]

According to Robert Ferrell, Short influenced the president's decision to remove McGrath from his post.

As McGrath remembered, "It was about six o'clock. Murphy and Joe are there. They are violent … blaming me for Morris. The whole thing was bitched up. They said the President was made the victim. 'You brought him down.' I said, 'Well you sons of bitches, I'll get rid of him. Don't think you can pull this … on me. I know what you're up to.'"[162]

Truman aide Kenneth Hechler remembers the confrontation with McGrath differently. In a chapter entitled "Korea, Communism and Corruption: MacArthur, McCarthy and McGrath," Hechler pointed to three liabilities in Truman's second administration: the pompous, egotistical general; the uncontrollable, drunken Wisconsin senator; and the lackadaisical, indolent attorney general. While he admitted that Morris had irritated a major segment of Washington elites with his shoddy methods of investigation, Hechler contended that it was McGrath who tried to force the president's hand regarding Morris's ill-fated questionnaire. Repeating Murphy's contention that by publicly (before the Chelf subcommittee) rejecting Morris, McGrath had in essence defied a presidential directive, Hechler believed that the only course was to oust McGrath. Like MacArthur, who had been insubordinate, Hechler averred, McGrath had disobeyed his commander in chief and needed to be dismissed for the sake of the president's reputation.[163]

Following the fateful meeting at the Washington airport, Hechler maintained that "McGrath continued the argument [with Murphy and Short] into the evening," and at the State Dinner for Queen Juliana at the Carlton, McGrath accused Murphy rather loudly of "trying to knife him."[164]

Solicitor General Philip B. Perlman served as an interim attorney general until the president could find a suitable official to take the job. Given the publicity surrounding McGrath's ouster, Truman's task was not an easy one. McGrath's successor, Philadelphia Judge James P. McGranery, who received Senate approval on May 21, willingly provided Kenneth B. Keating with the files necessary for the Chelf subcommittee to continue its investigation. While McGrath had resisted the Congressional hearings, McGranery "did cooperate to an extraordinary extent,"[165] allowing the subcommittee to conclude its investigation by October 1952. Its closing statements emphasized the "deplorable lack of knowledge" on the part of former attorney general McGrath, who responded to many queries about his department "in the most general terms." His own testimony a year earlier before King's group having revealed his extensive reliance on his assistants.[166]

In an interview following his ouster, McGrath half-jokingly replied to a query about his successor, Judge McGranery, advising the latter to wear his "asbestos suit" before he entered the White House. Throughout the ordeal, McGrath hinted, first to T. Lamar Caudle, and then later to friends, that a cabal to rid Truman of top Justice people, including him, was in the works. He had not dealt with the negative press well, but the major blow, Truman's personal call asking for McGrath's resignation, left him dumbfounded. It was obvious from the televised record of his exit interview that McGrath had aged, and had lost much of his confidence.

In many ways, the events that led to McGrath's downfall could have been prevented. For one, President Truman's initial appointment of the Rhode Islander was poorly conceived. McGrath was miscast, and thus suffered under the scrutiny of a hungry press and eager Republican opponents who sought every opportunity to bring down the Democratic president.

Still, McGrath's inertia cannot be excused. Often absent during major investigations, he attempted to cover his misdeeds by becoming defensive and combative. His initial failure to cooperate with both the King and Chelf subcommittees exacerbated tension both within his department and between the executive and legislative branches.

It is also clear from his interview in 1955 that McGrath had not learned from the episode. He blamed his ouster on external forces and did not, at least publicly, consider how he could have prevented his downfall. The *Washington Sunday Star* in August 1952 reported that McGrath left "his political head rolling in the dust beside the aristocratic skull of Newbold Morris."[167] Had McGrath returned to his old office, the author exclaimed, he would "almost literally … not know the old place," since his successor, James P. McGranery, had made a clean sweep, either asking for or accepting the resignations of many top officials in the Department of Justice.[168]

Nonetheless, McGrath was, at least in part, following the direction set by the president, who also resisted Congressional interference. Resenting the endless committees and subcommittees, the president retaliated by refusing access to FBI records, setting the precedent for his cabinet to do the same. Thus, Truman must bear some responsibility for the mismanagement of the Bureau of Internal Revenue and the Department of Justice. By sending conflicting messages to McGrath and Morris relating to the delivery of the infamous questionnaire and other directives, Truman allowed the problem to escalate until the final showdown on April 2.[169]

In the end, McGrath's downfall was not only indicative of his ineptitude, but also of the failure of the system to meet the needs of an expanding tax base. Judging from McGrath's comments during his 1955 interview, he believed that much of the problem with the Bureau of Internal Revenue was out of his hands. Had the Department of Justice and the Bureau of Internal Revenue, among others, been streamlined to meet the needs of a modern political and economic infrastructure, some of the "mess in Washington," including the debacle with Caudle and McGrath, might have been avoided.

By the time Truman implemented an effective reorganization of the Bureau of Internal Revenue, which included legislation to replace the 64 appointed collectors with 25 districts run by a district commissioner, the employees of which were all chosen from a pool of civil service applicants, the damage had already been done. The reform legislation, which was signed into law in March 1952, allowed for only one appointed officer, the commissioner of internal revenue, who resided in Washington. Additionally, and most importantly, a "strong, vigorous inspection service" was instituted and remained "completely independent of the rest of the Bureau," so that "operations and management of the Bureau" was kept "under continual scrutiny and appraisal."[170] Thus, McGrath's dismissal ultimately brought about positive appraisal of the division, and forced much needed change.

For McGrath, however, the change came too late. A more proactive attorney general might have vigorously called for, and participated in, reorganization efforts, but by the time McGrath assumed the head of the Justice Department, consistent and rigorous rooting out of corruption was needed, and that was just not McGrath's style.

In conclusion, the Rhode Islander's fight for his self-respect came too late, and his insatiable ambition cost him dearly. Although he had perfected the art of accommodation, he never built a reserve to cope with the possibility of failure, since he had only known political success. Insulating himself from criticism, in part by allying with strong, affluent benefactors like Peter Gerry and Theodore Francis Green, he never learned to deal with public rejection. When adversity had struck in the past, he sought protection and advice from Green. In addition, his ownership or interest in major radio stations in Rhode Island had shielded him from anything but perfunctory commentary on his performance as governor from his critics.

Having achieved the party unity he desired in 1940 in Rhode Island, McGrath captured the governor's seat for three consecutive two-year terms: 1940, 1942, and 1944. As war clouds loomed in 1940 and 1941, the airwaves piped out political and patriotic propaganda urging Rhode Islanders to unite, and despite some setbacks, they complied. Peacetime brought more success for McGrath, but his unfortunate decision to run for the Senate in 1946, an office left vacant by Peter Gerry, left leading Democrats in Rhode Island who sought the same seat bitter and frustrated.

As attorney general, McGrath's inattention to important judicial matters opened him up to criticism and more importantly weakened the Justice Department and the authority of the president. In the end, neither Harry Truman nor Theodore Francis Green could save him. He was made to serve as the scapegoat for the "mess in Washington,"[171] by definition an insidious cancer much broader in scope than the failure of one attorney general. McGrath's poor performance was a symptom, rather than the cause, of the chaotic atmosphere in the nation's capital.

Epilogue

Mourned by Rhode Island Senators Claiborne Pell and John O. Pastore, by Lieutenant Governor Giovanni Folcarelli and Attorney General J. Joseph Nugent, fondly remembered by former president Harry Truman, and honored by Ireland's official representative Frank Aikin and Ambassador William P. Fay, James Howard McGrath was lauded by more than 600 attendees when he was laid to rest at St. Francis Cemetery in Pawtucket, Rhode Island, on September 3, 1966. He was preceded in death by his old mentor, Theodore Francis Green, who passed on May 18, 1966, at the age of 98.[1]

Whether political ally, friend, or adversary, all present paid homage to the man who had served his party through the dark days of the Depression, his state as governor during the Second World War, and his country in the early Cold War years as United States solicitor general, senator, and attorney general.

Of the many in attendance, the Rev. William Paul Haas, president of Providence College, Governor John Chafee and Adjutant General Leonard B. Holland, former governors Dennis J. Roberts, John A. Notte, Jr., and Christopher Del Sesto, all noted that James Howard McGrath brought to his state recognition that was unmatched in modern history.

McGrath had been working throughout his last 14 years out of the public's eye. Serving as Carey Estes Kefauver's campaign manager during the latter's unsuccessful bid for the Democratic nomination in 1956, McGrath was able to keep his hand in politics. He returned to Rhode Island to work on behalf of the Armand Cote for governor campaign. Cote had served in McGrath's gubernatorial administration throughout the Second World War. Incurring the wrath of fellow Democrat Dennis Roberts, who also sought the title, McGrath eventually smoothed over the rough edges with Roberts.

McGrath had only just recently returned from Washington to spend time at his Point Judith home. At a board meeting for the First Federal Savings and Loan Bank, only two days before his death, McGrath appeared his old jocular self, exchanging barbs with the trustees. His public face, however, masked his inner turmoil.

Six years earlier in May 1960, McGrath had announced his intention to run for the Senate seat vacated by the aging Theodore Francis Green, who had first stepped down as the chairman of the Foreign Relations Committee in 1959, a post he had held since 1955. According to Senator Lyndon Johnson of Texas, Green was "one of the real patriots."[2] Other notable Rhode Islanders, including former governor Dennis J. Roberts, also praised him: "Senator Green has been a magnificent public servant.... It has been an honor for me to have been very closely associated with this great man during my years in public life."[3] Green knew when to step down. McGrath did not. Green ended his career on a high note. McGrath did not. McGrath's reputation suffered because he allowed his ambition to cloud his judgment, and he sought adulation at a high cost. From his first foray into politics, he had coveted power and prestige, always aiming to exceed the expectations of his father and his mentors. Never content to stay in any one position too long, he was constantly on the move, always planning his next conquest.

The *Providence Evening Bulletin* reported, "Although he has not been active in local politics for a number of years, Mr. McGrath ... has kept in touch with local affairs."[4] Despite the fact that his old nemesis, former governor Dennis J. Roberts, "will receive the Democratic endorsement for U.S. senator," McGrath pledged to "go all the way" in the 1960 election. He further criticized the Democratic state party as a "self-perpetuating system" that has moved "away from the people."[5] Although he maintained that "everything I have in this world is in Rhode Island," his critics thought otherwise, since his past sortie into national office took him away from the state, first when he resigned as governor in 1945 to serve as U.S. solicitor general, and then, when he resigned as senator in 1949 to accept the post as attorney general.[6]

Both McGrath and Roberts were surprised by the victory of young Claiborne Pell, whose wealth, vitality, and "fluent command of the French, Italian, and Portuguese languages " defeated McGrath and Roberts "by almost 2 to 1."[7]

The sixty-two-year-old Rhode Island politician had enjoyed a distinguished career, which brought him from the mill town of Woonsocket up through the political ranks to an appointment to Harry Truman's cabinet, as attorney general. Having served successfully as governor of Rhode Island through the dark days of World War II (1941–1945), as U.S. solicitor general (1945–1946), as senator (1947–1949), and as Democrat national chairman (1947–1949), McGrath's rise to power had been swift and steady. In 1949, however, when McGrath gave up his Senate seat to accept the position as attorney general, he hastened the beginning of the end to his public career. In hindsight, McGrath's tragic fall from grace on April 3, 1952, clearly was precipitated by a series of incidents that would make his forced resignation inevitable.

Evident throughout his rise was a systematic chipping away at his identity. McGrath's restlessness led to an obsessive self-promotion at the detriment of all else. By seeking praise from others, he never set aside enough time to cultivate his inner strength.

First as Democratic state chairman, McGrath followed the lead of his mentor Henry DeWitt Hamilton in orchestrating a coup to establish a police commission in Central Falls while assuring his election as the city's solicitor. Although he achieved the desired end, which enabled the Providence faction composed of Senator Gerry and General Henry deWitt Hamilton to burrow their way into the Blackstone Valley, the territory of "Boss" Tom McCoy, McGrath did so at great cost to his personal integrity and public credibility. His tenure as city solicitor of Central Falls in no way made up for the graft that resulted from the establishment of the Police Commission. Antagonizing city officials, especially Tom McCoy and Francis Condon, McGrath and Hamilton violated the home rule principle and through the commission encouraged gambling, bootlegging, and other nefarious activities. Even Governor Green's dismantling of the commission could not erase the damage that had already been done to the city, the state, and ultimately to McGrath's reputation. At this point, McGrath had made a choice, and continued to make similar choices throughout his life. In the end, his choices ruined him.

McGrath's success as United States district attorney overshadowed this earlier indiscretion, although his business interests compromised his duty to his office, as evidenced by his role in the Narragansett Race Track. His dismissal of five indictments, while legal in the proper sense, since no corrupt practices act existed in the state of Rhode Island, it did not eradicate the larger issue of private campaign contributions, which needed a greater hearing. While nearly all public officials at the time retained their legal clients, the practice as a whole objectified proper jurisprudence.

Nonetheless, James Howard McGrath bequeathed to his state a lasting legacy. His three two-year terms as governor produced a viable juvenile court bill, cash sickness legislation, a naval air base at Quonset Point, and a reformed tax structure. He campaigned on behalf of the oppressed; first in support of displaced persons and then in favor of civil rights for people of color. He brought his state proper recognition, and guided his constituency to a peaceful end to the world war, all the while maintaining order and economic stability.

Throughout his public service, he never forgot his ancestry. In speaking before the Friendly Sons of St. Patrick, on March 17, 1950, Attorney General J. Howard McGrath paid homage to his country: "We are, of course, grateful that we live in a land where so many young men and women of Irish ancestry have been able to rise to heights of eminence, enjoying glory and positions of honor and esteem."[8] Had he sold his soul for fame and riches? Some might say that he had, but when he returned to his roots; to Rhode Island, his home state; to the many friendships he had cultivated over the years; to his Catholic faith and his family, he finally knew that he was home. In the end, despite hardship and pain, he had earned his title as "Jim McGrath's Boy."

Appendix

Historians Weigh in on McGrath

While many scholars writing on the Truman presidency have praised J. Howard McGrath's contribution as Democratic national chairman, most have judged his tenure as attorney general severely. Four distinct categories emerge as important for this study.

The first group, comprised of Truman biographers, evaluated the performance of Attorney General McGrath as part of their report on Truman. A second group focuses on the 1948 election and includes insight into the inner workings of the Democratic National Committee and the Truman cabinet, and a third, smaller coterie assesses the contributions made by the Department of Justice to the national security state. The final group offers commentary almost exclusively on the mounting corruption evident in the Truman administration, most specifically in the Reconstruction Finance Corporation, the Bureau of Internal Revenue, and the Department of Justice. These historians have claimed that J. Howard McGrath's role was crucial, since his actions determined how both contemporaries and subsequent generations would view the Truman legacy.

Biographies of President Truman

Early Truman biographers detail the president's personal and political life, and in doing so, have pointed to McGrath's lackadaisical approach to his duties as head of the Justice Department. In addition, they judge his contribution to anti–Communist hysteria as detrimental to the president. They argue that his failure to stem the tide of money laundering, extortion, and tax fraud is a glaring example of the failure of American government to protect its citizens from both internal and external threats.

Without fail, however, these historians view McGrath's tenure as attorney general with its endemic corruption and mismanagement, as the low point of the Truman presidency. During the two decades following the death of the president in 1972, at least three substantial treatments of his tenure in office were published. Robert Donovan, Harold Gosnell, and Bert Cochran all minimize the Rhode Islander's performance as national chairman for the Democratic Party and focus on his less appealing two-and-a-half years as attorney general.

Washington correspondent Robert Donovan's two-volume study of the Truman presidency, published in 1977 and 1982, offers a generally balanced account of the early postwar years. Donovan, however, limits his discussion of McGrath to his role as a spokesman for the president, rather than as an agent of social change. Donovan, unlike other historians of the period, omits Chairman McGrath's measured performance against the fury of the Southern governors months before the November 1948 election, when he admirably championed the president's civil rights platform.[1]

In his second volume, Donovan challenges President Truman's assertion that the problems in the Bureau of Internal Revenue were holdovers from the Roosevelt presidency. He maintains that Truman should shoulder the blame, since he "had had a hand in staffing the Bureau of Internal Revenue in a manner that was to breed trouble,"[2] especially in his support of Robert E. Hannegan as commissioner of internal revenue, whom he described as a "wardheeler of low ethical standards and lower qualifications for commissioner of internal revenue." Donovan concludes that Hannegan eventually brought shame to the agency, because he appointed men of questionable moral character.[3] All in all, Donovan faults the president, who "never really got a grip on the department [of Justice]," and allowed it to degenerate into chaos and corruption.[4] Implicitly, McGrath's poor response to graft and corruption has, according to Donovan, become part and parcel of Truman's inability to manage his office.

Bert Cochran, a former professor at the New School for Social Research, provides a glimpse of Harry Truman's relationship to J. Howard McGrath; first describing the attorney general as a congenial host of the president's all-night poker game, and then as the object of Truman's disenchantment. In both cases, however, McGrath emerges not as an active, viable cabinet member, but as an unfortunate, ineffectual cog in the president's mismanaged organization.[5]

More matter of fact than the preceding studies, Harold Gosnell in *Harry Truman and the Crisis Presidency* briefly points to Chairman McGrath's success in confronting the Southern governors prior to the Democratic Convention in Philadelphia, but he fails to mention the president's decision to exclude McGrath from the important "Whistle Stop Campaign," in order to present a non-political image.

In one of his final chapters, "Investigations, Scandals, Security, and McCarthyism, 1947–1952," Gosnell infers that McGrath, and Truman's other so-called friends, "sold [Truman] down the river." He also theorizes that because Special Investigator Newbold Morris believed that he "was working for the President," and McGrath assumed that Morris was under his jurisdiction, Truman should have been clearer in his directives to avoid the debacle that ultimately occurred.[6]

Nonetheless, he does not excuse McGrath, stating: "His political credentials were impeccable after the successful election of 1948, but his legal qualifications were questioned by some…. McGrath was very ambitious, and he had hoped that he might be appointed to the Supreme Court."[7]

Others have made similar observations, especially the *Providence Journal*, which at one point predicted that McGrath would be next in line for the vice presidency.[8] No evidence exists that has proven that the president ever considered this possibility.

During the 1990s and 2000s, three substantive Truman biographies written by David McCullough, Robert Ferrell, and Alonzo Hamby also made major contributions to the historiography of the period, and have in varying degrees told similar stories of the days leading to McGrath's ouster.

Yale scholar David McCullough straddled popular and scholarly history in his massive biography of President Truman, published in 1992. Noting McGrath's importance to the campaign, McCullough contends that McGrath had a hand in coaxing the president to choose Alben Barkley of Kentucky as his running mate. McCullough states that Barkley, "the old warhorse politician," was praised by McGrath for his rousing convention speech in July 1948. This, in part, prompted Truman's response: "If Barkley was what the convention wanted … then Barkley was his [Truman's] choice, too."[9]

McCullough also credited McGrath, Publicity Director Jack Redding, and the Democratic National Committee with working diligently, despite predictions from leading sources that the Republicans would emerge victorious in the 1948 national election.[10] On the other hand, McCullough emphasizes the challenges faced by the president in retaining McGrath as attorney general, quoting from Truman's press secretary Roger Tubby: "McGrath, Korean truce talks … the steel, telegraph and telephone strikes, and his decision not to run again have been among the recent events draining on his emotional reserves … we were urging him to take a week off."[11]

Robert Ferrell, in *Harry S Truman: A Life*, offers a scathing appraisal of McGrath, but is equally critical of Truman's delay in meeting the crisis in the Bureau of Internal Revenue and the Department of Justice. In a chapter entitled "Nadir," Ferrell quoted the oft-repeated line from Truman that "Howard McGrath is a fine fellow but he can't do the job," asserting that "the department of justice should have protected the president against the five percenters, trouble in the RFC, and the crooks in the BIR." Ferrell observes that Truman "needed a scapegoat, and McGrath was at hand," implying that the failure was as much Truman's as it was McGrath's.

Remarking that the elevation of McGrath's predecessor, Tom Clark, to the Supreme Court "virtually dictated that McGrath would become the new head of the justice department," Ferrell intimates that Truman chose McGrath because of his religion. Since Tom Clark, a Presbyterian from Texas, replaced the deceased Supreme Court Justice Frank Murphy, an Irish Catholic, Truman had to balance his appointees by choosing a Catholic for the Justice Department. He then notes that the president would deny such allegations, claiming that religion was not a litmus test for office.[12]

Remarking that the McGrath appointment was a "mistake," Ferrell assesses that although he was "intelligent, sensible, and modest," he "lacked Clark's drive." Thus, Truman's decision to oust Assistant Attorney General Caudle of the Tax Division and his decision to replace his lethargic attorney general "by the end of 1951" with someone more energetic were only thwarted because the president's top choices refused the position.[13]

Alonzo Hamby was no less critical of Truman's response to corruption in his administration. In his initial study, *Beyond the New Deal: Harry S. Truman and American Liberalism*, written in 1973, Hamby concludes that Truman replied half-heartedly when rumors of graft surfaced. Instead, Hamby writes, the president characterized the Congressional probes of the Reconstruction Finance Corporation, the Internal Revenue Bureau, and the Department of Justice as the machinations of "McCarthy-like senators seeking to embarrass the administration and grab publicity for themselves,"[14]

Hamby also questions Truman's decision to allow his attorney general, J. Howard McGrath, "an administrative lightweight," to remain in office despite numerous complaints from the public and private sectors that McGrath failed to act when he was confronted with allegations against officers of the Internal Revenue Bureau and Department of Justice.[15]

Twenty years later, in his exhaustive biography of the president, Hamby took advantage of additional source material to reevaluate his assessment of the scandal. In *Man of the People: A Life of Harry S Truman*, Hamby contends that the president agreed to retain McGrath only out of a desire to soothe the Catholic hierarchy during an election year. Forced to acquiesce after his aides, "especially Charlie Murphy," urged him to fire his attorney general, Truman secretly campaigned to dismiss McGrath, but held back when leading Catholics, including Cardinal Francis Spellman, and McGrath ally Senator Green, pressured him to give the beleaguered attorney general another chance.[16]

Accordingly, some of the president's closest advisers blamed the problems existing within the Bureau of Internal Revenue on Attorney General McGrath, forcing the president to act: "His [McGrath's] rise had been based on neither charisma nor extraordinary energy. Good connections, a get-along, go-along attitude, and a powerful patron—venerable Rhode Island senator Theodore Francis Green—had paved the way for him."[17]

Critical of Newbold Morris, McGrath's choice to head the investigation, Hamby was circumspect about the relationship between the attorney general and the president, remarking that Truman was "hurt" by his decision to oust McGrath. Nonetheless, Hamby's overall conclusions remain the same. McGrath was inept, and Truman's lack of resolve compounded an already disturbing chapter in American history.[18]

The 1948 Election

A number of tracts have been written exclusively on the 1948 election. One in particular is the political study of the 1948 election by publicity director John Redding, whose *Inside the Democratic Party*, published in 1958, affords McGrath a central role in orchestrating Truman's win. Redding places McGrath, his immediate superior, at the core of campaign decision-making. McGrath, who provided the introduction to Redding's *Inside the Democratic Party*, declared proudly that "both Redding and I had our finest hour in 1948." Dejected by the harsh criticism he received from both Democrats and Republicans after his unceremonious firing nearly six years earlier, McGrath was heartened by his former subordinate's praise of his even-handed performance as Democratic national chairman.[19]

In 1968, Irwin Ross recognized the contributions McGrath made to the party, but he dismissed McGrath's optimism leading up to the election as "the ritual expected of a national chairman."[20] Ross, formerly a journalist with the *New York Post*, reported that McGrath "became confident of victory only in the latter part of October, because of the tremendous crowds which Truman was attracting."[21]

In *Truman and the 80th Congress*, Susan M. Hartmann reviews the president's relationship to Congress. At the same time, she points to McGrath's support of the president's initiative for national health care. While the legislature was willing to authorize a measure for federally funded health care for the poverty stricken, Truman instead desired nationwide insurance for all, regardless of their economic status. The issue would become a hot topic during the 1948 campaign.[22]

Sean Savage, Zachary Karabell, and David Pietrusza have penned formidable tracts that represent the more recent scholarship on the upset election of 1948. These studies place McGrath in a positive light, showing him to be an active, organizational dynamo, who campaigned rigorously and systematically for the president.

In promoting his work, Sean Savage states, "no previous book exclusively and comprehensively devotes its content and purpose to a detailed analysis of Harry S Truman's relationship with the Democratic party."[23] Given this premise, it is not surprising that Savage devotes considerable attention to Democratic National Chairman McGrath, contending that the president's "approach to and behavior as a party leader reflected the internal conflicts that he experienced in his own relationship with the Democratic party and in his goals for the party."[24] In Savage's estimation, the president chose McGrath because he was more conservative than some of the other possibilities, namely Rhode Island liberal Gael Sullivan.[25]

On McGrath, Savage affords the chairman his due by recognizing the difficulty of electing Truman during the early postwar period. "As the party spokesman for Truman's policy positions, McGrath's most challenging task … was his effort to maintain the active support of Southern Democrats who were loyal to Truman's candidacy but who also opposed the party's civil rights platform."[26]

Finally, Savage points to McGrath's frustration with the president and his close advisers, namely Clark Clifford, because of their exclusion of the DNC from the all-important decision-making process relating to party patronage.[27] Although McGrath would later deny it, his resistance to some of the president's appointments has been well documented.[28]

Recent publications by David Pietrusza and Zachary Karabell focus exclusively on the Truman upset in 1948. In doing so, they target a number of individuals who orchestrated the Democratic victory in November. In both studies, McGrath appears as an important player in the Republican defeat.

David Pietrusza, in *1948: Harry Truman's Improbable Victory and the Year That Transformed America*, introduces his readers to a host of characters, both Democrat and Republican, that marked the 1948 run for the presidency. Crediting McGrath with standing up to the Southern governors in support of the president's civil rights plank that February, Pietrusza also remarks that "in planning for Election Night, they [McGrath and Redding] had revealingly neglected to engage the Mayflower ballroom for any prospective victory celebrations," implying that the president's Democratic national chairman may not have been as buoyant about the election as other historians have argued.[29]

Zachary Karabell, in *The Last Campaign: How Harry Truman Won the 1948 Election*, argues that the 1948 campaign was a turning point in election history. "Americans didn't know when they went to the polls in 1948 that they were at the end of something." Lamenting that "America didn't realize that something precious, something vital, was about to be lost, perhaps forever," Karabell notes that for the "last time in this century … an entire spectrum of ideologies was represented … [and] debated and discussed in the mainstream media."[30]

In comparing the two campaigns, those of Thomas Dewey and Harry Truman, Karabell finds the Dewey organization wanting. Praising Truman's staff, he wrote that McGrath, Redding, and Truman's advisors "had created the first modern campaign team."[31] Karabell notes that their thorough preparation enabled the president to campaign vigorously and confidently, "with the benefit of intensive prior research and information."[32]

Other historians have focused on the president's civil rights platform, an initiative McGrath heartily endorsed. Michael Gardner in *Harry Truman and Civil Rights: Moral Courage and Political Risks* attempts to rehabilitate the image of the president regarding civil rights. Raised in Missouri, where his ancestors were confirmed Confederates, Truman appeared an unlikely proponent of desegregation. Nonetheless, Executive Order #9980, creating the committee on civil rights resulted in path-breaking legislation.

In Gardner's study, McGrath emerges as a spokesperson for the president's omnibus legislation, which was introduced to the 81st Congress. The bill, which included an anti-lynching law, an anti-poll tax bill, and a measure establishing a standing FEPC, an agency that would end institutionalized bigotry, was bound to fail because of the bloc of Southern Democrats and conservative Republicans who chafed under this expansion of the federal government. However, it illustrated Truman's commitment to the well-being of African Americans.[33]

Preferring to focus on the role of the Supreme Court in advancing the president's agenda on civil rights, Gardner emphasizes the deep friendship between Frederick M. Vinson, whom Truman appointed as chief justice, and the president. Vinson, who hailed from Georgia, shared the president's outlook on the plight of the people of color. As attorney general, McGrath, according to Gardner, had a hand in helping the president advance his civil rights agenda.[34]

Kari Frederickson, in *The Dixiecrat Revolt and the End of the Solid South, 1932–1968*, frames her argument through the lens of states' rights activism. Strom Thurmond and other Southern icons fought against the "expanding liberal state" by campaigning in favor of "local self-government." Although the Dixiecrats only captured four Southern states, Frederickson argues that the movement was nonetheless significant. By "encourage[ing] voters to question their traditional political allegiance to the national Democratic Party," it "inaugurated a highly experimental era in which conservative white southerners used the movement's organizational and ideological framework to experiment with new political institutions."[35]

Equally important, the Dixiecrats "legitimized … the use of red baiting in combination with race baiting."[36] Frederickson argues that race was still a viable topic and accounts for the defeat of Strom Thurmond, a Dixiecrat, in the 1950 primary race for the U.S. Senate in South Carolina. She claims that Southerners wanted the assurance of protection against federal mandates for racial equality, an assurance that the Dixiecrats could no longer give. It was the Dixiecrats that voters abandoned, not racism.[37]

In Frederickson's book, McGrath appears as a spokesperson for the president's civil rights platform, although the two debated over patronage in Mississippi, with McGrath seeking to appease the Southerners after the election, and Truman unwilling to compromise on the issue of the Southern defectors.[38] This disagreement is important, although Professor Frederickson does not pursue it, in that it illustrates the division between Truman and his Democratic national chairman.[39]

In *Eyes Off the Prize: The United Nations and the African American Struggle for Human Rights, 1944–1955*, Carol Anderson challenges Harry Truman's commitment to rights for African Americans. She points out, "For too long, civil rights has been heralded as the "prize" for black equality." Instead, the African American leadership should have held out, not just for civil rights, but for human rights. In her estimation, groups like the NAACP settled for the scraps given them by politicians like Harry Truman and Eleanor Roosevelt.[40] She claims that the Cold War dampened the fight for civil rights and "systematically eliminated human rights as a viable option for the main African American leadership."[41]

Thus, the 1948 civil rights platform serves as an example of "the politics of symbolic equality."[42] In other words, white America's "commitment" to people of color was driven by the political climate. In the case of the 1948 election, Truman relied on the Clifford-Rowe plan to wrench the black vote from the Republicans, "the party of Lincoln," by delivering on civil rights. Since African Americans held the all-important majority in New York, Illinois, Pennsylvania, Ohio, and Michigan, Harry Truman had no choice but to strike at the core of racial inequality. However, when he called for desegregation, an anti-lynching law, and a federal FEPC, Southerners threatened to bolt. Following a meeting between McGrath and the Southern leadership that February 1948, Truman realized that he had to back down.

The National Security State

Although historian Daniel Yergin in 1977 directed his attention to the president's foreign rather than domestic policies, his study lays the foundation for an understanding of the national security state and how it would come to direct the political scene in the United States. In *Shattered Peace: The Origins of the Cold War and the National Security State*, Yergin remarks that "the confrontation [between the United States and the Soviet Union] brought about fundamental changes in American life, [including] a permanent military readiness in what passed for peacetime."[43]

According to Yergin, "the men guiding U.S. policy in the 1940s had witnessed events in their own lifetimes that provided a compelling impetus for once again trying to make Woodrow Wilson's enterprise work."[44] In their attempts to make the world safe for democracy, statesmen like President Roosevelt desired to eradicate "Nazism, communism and colonialism," and in doing so were "truly seeking to abolish the very substance of world politics—balance of power, spheres of influence, power politics." Yergin argues that FDR, "a renegade Wilsonian," employed "traditional means to achieve Wilsonian ends."[45]

Since the Americans, according to Yergin, desired these altruistic, Wilsonian ends and the Soviets sought to "create a sphere of influence, a glacis, out of bordering countries," an inevitable clash was bound to occur. The national security state emerged from this debate over how best to handle the Soviet threat.[46]

Another group of scholars writing during the Cold War and afterward noted the pernicious influence of growth in power of the FBI and its director J. Edgar Hoover. Promoted by many attorneys general, including McGrath and his predecessor Tom Clark, Hoover as director of the FBI was moving America closer to a national police state. Attorneys General Clark and McGrath, among others, were careful to praise the FBI's vain director at every turn. McGrath, technically Hoover's superior, gave him a wide berth when it came to surveillance, thereby encouraging the expansion of the security state, and ultimately stepping on the Constitutional rights of many American citizens.

Athan Theoharis, Professor Emeritus at Marquette University and the foremost authority on the Federal Bureau of Investigation, has written several books on the rise of the security state. Theoharis sees J. Howard McGrath as a central factor in the growth of the power of the state, especially in the use of electronic surveillance during the early Cold War. He writes: "The Department of Justice—and in particular Attorneys General Tom C. Clark and J. Howard McGrath and FBI Director J. Edgar Hoover—exercised a strong influence on popular American attitudes during the postwar security debate."[47]

Accordingly, Theoharis concludes that the department often acted "independent[ly] ... indeed, sometimes at clear cross-purposes against—the main principles of Truman's policy."[48] In his book, Theoharis takes aim at McGrath's oratory, which heightened the fear against Communist infiltration, and highlights the inherent problem with the Justice Department's security policy, observing that "McGrath's rhetoric, [failed] to distinguish between communist ideology and actual espionage." Theoharis argues that the attorney general "significantly altered the framework within which the general public evaluated loyalty procedures."[49] Thus, McGrath, as the prime actor in President Truman's domestic policy concerning Communist subversives, helped to formulate Cold War policy through his support of a virtual police state to combat Russian aggression overseas and on American shores.

In *From the Secret Files of J. Edgar Hoover*, Theoharis includes "Personal and Confidential Memos" between the director and Attorney General McGrath. He prefaces his edited volume with a caveat that the files were "maintained separate from the FBI's central records system," but he was unable to obtain a complete record of the source because many documents, such as the Tolson File memoranda, were "regularly destroyed every six months." Thus, it is impossible to find a complete record of Hoover's correspondence with McGrath, President Truman, or his FBI agents.

In one of his surviving letters to McGrath, Hoover justifies the use of wiretaps, writing, "The FBI today has the gravest responsibility for protection of the national security of our country." Because of internal and external threats, Hoover believed that the Bureau should use all methods available and placed a request to Attorney General McGrath for authorization to use taps when deemed necessary. McGrath's response, although couched in legalese, gave tacit approval to Hoover's appeal: "The records do not indicate that this question dealing with microphones has ever been presented before; therefore, please be advised that I cannot authorize the installation of a microphone involving a trespass under existing law."[50]

McGrath's weak response, "I cannot authorize the installation," left room for the wily Hoover to sanction tapping in certain instances, while McGrath was merely following the prescribed policy as laid down by his predecessors. The attorney general's qualified support, though limited, was a first step to Hoover's growing interference in the private lives of several individuals.[51]

In fact, Richard Gid Powers, in *Secrecy and Power: The Life of J. Edgar Hoover*, credits Hoover with blocking the appointment of McGrath's potential successor as attorney general because he feared that a new justice head would not be as pliable. Powers maintains that "Hoover's success leading the government drive against Communists effectively discredited the Justice Department," thereby "g[iving] him what amounted to a veto over Truman's replacement for the feckless and embattled J. Howard McGrath."[52]

The declassification of many files in the Bureau of Investigation led to shocking discoveries that shed new light on this period and the motivations of the president, the Department of Justice, and its investigative arm, the FBI. Especially crucial to a study of this period was the discovery of the VENONA files in 1995, which opened up a whole new series of documents.

The Truman Library has held several symposia that have emphasized important issues from the Truman presidency. In 2011, a conference on civil liberties brought premier historians and political scientists of the era to Independence, Missouri. In his introduction to the symposium, the Library's director, Dr. Michael J. Devine, observed that while "loyalty oaths and background security checks for federal employment are now considered routine" especially after the terrorist attacks on 9/11, these procedures "had arisen only occasionally" before the onset of the Second World War.[53] Nonetheless, he contends that the Truman era set the standards for the modern security state: The cooperation of Justice Department leaders, predominantly Attorneys General Clark and McGrath, with the FBI encouraged the future adoption of surveillance methods.[54]

Also included in the Truman Library symposia, historian Michael Belknap revised his earlier stand in relation to the Smith Act passed on June 29, 1940. Admitting that his earlier work had underplayed the pervasiveness of the Communist threat, Belknap explains that internal espionage had a hand in intensifying the early Cold War.

The Smith Act (76th Congress, June 29, 1940) made it illegal to advocate the overthrow of the government. The 1951 Supreme Court decision was based on unsubstantiated evidence, and was therefore invalid. *Eugene Dennis, et. al v. U.S.* (341 U.S. 494) 1951, upheld the ruling of the lower courts in declaring that Dennis, the general secretary of the Communist Party and his compatriots, violated the Smith Act.

Belknap concludes that the "Smith Act story, while badly flawed, is not completely wrong." He declares that "although many Communists were dangerous, the Communist Party's teaching and advocacy were not." Since the government's overthrow is "a great evil," talking about it in a way that might instigate treasonous activity, "could be suppressed." The Dennis decision was overturned in 1968 in the Brandenburg case, which declared that the prohibition of speech may only be federally enforced if the subject is "inciting or producing imminent lawless action and is actually likely to product it."[55]

Corruption During the Truman Presidency

Former special assistant to the attorney general Newbold Morris, in *Let the Chips Fall: My Battles Against Corruption*, which was published in 1955, three years after McGrath fired him as special assistant attorney general, explained that his failure to uncover corruption in the government occurred because of McGrath's campaign to block his efforts to obtain vital evidence. While others, particularly Frank Chelf, who headed the House investigation against the Department of Justice, made similar claims, Morris, unlike Chelf, had an agenda in publishing his work. Morris writes, "Before leaving [my initial meeting with President Truman and McGrath] I told the President and the Attorney General that I would like to work quietly, avoiding publicity. But this was an impossible hope."[56]

This statement is in sharp contrast to contemporaries who characterized

Morris as a publicity-seeker out to make a name for himself. The charge was given further fuel when Morris appeared on *Meet the Press* in early 1952. According to his recollection, Morris was misquoted on whether he would have appointed either mayor William O'Dwyer or General Harry Vaughn ambassador to Mexico, Truman's close friend and military aide. When Morris "replied in the negative," newspaper reporters immediately rushed to press with statements accusing the new special assistant of leveling barbs against the president of the United States. According to Morris, his words were misrepresented in order to build a case against him. Emerging from his semi-autobiographical account as an embattled crusader, he urged the "hundreds of … fellow citizens who have joined me in the fight for good Government often without hope of victory and always without hope of material reward," to keep on fighting.[57]

Morris also faulted Congress for refusing to grant him subpoena power, which, along with McGrath's recalcitrance, stymied Morris's attempts to uncover evidence against the department. Doomed from the start, Morris was the object of a "whitewash," perpetrated by none other than Attorney General J. Howard McGrath.[58]

While Morris exonerates President Truman and places full responsibility on "corrupt politicians," like McGrath, journalists Blair Bolles and Jules Abels denounce both the president and the attorney general for their actions during the early Cold War. According to Bolles, Truman erred when he based his Justice Department appointments on political considerations, rather than on legal expertise. In doing so, he branded McGrath inept and ineffectual in his role as attorney general and dismissed his contributions to the Truman victory in 1948.

Abels in *The Truman Scandals* and Bolles in *How to Get Rich in Washington: Rich Man's Division of the Welfare State* offer scathing critiques of the Truman presidency and by association McGrath's tenure as attorney general. Branding the president, a two-bit politician who surrounded himself with corrupt officials and half-witted cronies, Abels and Bolles overlook the president's early successes in foreign policy, focusing instead on his domestic failures, including his appointment of J. Howard McGrath as attorney general.

Abels paints a sorry picture of a president reeling between numerous tax scandals unearthed by the legislature, and a string of ousters, culminating in the firing of his attorney general, J. Howard McGrath. According to Abels, "McGrath had shown total apathy for the anti-corruption campaign." Forced to act by the president, McGrath hired New York Republican Newbold Morris as a special assistant. Given the task to clean up the Justice Department, Morris found his job impossible because of a number of road blocks imposed by Congress and by McGrath. When Morris fell under suspicion for allegedly selling tankers to Nationalist China at a significant profit (which he emphatically denied), he was considered vulnerable and subject to bribery and coercion. According to Frank Chelf, chairman of the House subcommittee to investigate the Department of Justice, the Morris appointment "might justifiably be interpreted as an attempt to appoint to office a man who might be susceptible to pressure."[59] In the end, however, Abels writes that McGrath served as an unwilling scapegoat for the president's failures.[60]

Writing at the height of the scandals, Blair Bolles exposed the level of corruption that ran rampant in Washington. Stating plainly that "when nations mature, they grow tolerant of evil," he found the "anything goes" attitude among the country's public figures disturbing.[61] While not targeting McGrath specifically, Bolles remarked, "In the modern atmosphere, the use of public office for private profit seems like a natural thing."[62] Given Republican presidential candidate Harold Stassen's accusations that McGrath had earned millions while serving the public, the comment struck at the heart of the attorney general's weakness. In fact, McGrath specifically referenced Bolles's tract in his statement before the Chelf Subcommittee in 1952 shortly before his ouster.[63]

One important study, which appeared in 1984, was Andrew Dunar's *The Truman Scandals and the Politics of Morality*, which developed from his much larger dissertation. Dunar, who, after painstaking research, concludes that the president, while courageous, competent, and bold, suffered from his "connection with the underside of American politics."[64] The president's duality was evidenced by his statesmanship on the one hand and his "cronyism" on the other.[65] In appointing McGrath as attorney general, Dunar concludes that Truman had opted for a crony rather than a statesman. Ultimately, he believed the McGrath ouster was "a painful decision, for McGrath was honorable and loyal and unmistakably one of Truman's men."[66] To Dunar, Truman suffered from a limited view of people, which categorized them as either "friends or foes, his people or others." His narrow understanding of human nature exacerbated the scandals and caused him to hesitate rather than act decisively. Dunar then categorized the McGrath incident as representative of a long line of messy firings that could have been handled more efficiently.[67]

History has judged J. Howard McGrath an effective Democratic national chairman but a poor attorney general. His efforts on behalf of President Truman exhibit a forthright, workmanlike performance, which contributed to success at the polls, and his tenure as head of the Department of Justice an unfitting end to an otherwise productive career.

Chapter Notes

Acknowledgments

1. Maureen Moakley and Elmer Cornwell, *Rhode Island Politics and Government* (Lincoln: University of Nebraska Press), 3.

Preface

1. "McGrath Chosen State Chairman in Green's Place"; "J. Howard McGrath Is Made Chairman of State Democrats," *Providence Journal*, October 7, 1930.

2. "Crime Master a Victim of Squeal of His Stooge," *Boston Herald*, May 5, 1935.

3. Cass R. Sunstein, *The Second Bill of Rights: FDR's Unfinished Revolution and Why We Need It More Than Ever* (New York: Perseus Books, 2004), 27.

4. According to statistics compiled by Mc-Grath's campaign team, "the percentage of voters who failed to have their ballots recorded was 7%" in 1940, "in 1942, 4% and in 1944, 3½%. Under the former paper ballot plan the blanks and defectives averaged 8 to 10%." "Comparison—Actual Votes Cast for Governor and Protective Counter Reading of Ballots Cast in Voting Machines," Folder "Election 1944," J. Howard McGrath Collection, Special and Archival Collections, Providence College, Providence.

5. Henry H. Smith, "With Howard, Howard Comes First," *The Nation*, November 17, 1951, 421–423.

6. Folder, "Rhode Island: OPA Forum: The State of Rhode Island and the OPA," J. Howard McGrath Papers, Folder, "OPA Forum Program," April 27, 1943, Harry S Truman Presidential Library, Independence, MO.

7. Qtd. in Alonzo Hamby, *A Life of Harry S Truman: Man of the People* (New York: Oxford University Press, 1995), 592.

8. Alden Hatch, "Democratic Repairman:

The New National Committee Chairman, Senator J. Howard McGrath has a tough job of Political Welding," *Colliers Weekly*, March 27, 1948, 18–19.

Chapter 1

1. A political machine is an organization that doles out employment and other favors in exchange for votes and other forms of support.

2. Elmer E. Cornwell, "City Bosses and Political Machines," *The Annals of the American Academy of Political Science* 353 (May 1964): 28.

3. Evelyn Savidge Sterne, *Ballots and Bibles: Ethnic Politics and the Catholic Church in Providence* (Ithaca: Cornell University Press, 2004), 7.

4. By the early nineteenth century, these entrepreneurs introduced woolens into their thriving textile industry. William J. Jennings, Jr., "The Prince of Pawtucket: A Study of the Politics of Thomas P. McCoy," Providence College, 1985, 2; William G. McLoughlin, *Rhode Island: A History* (New York: W. W. Norton, 1986), 2nd edition, 114–123.

5. Maureen Moakley and Elmer Cornwell, *Rhode Island Politics and Government* (Lincoln: University of Nebraska Press, 2001), 24–25.

6. Robert A. Wheeler, "Fifth Ward Irish: Immigrant Mobility in Providence, 1850–1870," *Rhode Island History* (Spring 1973): 52–61.

7. Kerby A. Miller, *Emigrants and Exiles: Ireland and the Irish Exodus to North America* (New York: Oxford University Press, 1985), 38.

8. *Ibid.*, 39.

9. Neil Hegarty, *The Story of Ireland: A History of the Irish People* (New York: St. Martin's Press, 2011), 205–208.

10. Patrick T. Conley, *The Irish in Rhode Island: A Historical Appreciation* (Providence: The Rhode Island Heritage Commission, 1986),

16; Elmer E. Cornwell, Jr., "Party Absorption of Ethnic Groups: The Case of Providence, Rhode Island," *Social Forces* 38, no. 3 (March 1960), 206.

11. Cornwell, "Party Absorption," 124.

12. Henry Bowen Anthony, "Limited Suffrage in Rhode Island," *The North American Review* 137, no. 324 (November 1883): 417.

13. *Ibid.*

14. Hoppin won three consecutive races: in 1854 against Democrat Francis M. Dimond, in 1855 against Democrat Americus V. Potter, and in 1856 also against Potter. Ernest L. Sprague, *Rhode Island Manual with Rules and Orders for the Use of the General Assembly of the State of Rhode Island. 1927-1928* (Providence: E.L. Freeman Company, 1928), 118.

15. Patrick T. Conley, *Rhode Island in Rhetoric and Reflection: Public Addresses and Essays* (East Providence: Rhode Island Publications Society, 2002), 266-270; Donald D'Amato, "The Division of Warwick in 1913," *Warwick Beacon*, May 17, 1990, Warwick Public Library, Warwick.

16. Conley, *The Irish in Rhode Island: A Historical Appreciation,* 10-11.

17. Kerby Miller and Paul Wagner, *Out of Ireland: The Story of Irish Emigration to America* (Washington, D.C.: Elliott & Clark, 1994), 14.

18. Norman knight Richard De Clare, the Second Earl of Pembroke (Strongbow), wed Irish princess Aoife Ni Diarmait at Christ Church Cathedral in Waterford. Hegarty, *The Story of Ireland*, 64-65.

19. Lawrence J. McCaffrey, *The Irish Catholic Diaspora in America* (Washington, D.C.: The Catholic University of America Press, 1997), 75-76. "Ireland Births and Baptisms. 1620-1881," index, *Family Search*, accessed July 17, 2014, http://familysearch.org/pal:/MM9.11/F5tp-24F: Edmond McGrath in entry for James McGrath, 27 October 1873; Waterford, Waterford, Ireland, reference; FHL microfilm 255891. Midwest Genealogical Society, Lee's Summit, MO.

20. Stephen Puleo, *A City So Grand: The Rise of an American Metropolis, Boston, 1850-1900* (Boston: Beacon Press, 2010), 78.

21. McCaffrey, *The Irish Catholic Diaspora,* 71.

22. "U.S. Supreme Court Common Pleas Division," Providence, October 25, 1894.

23. Marcel P. Fortin, ed., *Woonsocket RI: A Centennial History, 1888-1988* (Woonsocket: Woonsocket Centennial Committee, 1988), 11.

24. Dr. A.P. Thomas, *Woonsocket: Highlights of History: 1800-1876* (Woonsocket: Woonsocket Opera House Society, 1976), 1-5.

25. Miller and Wagner, *Out of Ireland*, 94.

26. "M'Grath to be Honor Guest at I.O.F. Dinner," *News Tribune*, May 12, 1930.

27. Fortin, *Woonsocket*, 5; "John G. May," Vol. NS, U.S. District Court, Providence, 1903-1906; "Providence Death Index: John Gideon May, accessed 02/2015," https://familysearch.org/ark:/61903/1:1:f848-X5M.

28. "John G. May," https://familysearch.org.

29. *Names and Places of Nova Scotia* (Bellevile, Ontario: Mika Publishing Company, 1974), 577-578.

30. 1838 Census, accessed 06/25/2016, http://www.rootsweb.ancestry.com/—nspictou/census/cen1838pictou.

31. The 1851 census lists the property holdings of the Mahys: one store, barn and outhouse, 30 bushels of potatoes, one "neat cattle," one "milch cow," 20 yards of cloth "not fulled," 20 pounds of butter "manufactured." Accordingly, two children matriculated at the local schoolhouse, and the family raised enough money to purchase a pew # 17.5 by 1844 at the local Presbyterian church. This information was provided courtesy of Barbara Carroll, genealogist and spouse of J. Austin Carroll, maternal cousin of J. Howard McGrath.

32. "Death Registered in Providence," *Providence City Archives* 26, February 1919, 291.

33. "James J. McGrath Dead in this City," *Providence Journal*, October 26, 1931.

34. Milton MacKaye, "He'll Sink or Swim with Harry", *Saturday Evening Post*, May 29, 1948.

35. The first known American court was established in New York in 1864, more than a century after its founding in Knaresborough, England, in 1745. Setting forth its bylaws and "declaring" its independence from the British High Court, the American foresters of Brooklyn, New York, declared "that the New York and Brooklyn United Districts, herein by its delegates assembled, do hereby declare its independence in Forestry by severing its allegiance to and all connection with the High Court and the Executive Council of England of the Ancient Order of Foresters." M.D. Oronhyatekha, *History of the Independent Order of Foresters* (Toronto: Hunter, Rose, and Company, 1894), accessed 11/24/2017, https://archive.org/stream/historyofindepen00tororich/historyofindepen00tororich_djvu.txt24; Warren Potter and Robert Oliver, *Fraternally Yours: A History of the Independent Order of Foresters* (London: The Queen Anne Press Limited, 1967), 16-20.

36. "Independent Foresters Hold Public Installation," Folder, "Clippings, 1924-1932," J. Howard McGrath Collection, Special and Archival Collections, Providence College, Providence.

37. McGrath's mother, Ida May, was born in Providence, but the Mays originated from Pictou, Nova Scotia, where her grandfather worked as a cordswainer. John Austin Carroll, cousin, phone interview with author, August 2, 2007.

38. "Obituary," *Providence Visitor*, January 31, 1919.

39. "Woodrow Wilson's War Message," accessed 09/13/2017, http://wwi.lib.byu.edu/index.php/Wilson's_War_Message_to_Congress.

40. "Principles of Contagious Disease Control: Manuscript Notes," B-29, Series 2, MSS 343, Papers of Charles V. Chapin, Rhode Island Historical Society, Providence.

41. "Quidneck Resident Died Suddenly," *Providence-News*, September 11, 1918.

42. "Honor Roll, LaSalle Academy," *Providence Visitor*, January 17, 1919.

43. *Ibid.*

44. K.S. Bartlett, "When Atty. Gen. Nominee J. Howard McGrath Was 16 He could 'Out-Orate' His Foresters Organizing Father," *Daily Boston Globe*, August 7, 1949. ProQuest Historical Newspapers.

45. Milton MacKaye, "He'll Sink or Swim with Harry," Folder, "1949–51," Democratic National Committee Papers, Harry S Truman Presidential Library, Independence, MO.

46. Years later, archivist Matthew Smith received a letter from one of McGrath's fellow graduates. Letter from John E. Farrell to Head Archivist Matthew J. Smith, December 18, 1984, Folder, "General College: PC Commencement, 1926," Special and Archival Collections, Providence College, Providence; *The Maroon and White*, June 1922, LaSalle Academy, Providence.

47. Bartlett, "When Atty. Gen Nominee J. Howard McGrath Was 16."

48. *The Maroon and White*, June 1922, LaSalle Academy, Providence.

49. "Providence College Annual Catalogues, Volumes 1–13," Annual Catalogue, 1919–1920, Special and Archival Collections, Providence College, Providence, 11.

50. "Matthew Harkins, D.D. Bishop of the Diocese of Providence to the Dominican Fathers," Province of St. Joseph, October 9, 1915, Special and Archival Collections, Providence College, Providence.

51. Providence College Catalogue, 1918–1919, Special and Archival Collections, Providence College, Providence, 8.

52. Providence College Catalogue, 1925–1926, Special and Archival Collections, Providence College, Providence, 4, 12.

53. Providence College Catalogue 1924, Special and Archival Collections, Providence College, Providence.

54. Paul F. Healy, "The Story of Two Irishmen," *Extension* (December 1947): 7, 50, 52, 54;
James MacGregor Burns, *Roosevelt: The Lion and the Fox* (New York: Harcourt, Brace & World, 1956), 28–29.

55. "The New Attorney General: A Pictorial Biography," *Providence Sunday Journal*, August 28, 1949.

56. "First Prize Goes to Miss McKay: Her Vote is 13,163,500; J. H. McGrath Comes Second," *News-Tribune*, n.d., J. Howard McGrath Collection, Special and Archival Collections, Providence College, Providence. Gael Sullivan left Rhode Island after he graduated from Providence College to pursue a study of economics in the Midwest. Subsequently, he became part of Mayor Edward Kelly's team in Chicago. Following the war, he was slated by the Democrat powerbrokers to assume the responsibility as executive director and partnered with McGrath when the latter accepted the post of Democrat national chairman in 1948. "He'll Sink or Swim with Harry," *Saturday Evening Post*, May 29, 1948, 20.

57. "First Prize Goes to Miss McKay," *Providence News Tribune*, n.d. "James McGrath Dead in this City," *Providence Journal*, October 26, 1931, 10.

58. Healy, "The Story of Two Irishmen," 7.

59. J. Howard McGrath, *The Power of the People* (New York: Julian Messner, 1948), 28–29.

60. "Education Based Upon Faith Urged in Baccalaureate," *Providence Journal*, June 7, 1926.

61. *Ibid.*

62. Boston University Bulletin, 1929; *Bostonia: The Boston University Alumni Magazine*, Howard Gotlieb Archival Research Center, Boston University, Boston, December 1940.

63. "Speech: Dean Elwood H. Hettrick," 8, Folder, "Reception Honoring Honorable J. Howard McGrath, Attorney General of the United States," November 12, 1949, "J. Howard McGrath: Speeches, May 1945–Dec. 1951," J. Howard McGrath Collection, Special and Archival Collections, Providence College, Providence.

64. A. Rosen, Memorandum for the Director, October 3, 1945, Record Group #1, "J. Howard McGrath," File # 622–59475, Athan Theoharis Collection, Marquette University, Milwaukee.

65. "Estelle Cadorette will Wed J. Howard McGrath," n.d. "DePasquale Honored on Return from Honeymoon," n.d. J. Howard McGrath Collection, Special and Archival Collections, Providence College, Providence.

Chapter 2

1. Erwin L. Levine, *Theodore Francis Green: The Rhode Island Years, 1906–1936*

(Providence: Brown University Press, 1963), 7–10.

2. John D. Buenker, "The Politics of Resistance: The Rural-Based Yankee Republican Machines of Connecticut and Rhode Island," *The New England Quarterly* 47, no. 2 (June 1974): 214.

3. Ernest L. Sprague, "Article of Amendment, Article VII," *Manual with Rules and Orders for the Use of the General Assembly of the State of Rhode Island, 1925–1926* (Providence: E.L. Freeman, 1926), 49.

4. J. Hector Paquin, "Article VII of the Rhode Island Constitution, April 1888," *Manual with Rules and Orders for the Use of the General Assembly of the State of Rhode Island, 1939–1940* (Providence), 45.

5. Before 1888, the Rhode Island Constitution only barred those without real estate from voting for local council officers in Providence. At the time, the immigrant population only threatened the state capital. *Ibid.*, 7.

6. William Jennings, "The Prince of Pawtucket: A Study of the Politics of Thomas P. McCoy" (PhD diss., Providence College, 1985), 62.

7. *Ibid.*, 66.

8. However, Noel Ignatiev in his compelling study of Irish immigration contended that O'Connell, as a newly elected member of Parliament (made possible by the Catholic Emancipation Act of 1829), supported anti-insurrectionism as he rallied in support of British rule. Noel Ignatiev, *How the Irish Became White* (New York: Routledge, 1995), 19–25.

9. D'Amato, "The Division of Warwick in 1913."

10. *Ibid.*, 67–68.

11. McCoy finally succeeded in putting the amendment over in the General Assembly. McLoughlin, *Rhode Island*, 188; Matthew J. Smith, "The Real McCoy in the Bloodless Revolution of 1935," *Rhode Island History* (Summer 1973), 71–72.

12. David Patten, *Rhode Island Story: Recollections of 35 Years on the Staff of the Providence Journal, and Evening Bulletin*, (Providence: The Providence Journal, Company, 1954), 87–100.

13. Jennings, "The Prince of Pawtucket," 70.

14. "Young Women Meet," n.d. "Clippings: 1924–1932," J. Howard McGrath Collection, Special and Archival Collection, Providence College, Providence.

15. Smith, "The Real McCoy," 75–76.

16. Sultzer's public dispute with powerful Tammany boss Charles Murphy resulted in the former's impeachment. Led by a Tammany-backed committee, its members discovered that the governor failed to report campaign contributions, and instead diverted the funds to his private account. Terry Golway, *Machine Made: Tammany Hall and the Creation of Modern American Politics* (New York: Liveright Publishing Corporation, 2014), 214–216.

17. The *New York Times* charged that the Guard under Hamilton "has become a haven for jobs." "Adjutant General to Clean House," *New York Herald*, January 13, 1913; "Tammany Seeks Jobs in National Guard," *New York Times*, January 20, 1913. Papers of Henry DeWitt Hamilton, John Hay Library, Brown University, Providence.

18. "Neither Side Sure of Rhode Island," Personal Scrapbook 4, Aug. 30, 1919–Nov. 9, 1925, *New York Times*, October 20, 1920. Hamilton Papers, John Hay Library, Providence.

19. Robert S. Allen and William V. Shannon, *The Truman Merry-Go-Round* (New York: The Vanguard Press, 1950), 99.

20. Erwin L. Levine, *Theodore Francis Green: The Rhode Island Years, 1906–1936* (Providence: Brown University Press, 1963), 112.

21. Smith, "The Real McCoy," 76.

22. "Hall 'Revolts' When Democrats Ignore Demand for $2500," *News-Tribune*; "Hall Challenges Democratic Head," *Providence Evening Bulletin*, May 20, 1930; "Full Text of Statement Made by Colonel Quinn," *Providence Journal*, n.d.; "Denounce Hamilton's Methods—Fear Continued Influence: Seen as Cause of Defeat," *Providence Journal*, n.d.; J. Howard McGrath Collection, Special and Archival Collections, Providence College, Providence.

23. "State Democrats Re-Elect McGrath Committee Chief," *Providence Journal*, November 25, 1930; "McGrath Election Further Opposed," *Providence Evening Bulletin*, November 24, 1930; "McGrath, Re-elected, Promises Vigorous Drive by Democrats," *News-Tribune*, November 25, 1930.

24. "Democrats Elect Theodore F. Green in Stubborn Fight," *Providence Journal*, January 9, 1929, 1.

25. DePasquale had been Democratic state chairman in 1928, before Green was "unanimously" elected for the same post. "Further Discord Hits Democratic Ranks in State," *Providence Journal*, September 5, 1930.

26. Levine, *Theodore Francis Green: The Rhode Island Years*, 91–106, 116–117; "Democrats Elect Theodore F. Green in a Stubborn Fight," *Providence Journal*, January 9, 1929, 1.

27. Levine, *Theodore Francis Green: Rhode Island Years*, 112.

28. "Patrick Quinn to Franklin Delano Roosevelt," Folder, "FDR General Political Correspondence 1920–1928," Franklin Delano Roosevelt Papers, Hyde Park, NY.

29. Levine, *Theodore Francis Green, Rhode Island Years*, 116–117.

30. "Traitor Hall," *News-Tribune*, May 15, 1930; "Hall Revolts When Democrats Ignore Demand for $2500," *News-Tribune*, May 15, 1930.

31. Folder, "Rhode Island, Before Election, A-Z," Letter from Eddie Dowling to Louis Howe, June 15, 1934, Folder, "Democratic Party National Committee, 1928–1948," Franklin Delano Roosevelt Presidential Library, Hyde Park, NY.

32. "McGrath to Organize First Voters in State," *Providence Journal*, September 11, 1928, 24; "Political and Private," December, 1929, MSS 276, Harvey Almy Baker Papers, Rhode Island Historical Society, Providence.

33. "House Passes Three Redistricting Bills," *Providence Journal*, March 22, 1930, 1.

34. "Duffy Assails Democratic Vote Dodgers," *News-Tribune*, March 25, 1930.

35. "McGrath Attacks Absentee Sextet," *Providence Journal*, March 22, 1930.

36. *Ibid.*; "House Democrats Deny Selling Out," *Providence Journal*, March 26, 1930, 9.

37. Henry Benoit to Harvey Almy Baker, "Political and Private," MSS 276, Harvey Almy Baker Papers, Rhode Island Historical Society, March 31, 1930.

38. "Berarducci Denies Pelkey Influenced Absence in House," *Pawtucket Times*, March 25, 1930; "House Democrats Deny Selling Out," *Providence Journal*, March 26, 1930, 9; "Berarducci Denies Pelkey Influenced Absence in House," *Pawtucket Times*, March 25, 1930; *Rhode Island Manual 1933–1934*.

39. "Sullivan Raps M'Grath for Public Attack," *News-Tribune*, March 27, 1930; "McGrath Accused on Floor of House," *Providence Evening Bulletin*, March 27, 1930.

40. Sullivan was so incensed by McGrath's accusation and by the domination of Gerry's machine that he refused to seek reelection in November. By urging every Democrat to oppose the candidacy of Gerry, he openly broke with the state organization. "Further Discord Hits Democratic Ranks in State," *Providence Journal*, September 5, 1930; "McGrath Accused on Floor of House," *Providence Evening Bulletin*, March 27, 1930, 11.

41. Kiernan and Flynn charged that the Republicans hurriedly redistricted before the publication of the 1930 census, which would have favored the Democrats. "McGrath Accused on Floor of House," *Providence Evening Bulletin*, March 27, 1930, 11.

42. Mary Keenan was sister of the late Luke Keenan, former architect of the Democratic Party and Gerry confidant. Manzi was endorsed as Democrat leader in Johnston by a

vote of 48 to 36. "Johnston Insurgents Hold Meeting," *Providence Journal*, October 16, 1930.

43. *Ibid.*; "Says Miss Keenan is Party Leader," *Providence Evening Bulletin*, October 15, 1930, 2.

44. "Fox, Manzi and Iannuccilli Have Resigned from Democratic Town Committee," *Providence Journal*, January 4, 1932.

45. The state organization allocated five hundred dollars to North Providence, a paltry sum according to city councilman Charles Hall. Hall further complained, "Gerry, to further his own interests, has cut the political throats of Toupin [Felix], Gainer and Green, successively. But by no stretch of the imagination is he big enough to repeat on North Providence Democrats and get away with it." "Traitor Hall," *Providence News Tribune*, May 15, 1930, 1; "Hall 'Revolts' When Democrats Ignore Demand for $2500," "Hall Challenges Democratic Head," *News-Tribune*, May 15, 1930, 1; *Providence Evening Bulletin*, May 20, 1930.

46. North Providence turned out for Republican governor Case in 1930, even though they supported French Canadian Democrat Alberic Archambault in 1928. Stefano Luconi, *The Italian-American Vote in Providence, Rhode Island, 1916–1948* (Madison, NJ: Fairleigh Dickinson University Press, 2004), 68; "Hall 'Revolts,'" *News-Tribune*, May 15, 1930, 1.

47. "Traitor Hall," *News-Tribune*, May 15, 1930.

48. McGrath further alienated North Providence Italians by paying registration monies directly to the chairman of the town committee rather than to the town treasurer, Joseph Maresca. Levine, *Theodore Francis Green: Rhode Island Years*, 114.

49. Levine, *Theodore Francis Green: Rhode Island Years*, 114; "Hall Challenges Democratic Head," *Evening Bulletin*, May 20, 1930.

Chapter 3

1. Henry H. Smith, "With Howard, Howard Comes First," *The Nation*, November 17, 1951, 421–423.

2. "Central Falls Wide Open, Journal, Finds," *Providence Evening Bulletin*, February 13, 1931; "House Passes Police Bill; Women of Central Falls Demand Case Order Hearing," *Providence Journal*, February 18, 1931; "Wide Open Town," *News-Tribune*, February 14, 1931.

3. A similar bill was approved by the General Assembly on April 10, 1931. The measure called for a Board of Public Safety in Providence composed of three members appointed by the governor. Like the Central Falls bill, the Providence Board was controversial because it

stripped local politicos of the power of patronage. Ironically, McGrath concealed his complicity in the Central Falls scandal by publicly denouncing both bills. After five years of protest from several fronts, the Providence bill was overturned as a result of the "Bloodless Revolution." Norma LaSalle Daoust, *The Perils of Providence: Rhode Island's Capital City During the Depression and New Deal* (Ann Arbor: University Microfilm, 1982) 54; "Plan Fight Against Safety Board Law," *Providence Journal*, April 13, 1931; Louis W. Cappelli, *Manual with Rules and Orders for the Use of the General Assembly of the State of Rhode Island: 1935–1936* (Providence: E.L. Freeman Company, 1936), 339.

4. According to the Central Falls city charter, the council must meet to vote in the city solicitor. In response to the Hamilton/McGrath cabal, Republicans attempted to postpone the joint election of city solicitor and probate judge until August so that Nolan would have enough time to relocate to the city. The delay, however, was dismissed on the grounds that it too violated the provisions of the charter. "Circumvention of Kennedy Bill by Group in City Council Frustrated," *Providence Journal*, January 17, 1931.

5. McCoy had established his own bloc of local notables including Harry Curvin, Commissioner of Public Works A. J. Lamarre, and U.S. Congressman Francis Condon. Vernon C. Norton, *A Common Man for the Common People: The Life of Thomas P. McCoy, 1883–1945* (Pawtucket: By the author, 1946), 39; Jennings, 102; "McGrath Out for Post as Solicitor," *Providence Journal*, January 17, 1931; "Method Sought to Defeat Aims of Kennedy Act," *Providence Journal*, January 16, 1931; "Circumvention of Kennedy Bill by Group in City Council Frustrated," *News Tribune*, January 17, 1931; "McGrath Opposes Kennedy Bill," *Evening Bulletin*, February 3, 1931; "Solicitor McGrath to Protest Police Commission Bill Today," *News-Tribune*, February 3, 1931.

6. "Elections," *Providence Journal, Bulletin, Almanac 1930: A Reference Book for the State of Rhode Island* (Providence: The Providence Journal Co., 1930).

7. "Condon Urges City Committee Chairman to Work for Defeat of Police Commission Measure," *Pawtucket Times*, January 30, 1931; "Kennedy Exposes Men Behind Police Bill, "*Providence Journal*, December 22, 1933, 1, 6; "Text of Kennedy's Statement Charging G.O.P. Democratic Deal for Passage of Central Falls Police Bill," 6.

8. "Quinn Asserts Hamilton Offers 'Strange Picture,'" *Providence Evening Bulletin*, February 11, 1931; "Central Falls Wide Open, Journal,

Finds," *Providence Evening Bulletin*, February 13, 1931.

9. Ironically, Senator (later Mayor) Cadorette publicly denounced the bill and registered a "nay" vote in the Senate. According to Case, Cadorette almost immediately approached him about appointing Kennedy to the commission. Cadorette, who was J. Howard McGrath's father-in-law, refused to comment on Case's allegations, dismissed the *Journal's* reporter probes with a blunt "no comment." "Case Supports Kennedy Story on Police Bill," *Providence Journal*, December 23, 1933, 1.

10. "Case Supports Kennedy," 1.

11. "Ex-Central Falls Councilman Admits General Hamilton at Conference in Lavell's Home," *Evening Bulletin*, December 22, 1933; "Condon Urges City Committee Chairman to Work for a Defeat of Police Commission Measure," *Pawtucket Times*, January 3, 1931.

12. "McGrath Flays Quinn, Suggests He Resign," *Providence Journal*, February 12, 1931, 1.

13. Democrat Robert Quinn judged the November 1934 election results in Portsmouth and South Kingstown fraudulent. Under the Rhode Island Constitution, Quinn as president of the Senate could refuse to allow the two Republican senators from these respective towns to assume their seats until the votes were recounted. The results produced two more Democratic senators, thus changing the makeup of the Republican-dominated upper house. This famous "Revolution" was a turning point in the state's political history, as Green, Quinn, and other notables, including McGrath and McCoy, succeeded in defeating one of the last holdovers of Republicanism. Robert E. Quinn interview, July 24, 1972, F4, 11–12; Special and Archival Collections, Providence College, Providence.

14. "Former Governor Case Supports Kennedy Story on Police Measure; Hamilton Declared at Meeting in Lavell's Home," *Providence Journal*, December 23, 1933, 2.

15. *Ibid.*

16. "Former Governor Case," 2.

17. "Kennedy Exposes Men," 6; "Central Falls Wide Open, Journal Finds," *Evening Bulletin*, February 13,1931; McGrath's connection to Lavell, his son-in-law J. Clifden O'Reilly, and others did not end with this incident. Their business and legal ties carried on into McGrath's national career.

18. "Wide Open Town," *News-Tribune*, February 14, 1931.

19. "Kennedy Exposes Men," 6.

20. *Ibid.*

21. Nonetheless, Green did appoint a new commission in January of 1933 with McGrath's father-in-law Joseph Cadorette named as chair-

man. This new commission was instrumental in renaming Sherry-ally Collette as police chief. Jennings, "Prince of Pawtucket," 116n; "Kennedy's Expose Not Read by Green," *Providence Journal*, December 24, 1933, 3.

22. "McGrath Reveals Status of Police," *Providence Journal*, April 25, 1934.

23. "Statement of Former Senator Gerry." *The News-Tribune*, n.d.

24. "Smith is Endorsed by R.I. Democrats," *The News-Tribune*, May 2, 1932; "Gov. Roosevelt Anchors at Stonington, Conn.," July 13, 1932; "Former Gov. Al Smith Visits Providence," June 14, 1932; "McGrath at Al Smith Conference in N.Y."; June 9, 1932; "McGrath on Board Roosevelt's Yacht," July 13, 1932.

25. FDR's Stonington visit sealed Rhode Island's allegiance to him. "R.I. Promised to Roosevelt," *Boston Herald*, July 13, 1932; "R.I. Democrats Pledge Aid to Gov. Roosevelt," *Pawtucket Times*, July 13, 1932; "Roosevelt Looks for R.I. Victory, He Tells McGrath," *Providence Journal*, July 13, 1932.

26. "400 R.I. Democrats at Victory Dinner," *Providence Journal*, January 15, 1932; "Democrats' Victory Dinner Sounds Keynote of Triumph in November," *The News-Tribune*, January 15, 1932; "Democrats Hail Stand of Smith as Leaving Way Clear to Aid Candidacy," *The News-Tribune*, February 9, 1932; "Gerry Says R.I. Democrats Will Support Party Nominee," *Pawtucket Times*, July 2, 1932; "Statement of Former Senator Gerry," *The News Tribune*, n.d.; "R.I. Delegates Are Gratified at Wet Plank: Former Senator Gerry is Praised by Egan for His Efforts," *News-Tribune*, June 30, 1932; "Rhode Island Group Stands Resolutely with Al Smith," *News-Tribune*, July 1, 1932, 1; "Gerry Seconds Nomination of Smith to Head the Ticket: Declares Rhode Island Loves Him More than in 1928 Because of his Greatness in Defeat," *News-Tribune*, July 1, 1932.

27. Rhode Islanders gave Roosevelt a 27,058 plurality over Herbert Hoover in 1932. Kyvig, *Repealing National Prohibition*, 156–157. Louis W. Cappelli, *Manual with Rules and Orders for the Use of the General Assembly of the State of Rhode Island, 1933–1934* (Providence: E.L. Freeman Company, 1934), 234–235.

28. Kyvig, *Repealing National Prohibition.*, 158.

29. The textile industry suffered severely from worldwide depression. The state's reliance upon textile manufacturing made it especially vulnerable to layoffs and walkouts. From 1923 to the years prior to World War II, employment fell from 76,000 to 59,000. Jennings, 131–132; William G. McLoughlin *Rhode Island: A History* (New York: W. W. Norton, 1986), 196–197.

30. Jennings, 143.

31. "R.I. Delegates Plan to Start Return Trip," *News-Tribune*, July 2, 1932.

32. Erwin L. Levine. *Theodore Francis Green: The Washington Years, 1937–1960* (Providence: Brown University Press, 1971), 7.

33. According to a *Hartford Courant* editorial writer, Rhode Island should be commended for "boldly set[ting] itself in defiance of the law of the land, not by the will of its Legislature but by the will of its people"; "Rhode Island and Prohibition" as quoted in the *Providence Journal*, March 6, 1932.

34. "Beer Control Bill is Ready for Assembly," *News Tribune*, April 3, 1933.

35. "The Democratic State Platform 1932," J. Howard McGrath Collection, Special and Archival Collections, Providence College, Providence.

36. The Commission called for a "Beer Act" to mollify Rhode Islanders until repeal went into effect. This legislation was passed by April 7. It also authorized the formation of the Alcoholic Beverage Commission, which outlined the rules and regulations for Rhode Island Manufacturers including a stipulation that Rhode Island businesses must purchase beer exclusively from state dealers. From April 6 to January 25, 1934, the state collected $107,106.37 in service charges from the direct sale of liquor. "Liquor Board Calls for Saloon's Return," *Providence Journal*, February 6, 1934.

37. Levine, *Theodore Francis Green: Washington Years*, 150–151.

38. The governor then oversaw the formation of a five-person board, which directed the dispensing of liquor permits to five classes of drinking establishments, including restaurants and saloons. Ironically, the board reinstated home rule by allotting a portion of the beer tax to the cities and towns. To highlight the "bipartisanship" of the board, Green directed them to "let no outside influence affect your conclusions and recommendations." In reality, however, Green-ally J. Howard McGrath held sway with the Rhode Island Retail Alcoholic Beverage Association and was a prominent member on the ad hoc five-person board. Levine, 150–151; "State Control Planned to Ban Evils of Liquor," *News Tribune*, February 7, 1933; "R.I. Liquor Board Agrees on Repeal Convention Plan," *Pawtucket Times*, February 22, 1933; "Beer Control Bill is Ready for Assembly," *News Tribune*, April 3, 1933; *Report of the Bi-Partisan Commission to Study Pending Legislation in Congress Affecting the Manufacture, Possession, Transportation and Sale of Alcoholic Beverages and the Amendment and Repeal of the XVIIIth Amendment to the Constitution as made to the General Assembly March 14, 1933* (Providence: The Oxford Press, 1933).

39. "J. Howard McGrath in Line for U.S. District Attorney," *Providence Sunday Journal*, June 11, 1933; "McGrath Mentioned for Federal Post," *Providence Evening Bulletin*, June 10, 1933.

40. "United States Senator Election, 1936," *Providence Journal, Almanac 1937: A Reference Book for the State of Rhode Island* (Providence: The Providence Journal Co., 1937), 188–190.

41. Levine, *Theodore Francis Green: Rhode Island Years*, 177.

Chapter 4

1. "Rettich and Prosecutor are Study in Contrast," *Boston Traveler*, May 2, 1935, 6.

2. David Critchley, *The Origin of Organized Crime in America: The New York City Mafia, 1891–1931* (New York: Routledge, 2009), 73.

3. "Mystery Blonde Linked with Mob: 15,000 Go to Warwick for Glimpse of Villa," *Boston Globe*, May 6, 1935; John I. Taylor, Jr., "Bay State Man Sought in Slaying of One Gangster: Watch for Him in Worcester," *Boston Evening Globe*, May 2, 1935, 1; "Postal Robbery Hearing Finished," *Providence Journal*, May 10, 1935, 2.

4. Danny Walsh, local bootlegger, was supposedly held hostage by unnamed assailants. His brother Joseph allegedly paid $40,000 in exchange for Walsh, who never materialized. Rumors that his body was encased in cement and tossed off the coast of Block Island persist to this day. "Authorities Find Huge Arsenal in Warwick House," *Providence Journal*, April 28, 1935.

5. "Nearly Score of Crimes Declared Near Solution in Merola Slaying Raids," *Providence Sunday Journal*, April 28, 1935.

6. "Blackstone Forum Radio Address," Folder, "Crime Situation, Blackstone Forum," October 16, 1936, J. Howard McGrath Papers, Harry S Truman Presidential Library, Independence, MO.

7. The Volstead Act was drawn up by Republican congressman Andrew J. Volstead in order to enforce the provisions of the Eighteenth Amendment. It concurrently forbade the advertisement of intoxicating liquor, and authorized the confiscation of all vehicles used to transport the illegal substances. It was passed over an ailing President Wilson's veto. The act did not ban the use of intoxicating liquors in private homes. Edward Behr, *Prohibition: Thirteen Years That Changed America* (New York: Arcade, 2011), 78.

8. James Howard McGrath, "Broadcast Crime," J. Howard McGrath Papers, Harry S Truman Presidential Library, Independence, MO.

9. Patrick Hurley, "Opening Session," *Proceedings of the Attorney General's Conference on Crime*, December 10–13, 1934.

10. Henry L. Stimson, "An Address by Honorable Henry L. Stimson," *Proceedings of the Attorney General's Conference on Crime*, 11.

11. Franklin Delano Roosevelt, "An Address by His Excellency Franklin Delano Roosevelt," *Proceedings of the Attorney General's Conference on Crime*, 18–19.

12. Kenneth O'Reilly, "A New Deal for the FBI: The Roosevelt Administration, Crime Control, and National Security," *The Journal of American History* 69, no. 3 (December 1982): 642; "U.S. Officials to Seek Death for Rettich: U.S. to Invoke Lindbergh Law," *Boston Globe*, May 2, 1935.

13. Stimson, 8.

14. J. Edgar Hoover, "Detection and Apprehension, An Address by John Edgar Hoover," *Proceedings of the Attorney General's Conference on Crime*, Washington, D.C., December 10–13, 30.

15. J. Edgar Hoover, "Detection and Apprehension, An Address by John Edgar Hoover," *Proceedings of the Attorney General's Conference on Crime*, Washington, D.C., December 10–13, 1934, 30.

16. Edward J. Murphy, "Danny Walsh—What Happened: 25 Years after his Mysterious Disappearance State's Most Intriguing Mystery Still Unsolved," *Providence Sunday Journal*, February 2, 1958.

17. "Nearly Score of Crimes Declared Near Solution in Merola Slaying Raids: Authorities Find Huge Arsenal in Warwick House," *Providence Sunday Journal*, April 28, 1935.

18. The workers began searching the Warwick Neck home of Carl Rettich in April 1935 for the stolen Fall River money, and also dug up a small patch of Rettich's land in the hope of discovering the body of Danny Walsh. "Walsh's Body Sought Near Hideout of Gang after Tip by Prisoner," *Providence Evening Bulletin*, May 1, 1935.

19. Donald D'Amato, "Warwick Neck's 'Crime Castle,'" *Providence Journal*, 1985, 59.

20. *Ibid.*

21. Apparently, Rettich paid Walsh the $30,000, and Walsh hosted a get-together to celebrate Rettich's rite of passage for "making good" on his debts. "Bandit Gang 'Finger Man' Received Degree at Brown," *Evening Bulletin*, May 1, 1935; Murphy, "Danny Walsh—What Happened," *Providence Journal* (see above).

22. "Pin Murder on Rettich Gang," *Boston Post*, May 1, 1935.

23. *Ibid.*

24. Rettich had originally secured a boat, where the cash was to be hidden, but he found its owner suspect, and decided to postpone the robbery. As a result, Hornstein had to obtain new license plates, since the previous registration would expire by late January, the date whereby Rettich and his gang would steal the loot from the Fall River brinks truck. "*U.S. v. Rettich*: #12953," The National Archives, Waltham, MA.

25. "Weather Claims About 50 Lives," *Fall River Herald*, January 22, 1935, 1; "Testimony of Charles Wood," *U.S. v. Charles Harrigan*, # 12953, The National Archives, Waltham, MA.

26. Alfred J. Monahan, "Net Tautens as Mobmen Talk: Rettich Held in $125,000 to Avert Release—Steele Freed Under Heavy Guard: Gangdom Picks Pair for Death," Folder, "Clippings, 1935–1940," *Boston Globe*, May 1, 1935, 1, 12, J. Howard McGrath Collection, Special and Archival Collections, Providence College, Providence.

27. Fisher informed Hornstein that he could not obtain the money from Rettich for at least a few weeks, so he instead decided to borrow money from his sister Helen. "Testimony of Joseph Fisher," "Testimony of Herbert Hornstein," *United States of America v. Carl Rettich, Thomas Dugan, Charles Harrigan and John McGlone*, # 12953 and 12956, The National Archives, Waltham, MA.

28. "U.S. Outlines Case Against Rettich Gang," *Providence News-Tribune*, June 25, 1935.

29. "Mail Robbery Linked with Merola Slaying," *Providence Journal*, April 27, 1935.

30. *Ibid.*

31. "Pin Murder on Rettich Gang," *The Boston Post*, May 1, 1935.

32. Merola was a small-time thief; fined $400 for stealing two automobiles, he also figured prominently in an illegal gambling ring as a "strong-arm man." "Mail Robbery Linked with Merola Slaying," *Providence Journal*, April 27, 1935.

33. *Ibid.*

34. His death was ruled a homicide. "Trace Mail Loot to Rettich Gang," *Boston Post*, May 7, 1935; "Medical Examiner's Certificate of Death: Andino Merola," Norfolk County, Commonwealth of Massachusetts, Wrentham, MA.

35. "Walsh-Rettich Link is Found in Seized Ledgers," *Providence Evening Bulletin*, May 9, 1935

36. "Merola Buried as the Band Plays," *Providence Journal*, May 1, 1935.

37. Charles Simmons, "Czar Put on Scene of Mail Robbery: Federal Agents in Hub Accuse Mansion Head," *Boston Traveler*, May 1, 1935, 1.

38. "Officials Hoping to Pin Merola's Death on Rettich," *Providence Journal*, May 2, 1935, 1.

39. *Ibid.*

40. "Rettich in Custody: Faces Long Grilling," *Boston Globe*, April 30, 1935.

41. "Rettich Surrenders Here; $10,000 More Fall River Loot Dug Up at Warwick," *Providence Journal*, April 30, 1935, 1; "Rettich in Custody; Faces Long Grilling," *Providence Journal*, April 30, 1935.

42. Nat A. Barrows, "Hospital Visit Nets Gangster," *Boston Globe*, May 1, 1935.

43. *Ibid.*

44. Alfred J. Monahan, "Police Find New Gang Arsenal: Truck Linked with Holdup; Weapons Uncovered in Private Home; Police in Warwick Face Inquiry," *Boston Globe*, May 5, 1935.

45. "Police Shake Up Follows Liquor Drive in Warwick," *Providence Journal*, February 28 1932, 1; "Warwick Police Board Under Fire," *Providence Journal*, October 3, 1935, 1.

46. "Green to Insist Warwick Mayor Control Police," *Providence Journal*, May 13, 1935, 1.

47. "Crime Castle: Woman Tells of Rettich's Doings," *Providence Journal*, May 9, 1935, 1.

48. "Finish Roundup of Rettich Gang: 24th Arrest Made—Leaders Will Face Indictment for Murder and Kidnapping," *Boston Post*, May 2, 1935.

49. "Valuable Gems Discovered in Secret Vault," *Daily News*, May 3, 1935.

50. "Rettich Trial Opens as Defense Motions Fail in Boston Court," *Providence Evening Bulletin*, June 18, 1935.

51. Rettich also claimed that Dugan and McGlone stayed at his home three days prior to the robbery, and that Merola and Fisher asked him to borrow his truck "to move furniture the next day." He further alleged that he remained at "the wireless station … four or five hours" while the crime was being committed. Edward J. Kelley, "Carl Rettich Denies He took any Part in Mail Truck Robbery: Says He was in Warwick in Business Conference at Time of Crime," *Providence Journal*, July 4, 1935, 1.

52. Edward J. Kelley, "Rettich Trial Nears Close; Jury to Get Case on Wednesday," *Providence Journal*, July 6, 1935.

53. Edward Fitzgerald, "Fitzpatrick Calls Hornstein 'Judas' in Plea for Rettich," *News-Tribune*, July 9, 1935; Chester M. Potter, "Hornstein Bitterly Scored; U.S. Drops Case against Rubins," *Providence Evening Bulletin*, July 9, 1935.

54. Of note, the *Tribune* was owned by wealthy Democrat senator Peter Goelet Gerry, neighbor of Rettich, and mentor of J. Howard McGrath. The *Tribune* served as the Demo-

cratic sounding board and a balance to the Republican-based *Providence Journal.* "An Inspiring Victory," *Providence News-Tribune,* July 11, 1935.

55. Letter from James Breslin, post office inspector in charge, to J. Howard McGrath, September 6, 1940, Folder, "Resignations," Special and Archival Collections, Providence College, Providence.

56. The correction's officer noted Rettich's "Dull-Normal intelligence, mental age 13 years and 7 months; I.Q. 85," and recommended "maximum supervision." Admission Summary: Carl Rettich, Reg. # 46638-A," August 3, 1935, United States Penitentiary, Atlanta, Memorandum to the Warden, U.S. Penitentiary, Alcatraz, California, May 18, 1943, Department of Justice, San Francisco Penitentiary, San Francisco.

57. Rettich, Reg. # 46638-A, August 3, 1935.

58. Tom Mooney, "Mystery Solved? Remains could be lost rum-runner. Bones Found Near Church Could End 83-year saga of Danny Walsh," *Providence Journal,* December 16, 2016.

Chapter 5

1. McGrath blamed the defeat on Governor Quinn's fight with O'Hara and also cited his "several attacks on the Supreme and Superior courts," his bold move against O'Hara, which resulted in the elimination of his newspaper, the *News-Tribune* ("if the paper had continued to exist it would necessarily be Democratic" despite O'Hara's "vicious attacks on everybody who failed to do his bidding") and the governor's penchant for "surround[ing] himself with friends of no previous standing." Letter from J. Howard McGrath to James Farley, December 3, 1938, Official File (OF 300), Democratic National Committee, Franklin Delano Roosevelt Presidential Library, Hyde Park, NY; Copy of Letter in McGrath's File, Folder, "James A. Farley 1938," J. Howard McGrath Collection, Special and Archival Collections, Providence College, Providence.

2. "McGrath to Higgins," Folder, "Higgins," April 7, 28, 1937, J. Howard McGrath Collection, Special and Archival Collections, Providence College, Providence.

3. "Theodore Francis Green to James Farley," Folder 19, "Democratic National Committee: January–May 1939," Franklin Delano Roosevelt Presidential Library, Hyde Park, N.Y., January 4, 1939.

4. William Jennings, "The Prince of Pawtucket" (PhD diss., Providence College, 1985), 282.

5. McGrath wrote Peter Gerry, the former owner of the *Tribune,* regretting Gerry's loss of the paper, but praising the dedication of his former mentor. "We all owe you a debt of gratitude," since "if it had not been for the work done by the paper, our party would certainly not be as advanced in this State as it is." Letter, J. Howard McGrath to the Honorable Peter G. Gerry, March 20, 1937, Folder, "Gerry Peter G.," J. Howard McGrath Collection, Special and Archival Collections, Providence College, Providence; Jennings, "The Prince of Pawtucket," 281.

6. Jennings, "The Prince of Pawtucket," 283.

7. Mary C. N. Tanner, "Bridges Across the Chasm of Despair: The Depression Years in Rhode Island," *Rhode Island Yearbook* (1971), H-204.

8. *Ibid.,* H-204–205.

9. Leonard Jerome was the maternal grandfather of Winston Churchill. Steven A. Reiss, *The Sport Kings and the Kings of Crime: Horse Racing, Politics, and Organized Crime in New York, 1865–1913* (Syracuse: Syracuse University Press, 2011), 35–36.

10. *Ibid.,* 35.

11. As an example, in 1938, federal agents tracked down felon Raymond Patriarca at Narragansett Parkway on the evening of August 13, 1938, claiming that he stole between $15,000 and $20,000 worth of precious gemstones from a Boston, Massachusetts, jewelry establishment, Daniel Solder and Sons, Inc. However, according to William H. Edwards, "the association [Racing] in turn salved the conscience of objectors by presenting them with a gift to charity in the amount of $38,000." William H. Edwards, "Race Track 'War,'" *Rhode Island Yearbook,* 1971, H-210; "Patriarca Held for Hub Holdup," *Providence Journal,* August 14, 1938.

12. In an interview with former Speaker of the House Matthew Smith in 1972, Governor Quinn explained that Democratic reformers had lobbied to bring important legislation before the people, including a coveted constitutional convention. The final bill was a compromise between two earlier bills. Matthew J. Smith, "Interview with Judge Robert E. Quinn," July 31, August 7, 1972, Special and Archival Collections, Providence College; Vernon Norton, "The Pay-Off: An Epic in Rhode Island Politics or Eight Months with Walter E. O'Hara," published by author, 1941, Rhode Island Historical Society, Providence.

13. Norton, "The Pay-Off.

14. Reiss, *Sport Kings,* xiii.

15. Zechariah Chafee, *State House Versus Pent House: Legal Problems of the Rhode Island Race Track Row* (Providence: The Booke Shop, 1937), 2.

16. *Ibid.;* "Notables Attend Opening of Nar-

ragansett Race Track," *News-Tribune*, June 20, 1935.

17. O'Hara had reason to be proud. The park was the first to introduce the so-called "photo-finish" state-of-the-art photography that determined the winner in contested races, and the electronic starting gate, which prompted eager announcers to shout "and they're off." With this sort of state-of-the-art technology Narragansett Race Track quite possibly could have supplanted the more established parks in New York and New Jersey as destinations for wealthy horse aficionados. Jennings, "The Prince of Pawtucket," 283.

18. Following Quinn's defeat in 1938, Republican governor William Henry Vanderbilt conducted an investigation into alleged vote fraud in the 1936 Pawtucket elections, which forever tainted the reputation of Mayor Thomas P. McCoy, preventing his nomination for state office (see Chapter 7).

19. Governor Green was attending the inauguration of newly-elected President Franklin Delano Roosevelt in Washington, D.C. M. Randolph Flather, "Don't Bank on It: Bank Holiday for Rhode Island for Today, March 4 ordered by Acting Governor Quinn," *Rhode Island Yearbook, 1971*, H-198.

20. Governor Green was attending the inauguration of newly-elected President Franklin Delano Roosevelt in Washington, D.C. *Ibid.*

21. "McCoy Withdraws Racetrack Threat: Pawtucket Officials Visit Site, Decide Not to Insist Upon Labor from That City," *Providence Journal*, June 6, 1934, 1.

22. Since the Police Commission controversy, Supreme Court Judge Francis Condon was wary of McGrath's connivances with Central Falls boss Andrew Sherry. Jennings, "The Prince of Pawtucket," 201.

23. *Ibid.*, 283.

24. "Risks Political Future to Block Track Manager," *Providence Journal*, October 21, 1937, 1.

25. Zechariah Chafee, Jr., *State House Versus Pent House: Legal Problems of the Rhode Island Race-Track Row* (Providence: The Booke Shop, 1937), 3.

26. Jennings, "The Prince of Pawtucket," 260–261.

27. Chafee Jr., *State House versus Pent House*, 25–26.

28. "Track's Manager Guilty of Baiting State's Steward," *Providence Journal*, September 4, 1937, 1; "Board Ruling to Protect Public Cause of O'Hara Dispute," *Providence Journal*, September 5, 1937; "Six Counts Filed, Hearing Set for 1 P.M. Tomorrow," *Providence Journal*, September 9, 1937; "Quinn Wants Track License Revoked on 'Cussing' Charge: Order out

in Letters to Kiernan," *News-Tribune*, September 11, 1937.

29. "Track Manager Guilty," September 4, 1937; "Quinn Wants Track License Revoked," September 9, 1937.

30. The Racing Division subsequently exonerated O'Hara, ruling that "the fair preponderance of evidence does not show that the said Narragansett Racing Association, Inc., violated rule 463 of said division." "Board Ruling to Protect Public Cause," September 5, 1937.

31. "Track's Manager Guilty of Baiting State's Steward," *Providence Journal*, September 4, 1937, 1.

32. "Appendix E: Editorials and Comments from *Providence Journal*: Politicians and the Race-Track is the State Running the Track or is the Track Running the State," as quoted in Zechariah Chafee, *State House versus Pent House: Legal Problems of the Rhode Island Race Track Row* (Providence: The Booke Shop, 1937), 120–121.

33. "Risks Political Future to Block Track Manager," *Providence Journal*, October 21, 1937.

34. *Ibid.*, 8.

35. In the first of two Supreme Court cases, *Narragansett Racing Ass'n Inc. v. Kiernan et al.*, # 678, September 13, 1937, the justices ruled that the term "for cause" required substantial grounds in order to "support such action [dismissing O'Hara]." Thus, the court handed down a *per curiam* decision, which rejected Narragansett Racing Commissioner Kiernan's petition to "remove forthwith Walter E. O'Hara as an employee and official of said Narragansett racing Association, Inc." The justices ruled that the Racing Commission did not have enough proof to warrant O'Hara's removal. The court's ruling contradicted Attorney General John Hartigan, who believed final authority to remove O'Hara rested with the Racing Commission. *Narragansett Racing Ass'n v. Kiernan et al.*, # 678. *The Atlantic Reporter*, 1938; "Decision of Court Upholds O'Hara in Doorley Dispute: Evidence for Ouster not Legal," *News-Tribune*, September 13, 1937, Folder, "Clippings, 1935–1940," J. Howard McGrath Collection, Special and Archival Collections, Providence College, Providence.

36. "Eddie Higgins to J. Howard McGrath," July 11, 1937, Folder, "Higgins," J. Howard McGrath Collection, Special and Archival Collections, Providence College, Providence.

37. Governor Quinn was not the first Rhode Island executive to employ the National Guard to silence public disturbances. In 1925, then-governor Emory San Souci had marshalled the Guard to put down striking textile workers in the Blackstone Valley/Pawtuxet Valley.

38. James P. McCaffrey, "Troops Will Stop

Opening of Racing at Narragansett," *New York Times*, October 18, 1937.

39. "Commission Orders Audit of Race Track's Books; Quinn Says O'Hara is Out: Corps of Auditors to Probe Finances at 10 O' Clock Today," *Providence Journal*, September 5, 1937.

40. "Retail Store Trade Resumed Here after Labor Agreement is Reached in Parley with Director M'Mahon," *News-Tribune*, March 23, 1937.

41. Initially targeting the Outlet Company, Mr. Sylvia and the CIO eventually agreed to meet with the six major retailers. According to McGrath's summation of the case, "they [the Providence retailers] regarded the demands against the Outlet Company as demands against all of them," "Pre-1945 Legal Files," Folder 58, Memorandum of Department Store Labor Controversy, n.d., J. Howard McGrath Collection, Special and Archival Collections, Providence College, Providence.

42. McGrath's office collected the above amount from Cherry & Webb Company, the Shepard Company, the Outlet Company, the Boston Store, and Gladdings, Inc., all members of the Providence Department Store Retailers. "Retail Trade Board," Folder 58, "Legal Files," J. Howard McGrath Collection, Special and Archival Collections, Providence College, Providence.

43. "Retail Trade Board," Folder 58.

44. Edward J. Higgins to J. Howard McGrath, May 8, 1939, J. Howard McGrath to Edward J. Higgins, May 9, 1939, Folder 677, "Higgins," J. Howard McGrath Collection, Special and Archival Collections, Providence College, Providence.

45. From Mary M. McVey to McGrath, Frank Crook, Inc.; "Will of Frank F. Crook," December 31, 1948; "State of Rhode Island and Providence Plantations, Inventory (Resident Decedent)," General Laws, 1938, Chapter 43. December 1, 1950, date of death, Folder, "Frank Crook," J. Howard McGrath Collection, Special and Archival Collections, Providence College, Providence; "Conference Francis Crook and Edward J. Higgins," December 15, 1939, Folder 23, "Higgins—Correspondence—Wiretapping Case, 1939–1940," Edward J. Higgins Papers, Special and Archival Collections, Providence College, Providence.

46. Letter from Assistant to the Attorney General Joseph B. Keenan to J. Howard McGrath, May 22, 1937, J. Howard McGrath Collection, Special and Archival Collections, Providence College, Providence.

47. "Report from J. Howard McGrath to Assistant to the Attorney General Joseph B. Keenan," May 25, 1937. J. Howard McGrath

Collection, Special and Archival Collections, Providence College, Providence.

48. Letter from Joseph B. Keenan to John H. Rooney, Esquire, J. Howard McGrath Collection, Special and Archival Collections, Providence.

49. "Coercion," *News-Tribune*, August 18, 1937.

50. Letter from J. Howard McGrath to Eddie Higgins, August 19, 1937, J. Howard McGrath Collection, Special and Archival Collections, Providence College, Providence.

51. Letter from J. Howard McGrath to Assistant to the Attorney General Joseph B. Keenan, August 27, 1937, J. Howard McGrath Collection, Special and Archival Collections, Providence College, Providence.

52. "Risks Political Future to Block Track Manager: Governor Charges O'Hara Paid," *Providence Journal*, October 21, 1937, 1.

53. "McGrath to Drop Federal Charges on Track Gifts," *Providence Journal*, August 7, 1938; "McGrath Quashes Track Indictment," *Providence Journal*, August 10, 1938.

54. "McGrath to Drop Federal Charges," August 7, 1938; "McGrath Quashes," August 10, 1938.; "Race Track Political Contributions," *Providence Journal*, August 10, 1938.

55. Letter from J. Howard McGrath to Brien McMahon, Department of Justice, October 22, 1937, J. Howard McGrath Collection, Special and Archival Collections, Providence College, Providence.

56. He added that "the Court did not approve of the procedure followed by the Grand Jury in obtaining an audit of the books of the defendant corporation by accountants who worked under the supervision of a committee." "McGrath to Drop Federal Charges on Track Gifts," *Providence Journal*, August 7, 1938; "McGrath Quashes Track Indictment," *Providence Journal*, August 10, 1938.

57. For one, at various points during the jury's deliberations, only five of the required 16-member minimum required by law were sitting in judgment. More importantly, the language in the federal law proved troublesome for the jury, which found no statement expressly barring monetary contributions to a political committee. "McGrath to Drop Federal Charges on Track Gifts," *The Providence Journal*, August 7, 1938, 1; "Race Track Political Contributions," *Providence Journal*, August 10, 1938.

58. "Dooley Becomes Acting President Pending Election," *Providence Journal*, February 10, 1938.

59. "Race Track Political Contributions," *Providence Journal*, August 10, 1938, 8.

60. Letter from J. Howard McGrath to David Stern, J. Howard McGrath Collection, Special

and Archival Collections, Providence College, Providence.

61. In a letter to McGrath, Stern observed, "I honestly feel that the opportunity to give Providence a liberal newspaper is far from dead. I think the *Journal* will have to kill the *Star-Tribune*. And after the City has been under the dominance of one paper for a few months I think it will be far easier to get backing than it was last week." Letter to McGrath from Tom Stern," *Philadelphia Record*; Memorandum to Providence Journal Company, May 12, 1938; "Stern Withdraws Offer," *New York Times*, December 19, 1937; "Superior Court of the State of Rhode Island for the Counties of Providence and Bristol," *Walter E. O'Hara v. Providence Tribune, Co.*, Eq. # 14752, May 13, 1938, Folder 129, J. Howard McGrath Collection, Special and Archival Collections, Providence College, Providence.

62. "O'Hara Forwards Apology to Quinn for All Attacks," *Providence Journal*, March 29, 1938, 1.

63. *Ibid.*

64. Eddie Higgins to J. Howard McGrath, J. Howard McGrath Collection, Special and Archival Collections, Providence College, Providence.

65. "Walter E. O'Hara Killed in Crash," *Taunton Daily Gazette*, March 1, 1941; "Walter E. O'Hara, Former Narragansett Park Chief, Killed in Automobile Accident," *Providence Journal*, March 1, 1941; "Walter E. O'Hara Funeral is Held; Personal Estate Estimated at $50,000," *Providence Journal*, March 4, 1941; "Criminal Negligence Not Found in O'Hara Death; Judge Austin Reports," *Taunton Daily Gazette*, March 14, 1941.

66. Before the 1936 and 1938 elections, Rhode Island notables wrote Democratic National Chairman James Farley about the problems with local Democratic Party. See "Letters to Farley from James Kiernan, John M. Flynn, Francis B. Condon, Theodore Francis Green, Thomas Kennelly, and J. Howard McGrath, July–September 1936, December 1938," Folder, "Rhode Island," Democratic National Committee (OF 300), Franklin D. Roosevelt Presidential Library, Hyde Park, NY; Folder, "James A. Farley 1938," J. Howard McGrath Collection, Special and Archival Collections, Providence College, Providence.

Chapter 6

1. "Mayor McCoy's Phone Tapped; Wires Traced to Nearby Home; Police Quiz Edward L. Freeman," *Providence Journal*, November 28, 1939, 1.

2. Roy Olmstead, formerly a law enforcement officer, ran a bootlegging operation out of Seattle. Local police suspected him of wrongdoing so installed electronic surveillance devices on his home telephone lines. Intercepted conversations between Olmstead and his clients verified his guilt, but Olmstead argued that evidence obtained through the use of wiretaps violated his Fourth Amendment rights, and was thus inadmissible in court. The court rejected Olmstead's plea, so he appealed. The subsequent Supreme Court ruling upheld the decision of the lower court, arguing that Seattle police used proper methods in the subjugation of the criminal since "the evidence was secured by the use of the sense of hearing and that only." *Olmstead v. U.S.* 277 U.S. 438 (1928) http//supreme.justia.com, accessed October 27, 2017.

3. "Risks Political Future to Block Track Manager: Names McCoy, Handy, Pelkey as Recipients of Checks of up to $5000 Each," *Providence Journal*, October 21, 1937, 1; Jennings, "The Prince of Pawtucket," 285.

4. Jennings, "The Prince of Pawtucket, 285–286; Duane Lockard, *New England State Politics* (Chicago: Henry Regnery Company, Gateway Edition, 1959), 186.

5. William McLoughlin, *Rhode Island: A History* (New York: W. W. Norton, 1986), 195–197.

6. Smith, "The Real McCoy," 67; Jennings, "The Prince of Pawtucket," 130.

7. William A. Hasenfus, "Vanderbilt, William Henry," *Scribner Encyclopedia of American Lives*, Vol. 1, 1981–1985, 814–815.

8. *Ibid.*

9. Patrick T. Conley, *Rhode Island in Rhetoric and Reflection: Public Addresses and Essays* (Providence: Rhode Island Publication Society, 2002), 9.

10. *Ibid.*

11. According to J. R. Espinosa, of the Senate Interstate Commerce Subcommittee, Jackvony had been "objectionable to Mr. Vanderbilt [as a candidate for Attorney General] and they had a row about it." "Transcript of Louis Jackvony as transcribed by J. R. Espinosa," April 12, 1940, Senate Interstate Commerce Commission, Folder 25, "Wiretapping Hearing Testimony 1940," Edward J. Higgins Papers, Special and Archival Collections, Providence College, Providence.

12. "Efforts to Probe Jackvony Charge Blocked in the House," *Providence Journal*, January 18, 1930, 1.

13. Folder 20, "Committee on Election Frauds and Corrupt Practices, 1939–1940," William Henry Vanderbilt Papers, Archives and Manuscripts, University of Rhode Island, Kingstown.

14. Smith, "The Real McCoy," 76.

15. William Jennings, "The Prince of Pawtucket," 335; "Senate Votes $50,000 in Pawtucket Prove; House to Act Friday," *Providence Journal*, January 10, 1940, 1; "Jackvony to Get $50,000 to Probe Pawtucket Vote, "*Providence Journal*, January 18, 1940, 1; "J.R. Espinosa, "Wiretapping," April 12, 1940, 1–2; J. Howard McGrath Collection, Special and Archival Collections, Providence College, Providence.

16. Jennings, "The Prince of Pawtucket," 323–324; Folder 340, "Metcalf, Jesse H.," MSS 605, David Patten Papers, Rhode Island Historical Society, Providence; "Investigation of Alleged Wire Tapping: Hearings Before a Subcommittee of the Committee on Interstate Commerce, United States Senate, 76th Congress, 3rd Session, Pursuant to S. Res. 224, Part I" (Washington, D.C.: United States Government Printing Office), "Testimony of Louis V. Jackvony," 3–31, 271–278, Folder 26, "Wiretapping Hearing Testimony Photographs," Papers of Edward J. Higgins, Special and Archival Collections, Providence College, Providence.

17. U.S. Senate, "Testimony of William H. Vanderbilt," *Hearings Before a Subcommittee of the Committee of Interstate Commerce*, Part I, Sen. Res. 224, 222, "Correspondence: J. Howard McGrath, 1940," Papers of Edward J. Higgins, Special and Archival Collection, Providence College, Providence.

18. "Jackvony to Get $50,000 to Probe Pawtucket Vote," *Providence Journal*, January 18, 1940, 1; "Senate Votes $50,000 in Pawtucket Probe; House to Act Friday," *Providence Journal*, January 10, 1940, 1; "Jackvony Presents Goring Memo to Senate Wire-Tap Probers," *Providence Journal*, May 22, 1940; Jennings, 345; U.S. Senate, "Testimony of Louis Jackvony," 9–10, J. Howard McGrath Collection, Special and Archival Collections, Providence College, Providence.

19. U.S. Senate, "Testimony of Jonathan H. Harwood," "Investigation of Alleged Wire Tapping: Hearings before a Subcommittee of the Committee on Interstate Commerce, United States Senate, 76th Congress, 3rd Session, Pursuant to S. Res. 224," Folder 26, "Wiretapping: Hearing Testimony, Photographs, Apr. 1940," 126–127. Edward J. Higgins Collection, Special and Archival Collections, Providence College, Providence.

20. "Partial Report and recommendation of the September Grand Jury," J. Howard McGrath Collection, Special and Archival Collections, Providence College, Providence, 1–2.

21. "Chronological History of Rhode Island," *Journal Bulletin Almanac* (Providence: Providence Journal, Circulation Dept., 1941), 29; Chapter 2194, *1935–1936. Public Laws of the State of Rhode Island and Providence Plantations* (Providence: The Oxford Press, 1936), 54–61.

22. "Partial Report and Recommendation of the September Grand Jury," J. Howard McGrath Collection, Special and Archival Collections, Providence College, Providence.

23. *Ibid.*; *1935–1936. Public Laws of the State of Rhode Island and Providence Plantation* (Providence: The Oxford Press, 1936), 54–61.

24. According to the Pawtucket police report, Gillis noted that the work was unprofessional since the wire "lacks the usual twist." Notes, "On November 27, 1939," Folder, "Pawtucket Police Dept.—Miscellaneous Report," Edward J. Higgins Papers, Special and Archival Collections, Providence College, Providence.

25. Freeman had no knowledge of Barton's activities since he and his family were vacationing at their summer home in Bristol. He rented a room in his Pawtucket residence to Barton. Folder 40, "Pawtucket Police Dept. Miscellaneous Report," Edward J. Higgins Collection, Special and Archival Collections, Providence College, Providence; "Wiretapping: Copy of Pawtucket Police Department, Miscellaneous Report—Reference to Telephone of Mayor McCoy being Tapped," November 1939, Papers of Edward J. Higgins, Special and Archival Collections, Providence College, Providence, as quoted in Debra A. Mulligan, "Political Rivalry in Rhode Island: William H. Vanderbilt vs. J. Howard McGrath: The Wiretapping Case," *Massachusetts Journal of History* (2007): 59–61.

26. Hogan's most recent client was the notorious Walter O'Hara, of Narragansett Race Track fame.

27. Freeman would later testify that his close friend Harold Shippee approached him about renting his upstairs room to a Lee Edward Barton. Barton was identified as an employee of Shippee's client, Walter Meiss. Freeman discussed the matter with his wife, who agreed to rent their room to Barton at $3/per day. Folder 40, "Pawtucket Police Dept. Miscellaneous Report, 1939."

28. A Robert E. L. Umbach of Miami, Florida, also boarded at the Freeman home beginning in early November 1939. According to his statement, he met Lee Edward Barton a number of times, but they "never discussed the latter's employment." Report by Inspectors Hourigan & Hutton, Folder 40, "Pawtucket Police Dept. Miscellaneous Report, 1939"; "Freeman Denies He Aided Barton in Wiretapping," *Providence Journal*, January 7, 1940, 1.

29. "Pawtucket Police Dept. Miscellaneous Report, 1939"; "Wire-Tap Inquiry to Hear Barton," *Providence Journal*, February 13, 1941, 2;

"Barton Testifies in Wiretapping," *Providence Journal*, February 15, 1941, 5.

30. "Freeman Absolved by Judge Connell in Wire-Tap Case," *Providence Journal*, January 26, 1940, 1; "Freeman Denies He Aided Barton in Wiretapping," *Providence Journal*, January 7, 1940, 1; "Notes on Wiretapping," May 2, 1940; J. Howard McGrath Collection, Special and Archival Collections, Providence College, Providence, Rhode Island.

31. Freeman brought simultaneous suits in April against the governor and the New England Telephone and Telegraph Company for $500,000 each. Vanderbilt and Freeman settled out of court for an undisclosed amount. "Writ is Served on Vanderbilt," *Providence Journal*, April 11, 1940, 1; "Freeman Papers Accuse Governor," *Providence Journal*, May 16, 1940, 2; "Governor Denies Freeman Claims," *Providence Journal*, December 17, 1940, 1; "Freeman Absolved by Judge," *Providence Journal:* The Rhode Island Constitutional Convention, 1964–1969, "Wiretapping and the Law: A Report for the Committee on Personal Liberties," Mario R. Di-Nunzio. The Rhode Island Constitutional Convention, 1964–1969, Special and Archival Collection, Providence College, Providence.

32. "Jackvony to Give Wiretap Records to Jurors," *Providence Journal*, April 12, 1940, 1.

33. McCoy pushed for McGrath's removal as state chairman, for the "sake of harmony." "Democratic State Officials Probe Pawtucket Fight," *Pawtucket Times*, April 26, 1932, 1; "M'Grath and M'Coy Clash in Pawtucket," *News-Tribune*, September 21, 1932; "McCoy's Move to Oust McGrath Menaces Democratic Harmony as State Convention is Opened," *Providence Evening Bulletin*, October 7, 1932.

34. "J. Howard McGrath to Edward J. Higgins," May 9, 1939, Folder, "Higgins," J. Howard McGrath Collection, Special and Archival Collections, Providence College, Providence.

35. Jackvony testified that he "requested Mr. McGrath to submit to me the evidence in his possession respecting Mr. Goring's activities in connection with the tapping of telephone wires," 1. "Testimony of Louis V. Jackvony," 17. *U.S. Senate Hearings*, J. Howard McGrath Collection; Affidavit Louis V. Jackvony, Folder 25, "Wiretapping Hearing Testimony," Edward J. Higgins Papers, Special and Archival Collections, Providence College, Providence.

36. "Wiretapping Paraphernalia Seized in Turks Head Raid," *Providence Journal*, December 2, 1939, 1.

37. He resided for most of the year in Portsmouth, Rhode Island.

38. "Jury to Receive Evidence Today on Wiretapping," *Providence Journal*, December 5, 1939, 1.

39. Memo to Louis V. Jackvony from Matthew Goring, December 4, 1939, J. Howard McGrath Collection, Special and Archival Collections, Providence College, Providence.

40. *Ibid.*

41. "Goring Talks, Urges Pawtucket Inquiry Be Carried Through," *Providence Journal*, December 21, 1939; "Wiretapping, Statement by Louis V. Jackvony," May 22, 1940, "Jackvony Presents Goring Memo to Senate Wire-Tap Probe," May 22, 1940, 9, Edward J. Higgins Papers, Special and Archival Collections, Providence College, Providence.

42. Letter from J. Howard McGrath to the attorney general, February 2, 1940, J. Howard McGrath Collection, Special and Archival Collections, Providence College, Providence.

43. "Governor Promises Report of Labor Survey as Aid to Solving Relief Problem," *Providence Journal*, January 3, 1940, 9.

44. "Governor Vanderbilt to Meet Members of the Committee," *Providence Journal*, March 12, 1940, William H. Vanderbilt Papers, University of Rhode Island, Kingstown; "Governor Offers to Pay Chaffee's Probers Himself," *Providence Journal*, March 13, 1940; "Chaffee Board Democrats Backs Governor in Row," *Providence Journal*, March 14, 1940; "Pay by Governor Termed Illegal," *Providence Journal*, March 21, 1940.

45. "Salaries of State Officials," *Providence Journal Almanac, 1941: A Reference Book for the State of Rhode Island* (Providence: Providence Journal, 1941), 196.

46. *Ibid.*

47. "Vanderbilt to be Dropped, Says Chiefs," *The Italo-American Tribune*, March 14, 1940.

48. From Chairman Alfred G. Chaffee to Governor William Henry Vanderbilt, March 20, 1940, William Henry Vanderbilt Papers, Archival and Manuscripts, University of Rhode Island, South Kingston.

49. From Chairman Alfred G. Chaffee to Governor William Henry Vanderbilt, March 20, 1940, From William Henry Vanderbilt to Alfred G. Chaffee, March 20, 1940; From William Henry Vanderbilt to Louis Jackvony, March 27, 1940; From Louis Jackvony to William Henry Vanderbilt, April 2, 1940; From William Henry Vanderbilt to Louis Jackvony, April 4, 1940; From Louis Jackvony to William Henry Vanderbilt, April 5, 1940. William Henry Vanderbilt Papers, Archives and Manuscripts, University of Rhode Island, North Kingstown.

50. "From Vanderbilt to Jackvony, March 27, 1940; "From Jackvony to Vanderbilt, April 2, 1940; From Vanderbilt to Jackvony, April 4, 1940; From Jackvony to Vanderbilt, April 5, 1940.

51. "Election Frauds 1939–1940: Committee

on Elections, Frauds and Corrupt Practices," January 23, 1940, 9; William Henry Vanderbilt Papers, Archives and Manuscripts, University of Rhode Island, Kingstown; "Charges of Fraud Reported Before," *Providence Journal*, February 13, 1940, 6; "Chaffee Now Laws Claim to Hand in Urging Election Laws Changes," *Providence Journal*, March 7, 1940, 6; Jennings, 337–338; "Results of Grand Jury Investigation into Municipal Corruption and Wire Tapping Contained in Final Report," *Providence Journal*, June 29, 1940.

52. The act reads as follows: "An act authorizing the use of voting-machines at state, city, and town elections, and regulating the use of the same. Chapter 2195, H 647–*1935–1936 Public Laws of the State of Rhode Island and Providence Plantations* (Providence: The Oxford Press, 1936), "Election Frauds 1938–1940: Committee on Elections, Frauds and Corrupt Practices," January 23, 1940, 9; "Charges of Fraud Reported Before," February 13, 1940, 6. William Henry Vanderbilt Papers, Archives and Manuscripts, University of Rhode Island, Kingstown.

53. "5277 Irregular Votes Charged," *Pawtucket Times*, January 23, 1940, 1; "Tentative Jury Selected to Try Little and Others for Election Conspiracy: Many of Panel Challenged by State, Defense," *Pawtucket Times*, January 26, 1940, 1, 2; Jennings, "The Prince of Pawtucket," 345–346.

54. Meanwhile, a distraught Lee Barton, running from authorities since the story broke the previous year, requested (through an intermediary) a meeting with Senator Green and District Attorney McGrath. The intermediary, according to Higgins, revealed that Barton "was on the verge of a nervous breakdown and believes that he is to be made the goat and sent to jail." The unnamed go-between also stated that Barton had been relieved of his duties at the detective agency. "Merits of Pawtucket Fraud Accusations are Undecided," *Providence Journal*, June 19, 1941. Edward J. Higgins to J. Howard McGrath, J. Howard McGrath Collection, Special and Archival Collections, Providence College, Providence.

55. In his testimony before the Senate Subcommittee, McGrath revealed that he "caused a $6900 deposit to be traced by the Federal Bureau of Investigation." Folder 26, "Statement of U.S. Attorney J. Howard McGrath," Investigation of Alleged Wire Tapping: Hearings Before a Subcommittee of the Committee on Interstate Commerce: United States Senate, 76th Congress, 3rd Session, Pursuant to S. Res. 224, April 9, 1940; "Testimony of J. Howard M'Grath," Edward J. Higgins Papers, Special and Archival Collections, Providence College, Providence.

56. Memorandum to Judge Biddle, Acting Attorney General of a Conference by J. Howard McGrath, United States Attorney for the District of Rhode Island, and Whiting Willauer, Special Assistant to the Attorney General, with Governor William H. Vanderbilt, His Secretary James B. Hart, and Horace Weller, Director of the State Department of Business Regulation, and Personal Counsel to the Governor, Folder 22, "Correspondence, J. Howard McGrath," Edward J. Higgins Papers, Special and Archival Collections, Providence College, Providence.

57. "F.B. Bielaski Paid $13,597 for Probe," *Providence Journal*, May 23, 1940, 1.

58. *Ibid.*

59. *Ibid.*

60. Despite Jackson's statement, McGrath challenged his department's position on wiretapping and vowed to alter existing laws. Accordingly, Order No. 3343, issued on March 15, prohibited the use of wiretapping by the Federal Bureau of Investigation. "Statement by U.S. Attorney J. Howard McGrath," April 9, 1940; Memorandum to Judge Biddle, Acting Attorney General of a Conference Had at about 2:00 p.m., March 27, 1940; "McGrath Drops Wire Tap Probe," *Providence Journal*, April 10, 1940, 11; Folder 22, "Higgins Correspondence, J. Howard McGrath, 1940." Edward J. Higgins Papers, Special and Archival Collection, Providence College, Providence.

61. On December 4, 1939, Jackvony wrote Matthew Goring to inquire about Barton and Bielaski. Demanding that Goring submit "all information in [his] possession with reference to wire-tapping of Mayor McCoy's home and my home," Jackvony could not understand why "it was not given to me by you." Letter from Louis V. Jackvony to Matthew W. Goring, Folder 24, "Correspondence/Reports—Wiretapping Case, 1940," Edward J. Higgins Collection, Special and Archival Collections, Providence College, Providence.

62. "Vanderbilt Says He Paid," *Providence Evening Bulletin*, April 10, 1940, 1; "Goring Defends Probe Activities," *Providence Journal*, May 29, 1940, 1.

63. "Prosecutor Notes Executive's Stand of Tap Plot Link," *Pawtucket Times*, April 11, 1940, 1.

64. *Ibid.*

65. "Wire Tap Inquiry Given Approval," *Providence Journal*, March 1, 1940, 2.

66. "Wiretapping: Statement of Theodore Francis Green on Introducing in the Senate a Resolution on Wiretapping," J. Howard McGrath Collection; "Wiretap Hearings Start Tomorrow," *Providence Journal*, January 3, 1940; "Wire Tap Inquiry asked in Senate," *Providence Journal*, November 17, 1940.

67. "Eddie Higgins to Father Deery," May 2,

1940, Edward J. Higgins Papers, Special and Archival Collections, Providence College, Providence.

68. Memorandum from Eddie Higgins to Theodore Francis Green, February 20, 1940, Folder 22, "Correspondence: J. Howard McGrath," Edward J. Higgins Papers, Special and Archival Collections, Providence College, Providence; Memorandum from Eddie Higgins to J. Howard McGrath, Folder 677, "Higgins, Edward J." February 25, 1940, J. Howard McGrath Collection, Special and Archival Collections, Providence College, Providence.

69. "Governor Takes Stand to Defend Wire Taps Role," *Pawtucket Times*, May 28, 1940.

70. "Investigation of Alleged Wiretapping," May 21–June 12, 1940, Edward J. Higgins Papers, Special and Archival Collections, Providence College, Providence.

71. *Ibid.*

72. Letter from Sevellon Brown to J. Edgar Hoover, February 8, 1940, Folder 22, "Correspondence: J. Howard McGrath," Edward J. Higgins Papers, Special and Archival Collections, Providence College, Providence.

73. Letter from J. Edgar Hoover to Sevellon Brown, February 15, 1940, Folder 22, "Higgins Correspondence: J. Howard McGrath, 1940," Edward J. Higgins Papers, Special and Archival Collections, Providence College, Providence.

74. *Ibid.*

75. *Ibid.*

76. *Ibid.*

77. Letter from Eddie Higgins to Senator Theodore Francis Green, May 29, 1940, Folder 23, "Higgins: Correspondence—Wiretapping Case 1939–1940," Edward J. Higgins Papers, Special and Archival Collections, Providence College, Providence.

78. "Says Sen. Green Instigated Wiretapping Probe," *Newport Herald*, June 7, 1940; "Editor Blames Green for Probe," *Providence Journal*, June 7, 1940.

79. "Editor Blames Green for Probe," *Providence Journal*, June 7, 1940.

80. Statement of Theodore Francis Green of Rhode Island, March 13, 1940. Folder 19, "Higgins Correspondence—Theodore Francis Green, 1940," Edward J. Higgins Papers, Special and Archival Collections, Providence College, Providence.

81. Letter to the director from J. H. McGuire, Special Agent in Charge, Record Group 1, "J. Howard McGrath," File #62–59475, August 19, 1940. Athan Theoharis Collection, Marquette University, Milwaukee.

82. Democrat James Kiernan attempted to ally with McGrath in exchange for the lieutenant governorship, but McGrath refused to commit, telling Eddie Higgins that he "had not yet taken any position on this matter and would not do so until [he] had a chance to talk it over with the Senator." Still, he continually assured Higgins that various point persons, such as Andrew Sherry in Central Falls, who "seems to think that we will have little trouble in the Blackstone Valley" for "our program," would support McGrath's coup against former Governor Quinn for the top spot in the 1940 election. Kiernan later expressed his interest in the Democratic state chairmanship; McGrath acknowledged Kiernan's "desire with respect to the State Chairmanship," promising "not [to] make a commitment in this regard without seeing and talking with you." Letter from J. Howard McGrath to Eddie Higgins, May 9 1940, Folder, "Higgins," J. Howard McGrath Collection, Special and Archival Collections, Providence College, Providence; Letter from J. Howard McGrath to James H. Kiernan, April 8, 1947, Folder, "Personal—March–May, 1947," J. Howard McGrath Papers, Harry S Truman Presidential Library, Independence, MO.

83. "Elections," *Journal-Bulletin Almanac, 1942*, 229–238.

84. Letter from J. Edgar Hoover to J. Howard McGrath, 62–59475, November 9, 1940, "J. Howard McGrath," Athan Theoharis Collection, Marquette University, Milwaukee.

85. Memo from Eddie Higgins to McGrath, February 25, 1940, J. Howard McGrath Collection Special and Archival Collections, Providence College, Providence.

86. "Barton Testifies in Wire Tapping," *Providence Journal*, February 15, 1941, 5.

87. Letter from President Roosevelt to Hon. Thomas H. Eliot, M.C. in *Hearings before Subcommittee, No. 1.* of the Committee on the Judiciary House of Representatives Seventy-Seventh Congress, 1st Session: H.R. 2266 and HR 3099, J. Howard McGrath Collection, Special and Archival Collection, Providence College, Providence.

88. DiNunzio, "Wiretapping," Rhode Island Constitutional Convention, 4.

Chapter 7

1. Erwin L. Levine, *Theodore Francis Green: The Washington Years, 1937–1960*, vol. 2 (Providence: Brown University Press, 1971), pp. 94–95.

2. According to Levine, Walsh was an ally of Peter Gerry, who Green believed was "spreading rumors impugning his ability to secure benefits for Rhode Island." *Ibid.*

3. Brinkley, *The End of Reform: New Deal Liberalism in Recession and War* (New York: Vintage, 1995), 175–176.

4. "Welcome Aboard: Quonset Point. Unofficial Directory and Guide" (Boone Publications, 1968), 3.

5. Thomas P. Slater, "The History of Quonset Point Naval Air Station, 1939–1973," Providence College, 1983, 10.

6. "Green Proposes Priority Status for R.I. Air Base," *Providence Journal*, January 26, 1939, 1.

7. Sean Paul Milligan, *Quonset Point Naval Air Station* (Charleston, SC: Arcadia, 1996), 7.

8. "U.S. Takes Possession of 379 Acres at Quonset," *Providence Journal*, July 10, 1940, 11.

9. Christian McBurney, Chapter 3, "The Naval Air Station at Quonset Point and the Naval Auxiliary Air Fields at Charlestown and Westerly," in Christian McBurney, Brian L. Wallin, Patrick T. Conley, John W. Kennedy, and Maureen Taylor, *World War II Rhode Island* (Charlestown, SC: The History Press, 2017), 31.

10. Letter from Frank Knox to President Franklin Delano Roosevelt, December 15, 1939, Folder, "President's Secretary's File, Departmental File, Navy: Knox, Frank: 1939–41," President's Secretary's Files (PSF), Papers of Franklin Delano Roosevelt, Franklin Delano Roosevelt Presidential Library, Hyde Park, NY.

11. Jean Edward Smith, *FDR* (New York: Random House, 2007), 426.

12. Alfred C. Farrell, "Quonset Point Anniversary," *Providence Sunday Journal*, July, 1960.

13. The act also approved a buildup of 135,000 tons of capital ships, nullifying the Washington Naval Treaty of 1921–1922. Richard B. Morris, ed., *Encyclopedia of American History*, 6th ed (New York: Harper & Row, 1982), 424.

14. Admiral Leahy was relieved of his position in August 1939. *Building the Navy's Bases in World War II: History of the Bureau of Yards and Docks and the Civil Engineer Corps: 1940–1946*, Vol. 1 (Washington, D.C.: U.S. Government Printing Office, 1947), 27.

15. "Report of the Board appointed to report upon the need, for purposes of national defense of additional submarine, destroyer, mine, and naval air bases on the coasts of the United States, its Territories, and Possessions," 76th Congress, 1st Session, December 27, 1938.

16. Rhode Island adjutant general Herbert Dean and Senator Green were the only two officials from the state privy to Hepburn's conclusions. "Naval Air Station at Quonset Point Urged to Congress," *Providence Evening Bulletin*, January 3, 1939, 1; "House Naval Committee Recommends Quonset Base," *Providence Journal*, March 29, 1939, 12; "Purchase of Land at Quonset Voted by Senate Group," *Providence Journal*, April 11, 1939, 1.

17. The presence of a federal base on state property meant that millions of dollars would be funneled into the state. Thus, Adjutant General Dean supported Vanderbilt's plan to "donate" the said territory to the government so that construction of the base could be "expedite[d]." "Naval Air Station at Quonset Point Urged to Congress," *Evening Bulletin*, January 3, 1939, 1, 13; "Governor Urges State Give Land for Plan Field," *Evening Bulletin*, January 4, 1939, 1; "Government's Evaluations Stun Quonset Point Property Owners," *Providence Journal*, July 11, 1940; "Quonset Point Naval Station: 244.60 acres from State of Rhode Island," "George Troy, Assistant United States Attorney to Norman M. Littell, Assistant Attorney General," December 11, 1939 and December 20, 1939, J. Howard McGrath Collection, Special and Archival Collections, Providence College, Providence; "Welcome Aboard: Quonset Point," *Unofficial Directory and Guide* (Boone Publications, 1968).

18. Sandager, who chafed amidst delays on funding for Quonset Point, badgered Chairman of the Naval Committee Carl Vinson of Georgia to move on allocating funding for the base. Vinson initially delayed on Quonset because, according to Sandager, the Georgia congressman wanted to secure his home state as the site for the southern base rather than Jacksonville, Florida, the location recommended by the Hepburn committee. Additionally, however, Vinson and the naval committee harbored a grudge against Sandager, who fervently opposed appropriations for the Guam base, fearing Japanese attack. Even so, he recommended that Vanderbilt write a "persuasive" letter reminding the committee of the virtues of Quonset. A week later, Sandager visited Rhode Island with "several men from the Naval Affairs Committee," and would offer the state a chance "to put on an act for their benefit" in support of the Quonset base. Letters: Sandager to Vanderbilt, Folder 224, February 17, 18, 22, 1939, William H. Vanderbilt Papers, Manuscripts and Archives, University of Rhode Island, North Kingstown; Levine, *Theodore Francis Green*, pp. 95–96.

19. "Naval Air Station at Quonset Point Urged to Congress," *Evening Bulletin*, January 3, 1939, 1; "House Naval Committee Recommends Quonset Base," *Providence Journal*, March 29, 1939, 12; "Purchase of Land at Quonset Voted by Senate Group," *Providence Journal*, April 11, 1939, 1.

20. The Walsh-Vinson Bill, named for Senator David I. Walsh of Massachusetts, chairman of the Senate Naval Affairs Committee, and Representative Carl Vinson of Georgia, chairman of the House Naval Affairs Commit-

tee since 1931, allocated $65,000,000 for the construction of new air bases from Alaska to Puerto Rico. "Naval Air Station at Quonset Point," January 3, 1939; "House Naval Committee Recommends," March 29, 1939; "Purchase of Land at Quonset Voted," April 11, 1939; Samuel Eliot Morison, *The Two-Ocean War: A Short History of the United States in the Second World War* (Boston: Little, Brown, 1963); "Quonset Project Voted by House," *Providence Journal*, April 21, 1939, 13.

21. "Purchase of land at Quonset Voted by Senate Group," *Providence Journal*, April 11, 1939, 1.

22. "Quonset Owners Ask Square Deal," *Providence Journal*, July 15, 1940, 1; "Acquisition of Land for Naval Air Base at Quonset Point, Rhode Island," J. Howard McGrath to Mr. Norman M. Littell, assistant attorney general, July 30, 1940, J. Howard McGrath Collection, Special and Archival Collections, Providence College, Providence.

23. "U.S. Take Possession of 379 Acres at Quonset," *Providence Journal*, July 10, 1940.

24. "Government's Evaluations Stun Quonset Point Property Owners," *Providence Journal*, July 11, 1940.

25. Their due included either an investigation by a commissioner, or a hearing in the federal district court. Estimates from navy officials as to completion of the project ranged anywhere from two to three years. "U.S. Takes Possession of 379 Acres at Quonset," *Providence Journal*, July 10, 1940, 11; "Quonset Condemnation Steps Taken by U.S.," *Newport Daily News* July 9, 1940, 1.

26. "Government's Evaluations Stun Quonset Point Property Owners," *Providence Journal*, July 11, 1940.

27. On July 23, 1940, the *Newport Daily News* randomly reported that two noted Quonset residents were paid sums that exceeded the 1939 valuation for their property. Prominent businessman Frank L. Murray was paid $61,200 for 455 lots originally quoted at $7,000. Two realtors, Howard V. Allen and George R. Hanaford, were awarded the exorbitant price of $56,000 for 271 lots and 17 acres, a portion of the latter considered "marsh land," which in 1939 was only valued at $6,000. "U.S. Offers to Quonset Owners Exceed Value," *Newport Daily News* July 23, 1940, 3; "Fairness Pledged Quonset Colony," *Providence Journal*, July 22, 1940.

28. Memorandum to Quonset Colony Owners by J. Howard McGrath: Proposed Statement to be Issued by the United States Attorney at Providence, Rhode Island, re: Future Proceedings in Land Condemnation at Quonset Point, July 30, 1940, "Fairness Pledged Quonset Colony," *Providence Journal*, July 22, 1940.

29. "Quonset Claims Filed," *Newport Daily News* August 16, 1940, 3.

30. J. Howard McGrath to Norman Littell, July 30, 1940, Folder, "Correspondence," McGrath Collection, Special and Archival Collections, Providence College, Providence.

31. *Ibid.*; Memorandum to Quonset Colony Owners by J. Howard McGrath.

32. J. Howard McGrath to Norman Littell, assistant attorney general, July 30, 1940, Folder, "Correspondence," McGrath Collection, Special and Archival Collections, Providence College, Providence.

33. *Ibid.*

34. The navy appointed three realtors who investigated and quoted sums for each case independently. McGrath is suggesting here that his office push the lowest possible figure of the three for each property in question. J. Howard McGrath to Norman M. Littell, assistant attorney general, August 15, 1940, Folder, "Correspondence," J. Howard McGrath Collection, Special and Archival Collections, Providence College, Providence.

35. *Ibid.*

36. By the end of August, 383 of the 400 were set to appear in U.S. district court. "Quonset Owners Urged to Protest," *Providence Journal*, September 1, 1940, 5; "McGrath Enters R.I. Gubernatorial Race," *Newport Daily News* August 23, 1940, 1; "Quonset Body Named," *Newport Daily News* August 26, 1940, 9; "Navy Gets Prices on Quonset Water Supply," *Newport Daily News* September 4, 1940, 9.

37. Alfred C. Farrell, "Quonset Point Anniversary," *Providence Sunday Journal*, July 1961.

38. McBurney, "Naval Air Station," 32–33.

39. *Ibid.*

40. "Men and Money Mobilized to Build Base at Quonset," *Providence Journal*, July 13, 1940, 3; "Quonset Point Due to Help Jobless," *Providence Journal*, July 14, 1940, 11; "25,189,000 Contract for Navy Work in R.I.," *Newport Daily News*, July 12, 1940, 1; "Need for Speed Seen in Quonset Work," *Newport Daily News*, July 13, 1940, 1; "Excavation Begun at Quonset Point," *Providence Journal*, July 25, 1940.

41. "Newport Naval Expansion Considered, President Said," *Newport Daily News*, August 11, 1940, 1; "Quonset Colony Has Until Sept. 6," *The Evening Bulletin*, August 19, 1940.

42. "Quonset Station Gets More Land," *Providence Journal*, September 13, 1940, 7.

43. "Activity at Quonset Point Makes Base a 'Boom Town,'" *Providence Journal*, September 1, 1940, 5.

44. "Quonset Colony Sees Life Begin," *Providence Journal*, September 10, 1941, 5.

45. *Ibid.*

46. J. Howard McGrath to Edward J. Higgins,

et. al, Folder, "Eddie Higgins," 1942, J. Howard McGrath Collection, Special and Archival Collections, Providence College, Providence.

47. Rhode Island was chosen as a site for several reasons. Green's support of FDR was certainly a factor, as well as the vociferous denunciation of the Roosevelt administration by Senator David I. Walsh of Massachusetts, chairman of the powerful Naval Affairs Committee. In June 1940, Walsh warned that if FDR ordered torpedo and sub chasers to Great Britain, he would "threaten criminal prosecution," citing Section 3 of the Espionage Act of June 15, 1917, which stated that neutral nations were forbidden "to send out of jurisdiction of the United States any vessel built, armed or equipped as a vessel of war." David I. Walsh Collection, College of the Holy Cross, Worcester, MA. Although the board initially believed that the land was inadequate for a major base, they believed that after "dredging and filling" the location would adequately meet the needs of the United States Navy. "Report on Need of Additional Naval Bases to Defend the Coasts of the United States, Its Territories, and Possessions: Letter from the Secretary of the Navy," 76th Congress, 1st Session, The House of Representatives, The Hepburn Report," The National Archives, Washington, D.C.

48. John P. Forbes, "Quonset Naval Air Station, $30,000,000 Project Built Within Year, Opens Today," *Providence Journal*, July 12, 1941, 1.

49. The Naval Expansion Bill of 1940 (52 Stat. # 401) finally passed both houses of Congress in July 1940, and sanctioned the expansion of the United States Army and Navy. "President Gets Naval Expansion Bill," *Providence Journal*, July 11, 1940.

50. "Navy Department #3," Chronological File, Folder 170, May 22, 1941, Theodore Francis Green Senate Papers, Library of Congress, Washington, D.C.

51. Christian McBurney, "Seabees, Pontoons and Quonset Huts at Davisville," in Christian McBurney, Brian L. Wallin, Patrick T. Conley, John W. Kennedy, and Maureen A. Taylor, *World War II Rhode Island* (Charlestown, SC: The History Press, 2017), 50–51.

52. "Text of Governor's Speech," *Providence Journal*, January 8, 1941.

53. "Colonists Would Never Know Quonset Today," *Providence Journal, Special Edition* June 26, 1974, 5.

Chapter 8

1. According to the author, "...Roosevelt, if he is renominated ... will be elected and will carry Rhode Island, if, McGrath is the candidate." "Green for Governor Washington newspaper joke—*Lookout* August 17, 1939," Folder "Miscellaneous—Material Campaign 1940," J. Howard McGrath Papers, Harry S Truman Library, Independence, MO.

2. See previous chapter.

3. The campaign material listed various measures vetoed or ignored by Republicans, including passage of a Corrupt Practices Act. "Dear Voter," November 4, 1940, Folder, "Miscellaneous—Material Campaign 1940," J. Howard McGrath Papers, Harry S Truman Presidential Library, Independence, MO.

4. "Statement by J. Howard McGrath," September 27, 1940, Folder "Miscellaneous Material—Campaign 1940," J. Howard McGrath Papers, Harry S Truman Presidential Library, Independence, MO.

5. Quinn interview with Matthew J. Smith, August 7, 1972, Special and Archival Collections, Providence College, Providence, 7–9.

6. Letter from William Pelkey to J. Howard McGrath, Folder, "Material Furnished by Pelkey," J. Howard McGrath Collection, Special and Archival Collections, Providence College, Providence.

7. *Ibid.*

8. J. Howard McGrath to Eddie Higgins, May 3, 1939, J. Howard McGrath Collection, Special and Archival Collections, Providence College, Providence.

9. See Chapter 6.

10. Green had recently been admitted to the hospital for undisclosed surgery. His secretary wrote, "He is coming along grand and is as busy as a bee in his limited way." Memorandum from Edith S. W. to Frances Cohen, May 6, 1940, May 17, 1940, May 22, 1940, Folder, "Correspondence with Green's Office," J. Howard McGrath Collection, Special and Archival Collections, Providence College, Providence.

11. Lincoln Steffens, "A State for Sale," *McClure's Magazine*, 1905; "McGrath Reveals Plans for State," *Providence Journal*, December 18, 1940, 5.

12. "Text of Governor's Speech," *Providence Journal*, January 8, 1941.

13. "McGrath Proposes Two Basic Changes in Assembly Rules," *Providence Journal*, December 19, 1940, 1.

14. *Ibid.*

15. The preamble to the Republican bill read, "The purpose of this act is to guarantee to all citizens a fair and equal opportunity for public service." Folder 19, "Civil Service Reform," William Henry Vanderbilt Papers, Manuscripts and Archives, University of Rhode Island Archives, Kingstown.

16. In advertising for these positions, DeVoe

announced that "some of these jobs pay fair salaries, in fact, nine classes pay $3000 or more ... and one of them goes to $6000 a year." "Announcement from Maxwell A. DeVoe, Director Department of Civil Service," October 10, 1940, Folder, "Civil Service Materials," J. Howard McGrath Papers, Harry S Truman Presidential Library, Independence, MO.

17. McGrath based his criticism on correspondence initiated between Senator Theodore Francis Green and the United States civil service commissioner, the latter finding "the Rhode Island Civil Service Act ... satisfactory for administrative purposes." The U.S. Commission found fault with Section 12 of the Rhode Island legislation, which called for a single candidate named by the director. Additionally, the commissioner questioned the soundness of forcing existing government employees to sit with the general public for a competitive examination. Instead, he recommended that existing government workers whose jobs fall within the civil service to sit for a "non-competitive" examination. See above. Letter: United States Civil Service Commission to Honorable Theodore Francis Green, September 6, 1939, Folder, "Civil Service Materials," J. Howard McGrath Papers, Harry S Truman Presidential Library, Independence, MO.

18. Unnamed speech, n.d., Folder, "Civil Service Materials 1939," J. Howard McGrath Papers, Harry S Truman Library. Independence, MO.

19. The Broomhead Bill required the potential director to sit for the merit examination before making application. "House Gets McGrath's Bill to Change R.I. Civil Service," *Providence Journal*, March 5, 1941, 1.

20. Democrats capitalized on Republican alliance with industry, McGrath was sensitive to the needs of Rhode Island industry and, like Roosevelt, recognized the vital role business played in war and postwar reconversion. Cass R. Sunstein, *The Second Bill of Rights: FDR's Unfinished Revolution and Why We Need It More Than Ever* (New York: Basic Books, 2004), 49.

21. "McGrath Proposes Two Basic Changes in Assembly Rules," *Providence Journal*, September 19, 1940, 1.

22. "Compromise Mark Final Adjournment of R.I. Legislature," *Providence Journal*, May 2, 1941, 1.

23. Folder, "Speeches, 1941," July 2, 1941, J. Howard McGrath Collection, Special and Archival Collections, Providence College, Providence; "Governor Warns the State to Save," *Providence Journal*, July 5, 1941, 5.

24. "Governor Warns States to Save," *Providence Journal*, July 5, 1941.

25. The governor consistently championed the importance of his state especially when rationing went into effect. Six months prior to the Pearl Harbor attack, McGrath held a meeting of local industrialists to ensure that they would not undergo undue hardship because of the call to national defense. "Governor Warns the State to Save," *Providence Journal;* "Bonds-War Workers Obligations: Address by Governor J. Howard McGrath at the Annual Banquet of the Olneyville Business Men's Association," January 20, 1943, J. Howard McGrath Papers, Harry S Truman Presidential Library, Independence, MO.

26. "Address by Governor J. Howard McGrath ... Olneyville Business."

27. Senator Peter Gerry wrote McGrath upon the latter's decision to run for governor. "Of course, I have watched with interest the part you have played since entering politics." Letter Senator Peter G. Gerry to J. Howard McGrath, August 29, 1940, Folder, "Peter G. Gerry," J. Howard McGrath Collection, Special and Archival Collections, Providence College, Providence.

28. "McGrath Reveals Plans for State," *Providence Journal*, December 18, 1940.

29. William O'Neill, *A Democracy at War: America's Fight at Home and Abroad in World War II* (New York: The Free Press, 1993), 10.

30. Frank Freidel, *Franklin Delano Roosevelt: A Rendezvous with Destiny* (Boston: Little, Brown, 1990), 418–420.

31. According to the *Military Code of Rhode Island*, the adjutant general carried the rank of a brigadier general and was appointed by the governor. *Military Code of Rhode Island* (Providence, 1940), 15, J. Howard McGrath Collection, Special and Archival Collections, Providence College, Providence.

32. The bill organizing the State Council of Defense was approved on May 7, 1941, and stipulated that the Council would meet "in times of emergency" to "assist in coordination of state and local activities" necessitated by military crisis. The governor would serve as chairman and appoint the eleven members of the council. H-725, "House Committee on Finance," Rhode Island State Archives. Providence; "McGrath to Call R.I. Guard Today for Home Service," *Providence Journal*, December 8, 1941, 12; "FBI Starts R.I. Roundup of German, Italian Aliens," *Providence Journal*, December 9, 1941, 1.

33. "McGrath to Call R.I. Guard Today for Home Service," *Providence Journal*, December 8, 1941, 12.

34. Fields Point Farm, located in the far southern section of Providence, was the site of a famous shore-dining hall, which specialized in New England clambakes. Patrick T. Conley

and Paul R. Campbell, *Providence: A Pictorial History* (Norfolk: Donning Company Publishers, 1982), 111.

35. "Rhode Island Acts Swiftly to Protect Defense Shops," *Providence Journal*, December 8, 1941, 12.

36. "Hundreds Storm Recruit Stations," *Providence Journal*, December 9, 1941, 9; "R.I. Congressmen Are All for War," *Providence Journal*, December 9, 1941, 13; "Rhode Island 22% for Entering War," *Providence Journal*, 2.

37. Throughout the 1920s and 1930s, a sizable number of Rhode Island Italians supported the Fascist pursuits of Benito Mussolini, but when the Japanese bombed Pearl Harbor, the Fraternal Sons of Italy issued a collective statement of support for President Roosevelt's declaration of war against the Axis powers. They promised to "so conduct themselves as to prove that no sacrifice in this historic hour of our nation is too great." "R.I. Sons of Liberty 'All-Out' for U.S.," *Providence Journal*, December 24, 1941, 2; "McGrath Offers to Aid Idle Aliens," *Providence Journal*, September 6, 1941, 9.

38. Luconi, *Providence*; "McGrath Offers to Aid Idle Aliens," *Providence Journal*, September 6, 1941; Folder, "Speeches," Statement for the Press, n.d., J. Howard McGrath Collection, Special and Archival Collections, Providence College, Providence.

39. O'Neill, *A Democracy at War*, 9.

40. "10,000 Will Work for R.I. Defense," *Providence Journal*, December; "Knudsen Favors 'Work or Fight' Program in Industry to Win War," *Providence Journal*, December 11, 1941, 12; "Civilian Defense Plans Progress," *Providence Journal*, December 11, 1941, 17.

41. "S.S. of D.," n.d., Folder, "Defense, State Council of," J. Howard McGrath Papers, Harry S Truman Presidential Library, Independence, MO.

42. James J. Landis, "Morale and Civilian Defense," *The American Journal, of Sociology* 47, no. 30 (November 1941): 331–332.

43. *Ibid.*, 331.

44. *Ibid.*, 337.

45. "If Air Raids Come," newspaper release, January 7, 1942, Folder 3, "Air Raid," Series III, MSS 231, Rhode Island State Records Collection, Rhode Island Historical Society, Providence.

46. *Ibid.*

47. "Warden News," East Providence, District 1, October 20, 1943, Folder, "Air Raid Wardens," MSS 231, Rhode Island State Records Collection, Rhode Island Historical Society, Providence.

48. "State Blackout Planned in May," *Providence Journal*, April 11, 1942, 1.

49. Examples of "on the air classrooms" were conducted on areas relating to the local chapter of President Roosevelt's Office of Price Administration, Franklin Delano Roosevelt Presidential Library, Hyde Park, NY.

50. Armand H. Cote, "Statistics of the Rhode Island Military," *Manual with Rules and Orders for the Use of the General Assembly of the State of Rhode Island, 1947–1948* (Providence: E.L. Freeman, 1948), 225.

51. On the Air Classrooms.

52. *Ibid.*

53. *Ibid.*

54. "To Order R.I. Schools and Public Buildings to Close Mondays to Save Fuel Supply," *Providence Journal*, January 16, 1943, 1; "Proclaims Fuel Emergency," *Providence Journal*, January 17, 1943, 6; "Full Text of Fuel Emergency Order," *Providence Journal*, January 21, 1943, 6.

55. "The Governor's Message," *Pawtucket Times*, January 7, 1942.

56. *Ibid.*

57. "65 Men Form Club," *Seabees Newsletter*, "Wash the Window Club," *Seabees Newsletter*, "Tow-Lines: Receiving Barracks, NABD, Davisville," Vol. 7–8, 1943, Rhode Island Historical Society, Providence.

58. Earl C. Webster, director of civilian defense, Memorandum: to Chairmen of Local Councils of Defense, July 9, 1943, Folder 3, Series III, "Air Raid: 1941–1944," Rhode Island State Government Records, Rhode Island Historical Society, Providence.

59. In addition, the State Council urged all industrial plants to refrain from blowing whistles, since "the blowing of mill whistles during the period of air raid drills confused Rhode Island citizens needlessly." To Rhode Island Industries and Business Establishments from William J. Harrington, Plant Protection Officer, May 12, 1943, State Council of Defense, MSS 113, Papers of Christopher Del Sesto, Rhode Island Historical Society, Providence.

60. Folder, "Inaugural Messages," McGrath "Inaugural Message to the General Assembly, 1943," January 1943, 5–9, J. Howard McGrath Collection, Special and Archival Collections, Providence College, Providence.

61. "Black Market Hit," *Providence Evening Bulletin*, December 9, 1943.

62. "Special Black Market Squad Gets First Job," *Woonsocket Call*, August 25, 1943, Folder 7, MSS 113, Christopher Del Sesto Papers, Rhode Island Historical Society, Providence.

63. "Cooperation of Local Police, Especially in Cities, Sought by OPA," *Pawtuxet Valley Times*, August 25, 1943, Folder 7, MSS 113, Christopher Del Sesto Papers, Rhode Island Historical Society, Providence, RI.

64. "OPA, Special Squad of Police and State Troopers Round up Gas Black Market Operators," *Providence Journal*, October 4, 1943; "3 More men Linked to 'Gas' Black Market," *Newport News*, October 4, 1943; "OPA Probe Traps Pawtucket Man in Gasoline Plot," *Pawtucket Times*, October 4, 1943, Folder 1, MSS 113, Christopher Del Sesto Papers, Rhode Island Historical Society, Providence; "20 Seized in Week in the 'Gas' Racket," Folder 2, MSS 113, Christopher Del Sesto Papers, Rhode Island Historical Society, Providence.

65. "Pleasure Car Tire Allocation is Cut," *Providence Sunday Journal*, August 27, 1944, Folder 2, MSS 113, Christopher Del Sesto Papers, Rhode Island Historical Society, Providence.

66. "Blow to Crush Ration Racket," *Boston Herald*, September 16, 1944, Folder 5, MSS 113, Christopher Del Sesto Papers, Rhode Island Historical Society, Providence.

67. *Ibid.*

68. Memorandum to All Local War Price and Rationing Boards from Christopher Del Sesto, state director, February 18 1944, Folder 6, MSS 113, Christopher Del Sesto Papers, Rhode Island Historical Society, Providence.

69. "OPA Continues Drive to Kill Black Market," *The Yard Arm*, July 19, 1944, Folder 6, MSS 113, Christopher Del Sesto Papers, Rhode Island Historical Society, Providence.

70. "Christopher Del Sesto, State OPA Director, Receives Roger," *Westerly Sun*, July 17, 1944; "Text of Citation Presented with Third 'Roger' Award for Outstanding Community Service," *Providence Journal*, July 17, 1944, Folder 23, MSS 113, Christopher Del Sesto Papers, Rhode Island Historical Society, Providence.

Chapter 9

1. The Board outlined a program of centralized postwar planning funded through taxation. Roosevelt integrated the report's concept of economic stability through full employment, education, federal housing, and universal health care in his Second Bill of Rights. Jytte Klausen, "Did World War II End the New Deal?" in Sidney M. Milkis and Jerome M. Mileur, eds., *The New Deal and the Triumph of Liberalism* (Boston: University of Massachusetts Press, 2002), 202.

2. "McGrath Desires Board to Handle State Sick Fund," *Providence Journal*, January 3, 1945, 1.

3. Cass R. Sunstein, *The Second Bill of Rights: FDR's Unfinished Revolution and Why We Need It More Than Ever* (New York: Basic Books, 2004), 12–13.

4. *Ibid.*

5. Alan Brinkley defined the "new-New Deal" as a gradual "redefinition of New Deal thought" that culminated during the postwar period. Brinkley, *The End of Reform*, 3.

6. "War Powers Bill to Face Revisions," *Providence Journal*, March 25, 1942; "McGrath Urges Party Harmony," *Providence Journal*, March 26, 1942.

7. *Ibid.*, 6.

8. See Debra Mulligan, "The 'Difficult Business' of Wartime Delinquency: Rhode Island and the Establishment of a Juvenile Court," *The New England Journal of History* (Fall 2015), 82.

9. "Address by Governor J. Howard McGrath at the War-Time, Health and Welfare Conference," Biltmore Hotel, February 10, 1943, Folder, "Health and Welfare Conference: War Time, Biltmore Hotel, Prov.," J. Howard McGrath Papers, Harry S Truman Presidential Library, Independence, MO.

10. *Ibid.*

11. J. Howard McGrath, "Address by Governor J. Howard McGrath at the War-Time, Health and Welfare Conference," Biltmore Hotel, February 10, 1943, Folder, "Health and Welfare Conference: War Time, Biltmore Hotel, Prov.," J. Howard McGrath Papers, Harry S Truman Presidential Library, Independence, MO.

12. *Ibid.*, "McGrath Urges Governors' Act to End Overlapping of Taxes," *Providence Journal*, May 30, 1944, 1.

13. McGrath, "Address … Health and Welfare Conference." See above.

14. "Text of Governor McGrath's Annual Message to Assembly as 1944 Session Opens," *Providence Journal*, January 5, 1944, 1. McGrath had initially proclaimed his support of the Four Freedoms on December 15, 1941, in a memorial of the 150th anniversary of the Bill of Rights via radio broadcast. In his speech, he reminded the citizens of the state, "Rhode Island withdrew its original reluctance because the supplementary Bill of Rights breathed life into our Constitution…. The first is freedom of speech and expression … everywhere in the world…. The fourth is freedom from fear." "Bill of Rights: Radio Address by Governor J. Howard McGrath on the Bill of Rights," WFCI, Papers of J. Howard McGrath, Harry S Truman Presidential Library, December 15, 1941.

15. According to Cass Sunstein, the "Four Freedoms" speech and the Atlantic Charter laid the foundation for the Second Bill of Rights. Sunstein, *The Second Bill of Rights*, 85.

16. "Text of Governor McGrath's Third Inaugural Address Before Assembly," *Providence Journal*, January 3, 1945.

17. J. Howard McGrath, "The Rhode Island

Plan of Hospital Insurance," Delivered at the Tri-State Hospital Assembly Dinner, Palmer House, Chicago, Folder, "Hospital Insurance, R.I. Plan Address in Chicago, May 11, 1944," J. Howard McGrath Papers, Harry S Truman Presidential Library, Independence, MO.

18. The minimum claim was set at $6.75 a week and the maximum, to those earning $1,800 or above, would be $18 a week. The bill, as published in the RI Public Laws in 1942, stipulated that if "funds are made available" from the federal government under "title III of the Social Security Act," the state may take advantage of these monies. Thomas H. Bride, "Rhode Island Cash Sickness Compensation Program," *American Journal, of Public Health* 39, no. 8 (August 1949), 1012; "Sickness Insurance— Rhode Island Creates First Plan for Sickness Compensation," *Recent Statute* (1942): 317.

19. Thomas P. McCoy was mayor of Pawtucket during the war, and a staunch Democrat. Mortimer Newton, chairman of the board, *Ninth Annual Report: 1944 of the Rhode Island Unemployment Compensation Board* (March 27, 1945), 8–10.

20. David M. Cameron, "R.I. First in the National with Sickness Benefits," *Providence Sunday Journal*, March 14, 1943; Thomas H. Bride, "Rhode Island Cash Sickness Compensation Program," *American Journal of Public Health* 39 (August 1949), 1011.

21. Each potential claimant would be required to submit an extensive form specifying the reasons for his/her unemployment and the nature of the illness in question. The applicant's doctor would thereby certify that all information was correct, whereby the form was mailed to the Unemployment Compensation Board. The medical director then reviewed the request to determine its validity. Bride, "Rhode Island Cash Sickness," 1012.

22. David M. Cameron, "R.I. First in the Nation with Sickness Benefits," *Providence Sunday Journal*, March 14, 1943.

23. Senator Theodore Francis Green had recently drafted a bill to expand social security benefits through additional contributions from workers. "R.I. Sickness Act Called Beginning," *Providence Journal*, February 5, 1943.

24. Folder, "R.I. Sickness Benefits Act," "Unemployment Compensation Board in R.I. Takes Issue with R.I. Medical Journal," *Pawtuxet Valley Daily Times*, November 20, 1943. J. Howard McGrath Collection, Special and Archival Collections, Providence College Archives, Providence.

25. "Sickness Benefit Revisions Likely," *Providence Journal*, December 12, 1944.

26. *Ibid.*

27. "Sickness Benefit Fund Faces Insol-

vency," *Providence Journal*, December 13, 1944, 17.

28. Mortimer Newton, chairman of the board, *Ninth Annual Report: 1944 of the Rhode Island Unemployment Compensation Board* (March 27, 1945), 8–10.

29. *Ibid.*; "Most Illness Aid Goes to Women," *Providence Journal*, February 26, 1944, 8; "Sickness Benefit Revisions Likely," *Providence Journal*, December 12, 1944, 15; "Governor to Get Sickness Aid Data," *Providence Evening Bulletin*, June 24, 1945.

30. "Deficit Budget," *Providence Journal*, April 20, 1944, 11; Selig Greenberg, "Sick Benefit Fund Faces Insolvency," *Providence Journal*, December 13, 1944, 17; "Cash Sickness Fund," *Providence Journal*, September 7, 1944, 11.

31. "Sick Benefit Act Changes Offered," *Evening Bulletin*, January 23, 1945; "Tighter Sickness Benefit Aid Urged by McGrath in House," *Woonsocket Call*, January 23, 1945; "Sickness Benefit Secrecy is Urged," *Providence Evening Bulletin*, January 24, 1945.

32. "Most Illness Aid Goes to Women," *Providence Journal*, February 26, 1944, 8.

33. "Opposition to UCB Reform Indicated," *Providence Journal*, January 15, 1945.

34. McGrath's suggestion of a board was finally implemented under the governorship of his successor, John O. Pastore. The new Cash Sickness Advisory Committee was composed of seven members, five chosen by the governor, with three representing labor, two the general public, and one the medical profession. "McGrath Desires Board to Handle State Sick Fund," *Providence Journal*, January 3, 1945; J. Howard McGrath, "Inaugural Message of J. Howard McGrath to the General Assembly," January 1945; "McGrath Acts to Safeguard Sick Benefits," *Pawtucket Times*, January 30, 1945; "Full Probe of Cash Sickness Law Asked," *Pawtuxet Valley Daily Times*, January 31, 1945.

35. "McGrath Acts to Safeguard," *Pawtucket Times*, January 30, 1945; "GOP Will Oppose Sick Fund Board," *Providence Journal*, February 13, 1945, 9.

36. "GOP Will Oppose Sick Fund Board," *Providence Journal*, February 13, 1945, 9; "Cash Sickness," *Providence Journal*, February 22, 1945, 13; "In the Day's Mail: Cash Sickness," *Providence Journal*, February 22, 1945, 13; "Opposition to UCB Reform Indicated," *Providence Journal*, January 15, 1945; "Board to Manage Cash Sick Fund Sought in Bill," *Providence Evening Bulletin*, January 30, 1945; "McGrath Acts to Safeguard Sick Benefits," *Pawtucket Times*, January 30, 1945.

37. "Cash Sickness," *Providence Journal*, February 22, 1945, 13.

38. *Ibid.*

39. "R.I. Jobless Aid Soars Rapidly," *Providence Journal*, August 22, 1945.

40. "500 Seek Jobless Benefits as City Plants Reconvert," *Woonsocket Call*, August 20, 1945.

41. "Sick Benefits Show Decline While Unemployed Costs Gain," *The Westerly Sun* September 13, 1945.

42. According to UCB report, 23,803 workers had filed for unemployment benefits since April 1944. *Ninth Annual Report: 1944 of the Rhode Island Unemployment Compensation*.

43. "Openings Exceed R.I. Jobless Total," *Providence Journal*, September 25, 1945.

44. Chapter 1948, *Public Laws of R.I. 1947* (Providence: The Oxford Press, 1947); William M. Blair, "Report from the Nation: The Trends in Five Sections of the Country," *New York Times*, February 23, 1947.

45. John O. Pasture, "Annual Message of John O. Pastore, 1946," Folder 2, "1946," John O. Pastore Papers, Special and Archival Collections, Providence College, Providence.

46. "Governor Offers Health Insurance Program for R.I.," *Providence Journal*, January 5, 1944, 1.

47. J. Howard McGrath, "Inaugural Message of J. Howard McGrath," January Session, 1944, 12, Folder, "Inaugurals," J. Howard McGrath Collection, Special and Archival Collections, Providence College, Providence.

48. J. Howard McGrath, "Inaugural Message of J. Howard McGrath," January Session, 1944, 10, Folder, "Inaugurals," J. Howard McGrath Collection, Special and Archival Collections, Providence College, Providence.

49. The bill also called for national unemployment insurance, extension of elderly and disability insurance, extensive benefit packages for veterans, and a reform of federal grants-in-aid to each of the forty-eight states. J. Joseph Huthmacher, *Senator Robert F. Wagner and the Rise of Urban Liberalism* (New York: Athenaeum, 1968), 292.

50. *Ibid.*

51. "Health Council Elects Officers," *Providence Journal*, February 6, 1944, 19; "Investigate First," *Providence Journal*, January 12, 1944, 9; "Governor Moves for Health Study," *Providence Journal*, January 12, 1944, 2.

52. "Dr. Sullivan Says Health Council Plans Complete Insurance Study," *Providence Journal*, February 10, 1944, 1.

53. "Health Council's Work," *Providence Journal*, February 9, 1944.

54. "Health Council Elects Officers," *Providence Journal*, February 6, 1944; "McGrath Awaits Hospital Report: Dr. Ruggles Says Compulsory Insurance Law Proposal Should be Ready Soon," *Providence Journal*, November 23, 1944.

55. "The Governor's Inaugural Message," January 2, 1945, 20, Folder, "Inaugurals," J. Howard McGrath Collection, Special and Archival Collections, Providence College, Providence.

56. At the time, the governor supported a continuation of the single-payer Blue Cross model, whereby current employees paid into the fund. He further suggested that the workers could opt to transfer to the state insurance plan if the General Assembly adopts it. "McGrath Desires Sick Fund Board," *Providence Journal*, January 3, 1945.

57. *Ibid.*

58. "State May Lead the Way in Hospital Insurance for All," *Westerly Sun*, January 3, 1945.

59. "R.I. Health Plan Delay Advocated," *Providence Journal*, February 20, 1945.

60. *Ibid.*

61. *Ibid.*

62. "McGrath Favors Wider Security," *Providence Journal*, July 4, 1945, 4.

63. J. Howard McGrath, "Address by Governor J. Howard McGrath at the General Luncheon of Governors' Conference: Developing an Adequate Social Security Program," Mackinac Island, Michigan, July 3, 1945, Folder, "Social Security: Governors Conference, Mackinac Island," *The Providence Journal*, July 3, 1945. J. Howard McGrath Papers, Harry S Truman Presidential Library, Independence, MO.

64. "Social Security: Governors Conference, Mackinac Island," *The Providence Journal*, July 3, 1945.

65. McGrath warned that "unless we can provide social and economic security in this, the wealthiest of nations, our failure will largely prevent the economic recovery of a devastated world." James A. Hagerty, "Governors Move to Back Charter," *New York Times*, July 4, 1945, 7.

66. According to Wagner biographer J. Joseph Huthmacher, Roosevelt failed to "prod a reluctant Congress into concretely preparing for the kind of postwar America that his new 'bill of rights' envisioned." Huthmacher, *Senator Robert F. Wagner*, 291.

67. Donald W. Smith, "The Wagner-Murray-Dingell Bill (1945): Senate Bill 1050, H.R. 3293," *The American Journal of Nursing* (November 1945): 933.

68. Nonetheless, Huthmacher also observed that the Wagner Bill contributed substantially to the final GI Bill of Rights. Huthmacher, *Senator Robert F. Wagner*, 293–295.

69. The Servicemen's Readjustment Act of 1944 also allotted $20 per week for unemployment compensation for one year, granted up to four years of educational benefits for veterans, and pledged half of all loans for farms,

businesses, and housing to veterans. Glenn C. Altschuler and Stuart M. Blumin, *The GI Bill: A New Deal for Veterans* (New York: Oxford University Press, 2009), 71.

70. John O. Pastore, "Annual Message of Gov. John O. Pastore, 1946," 5, Folder, 1, "1946: Speeches," Papers of John O. Pastore, Special and Archival Collections. Providence College, Providence.

71. *Ibid.*, 6.

72. Chapters 581 and 1185, *Acts and Resolves of the General Assembly* Providence, 1915.

73. "Text of the Governor's Speech," *Providence Journal*, January 8, 1941; "Juvenile Court Plan Backed," *Providence Journal*, January 8, 1941.

74. "Nippon's Warplanes Blast Naval, Army Bases at Honolulu," *Providence Journal*, December 8, 1941, 1.

75. "R.I. Children's Court Association Formed to Consolidate Efforts," *Providence Journal*, January 11, 1941, 11.

76. Rhode Island industries employed a number of women. According to Christian McBurney, after the attack on Pearl Harbor, women "by the thousands were needed to fill jobs left behind in manufacturing plants." In the process of conversion to meet the needs of overseas campaigns in Europe and the Pacific, these plants were forced to hire women in industrial or clerical jobs. Quonset Naval Air Base and other such industries hired women to keep the books; women comprised the majority of laborers at Brown and Sharpe, Walsh-Kaiser Industries, and McGrath's personal friend, Antoine Gazda's plant, where women "assembled the famous Oerlikon-Gazda 20-millimeter antiaircraft guns." Christian McBurney, "Women at Work Outside the Home," in Christian McBurney, Brian L. Wallin, Patrick T. Conley, et al., *World War II Rhode Island* (Charleston, SC: The History Press, 2017), 89–91.

77. The district courts committed 255 children to the State Home during the 1943–1944 fiscal year. "Children's Court Report Released," *Providence Journal*, March 1, 1944, 5.

78. According to a report issued by the Junior League in February 1944, 12 individual district court judges throughout the state collectively heard 481 cases of wayward or delinquent youths in 1941, 537 in 1942, and 820 in 1943. In advocating for the bill, Sixth District Court Judge DePasquale cited the rise in the number of young offenders (17 and younger) brought to him—339 in 1941, 437 in 1942, and 503 in 1943—he contended that the gravity of the situation required a full-time body to handle the rising number of wayward and delinquent youth. *Ibid.*

79. Mrs. Marion Yatman, Providence Repub-

lican, and Katherine T. Shunney, Woonsocket Democrat, reintroduced the measure in 1942 and 1943, respectively. At one point, 50 amendments were introduced into the House of Representatives; among them, whether the governor would have the power to name justice and associate justice without Senate confirmation. "A Children's Court," *Providence Journal*, March 22, 1944; G. Richmond Carpenter, "R.I. Senators Do an About Face on Children's Court," *Providence Journal*, March 12, 1944.

80. "*Visitor* Opposes Child Court Bill," *Providence Journal*, March 17, 1944, 1.

81. *Ibid.*

82. "Senate Accepts Amendments by House," *Providence Journal*, April 7, 1944.

83. Richard John Maiman, "'Constitutionalizing' the Juvenile Court: The Impact of *In re Gault* in Rhode Island," PhD Diss., Brown University, 1972, 39.

84. "Rhode Island Public Laws"; "McGrath Pleased by Senate Action," *Providence Journal*, March 12, 1944, 12; "Court Bill Reported with Senate Approved Broomhead Juvenile Court," *Providence Journal*, March 20, 1944, 1; State of Rhode Island, in General Assembly, "An Act Creating a Children's Court for the State of Rhode Island," January Session, 1944, 2–3.

85. Critics feared that children who were not afforded trial by jury would suffer at the hands of an arbitrary judge. The establishment of a family court in 1961 attempted to allay some of these concerns.

86. "The Voters' Log" III, no. 8 (April 1944), MSS 21, League of Women Voters, Rhode Island Historical Society, Providence.

87. Assured that Republican deputy leader John G. Murphy would be named judge or associate judge, floor leader Richard D. Windsor and Murphy teamed to oppose the final Juvenile Court Bill. "Juvenile Court Appointments: Selection of McCabe and Littlefield Pleases Most Everyone Except Republicans Who Feel They were Left Out in the Cold," *Providence Journal*, April 16, 1944, 5.

88. Rhode Island's population, according to the 1940 Census, was 713,346. *Rhode Island Manual*, 1941; Mary Gertrude Honan, "An Inquiry into the Work of the Juvenile Court of the State of Rhode Island," Master's Thesis, Rhode Island College of Education, June 1949, 11–12.

89. *Ibid.*

90. "McGrath Desires Board to Handle State Sick Fund," *Providence Journal*, January 3, 1945.

91. Irvin L. Child and Marjorie Van De Water, eds., *Psychology for the Returning Serviceman: Infantry Journal* (Washington, D.C.: The Infantry Journal, 1945), 1–2.

92. Metcalf was disappointed when the federal government decided to build the hospital in Connecticut. "For Veterans' Hospital in RI," *Providence Journal*, March 9, 1943; "Veteran Hospital Sought for State," *Providence Journal*, April 1, 1937.

93. Many soldiers traveled to Rutland, Massachusetts, or similar facilities in Maine, Connecticut, and New York.

94. U.S. Congress, Senate, February 9–March 21, 1944. 78th Cong., Bills Introduced. *Congressional Record—Senate*, 1944. 2nd sess., Vol. 90, Pt. 2.

95. Frederic W. Collins, "Veterans' Hospital in R.I. Seen 'Practically Assured,'" *Providence Journal*, February 10, 1944.

96. Francis Chapman, "What Veterans Should Know," *Providence Journal*, April 30, 1945, 8.

97. "More Psychiatric Clinics Proposed," *Providence Journal*, October 9, 1945, 12; Francis Chapman, "What Veterans Should Know," *Providence Journal*, April 30, 1945, 8.

98. "Veterans' Center," *Providence Journal*, February 23, 1945.

99. Chapter 1395, *The Public Laws of Rhode Island*, 293–295.

100. *Ibid.*

101. "Veteran Hospital Sites Considered," *Providence Journal*, June 5, 1944; "Comstock Site Favored for R.I. Vets' Hospital," *Providence Journal*, June 19, 1944, 1.

102. "Coggeshall Hits Bristol Measure," *Pawtucket Times*, February 12, 1943.

103. "Hospitals in Rhode Island," *Journal-Bulletin Almanac* (Providence: Providence Journal, 1950), 211.

104. Even at that stage, many health care professionals linked physical illness to emotional/mental disturbances. Soldiers complaining of gastro-intestinal difficulty, headaches, numbness, and dizziness were in some cases deemed "psychosomatic." The *Providence Journal* estimated that the Chapin clinic psychologists treated 45% of all disabled veterans for some form of "psychoneurosis." Chapman, "What Every Veteran Should Know."

105. *Ibid.*

106. *Ibid.*

107. *Ibid.*

108. Sunstein, *The Second Bill of Rights*, 13.

109. *Ibid.*, 15.

110. "Governor Names Postwar Group"; *Providence Journal*, November 18, 1943; "McGrath Pledges to Back Planners," *Providence Journal*, December 18, 1943.

111. "Governor Names Postwar Group," November 18, 1943; "McGrath Pledges to Back Planners," December 18, 1943.

112. McGrath was instrumental in securing

a safe haven for Gazda and his wife during the war and postwar periods. Patrick T. Conley, "Liberty Ships and More: Civilian Workers and Manufacturers Bolster the War Effort," in Christian McBurney, Brian L. Wallin, Patrick T. Conley, John W. Kennedy, and Maureen A. Taylor, *World War II Rhode Island* (Charleston, SC: The History Press, 2017), 79; "Fires 1st Shot from Gazda's New Anti-Aircraft Gun," *Providence Evening Bulletin*, January 25, 1943, 19; "Accepts 35 Patent Models Given to the State by Antoine Gazda," *Providence Journal*, December 14, 1944, 6.

113. Robert L. Andresen, *Providence Shipyard: Walsh-Kaiser Company, Inc. 1943–1945* (Providence: Bank Lithograph Company, 1945), 9, from the private collection of Dr. Patrick T. Conley, Bristol, RI.

114. *Ibid.*, 5–6.

115. George H. Kellner and J. Stanley Lemons, *Rhode Island: The Ocean State* (Sun Valley, CA: American Historical Press, 2004), 136; Patrick T. Conley, *An Album of Rhode Island History, 1636–1986* (Norfolk: Donning Company Publishers, 1986), 212; "Walsh-Kaiser Co. Takes Control of Shipyard Without Ceremony: Officials Promise Full Report Early This Week on Plans for Reorganization; Several Top Rheem Men Remain to Close Business," *Providence Journal*, March 1, 1943; "Walsh-Kaiser Co. Begins Hiring Men," *Providence Journal*, March 2, 1943.

116. "MacLeod Assails McGrath Delay in Acting to End Shipyard Tie up," *Providence Journal*, September 7, 1944.

117. *Ibid.*; "Governor Visits Duke of Windsor," *Providence Journal*, May 21, 1941; Gerry Goldstein, "J. Howard McGrath had a Style All His Own," *Providence Journal*, January 11, 1989.

118. "McGrath to Meet Yard Union Chiefs," *Providence Journal*, September 29, 1944.

119. "McGrath Assails Shipyard Strike as 'Indefensible': Recent Boilermakers' Tie-up Hit at R.I. AFL Dinner for Congressman Fogarty," *Providence Journal*, September 4, 1944.

120. *Ibid.*

121. "McGrath, Roosevelt Widen Margin by Service Ballots," *Providence Journal*, December 14, 1944.

122. "Post War Planning," Providence Chamber of Commerce, Folder, "Post War Planning," February 1, 1944, J. Howard McGrath Papers, Harry S Truman Presidential Library, Independence, MO.

123. *Ibid.*

124. "Rhode Island Veterans Retraining and Reemployment Committee," *State of Rhode Island and Providence Plantations*, Annual Report 1946.

125. "Appointments Made," *Providence Journal*, September 10, 1944.

126. G. Richmond Carpenter, "Vets Retain State Jobs," *Providence Sunday Journal*, August 26, 1945.

127. "R.I. Veterans Retraining and Reemployment Committees: Annual Report, 1946"; "Rhode Island's Educational and Training Opportunities for the Veteran" (Providence: Office of the Commissioner of Education, 1945).

128. "McGrath Gives Advice on V-J," *The Pawtucket Times*, August 13, 1945; J. Howard McGrath, "Proclamation: A Period of Thanksgiving for Total Victory," *Providence Journal*, August 15, 1945.

129. "McGrath Accepts Advance to U.S. Solicitor General; Pastore to Govern State: Truman's Choice Hits Democrats as Big Surprise," *Providence Journal*, September 29, 1945.

Chapter 10

1. J. Howard McGrath, "Third Inaugural Address," 3, Folder, "Annual Message, 1943," J. Howard McGrath Papers, Harry S Truman Presidential Library, Independence, MO.

2. "Rhode Island Governor Signs Soldier Vote Bill," *The National Legionnaire* (March 1944), Folder, "Soldier Vote, March, 1945," J. Howard McGrath Collection, Special and Archival Collections, Providence College, Providence.

3. Donald S. Inbody, *The Soldier Vote: War, Politics, and America* (London: Palgrave Macmillan, 2016), 1.

4. The Southern states especially complained that the Green-Lucas bill contradicted the laws of certain states that did not permit absentee balloting. "Text of the Governor's Speech," *Providence Journal*, January 5, 1944.

5. Inbody, *The Soldier Vote*, 2.

6. Charles P. Bennett, secretary of state, "Article IV," *Manual, with Rules and Orders, for the Use of the General Assembly of the State of Rhode Island, 1903* (Providence: E.L. Freeman & Sons, 1903), 44.

7. *Ibid.*

8. The Gallup Poll was established in 1935; John Morton Blum, *V Was for Victory: Politics and American Culture during World War II* (New York: Harcourt Brace & Company, 1976), 247–250.

9. Inbody, *The Soldier Vote*, 66–67.

10. Blum, *V Was for Victory*, 247.

11. Inbody, *The Soldier Vote*, 60–62.

12. Congress then authorized a new measure maintaining that a federal balloting procedure may be implemented if each respective state supported it. Although the president did not support it, he grudgingly accepted the bill and it passed without his signature. *Ibid.*; "Soldier Vote-1944 S. 1285, Public Law 277, 78th Congress," *Congressional Quarterly* I (1945).

13. Inbody, *The Soldier Vote*, 62–64.

14. Erwin Levine, *Theodore Francis Green: The Washington Years, 1937–1960*, vol. 2 (Providence: Brown University Press, 1971), 65–66; Inbody, 66–68.

15. Letter from Henry L. Stimson to Chairman Robert E. Hannegan, May 25, 1944, Folder, "Subject File: 1943–1992, War Ballot Commission, 1944," Papers of Robert E. Hannegan, Harry S Truman Presidential Library, Independence, MO.

16. J. Howard McGrath, "Annual Message of J. Howard McGrath, Governor of the State of Rhode Island and Providence Plantations to the General Assembly at its January Session, 1942," Folder, "Inaugural Message," J. Howard McGrath Collection, Special and Archival Collections, Providence College, Providence.

17. "Absentee Ballot," n.d. "Absentee Voter," Folder, "Absentee Ballot," Special Files, John E. Fogarty Collection, Special and Archival Collections, Providence College, Providence.

18. "998 Requesting Absentee Ballots," *Providence Journal*, October 14, 1942, 18.

19. "Governor Seeks Complete Army Absentee Voting," *Providence Journal*, March 17, 1943.

20. *Ibid.*

21. *Ibid.*

22. "Service Ballot Plan Presented," *Providence Journal*, January 5, 1944, 1.

23. *Ibid.*

24. Memo to Governor McGrath from William Pelkey, Folder, "Material furnished by Pelkey," n.d., J. Howard McGrath Collection, Special and Archival Collections, Providence College, Providence.

25. Letter Joseph A. McMahon to Fred C. Kilguss and letter Fred C. Kilguss to Joseph A. McMahon, Folder, "Miscellaneous 'Mc,'" February 4, 18, 1944, J. Howard McGrath Collection, Special and Archival Collection, Providence College, Providence.

26. "State Convention Adopts Proposal for Service Vote," *Providence Journal*, March 29, 1944.

27. *Ibid.*

28. *Ibid.*

29. *Ibid.*

30. *Ibid.*

31. That record was broken by Democrat Claiborne Pell in 1960, when he defeated Republican Raoul Archambault for the Senate seat made vacant by aging senator Theodore Francis Green's retirement. Pell won with a plurality of 153,986. G. Wayne Miller, *An Un-*

common Man: The Life and Times of Senator Claiborne Pell (Lebanon, NH: University Press of New England, 2011), 32.

32. In Rhode Island, President Roosevelt received 174,431 and Governor Thomas Dewey of New York, 123,517. Governor McGrath had no trouble defeating his opponent, Norman D. MacLeod, 178,812 to 116,032. "McGrath, Roosevelt Widen Margin by Service Ballots," *Providence Journal*, December 14, 1944, 1, 2.

Chapter 11

1. The establishment of United Nations Relief and Rehabilitation Administration was the result of a meeting between the United States and Great Britain in Bermuda for the "determination of the American people, in the midst of war, to do their part in binding up the wounds of those nations most sorely stricken by the war." Harry S Truman to Herbert H. Lehman, director general of UNRRA (November 8, 1945) as quoted in Eleanor Baldwin Tripp, "Displaced Persons: The Legislative Controversy in the United States, 1945–1950," MA Thesis (Columbia University, 1966), 28; Gerard Daniel Cohen, *In War's Wake: Europe's Displaced Persons in the Postwar Order* (New York: Oxford University Press, 2012), 3–4.

2. Kay Stokey, "Mrs. McGrath Relaxes at Pier," *Washington Post*, December 23, 1945.

3. *Ibid.*

4. *Ibid.*

5. Milburn P. Akers, "How the Capital Whirls Merrily" *The Chicago Sun*, March 9, 1949, Folder, "J. Howard McGrath File, McGrath after the Presidential Election, 1948—DNC Clippings," Democratic National Committee, Harry S Truman Library, Independence, MO.

6. "The New Solicitor General," *Springfield Daily Republican*, October 1, 1945, Folder, "Solicitor General, 1946, Desk Corres. Clippings—Senatorial," J. Howard McGrath Papers, Harry S Truman Presidential Library, Independence, MO.

7. "Unexpected, But Good," *Hartford Times*, October 1945, Folder, "Solicitor General, 1946, Desk Corres. Clippings—Senatorial," J. Howard McGrath Papers, Harry S Truman Presidential Library, Independence, MO.

8. "McGrath Favored by Senate Group," *Providence Journal*, October 2, 1945, 3.

9. Letter from Charles Fahy to J. Howard McGrath, October 25, 1945, Charles Fahy Papers, Franklin Delano Roosevelt Presidential Library, Hyde Park, NY.

10. "J. Howard McGrath," File Number 62–59475, Section 1, "Office Memorandum to the Director from A. Rosen," October 3, 1945, Athan Theoharis Collection, Department of Special Collections and University Archives, Marquette University, Milwaukee.

11. McGrath upheld the decision of the controversial Philippines War Tribunal, which took place in December, 1945, the first trial that dealt with war crimes of the Pacific Theater. As a result of his ruling, Generals Homma Masaharu and Yamashita Tomoyuki, the so-called "Tiger of Malaya," were executed for crimes against humanity and hanged in February 1946. In the high-profile case, Solicitor General McGrath heard the evidence following a hasty trial that took place in the Philippines, where five prosecutors pronounced the Japanese generals guilty of war crimes. Appealing the verdict, death by hanging, Yamashita was denied a stay of execution by McGrath, who regarded the Philippine tribunal as a legal arm of the president of the United States. This case served as a benchmark for a heretofore unrecognized dictum: command accountability.

In the Tidelands Controversy, McGrath supported the president's position, which pitted Truman ally and oil tycoon William Pauley, who was of late the Democratic state chairman of California against the secretary of the interior, the curmudgeonly Harold Ickes. Ickes resigned over the dispute. Pauley argued that the Tidelands, or the oil beds beneath the ocean floor, was bound by the state, while Ickes believed that the federal government should have jurisdiction over this resource. Again, the concept of federalism played a major role in determining whether the state's position would claim victory over the federal government. Ernest R. Bartley, *The Tidelands Oil Controversy: A Legal and Historical Analysis* (Austin: University of Texas Press, 1953), 255–256; "Yamashita Files: New Plea in U.S.," *New York Times* December 8, 1945; Allan A. Ryan, *Yamashita's Ghost: War Crimes, MacArthur's Justice, and Command Accountability* (Lawrence, KS: University Press of Kansas, 2012), 264, 274, 279.

12. "McGrath to Take Oath Tomorrow," *Providence Journal*, October 7, 1945, 1, 4.

13. "McGrath's Move Puts Problem Before Party," *Providence Journal*, October 14, 1945; "Ex-Gov. McGrath Demands Journal, Name Informant," *Providence Journal*, October 7, 1945, 1.

14. While Gerry campaigned for McGrath in 1944, he refused to support FDR. Of McGrath, Gerry stated, he [McGrath] has exhibited "great tact and patience" in his administration of the state during the war. "Gerry Campaigns for Gov. McGrath," *Providence Journal*, November 2, 1944, 9; David M. Cameron, "Gerry Senate Career Ends: Relin-

quishes Seat to McGrath after 26 Years in Capitol," *Providence Evening Bulletin*, January 3, 1947.

15. "Democratic Politics," *Providence Journal*, October 5, 1945, 15; "McGrath to Leave State Post Today: Pastore Will Succeed to R.I. Gubernatorial Chair at Informal Ceremony," *Providence Journal*, October 6, 1945; "Ex-Governor McGrath Demands Journal, Name Informant," *Providence Journal*, October 7, 1945, 1, 14.

16. "Ex-Gov, McGrath Demands Journal, Name Informant," *Providence Journal*, October 1, 1945, 1.

17. Jonathan Bell, *The Liberal State on Trial: The Cold War and American Politics in the Truman Years* (New York: Columbia University Press, 2004), 20; Alan Brinkley, *The End of Reform: New Deal Liberalism in Recession and War* (New York: Vintage, 1995), 227–235.

18. Bell stated that liberals like Helen Gahagan Douglas "saw their commitment to social democracy held up as a liability not only by anti-statist Republicans but also by their colleagues in the Democratic Party." The same can be said for the face-off between Green and Gerry. Nonetheless, local politics had a hand in their unspoken conflict as well. Alan Brinkley, *The End of Reform*, 235–245; Bell, *The Liberal State on Trial*, xiv–xv.

19. Jonathan Bell, *The Liberal State*, 4–5, 11, 68–69.

20. Robert Quinn challenged McGrath for the Democratic nomination, and stated that "McGrath had given me his word at that time, you know that he would not run for senator. We had sat down with him, John Fogarty and I sat down and had gotten his word on it that he would not run. The minute Gerry withdrew as a candidate, why he [McGrath]became a candidate ... I think Howard really maybe used me to drive Gerry out." The Honorable Robert Quinn interviewed by Matthew J. Smith, August 7, 1972, Special and Archival Collections, Providence College, Providence. "Truman's Letter Praises McGrath," *Providence Journal*, October 26, 1946.

21. As senator, McGrath would serve on three committees: the Judiciary, the District of Columbia, and the Special Committee Investigating the National Defense Program. "McGrath Pledges Truman Support," *Providence Journal*, October 8, 1946; Letter from J. Howard McGrath to Mr. Wallace Dickson, director of publicity, February 4, 1947, Folder, "Personal, January–February 1947," J. Howard McGrath Papers, Harry S Truman Presidential Library, Independence, MO.

22. "Federal Official Boosts McGrath," *Providence Journal*, October 30, 1946; "Hannegan

Aide Claims Truman Wants M'Grath," *Pawtucket Times*, October 30, 1946; "Capital Needs McGrath, Postal Official States," *Newport Daily News*, October 30, 1946.

23. "United States Senator Election, November 5, 1946," *Journal Bulletin Almanac*, 264; Armand Cote, *Manual with Rules and Orders for the Use of the General Assembly of the State of Rhode Island, 1947–1948*, 347.

24. Tripp, "Displaced Persons: The Legislative Controversy," 28.

25. *Ibid.*

26. The quotas as mandated by earlier legislation had not been met during the Second World War. This factor proved instrumental for McGrath, who argued that the unused quotas could be used to help the displaced. Tripp, "Displaced Persons: The Legislative Controversy," 30; *The Displaced Persons Commission: First Semi-Annual Report to the President and the Congress*, February 1, 1949, 4.

27. Eleanor Baldwin Tripp, "Displaced Persons: The Legislative Controversy in the United States, 1945–1950," MA thesis (Columbia University, 1971), 34–36.

28. Charging that UNRRA employed "a substantial pro-Soviet infiltration ... and that the UNRRA Administration has employed various pressures to induce repatriation," the Refugees Defense Committee et al. issued a report, which they presented to Secretary of State George Marshall outlining their goals for a just integration of displaced persons in the United States. "Petition on the Repatriation Drive currently being carried on by the authorities in Charge of the Displaced Persons," May 14, 1947, in Folder, "Corres. Re: Displaced Persons Apr. 1–7 1948—Senatorial," J. Howard McGrath Papers, Harry S Truman Presidential Library, Independence, MO.

29. Complicating matters further, a detailed study was conducted by Abraham G. Duker, who was a noted "political analyst in the Office of Strategic Services, and a member of the staff of the U.S. Chief Counsel for the Prosecution of the Axis Criminality." He concluded that some groups, which included Ukrainian volunteers, Croats and Slovaks, and others who traveled under the moniker of 'displaced persons' "willingly served in the German police." In order to prevent former Nazi collaborators or officers from entering displaced persons camps, Duker suggested a close vetting process before any camp residents would be allowed to enter the United States. The proof for Duker's allegations was found in the Nazi archives, and in interviews with the victims of Nazi atrocities. Abraham G. Duker, "Summary of the Statement on "the Need for Screening Displaced Persons Applying for Entry into the

United States," June 1, 1948, Folder, "Corres. Re: Displaced Persons- May–Dec. '48—Senatorial," J. Howard McGrath Papers, Harry S Truman Presidential Library, Independence, MO.

30. Leonard Dinnerstein, *America and the Survivors of the Holocaust* (New York: Columbia University Press, 1982), 39.

31. Dean Harrison as quoted in Allis Radosh and Ronald Radosh, *A Safe Haven: Harry S Truman and the Founding of Israel* (New York: Harper Perennial, 2010), 93.

32. President Truman at first appeared lukewarm toward the idea of a Jewish homeland in Palestine. Tripp, "Displaced Persons: The Legislative Controversy," 34. Madeline Lorimer, CSA, BA, MA, "America's Response to Europe's Displaced Persons, 1948-1952: A Preliminary Report," PhD diss. (Saint Louis University, St. Louis, 1964), 36–37.

33. Folder, "Corres. Re: Displaced Persons—947—Legislation S. Res. 137 Immigration—Senatorial," 80th Congress: 2nd Session Report—No. 950, "Displaced Persons in Europe: Report of the Committee on the Judiciary Pursuant to S. Res. 137. A Resolution to Make an Investigation of the Immigration System," McGrath Papers, Harry S Truman Presidential Library, Independence, MO.

34. "Displaced Persons in Europe: Report of the Committee on the Judiciary: A Resolution to Make an Investigation of the Immigration System," Pursuant to S. Res. 137 (Report No. 950), 80th Congress, 2nd Session, March 2, 1948.

35. Letter to Mr. Joseph Joslow from Cecilia R. Davidson, Folder, "Gen Immigration," *Citizens Committee on Displaced Persons*, August 7, 1947. *Congressional Record* 93, no. 144 (July 25, 1947). JDC Archives, New York.

36. Susan M. Hartmann, *Truman and the 80th Congress* (Columbia: University of Missouri Press, 1971), 174–175.

37. *Ibid.*, 36–37, 64–65, 72.

38. "Displaced Persons," March 1, 1948, Folder "Corres: Re: Displaced Persons Mar 1-16, 48, Senatorial," J. Howard McGrath Papers. Harry S Truman Presidential Library, Independence, MO.

39. "H.R. 2910 in the House of Representatives," April 1, 1947, Folder, "Corres. RE: Displaced Persons—1947, Legislation HR 2910 AD, of Dis. Pers., to D.S.—Senatorial," J. Howard McGrath Papers, Truman Presidential Library, Independence, MO.

40. *Ibid.*, 38–39.

41. Revercomb was a committed restrictionist/isolationist, and opposed American entry in the United Nations. *Ibid.*, 65.

42. Hartmann, *Truman and the 80th Congress*, 175.

43. *Ibid.*, 67–68.

44. Folder, "Corres. Re: Displaced Persons,—Senatorial," J. Howard McGrath Papers, Harry S Truman Presidential Library, Independence, MO.

45. Letter from the Members of the Lithuanian Camp Committee to J. Howard McGrath, n.d., Folder, "Corres Re: Displaced Persons, April 1-7 1948—Senatorial," J. Howard McGrath Papers, Harry S Truman Presidential Library, Independence, MO.

46. "Senator McGrath Back from Europe," *Providence Journal*, October 26, 1947, 1.

47. "McGrath Asks U.S. to Admit DP's by Adjusting Immigration Quotas," *Providence Journal*, October 18, 1947, 1.

48. Harold N. Graves, Jr., "McGrath Asks Quick Aid to France to Halt Reds," *Providence Evening Bulletin*, October 28, 1947, 8.

49. *Ibid.*

50. "McGrath Urges U.S. to Fill Immigration Quotas with DPs," *Washington Post*, November 3, 1947, Folder, "Displaced Persons, Desk Corres. Clippings—Senatorial," J. Howard McGrath Papers, Harry S Truman Presidential Library, Independence, MO.

51. Leonard O. Warner, "R.I. Senators Disclosed as Saviors of 14 Monks," *Providence Journal*, January 20, 1948; "14 Monks Saved from Reds through R.I. Senators' Aid," *Providence Evening Bulletin*, January 20, 1948.

52. Warner, "R.I. Senators Disclosed," January 20, 1948; "14 Monks Saved from Reds," January 20, 1948.

53. Warner, "R.I. Senators Disclosed," January 20, 1948; "14 Monks Saved from Reds," January 20, 1948.

54. Warner, "R.I. Senators Disclosed," January 20, 1948; "14 Monks Saved from Reds," January 20, 1948.

55. Telegram from Senator Pat McCarran to J. Howard McGrath, care of Fred Kilguss, December 13, 1948; Response from J. Howard McGrath to Honorable Pat McCarran, December 15, 1948; Folder, "Corres. Re: Displaced Persons, May–Dec. '48—Senatorial," J. Howard McGrath Papers, Harry S Truman Presidential Library, Independence, MO.

56. "Displaced Persons," *Congressional Quarterly Almanac 1948*, 193.

57. Cohen, *In War's Wake*, 18–19.

58. J. Howard McGrath in the *Congressional Record* CXIV (May 12, 1948), 5687, as quoted in Sister M. Madeline Lorimer, CSA, BA, MA, "America's Response to Europe's Displaced Persons, 1948-1952: A Preliminary Report" PhD diss. (Saint Louis University, 1964), 151.

59. Bill introduced by Mr. McGrath and Mr. Hatch, "S. 2901 in the Senate of the United States," July 28, 1948, Folder, "Amend. Dis-

placed Persons Act. S2901, Bills Intro. By Sen. McGrath, Senatorial," J. Howard McGrath Papers, Harry S Truman Presidential Library, Independence, MO.

60. J. Howard McGrath, qtd. in Lorimer, "America's Response to Europe's Displaced Persons," 166.

61. *Ibid.*, 168.

62. *Ibid.*; "Displaced Persons," *Congressional Quarterly Almanac 1948*, 193.

63. "Displaced Persons," *CQ Almanac 1948*, 193.

64. *Ibid.*

65. Emanuel Celler, *You Never Leave Brooklyn: The Autobiography of Emanuel Celler* (New York: The John Day Company, 1953), 96–97.

66. Maurice R. Davie, "Immigration and Naturalization," *The American Jewish Year Book* 51 (1950): 127–33; Wyman, *DPs*, 194–200.

67. "Displaced Persons Still Displaced," *Social Service Review* 23, no. 2 (June 1949), 234–235, accessed March 5, 2017, http://www.jstor.org/stable/30018271.

68. "To Cooperating Organizations, Local Citizens Committees, and Friends of the Citizens Committee on Displaced Persons from William S. Bernard, Secretary," December 8, 1948.

69. "Displaced Persons," *Congressional Quarterly Almanac* 1948, 193–195; "McGrath Proposes Plan to Admit Employable DP's," October 19, 1947, Folder, "Desk Corres. Clippings—Senatorial," J. Howard McGrath Papers, Truman Presidential Library, Independence, Missouri.

70. Michael J. Ybarra, *Washington Gone Crazy: Senator Pat McCarran and the Great American Communist Hunt* (Hanover, NH: Steerforth Press, 2004), 460.

71. *Ibid.*, 460–461.

72. *Ibid.*, 464–466.

73. McCarran admitted to his daughter Mary that when he stepped foot on "holy ground where dear old grandma was a girl" he "had a little silent cry all to myself." Ybarra, *Washington Gone Crazy*, 476–477; Ben Shepard, *The Long Road Home: The Aftermath of the Second World War* (New York: Anchor Books, 2010), 381.

74. Oliver Pilat, "McGrath Will Carry Ball for an Open Door to DPs," *Washington Post*, December 2, 1948, Folder, "Displaced Persons, Desk Corres. Clippings—Senatorial," J. Howard McGrath Papers, Harry S Truman Presidential Library, Independence, MO.

75. Ybarra, *Washington Gone Crazy*, 462.

76. Dinnerstein, *America and the Survivors*, 220.

77. Ybarra, *Washington Gone Crazy*, 464–465.

78. Dinnerstein, *America and the Survivors*, 99–100.

79. A total of 300,000 DPs, who had been under custody of the IRO, 54,744 German refugees, 18,000 Polish veterans of the war, who had been residing in England 10,000 Greeks, 2,000 from Venezia-Giulia, 4,000 Chinese from Shanghai, 500 who escaped from Eastern Europe, and 10,000 war orphans. *Congressional Quarterly Almanac 1950*, 81st Congress, 2nd Session, Volume VI, 225; Wyman, *DPs*, 194–195.

80. "J. Howard McGrath to Secretary of State Dean J. Acheson," October 20, 1950.

81. *Ibid.*

Chapter 12

1. "I'm Just Wild About Harry" was a song written in the 1920s by Eubie Blake. Library of Congress."

2. "Methods of Democratic Chief McGrath, Who Never Lost an Election: Organize, Get Around, Avoid Control by Labor but Seek its Help," *The United States News and World Report* 23, no. 20 (November 14, 1947), 56–59.

3. Sean Savage, *Truman and the Democratic Party* (Lexington: University Press of Kentucky, 1997), 65.

4. Zachary Karabell, *The Last Campaign: How Harry Truman Won the 1948 Election* (New York: Vintage, 2001), 8.

5. "Hannegan Quits; McGrath to Get Chairmanship: Change to be Made at Meeting Oct. 29; Sullivan Also Resigns," *Evening Star*, September 27, 1947, Folder, "Miscellaneous Clippings—1947," J. Howard McGrath Papers, Harry S Truman Presidential Library, Independence, MO.

6. Redding, *Inside the Democratic Party*, 51.

7. *Ibid.*

8. "Hannegan Quits; McGrath to Get Chairmanship," *Evening Star*, September 27, 1947, Folder, "Miscellaneous Clippings—1947," J. Howard McGrath Papers, Harry S Truman Presidential Library, Independence, MO. Savage, *Truman and the Democratic Party*, 65–66.

9. "Hannegan Quits," September 27, 1947.

10. J. Howard McGrath to Harry S Truman, September 17, 1948, Democratic National Committee Records; "McGrath's Visit to R.I. Revealed as Move to Heal Democratic Rift," *Providence Journal*, October 1, 1947, Folder, "Miscellaneous Clippings- Senatorial, 1947," J. Howard McGrath Papers, Independence, MO.

11. "Gael E. Sullivan Is Dead at 51; Started Helicopter Mail Service," *New York Times*, October 28, 1956; Jack Redding, *Inside the Dem-*

ocratic Party; Jerry Greene of the *New York Daily News* contends that Sullivan believed "until the last minute" that he would get the job, and Massachusetts State Chairman John Cahill supported Federal Judge James P. McGranery as the new chairman. Ironically, though President Truman supported McGrath as chairman, he would in 1952 call on McGranery to replace McGrath as United States Attorney General. Jerry Greene, "Hannegan Out, Dems Battling Over No. 1 Job," *New York Daily News*, September 28, 1947.

12. Jack Redding, *Inside the Democratic Party* (New York: Bobbs-Merrill, 1958), 36–39; Arthur Krock, "Partisan Aim Rebuked," *New York Times*, March 19, 1947.

13. According to Redding, Sullivan apologized to Senator Pepper, who graciously accepted. Redding, *Inside the Democratic Party*, 36–39.

14. Redding contended that the Republican Party set out to frame Sullivan, who had returned from a party late one evening, nearly fell asleep at the wheel, swerving into the wrong lane, awaking in time to avoid an oncoming car. Witnesses who attended the party swore that Sullivan suffered from sleep deprivation, not drunkenness. Sullivan was taken to the police station, and spent the night in jail. Learning of the incident, a *Providence Journal* reporter leaked it to the press, thus initiating a round of damning stories meant to ruin him. Redding, *Inside the Democratic Party*, 36–39; 88–89.

15. *Ibid.*

16. Connelly recalled, "I had known him since about 1935 when he was Federal District Attorney in Providence, Rhode Island. When the vacancy occurred ... I recommended to Mr. Truman that he appoint Howard McGrath, and a fellow at that time who was administrative assistant to Senator Theodore Green, and who in my book at that point was the best politician on Capitol Hill, so our package was for Howard McGrath to make the speeches and let Eddie Higgins, who was Green's assistant, the other Senator from Rhode Island, do the work. Well, unbeknown to me, which Higgins later told me about, he couldn't take the job because he had an agreement with Senator Green that he couldn't leave him, that Green had set up some kind of a trust fund for him, as long as he would stay with him." Oral History interview with Matthew Connelly, Harry S Truman Presidential Library, Independence, MO.

17. Redding, *Inside the Democratic Party*, 97. "Democratic Chairman Quiet, Essentially a Compromiser," *St. Louis Star-Times*, October 1, 1947, Folder, "Miscellaneous Clippings—

Senatorial, 1947," J. Howard McGrath Papers, Harry S Truman Presidential Library, Independence, MO.

18. "Gael Sullivan to Robert Hannegan," Robert E. Hannegan Papers, September 30, 1947.

19. Zachary Karabell, *The Last Campaign*, 39–40.

20. Irwin Ross, *Inside the Democratic Party*, 119; David McCullough, *Truman* (New York: Simon & Schuster, 1992), 621.

21. "Election Returns—November 3, 1948," accessed September 5, 2017, www.youtube.com/watch?v=Zck1wxiugaE.

22. In fact, McGrath planned to sell his Providence home to take up housekeeping in Washington. He explained, "For more than a year I have been looking for a new house to get better accommodations ... I haven't stayed in the Providence house two nights in the last two years." "M'Grath's Not Headin' for the Hills," *Providence Journal*, October 27, 1948; "McGrath Estimates his Holdings at Less than $200,000 in Story," *Providence Journal*, May 26, 1948.

23. "M'Grath's Not Headin' for the Hills."

24. Marie Chatham as quoted in Sean J. Savage, *Truman and the Democratic Party* (Lexington: University of Kentucky Press, 1997), 61.

25. V.O. Key, as quoted in Savage, *Truman and the Democratic Party* (Lexington: University of Kentucky Press, 1997), 59.

26. According to columnist Doris Fleeson, McGrath suffered from only a casual acquaintance with Truman. Doris Fleeson, "Boyle Handles Patronage," *Evening Star*, February 10, 1949, in William M. Boyle, Jr., Papers, "File: Scrapbook, 1948–49," Harry S Truman Presidential Library, Independence, MO.

27. Savage, *Truman and the Democratic Party*, 66–67.

28. Harold Emery Barto, "Clark Clifford and the Presidential Election of 1948," PhD diss. (Rutgers University, 1970), 5–51.

29. James F. King of the *Kansas City Star* reported that McGrath enjoyed a close link "to the big city politics of New York and Jersey City..., and has always been highly regarded by Tammany Hall. He will fit in adequately with the Kelly machine in Chicago and the other boss groups over the country." James F. King, "Woo Cities' Vote: Look to Labor Blocs," *Kansas City Star*, September 28, 1947; "McGrath Sees Truman; Says He'll Be Active as Party Chairman," *Kansas City Star*, October 1, 1947, J. Howard McGrath Papers, Harry S Truman Presidential Library, Independence, MO.

30. Gary A. Donaldson, *Truman Defeats Dewey* (Lexington: University Press of Kentucky, 1999), 21–22.

31. Radio Press Release, March 9, 1948, Folder, "Democratic National Committee File: Publicity Division Democratic National Committee press releases, February 13—April 20, 1948," John M. Redding Papers, Harry S Truman Presidential Library, Independence, MO; Barto, "Clifford and Presidential Election of 1948," 75.

32. William Batt complained that McGrath never consulted with his division, while James Barriere added that McGrath grudgingly "tolerated" the department because the president authorized it. Nonetheless, it proved a major cause of disagreement between Truman and his Democratic national chairman. Interview, William Batt to Jerry Hess; Interview James Barriere to Hess, Truman Library, Independence, MO; Jack Redding, *Inside the Democratic Party* (New York: Bobbs-Merrill, 1959), 119.

33. Stephen White, "Rhode Island's Junior Senator: J. Howard McGrath, New Democratic National Chairman, Has Moved Up Fast," *New York Herald Tribune*, October 14, 1947.

34. J. Howard McGrath, *The Power of the People* (New York: Julian Messner, 1948), 17.

35. Zachary Karabell, *The Last Campaign*, 41.

36. "Harry Truman and the Election of Clifford attached his name to the memorandum because of the President's alleged disdain for Roosevelt reformer Rowe." Folder, Confidential Memorandum to President, November 19, 1947, Clark M. Clifford Papers, Harry S Truman Presidential Library, Independence, MO; Harvard Sitkoff, "The Coming of Age of Civil Rights in American Politics," *The Journal of Southern History* 37, no. 4 (November 1971): 597–598, accessed July 27, 2009, http://www.jstor.org/stable/2206548.

37. Clifford memorandum as quoted in Harold Emery Barto, "Clark Clifford and the Presidential Election of 1948," PhD diss. (Rutgers University, 1970), 47.

38. *Ibid.*, 49.

39. Clark Clifford, et al., Memorandum for the President, November 1948, Student Research File, "B File," Harry S Truman Presidential Library, Independence, MO.

40. Clifford Memo, 8; Carol Anderson, *Eyes Off the Prize: The United Nations and the African American Struggle for Human Rights, 1944-1955* (New York: Cambridge University Press, 2006), 8, 113.

41. Clifford Memo, 8-10.

42. "Civil Rights and Southern Splits, Dixie Democrats to Present Protest to McGrath: Monday Opening Intra-Party Battle," *Providence Journal*, March 31, 1948; "McGrath Turns Back Civil Rights Attack by Dixie Governors," *Providence Journal*, February 24, 1948.

43. "Bolting Dinner Guests," *Providence Journal.*

44. "Dixie Group Cancels Dinner Plan, Blaming 'No Segregation Policy,'" *Providence Journal*, February 19, 1948.

45. "Pitchfork Ben" Tillman as quoted in David Pietrusza, *1948: Harry Truman's Improbable Victory and the Year That Transformed America* (New York: Union Square Press, 2011), 28-29.

46. *Ibid.*, 29.

47. *Ibid.*

48. *Ibid.*

49. "List of Questions Put to Senator McGrath by Dixie Leaders," *Providence Journal*, February 24, 1948.

50. "McGrath Turns Back Civil Rights Attack by Dixie Governors: Voices Flat 'No' to Appeal to Ditch Plan," *Providence Journal*, February 24, 1948.

51. Jack Redding, *Inside the Democratic Party*, 137.

52. *Ibid.*

53. Pietrusza, *1948*, 80.

54. Letter and insert from Tom Mulvany to J. Howard McGrath, March 6, 1948, Folder, "Civil Rights, 1947-48—Proposed Legislation," J. Howard McGrath Papers, Harry S Truman Presidential Library, Independence, MO.

55. "McGrath Asserts Truman to Press Civil Rights Plan," *Providence Journal*, February 23, 1948.

56. "Democrats' Finance Chief Quits Post: Geo. B. Hamilton, Georgia, Protests Civil Rights Program," *Providence Evening Bulletin*, February 28, 1948.

57. "McGrath Turns Back Civil Rights Attack by Dixie Governors," *Providence Journal*, February 24, 1948.

58. Pietrusza, *1948*, 82.

59. Folder, "Speech Material, Civil Rights," J. Strom Thurmond, "President Truman's So-Called Civil Rights Program before the Columbia Democratic Party Rally" (Columbia, SC, March 17, 1948), 4. James Roosevelt Papers, Franklin Delano Roosevelt Presidential Library, Hyde Park, NY.

60. *Ibid.*

61. After the announcement, the president incurred the wrath of the Zionists when he pledged his support for a UN trusteeship of Palestine after the termination of British control, contradicting his earlier decision to partition into both a Jewish and Arab state. Equally divisive, Truman also pressed the House and Senate to impose universal military training because of the threat of Communism in Europe. Irwin Ross. *The Loneliest Campaign: The Truman Victory of 1948* (New York: The New American Library, 1968), 70-72.

62. "Unnamed notation: March 8, 1948," Folder, "Clippings: Senator D.N.C. Chairman," J. Howard McGrath Papers, Harry S Truman Presidential Library, Independence, MO.

63. Clayton Knowles, "Statement of Governors," February 24, 1948. "South not 'in the bag' Governors retort to M'Grath Rebuff," *Providence Journal*, February 24, 1948, 1.

64. "Dixie Democrats to Present Protest to McGrath Monday Opening Intra-Party Battle," *Providence Journal*, March 31, 1949.

65. *Ibid.*

66. Letter from Mary McLeod Bethune, founder-president, National Council of Negro Women, Inc. to J. Howard McGrath, Folder, "Civil Rights, 1947–48—Proposed Legislation," J. Howard McGrath Papers, Harry S Truman Library, Independence, MO.

67. "Promise—and Performance," *New York Post*, February 3, 1948, Folder 10, Box "The Truman Administration's Civil Rights Program: The Report of the Committee on Civil Rights, and President Truman's Message to Congress" (February 2, 1948), #18 A, Student Research File, Harry S Truman Presidential Library, Independence, MO.

68. Carol Anderson, *Eyes off the Prize: The United Nations and the African American Struggle for Human Rights, 1944–1955* (Columbia: University of Missouri Press, 2003), 124.

69. Letter from Rick Dawson, secretary, The Tolerance Club of Dallas to J. Howard McGrath, Folder, "Civil Rights, 1947–48, Proposed Legislation," J. Howard McGrath Papers, Harry S Truman Presidential Library, Independence, MO.

70. Harold N. Graves, Jr., "A Party Divided: Dixie Revolt, Sniping at Truman, McGrath Bode Ill for Democrats," *Providence Evening Bulletin*, February 26, 1948.

71. "McGrath Gives Henry Wallace Virtual Invitation to Return to Ranks of Democratic Party," *Providence Journal*, February 19, 1948.

72. "McGrath Denies Southern Revolt," *Providence Journal*, May 3, 1948.

73. Ashley E. Holden, "M'Grath Extols Truman Record," *Spokane Review*, April 6, 1948, Folder, "Democratic National Committee, Western Trip, April 1948, Desk Corres. Clippings—Senatorial," J. Howard McGrath Papers, Harry S Truman Presidential Library, Independence, MO.

74. "McGrath Address at Auditorium Open to Public," *Oregon Journal*, April 7, 1948.

75. Stub Nelson, "McGrath Dem Leader Sees Basin; to Visit City," *Seattle Post*, April 6, 1948.

76. Paul Hauser, "Demo Chief Takes Blast at Wallace," *The Oregonian*, April 8, 1948, Folder, "Democratic National Committee: Western Trip: April 1948, Desk Corres. Clippings—Senatorial," J. Howard McGrath Papers, Harry S Truman Presidential Library, Independence, MO.

77. Fellow Rhode Islander and former Roosevelt crony Thomas Corcoran urged McGrath to persuade the president to refrain from pressuring justice Douglas to leave the Supreme Court. The justice, Corcoran explained, would feel obligated to fulfill his duty to the president, but would prefer to remain on the bench. Redding, *Inside the Democratic Party*, 171.

78. Vaughan, *Politics and Civil Rights*, 40–41.

79. Pietrusza, *1948*, 170.

80. "'Draft Ike' Move Boosted," *Providence Evening Bulletin*, July 1, 1948.

81. "McGrath Says Bolt Might Boomerang," *Washington Post*, May 13, 1948, Folder, "Civil Rights and Southern Splits, Desk Correspondence Clippings—Senatorial," J. Howard McGrath Collection, Harry S Truman Presidential Library, Independence, MO.

82. Paul R. Leach, "McGrath Sits Tight," *Chicago Daily News*, June 1948, Folder, "Democratic Convention, Philadelphia July, 1948, Desk Correspondence Clippings—Senatorial," J. Howard McGrath Collection, Harry S Truman Presidential Library, Independence, MO.

83. "Two Words by Truman Hailed on Par with his Main Address," *Woonsocket Call*, September 28, 1948, Folder 49, "1948: Speeches," John O. Pastore Papers, Special and Archival Collections, Providence College, Providence.

84. David McCullough, *Truman* (New York: Simon & Schuster, 1992), 635.

85. Tobin stated, "fellow delegates of this Convention, from the 48 states and the possessions, we are all Americans and under the law all Americans are entitled to their legal rights, regardless of race, regardless of creed, regardless of color." Truman eventually named Tobin secretary of labor on the advice of McGrath. Vincent A. Lapomarda, *The Boston Mayor Who Became Truman's Secretary of Labor* (New York: Peter Lang, 1995), 207. In an oral interview with Truman Library archivist Hess, Biemiller stated that he convinced young Humphrey to deliver his rousing speech in favor of civil rights, since the young senator-to-be feared that a strong stand would cost him the election. Hess interview with Biemiller, Harry S Truman Presidential Library, Independence, MO.

86. John Frederick Martin *Civil Rights*, 85.

87. "J. Howard McGrath Opening Speech: Democratic National Convention, July 12, 1948," J. Howard McGrath Papers, Harry S Truman Presidential Library; E. Edgar Brown, ed., *Democracy at Work: The Official Report of the*

Democratic National Convention Philadelphia, July 12–July 14, 1948, resulting in the nomination of Harry S Truman of Missouri for president and Alben W. Barkley for vice president.

88. Carol Anderson, *Eye off the Prize*, 124–125.

89. Redding, *Inside the Democratic Party*, 196–197; McCullough, *Truman*, 641–642.

90. Redding, *Inside the Democratic Party*, 198.

91. "United States Senate: 'Turnip Day' Session," accessed June 28, 2017, https://www.senate.gov/artandhistory/history/minute/Turnip_Day_Session.htm.

92. *Ibid.*

93. "J. Howard McGrath to Harry S Truman, September 17, 1948," Folder, "Democratic National Committee Records," J. Howard McGrath Papers, Harry S Truman Presidential Library, Independence, MO.

94. The president stated, "Crackpot Biemiller from Wisconsin offers a minority report on civil rights…. The Convention votes down States Rights and votes for the crackpot amendment to the Civil Rights Plank. The crackpots hope the South will bolt." Robert H. Ferrell, ed., *Off the Record: The Private Papers of Harry S Truman* (Columbia: University of Missouri Press), 143.

95. Brinkley, *The End of Reform*, 262.

96. "Chairman McGrath's Task," *U.S. News and World Report*, February 4, 1949, 40, Folder, "Magazine Articles, Comments on, 1948–49," J. Howard McGrath Papers, Harry S Truman Presidential Library, Independence, MO.

97. "Manuscript," Folder, "Manuscripts File: *Insider the Democratic Party*, Folder 3 of 5," John M. Redding Papers, Harry S Truman Presidential Library, Independence, MO.

98. *Ibid.*

99. *Ibid.*

100. In the case of Roosevelt, Pauley was correct, since Roosevelt nearly sabotaged the election with his indiscriminate support for General Dwight D. Eisenhower. The campaign to "Dump Truman," like the support for Eisenhower, fell by the wayside, and Roosevelt eventually backed the president. *Ibid.*

101. "Notes: Pearson, Pegler and other reporters," Folder, "Democratic National Committee File: Editorials and Columnists—statements regarding 1948 Presidential Campaign," John M. Redding Papers, Harry S Truman Presidential Library, Independence, MO.

102. *Ibid.*

103. Letter from Harry S Truman to J. Howard McGrath, January 7, 1949, Folder, "McGrath, J. Howard," PSF, Harry S Truman Presidential Library, Independence, MO.

104. "The Dixiecrat Purge," *Providence Journal*, December 15, 1948.

105. "Tip to Truman: Dixiecrats Set to Even Snubs," January 2, 1949; Folder, "Democratic National Committee, 1948 Desk Corres. Clippings, Senatorial," J. Howard McGrath Papers, Harry S Truman Presidential Library, Independence, MO.

106. McClellan was named chairman of the Expenditures Committee and retained his spot on the Public Works Committee. Jack Bell, "McGrath Sets out to Heal Party Wounds," *Providence Journal*, January 30, 1949.

107. *Congressional Quarterly Almanac*, 81st Congress, 1st Session, Vol. V (Washington, D.C.: Congressional Quarterly News Feature, 1949), 14.

108. Martin S. Hayden, "McGrath Admits Giving White, Negro Leader, 'Tonguelashing,'" *Washington Star*, March 16, 1949; Martin S. Hayden, "McGrath Admits Chastising Negro Head on Civil Rights: Says He was Angered by 'Turning Tail' Accusation in Letter Written by Walter White, NAACP Leader; Denies Report Fisticuffs Almost Occurred," *Providence Journal*, March 1949.

109. Hayden, "McGrath Admits Giving White," March 16, 1949; "McGrath Admits Chastising," March 1949.

110. Hayden, "McGrath Admits Giving White," March 16, 1949; "McGrath Admits Chastising," March 1949.

111. "A Form of Blindness," *DC Star*, March 17, 1949.

112. Letter from Walter White to J. Howard McGrath, March 15, 1949, Folder, "Walter White—1949, Misc. Senatorial," J. Howard McGrath Papers, Harry S Truman Presidential Library, Independence, MO.

113. In an interview with Truman archivist Noyes in 1955, McGrath refuted this claim, stating, "I might go to the President about an appointment, but we never took the position in the National Committee that we had a right to make appointments." "Interview with Associates of President Truman: McGrath, J. Howard and Charles Sawyer," Post Presidential Memoirs, Harry S Truman Presidential Library, Independence, MO; "Chairman McGrath's Task: To Find Jobs for Deserving Democrats and Hold Party Together by Organizing Methods that Won in '48," *U.S. News and World Report* 26, no. 5 (February 4, 1949), 39–40; "Party Indicates McGrath in Solid with Truman," *Providence Evening Bulletin*, January 22, 1949.

114. *Ibid.*, 40; "Party Indicates McGrath in Solid with Truman," *Providence Evening Bulletin*, January 1, 1949.

115. "Nation's New Money Man," *Chicago*

Times, January 31, 1948, Folder, "Clippings—Senator—D.N.C. Chairman," J. Howard McGrath Papers, Harry S Truman Presidential Library, Independence, MO.

116. Savage, *Truman and the Democratic Party*, 65–66; *Providence Evening Bulletin*, January 30,1948.

117. However, evidence from the Truman Library points to their friendly relationship after McGrath became Democratic national chairman. For example, McGrath refused to accept Hannegan's resignation as national committeeman of Missouri. Folder, "Hannegan, Robert E.," J. Howard McGrath Papers, Harry S Truman Presidential Library, Independence, MO; Robert S. Allen and William Shannon; "Chairman McGrath's Task," *U.S. News*, 40.

118. "Democrats Finance Chief Quits Post," *Providence Evening Bulletin*, February 28, 1948.

119. According to McFarland and Roll, Johnson accepted the position as finance director of the party in order to "be appropriately rewarded." Quite possibly, Truman would name him the next secretary of defense. Jack Redding, *Inside the Democratic Party*. George Dixon, "Washington Scene," King Features Syndicate, Inc., Folder, "Democratic National Committee, 1948 Desk Corres. Clippings, Senatorial," J. Howard McGrath Papers, Harry S Truman Presidential Library, Independence, MO; Keith D. McFarland and David L. Roll, *Louis Johnson and the Arming of America: The Roosevelt and Truman Years* (Bloomington: Indiana University Press, 2005), 134–138.

120. McFarland and Roll, *Louis Johnson*, 138.

121. "no name financial statement," Folder, "Clippings—Senator D.N.C. Chairman," J. Howard McGrath Papers, Harry S Truman Presidential Library, Independence, MO.

122. "$1,000,000 Promised Democrats in Drive for Victory in 1950," *D.C. Star*, April 4, 1949, Folder, "Democratic National Committee, 1948, Desk Clippings, Senatorial," J. Howard McGrath Papers, Harry S Truman Presidential Library, Independence, MO.

123. Robert S. Allen, "Oust-McGrath Growls Heard Despite Victory," November 7, 1948, Folder, "Democratic Campaign, General, 1948, Desk Corres. Clippings—Senatorial," J. Howard McGrath Papers, Harry S Truman Presidential Library, Independence, MO.

124. Drew Pearson, "Atomic Energy Tried for Farms," *Washington Merry-Go-Round, Washington Post*, January 24, 1949, Folder, "J. Howard McGrath File: McGrath After the Presidential Election, 1948," Democratic National Committee, Harry S Truman Presidential Library, Independence, MO.

125. Doris Fleeson, "Boyle Won't Upset McGrath Policies," *Washington Post*, August 10, 1949, Folder, "Newspaper Clippings—1949," J. Howard McGrath Papers, Harry S Truman Presidential Library, Independence, MO.

126. *Ibid.*

127. In Ohio, Robert Taft country, Republicans "feared the loss of the Senate seat"; in Indiana, Republican senator Homer E. Capehart was losing his battle against former a strong former governor, in Iowa Bourke Hickenlooper faced an almost assured loss, and Massachusetts Republican Joseph Martin was shocked by the election of Democrat Paul Dever. "Fair Deal Is Sound Policy on Pay-as-Go Basis'—McGrath: McGrath Builds for Vital Fight in '50 Election," *Illinois Democratic Newspaper: Public Service Leader*, March 18, 1949, 1, 3, Folder, "Magazines and Newspapers—1948," J. Howard McGrath Papers, Harry S Truman Presidential Library, Independence, MO.

128. "Fair Deal is Sound Policy on Pay-as-Go Basis'—McGrath: McGrath Builds for Vital Fight in '50 Election," *The Illinois Democratic Newspaper: Public Service Leader*, March 18, 1949, 1, 3, Folder, "Magazines and Newspapers—1948," J. Howard McGrath Papers, Harry S Truman Presidential Library, Independence, MO.

129. Randolph, who threatened that his people would institute a military boycott unless the president decided to desegregate the military, most probably "encouraged" the president's positive action on July 26, 1948.

Chapter 13

1. Milton MacKaye, "He'll Sink or Swim with Harry," *Saturday Evening Post* (May 29, 1948).

2. Alex Ray, *Hired Gun* (New York: University Press of America, 2008), 1.

3. *Ibid.*

4. Alonzo Hamby, *Man of the People: A Life of Harry S Truman* (New York: Oxford University Press, 1995), 589.

5. Robert Ferrell, *Harry S Truman: A Life* (Columbia: University of Missouri Press, 1994), 358; Robert Donovan, *The Tumultuous Years*, 380.

6. Robert J. Donovan. *Tumultuous Years: The Presidency of Harry S Truman, 1949–1953* (New York: W. W. Norton, 1982), 375.

7. In return, some sources claim that Johnson was promised the Defense Department. According to his biographers, McFarland and Roll, the reasons for Johnson's acceptance of Finance remain a mystery, since "no evidence has ever been discovered to substan-

tiate such a pact" (Truman's alleged promise to Johnson). Keith D. McFarland and David L. Roll, *Louis Johnson and the Arming of America: The Roosevelt and Truman Years* (Bloomington: Indiana University Press, 2005), 138.

8. "RI Senator Says He Will Give His Decision Shortly," *Providence Journal*, July 29, 1949.

9. Mr. Connelly stated that "Mr. McGrath was appointed to the Cabinet, and Mr. Truman thereby solved the problem of ignoring the Catholic people." Jerry N. Hess oral History Interview with Matthew J. Connelly, New York, November 28 and November 30, 1968, and August 21, 1968, Harry S Truman Presidential Library, Independence, MO.

10. Jerry N. Hess, oral interview Supreme Court Justice Thomas Clark, October 17, 1972, Harry S Truman Presidential Library, Independence, MO.

11. "McGrath Declines Comment on Stand; Opposition Reported to Stopgap Appointee," *Providence Journal*, July 30, 1949, 1.

12. *Ibid.*

13. "McGrath Development Stirs Speculation on Successor," *Providence Journal*, July 29, 1949.

14. Ickes would come to think differently of McGrath as time wore on. Harold L. Ickes, "To Tom, with Love," *Washington News*, September 22, 1949.

15. "Clark and McGrath," *Washington Post*, September 15, 1949.

16. *Ibid.*

17. "The President's Choices," *Providence Journal*, July 30, 1949, 7.

18. Nancy V. Baker, *Conflicting Loyalties: Law and Politics in the Attorney General's Office, 1789–1990* (Lawrence: University of Kansas Press, 1992), 94–95.

19. Brownell worked for much stronger civil rights legislation than Eisenhower had envisioned. Baker, *Conflicting Loyalties*, 68–69, 94–95.

20. *Ibid.*

21. In the past, cabinet officers retained their original salary. "Pending Cabinet Pay Increases Pose New Problem for McGrath," *Providence Journal*, July 30, 1949, 1.

22. The bill (HR 1689) was adopted following changes made in both Houses. HR 1689 constituted the first raise granted to cabinet members since 1925. Its passage resulted in an increase of $1,087,496.20 to the Executive Department payroll. "Executive Pay Raise," *Congressional Quarterly Almanac 1949*, 81st Congress, 1st Session, Vol. V, 567.

23. The two dissenters, Republicans Forrest C. Donnell of Missouri and Homer Ferguson of Michigan, refused to support the decision unless Clark would appear before the body to respond to queries concerning his actions while attorney general. "Clark Indorsed by 9–2 Vote in Senate Group," *Washington Post*, August 13, 1949.

24. "Jolt for McGrath ... Job at Justice Was a Quiet Door to Supreme Court ... Till Tax Case Made It a Hot Spot," *U.S. News and World Report* 31, no. 24 (December 14, 1951), 47–49.

25. Daniel S. Cheever and H. Field Haviland, Jr., *American Foreign Policy and the Separation of Powers* (Cambridge: Harvard University Press, 1952), 6.

26. Daniel Yergin, from *Shattered Peace* as quoted in *Interpretations of American History: Patterns and Perspectives* (New York: The Free Press, 1992), 413.

27. J. Howard McGrath as quoted in Athan Theoharis, "The Rhetoric of Politics," in Barton J. Bernstein, ed. (Chicago: Quadrangle Books, 1970), 215.

28. "M'Grath Given Church Honor," *Providence Evening Bulletin*, March 7, 1949; "Pontiff Names Senator McGrath as Knight of the Holy Sepulchre," *Providence Journal*, March 8, 1949; "To Honor McGrath," *Providence Evening Bulletin*, April 7, 1949; Robert D. Whitaker, "Senator McGrath Becomes Knight of Holy Sepulchre," *Providence Journal*, May 1, 1949.

29. Richard Gid Powers, *Secrecy and Power: The Life of J. Edgar Hoover* (New York: The Free Press, 1987), 58–60.

30. Daniel Cohen, *Joseph McCarthy: The Misuse of Political Power* (Brookfield, CT: The Millbrook Press, 1996), 15–16.

31. "Committee Chairman and Ranking Democrat, J. Parnell Thomas," *Congressional Quarterly* III (1947), 85–86.

32. Some historians question President Truman's commitment to internal subversion. Athan Theoharis in *Seeds of Repression* argued that Truman's attorneys general acted independently in rooting out Communism. See Theoharis, *Seeds of Repression* (Chicago: Quadrangle Books, 1971), 136–140.

33. "By Harry S Truman: Campaign Barbs That Won the Votes ... by 'Giving Hell' to 'Do-Nothings' and 'G.O.P. Platitudes,'" *Newsweek*, November 8, 1948, 5; "Folder, "Miscellaneous Clippings—1946," J. Howard McGrath Papers, Harry S Truman Presidential Library, Independence, MO.

34. Hatch Act. 55 Stat. 1148; 18 U.S.C. 611 as quoted in "The Report of the President's Temporary Commission on Employee Loyalty," August 2, 1939, Folder, "Subject File: 11943–1950," Papers of A. Devitt Vanech, Harry S Truman Presidential Library, Independence, MO.

35. Athan Theoharis, "The Rhetoric of Politics," 218–219.

36. *Ibid.*, 220–221.

37. John Earl Haynes and Harvey Klehr, *Early Cold War Spies: The Espionage Trials That Shaped American Politics* (New York: Cambridge University Press, 2006), 16.

38. Jacob Golos was born Jacob Raisen in the Ukraine in 1890, and immigrated to the United States in circa 1908. He became one of the founding members of the American Communist Party. John Earl Haynes and Harvey Klehr, *Venona: Decoding Soviet Espionage in America* (New Haven: Yale University Press, 1999), 93–94.

39. Curt Gentry, *J. Edgar Hoover: The Man and His Secrets* (New York: W.W. Norton, 1991), 341–343.

40. Haynes and Klehr, *Early Cold War Spies,* 71–73.

41. According to Michael R. Belknap, historians have until now underestimated the real danger that existed during the Cold War. "New evidence that has come to light … [which] suggests the CPUSA (American Communist Party) was far more menacing than I recognized in 1977." This new evidence, deciphered from the VENONA files, would have an impact on the United States, the president, and on the relationship between the Department of Justice under McGrath and the Federal Bureau of Investigation, labeled by him the "investigating arm of the Department." Michael R. Belknap, "The Smith Act Case," in Richard Kirkendall, ed., *Civil Liberties and the Legacy of Harry S Truman* (Kirksville, MO: Truman State University Press, 2013), 81.

42. Haynes and Klehr, *Venona,* 18–19.

43. Herbert Romerstein and Eric Breindel, *The Venona Secrets: The Definitive Expose of Soviet Espionage in America* (Washington, D.C.: Regnery History, 2000), 9–10.

44. J. Howard McGrath, "Government Employee Loyalty Records," *Vital Speeches of the Day,* April 15, 1950, 394–398.

45. File, "McGrath Files," Leslie E. Claypool, "McGrath in L.A. tells way to fight Communism," *Los Angeles Daily News,* October 16, 1950, Athan Theoharis Collection, Marquette University, Milwaukee.

46. "Nixon Challenges McGrath Speeches," *Los Angeles Times,* October 20, 1950, Folder, "Clippings July–Dec. 1950," J. Howard McGrath Papers, Harry S Truman Presidential Library, Independence, MO.

47. Andrew J. Dunar, *America in the Fifties* (Syracuse: Syracuse University Press, 2006), 41–42.

48. Leslie E. Claypool, "McGrath en route to S.F. after fighting L.A. Talks," *Los Angeles Daily News,* October 17, 1950, Athan Theoharis Collection, Marquette University; Lucy Freeman, "M'Grath Derides Communist Hunts," *New York Times,* April 27, 1950.

49. Gentry, *J. Edgar Hoover,* 264n.

50. Franklin Delano Roosevelt as quoted in "The Truman Presidency and the FBI," Athan Theoharis, 52. Richard Kirkendall, ed., *Civil Liberties and the Legacy of Harry S Truman* (Kirksville, MO: Truman State University Press, 2013).

51. Gentry, *J. Edgar Hoover,* 386.

52. William P. Rogers, "The Case for Wire Tapping," *The Yale Law Journal* 63, no. 6 (April 1954) 792–793.

53. "McCarthy Charges, Loyalty Probe," *Congressional Quarterly Almanac 1950,* 81st Congress, 2nd Session, 444–445; Bert Andrews, "McGrath, Hoover Oppose Giving Data," *New York Tribune,* March 28, 1950; Alfred Friendly, "'No Case' Against Lattimore, FBI Chief Hints to Probers," *Kansas City Post,* March 28, 1950, Folder, "Clippings Jan.–June 19," J. Howard McGrath Papers, Harry S Truman Presidential Library, Independence, MO.

54. Letter from Harry S Truman to J. Howard McGrath, March 20, 1950, Folder, "McGrath, J. Howard," PSF, Harry S Truman Presidential Library, Independence, MO.

55. *Ibid.*

56. J. Howard McGrath, "Statement of Attorney General J. Howard McGrath before Subcommittee of the Senate Committee on Foreign Relations" March 27, 1950, Papers of J. Howard McGrath, Harry S Truman Presidential Library, Independence, MO.

57. *Ibid.*; *Congressional Quarterly* (1950), 451–452.

58. "File 1: Letter to J. Howard McGrath from unnamed source," December 25 1950; "J. Howard McGrath File," J. Edgar Hoover, Athan Theoharis Collection, Marquette University, Milwaukee.

59. Athan Theoharis, "Truman Presidency and the FBI," in *Civil Liberties and the Legacy of Harry S Truman,* Richard S. Kirkendall, ed. Volume 9 (Kirksville, Missouri: Truman State University Press, 2013), 51.

60. Athan Theoharis. *The FBI & American Democracy* (Lawrence, Kansas: University Press of Kansas, 2004), 3.

61. Robert J. Donovan. *Tumultuous Years: The Presidency of Harry S Truman, 1949–1953* (New York: W. W. Norton & Company, 1982), 375.

62. *Ibid.*, 376.

63. Royal Little. *How to Lose $100,000,000 and Other Valuable Advice* (Boston: Little, Brown, and Company, 1979), 63.

64. On April 27, 1943, Little, according to *Fortune* magazine, "broke nearly every rule in the book" by gambling that his small rayon

company could be transformed from a single product industry into a fully diversified business model. He would realize substantial profits through the production of cotton cloth combined with "a well-styled, well-made line of branded consumer products," sold in the open market with the aid of a smartly fashioned advertisement campaign. He named his newly created conglomerate Textron, Incorporated, which he believed best represented "textile products made from synthetics." Through the benefit of a wartime economy and his acute business savvy, Little transformed New England's tired textile industry into a workable model. Little financed these ventures through loans secured from the First National of Boston and American Associates. The former was supportive of Little's ventures; the latter was a Little holding company. "Royal Little's Announcement," *Providence Journal*, September 16, 1945, 1; "Little's Charitable Trust Placed under 3 Trustees, Gov. McGrath Among Them," *Providence Journal*, September 16, 1945, 1; "Godfrey Simonds and B.R. Sturges Other 2 Members," *Providence Journal*, September 16, 1945, 1.

65. Letter from Benjamin Sturges to J. Howard McGrath, January 4, 1949; "Investigation of Closing of Nashua, N.H. Mills and Operations of Textron Incorporated. Report of a Subcommittee of the Committee on Interstate and Foreign Commerce United States Senate," February 18, 1949, Folder, "R.I. Charities Trust," Harry S Truman Presidential Library, Independence, MO.

66. This practice resulted in massive unemployment in the New England region, including the small Blackstone Valley villages of Manville and Esmond, Rhode Island, Dover, New Hampshire, and Taunton, Massachusetts. Residents of these communities renewed the fight against Textron and those considered complicit in its expansion. "Investigation of Closing of Nashua, N.H.Mills".

67. According to the *Providence Journal*, the Trust had amassed net assets of $1,000,000. The provisions of the trust's contract, as drawn up by Little's lawyers, instructed the trustees to transfer the net profit to the Providence Community Fund two years after Little's death, providing "the committee dispensing the income of the foundation" judged the payment "wise and practicable." The language of the contract was left purposely vague to allow the trustees broad power to pay the Community Fund as they saw fit. "Little's Charitable Trust Placed Under 3 Trustees, Gov. McGrath Among Them: Godfrey Simonds and B.R. Sturges Other 2 members," *Providence Journal*, September 16, 1945, 1; "Royal Little's Announce-

ment," *Providence Journal*, September 16, 1945, 1.

68. "McGrath-Simonds Statement," *Providence Journal*, September 16, 1945, 1.

69. "Tobey to Probe Textron Political Affiliations as Manchester Offers Aid," *New Hampshire Sunday News*, September 19, 1948, Folder, "Senatorial Records, Desk Correspondence," J. Howard McGrath Papers, Harry S Truman Presidential Library, Independence, MO.

70. He later discovered that Puerto Rico extended foreign business a 12-year moratorium on property and income taxes. "Tobey to Probe Textron Political Affiliations as Manchester Offers Aid," *New Hampshire Sunday News*, September 19, 1948, Folder, "Senatorial Records, Desk Correspondence," Papers of J. Howard McGrath, Harry S Truman Presidential Library, Independence, MO.

71. "Investigation of Closing of Nashua, N. H. Mills," 1.

72. *Congressional Quarterly* I (1945) (Washington, D.C.: Henrietta and Nelson Poynter, 1948), 118.

73. President Truman regarded Senator Tobey with disdain, since the latter, as a member of Estes Kefauver's highly publicized Senate committee, had intimated that Democrats and gangsters maintained an unholy secret alliance. Tobey also led a very spirited campaign as chairman of the Banking and Currency Committee against the Reconstruction Finance Corporation's decision to lend money to the Baltimore and Ohio Railroads. Sean J. Savage. *Truman and the Democratic Party* (Lexington: University Press of Kentucky, 1997), 185–186.

74. "Death of Textron '45 Probe Queried," *Providence Journal*, October 29, 1948.

75. "McGrath, Fogarty Join Pastore in Urging Congressional Probe of New England Mill Closings: Action is Inspired by Union Criticism of Textron Deals," *Providence Journal*, September 16, 1948.

76. *Ibid.* "Trustees' Meeting Not 'Mysterious,' McGrath Tells Textron Hearing," *Providence Evening Bulletin*, November 24, 1948.

77. *Ibid.*

78. Republican Senator Kenneth S. Wherry of Nebraska led another committee investigating small businesses simultaneously. "2nd Textron Probe Pledged," *Providence Evening Bulletin*, September 18, 1948; "Investigation of Closing of Nashua, N.H. Mills," 2.

79. "Statement by Royal Little, Textron President, Before Subcommittee of U.S. Senate," *Providence Journal*, October 27, 1948.

80. *Ibid.*

81. "Little Tells Why Textron Quit N.E.," *Providence Journal*, September 21, 1948.

82. *Ibid.*

83. *Ibid.*
84. Little explained that by shifting or selling Textron companies to charitable trusts and then in turn leasing these properties, he generated liquid income and increased production, which meant more profit, and subsequently more taxes to the government. "Statement by Royal Little, Textron President Before Subcommittee of U.S. Senate," *Providence Journal*, October 27, 1948.
85. "Investigation of Nashua Closing," 3.
86. "Tobey Not to Call Sen. McGrath Now," *Providence Journal*, November 11, 1948; "Trust Reform Proposals Would Go to McGrath's Committee," *Providence Evening Bulletin*, February 18, 1949.
87. "Probe Told about 'Intimate' Meeting in McGrath's Office on Tax Problems of Trustees," *Providence Journal*, November 11, 1948.
88. "Tobey to Probe Textron Political Affiliations as Manchester Offers Aid," *New Hampshire Sunday News*, September 19, 1948, Folder, "Textron, Inc. Desk Corres. Clippings-Senatorial," J. Howard McGrath Papers, Harry S Truman Presidential Library, Independence, MO; "Tobey Not to Call Sen. McGrath Now," *Providence Journal*, November 12, 1948.
89. Paul A. Kelly, "Defends Naming Paull, O'Keefe to Directorates," *Providence Journal*, September 18, 1952, 1; "Senate Committee Backs Tobey's Report on Textron," *Providence Evening Bulletin*, March 9, 1949.
90. "Senate Committee Backs Tobey's Report," March 9, 1949, 19; "Internal Revenue Code Lists Trust Exemptions," *Providence Evening Bulletin*, November 24, 1948.
91. "McGrath Says Tobey Errs on Trust Taxes," *Providence Evening Bulletin*, February 18, 1949, Folder, "Textron, Inc., Desk Corres.—Clippings, Senatorial," J. Howard McGrath Papers, Harry S Truman Presidential Library, Independence, MO.
92. *Ibid.*
93. Donald I. Rogers, "Tobey Backs Charity Foundation in N.H. Like One He Hit in R.I.," *Providence Journal*, November 2, 1948.
94. *Ibid.*, 2–3.
95. "Trust Reform Proposals Would Go to McGrath's Committee," *Evening Bulletin*, February 18, 1949.
96. Ferrell, *Harry S Truman*, 366.
97. Bert Cochran, *Harry Truman and the Crisis Presidency* (New York: Funk & Wagnalls, 1973), 249.
98. Milne, "Delaware Freshman," 1, 15.
99. "Historical Perspectives on the Federal Income Tax: 1939 The Internal Revenue Code and the Public Salary Tax Act," accessed September 3, 2017, www.taxhistory.com/1939.htm.

100. In 1943, Congress passed legislation that withheld a special tax on individual income earned. In essence, this act increased the number of taxpayers, as did the postwar economic boom. "Statement by the President," WHCF, Official File 21-D, "Bureau of Internal Revenue 1952–1953," Papers of Harry S Truman, Harry S Truman Presidential Library, Independence, Missouri.
101. Andrew Dunar, *The Truman Scandals and the Politics of Morality* (Columbia: University of Missouri Press, 1984), 96–97.
102. McGrath, accordingly, told the press that he and Moore never had this conversation. He later unearthed a "forgotten" office memorandum from Peyton Ford to Caudle proving Moore's allegation; he then sheepishly apologized to the judge claiming that he had "forgotten" about the memo. Fowler then asked, "How could McGrath forget that?" Fowler Harper, "The Record of J. Howard McGrath." *The Nation* (November 24, 1951), 443.
103. Harper, "The Record of J. Howard McGrath."
104. Andrew Dunar, "All Honorable Men: The Truman Scandals and the Politics of Morality," PhD diss. (University of Southern California, 1981), 229–230.
105. In addition to Williams's revelations, the famous Kefauver committee, established to expose and abolish organized crime, charged, "The federal government [was] being defrauded of many millions of tax revenues by mobsters engaged in organized criminal activities." Estes Kefauver further speculated that "there [was] doubt whether the Bureau of Internal Revenue has been making a real effort to check on the income tax returns of known gamblers and racketeers…. It [was] apparent … that returns [were] being submitted by gangsters and racketeers which the bureau would not accept from ordinary citizens." As a result, the Internal Revenue Bureau instituted a "rackets squad" under the direction of lifelong agent John B. Dunlap, from Dallas, Texas. Dunlap, who would later serve as commissioner of internal revenue, ably and efficiently discharged his duties. Dunar, *The Truman Scandals*, 98; "Delaware Freshman Senator Gives More Woe than GOP Does," *Providence Journal*, November 18, 1951.
106. "The Internal Revenue Service, 1946–1951," John W. Snyder Papers, Harry S Truman Presidential Library, Independence, MO.
107. *Ibid.*
108. "Commissioner Dunlap Tells of Shake-Up in Tax Bureau," *U.S. News and World Report*, December 14, 1951, 24.
109. *Ibid.*
110. Cabell Phillips, *The Truman Presidency*:

The History of a Triumphant Succession (New York: Macmillan, 1966), 40.

111. While Caudle served as U.S. attorney in North Carolina, he came under fire for allegedly accepting automobiles at reduced cost in exchange for "handling" the case of two known tax violators. Despite a subsequent FBI probe, where Caudle admitted his "indis[cretion]," Attorney General Clark still appointed him assistant attorney general. "Truman, McGrath and Hoover Meet," *Providence Journal*, December 13, 1951.

112. "The Friendliest People." *Time*, December 10, 1951, 21.

113. "Missouri Republican Asks Truman to Oust McGrath," *Providence Journal*, November 18, 1951.

114. "Testimony of J. Howard McGrath," 1663.

115. "Jolt for McGrath ... Job at Justice Was a Quiet Door to Supreme Court ... Till Tax Case Made It a Hot Spot," *U.S. News and World Report* 31, no. 24, December 14, 1951: 47–49. "Testimony of Hon. J. Howard McGrath, Attorney General of the United States," *Hearings before a Subcommittee of the Committee on Ways and Means House of Representatives*, Part 2, December 11, 1951, 1660.

116. "Testimony of J. Howard McGrath," 1660.

117. "Truman Seeks to End Dispute over Tax Files," *New York Herald Tribune*, November 25, 1951, Folder, "Harry S Truman File; Probes in Administration Tax Scandals," Democratic National Committee, Harry S Truman Presidential Library, Independence, MO.

118. Capitalizing on McGrath's devout Catholicism, Caudle presented him with a four-hundred-year-old relic, which was "carried by people in distress who were in the underground during the last war." T. Lamar Caudle to J. Howard McGrath, April 17, 1951, Attorney General Desk Correspondence, J. Howard McGrath Papers, Harry S Truman Presidential Library, Independence, MO; "Caudle, Coats, and Cars," *Newsweek*, December 10, 1951, 21.

119. "Scores Truman for Summary Firing of Caudle," *Providence Journal*, September 18, 1952.

120. "Justice Clark Writes Keating Reasons for Not Testifying," *Washington Star*, June 18, 1953, Athan Theoharis Collection, Marquette University, Milwaukee; "Truman, McGrath and Hoover Meet," *Providence Journal*, December 13, 1951.

121. *Investigation of the Department of Justice*, Report. H. Res. 50. 83rd Congress, 1st Session, 88.

122. "Caudle A Scapegoat, Chelf Probers Charge," *Louisville Times*, December 27, 1952, Chelf Papers, Western Kentucky.

123. Oliphant supposedly sent clients of the Bureau of Internal Revenue to "investigator, lobbyist, and influence peddler," Henry Grunewald in exchange for various gifts, monetary and otherwise. Dunar, *The Truman Scandals*.

124. Charles Oliphant to Harry S Truman, December 5, 1951, WHCF OF 174, Truman Papers, Harry S Truman Presidential Library, Independence, MO.

125. A *Providence Journal* editorial demanded that President Truman "issue a direct order to his attorney general to get busy with the broom..." or "insist that Mr. McGrath step aside for a man whom the country can trust to do the job." "Mr. McGrath's Turn," *Providence Journal*, December 2, 1951.

126. McGrath had just called for a grand jury probe based on affluent Chicago lawyer Abraham Teitelbaum's accusation that two unnamed federal men tried to extort $500,000 from him in exchange for a "tax fix." "McGrath Voices His Confidence in Legal Talent of Government: Cheered for Defense of Justice Dept.," *Providence Journal*, December 7, 1951, 1.

127. *Ibid.*

128. Joseph Hanlon, "Chelf Report Assails Delays by Justice Dept. in Fraud Cases: Recovered Only $300,000 of $21,000,000 in Claims certified by GAO, It Says—Calls Record 'Shameful,'" *St. Louis Post-Dispatch*, October 6, 1952, Papers of Frank Chelf, Manuscripts & Folklife Archives, Library Special Collections, Western Kentucky University, Kentucky.

129. Mr. Reed, "Investigation of the Department of Justice," 83rd Congress, 1st Session, Report No. 1079, August 1, 1953.

130. *Ibid.*; "Chelf Report Assails," October 6, 1952.

131. "Jolt for McGrath...," 48–49.

132. "Testimony of Peyton Ford," *Internal Revenue Investigation*, Part 2, 1276–285.

133. Andrew Dunar contends that Representative King urged the president to appoint a separate investigative committee as well. Dunar, *The Truman Scandals*, 111.

134. "Truman Has No Plans to Fire McGrath, McKinney," *Sacramento Beacon*, December 13, 1951.

135. "President's Talk to Murphy Held Cleanup Plan Key," *Providence Journal*, December 15, 1951, 1.

136. Dunar, *The Truman Scandals*, 111–112.

137. Robert S. Allen, "Commentator Gives 3 Men Credit for Saving McGrath Cabinet Job," *Providence Journal*, January 15, 1952, 3; "Advised Protégé not to Quit, then went to Truman," *Providence Journal*, January 12, 1952; "Jettisons Original Program of Special Com-

mission for Job," *Providence Journal*, January 11, 1952.

138. "McGrath Has Long Talk with Green," *Providence Journal*, January 5, 1952.

139. "Jettisons Original Program of Special Commission for Job," *Providence Journal*, January 11, 1952.

140. "'Drastic Action'" *Providence Journal*, January 11, 1952, 13.

141. In McGrath's later interview with David Noyes, he contended that Judge Learned Hand recommended two of his sons-in-law, one Norris Darrow and the other Newbold Morris. McGrath stated that he "sent a letter to Darrow and offered him the job." After a few days, Darrow refused the offer, claiming that his business partners "couldn't afford to let him do it because they had a lot of tax cases in their office." David Noyes, David Noyes interview with J. Howard McGrath, Folder, "McGrath, J. Howard, and Charles Sawyer—Interviews, February 24, 1955," Papers of William Hillman, Harry S Truman Presidential Library, Independence, MO.

142. Edward T. Folliard, "Cleanup Task Hampered, Truman Says," *Washington Post*, February 21, 1952, Folder, "Harry S Truman File: Statements on Justice Dept. Probe and McGrath," Records of the Democratic National Committee, Harry S Truman Presidential Library, Independence, MO.

143. "Statement by the President," February 14, 1952, Folder, "B File: The Truman Scandals, 8 of 11," Box 47, "The Truman Scandals," Student Research File, Harry S Truman Presidential Library, Independence, MO.

144. Morris was charged with investigating alleged wrongdoing and then "recommend[ing]" action "to the President and Attorney General for correction and prevention of improper or illegal acts." "Testimony of Newbold Morris," *Internal Revenue Investigation*, Part 4, Harry S Truman Presidential Library, Independence, MO.

145. "Report," Stephen Mitchell Papers, Harry S Truman Presidential Library, Independence, MO; Morris, *Let the Chips Fall*, 42–56.

146. Morris, *Let the Chips Fall*, 43.

147. Correspondence Stephen Mitchell to various friends and clients, March 13–27, 1952, Papers of Stephen A. Mitchell, Harry S Truman Presidential Library, Independence, MO.

148. Morris, *Let the Chips Fall*, pp. 15-16.

149. Dunar, *The Truman Scandals*, 112–113.

150. "Morris to Name Leading Lawyers as Prosecutors," *Providence Journal*, March 3, 1952, 1.

151. "McGrath to Get 1st Income Quiz," *Providence Journal*, March 7, 1952, 1.

152. Begun while McGrath was Democratic national chairman, the media attempted to prove that he held ownership in Yellow Cab Company. James Kiernan, still smarting after the party ignored him in his bid for Democratic state chairman, intimated that McGrath and the "mushrooms in both parties are taking over." "McGrath Taxi Link Denied," *Providence Evening Bulletin*, May 28, 1948; "McGrath Estimates His Holdings at Less than $200,000 in Story," *Providence Journal*, May 26, 1948; "McGrath Quizzed on Finances by Harold Stassen," *Providence Journal*, February 22, 1952, 1.

153. Donovan, *The Tumultuous Years*, 378.

154. "McGrath Believes His Race and Religion at Stake in Probe," *Providence Journal*, March 17, 1952, 1.

155. Bearing the stamp "Security Information—Secret," the document cites a number of individuals who allegedly leaked secrets to the Soviet Union on "atomic bomb production, and the number stockpiled," in "the field of aeronautics in the United States," in the "production of anti-biotics—penicillin, streyptomicin, terramicin, aureomicin, cloromyciden and bacitracin," and in international relations. According to the document, the Soviets had targeted the American State Department, intelligence and counterintelligence, and other areas "so diverse [in] nature that it is doubtful that they can be defined in very specific terms." Whether McGrath meant to expose this information is unknown, but the attorney general, expended much of his time on this issue. Ferrell, *Harry S Truman*, 368; "Security," J. Howard McGrath Collection, Special and Archival Collections, Providence College, Providence.

156. Since McGrath was away, Morris left the questionnaire with Solicitor General Philip Perlman. "McGrath's Tax Returns Sought by Investigation," *Providence Journal*, March 16, 1952, 1.

157. McGrath told interviewer David Noyes that the president agreed with him. According to McGrath, Truman supported his decision, commenting that "I agree with you.... We can't have that kind of stuff happening in this government.... You don't have to do anything about it. I am going to tell this guy to go home." David Noyes, interview with J. Howard McGrath, Folder, "McGrath, J. Howard, and Charles Sawyer—Interviews, February 24, 1955," Papers of William Hillman Memoirs File, Harry S Truman Presidential File, Independence, MO. The president, however, stated that he did not speak to McGrath before the latter fired Morris. Dunar, *The Politics of Morality*, 118.

158. Chelf Subcommittee, 14; Donovan, *The Tumultuous Years*, 379.

159. Donovan, *The Tumultuous Years*, 380.

160. Dunar, *The Truman Scandals*, 118.

161. *Ibid.*; Ferrell, *Harry S Truman*, 367–368.

162. Ferrell, *Harry S Truman*, 368.

163. Kenneth Hechler, *Working with Truman: A Personal Memoir of the White House Years* (New York: G. P. Putnam's Sons, 1982), 197–210.

164. *Ibid.*

165. Memo to Harry Barnard, March 19 to August 12, 1952, General Political Files, Mitchell Papers, Harry S Truman Presidential Library, Independence, MO.

166. "Testimony of J. Howard McGrath," Internal Revenue Investigation, "Former Attorney General McGrath," Folder, "General Political Files," Mitchell Papers, Harry S Truman Presidential Library, Independence, MO.

167. "Review of the Week: Justice Gets an Overhauling," *Washington Sunday Star*, August 17, 1952, Papers of Frank Chelf, Manuscripts & Folklife Archives, Library Special Collections, Western Kentucky University.

168. *Ibid.*

169. Morris would later contend that the "political system was too strong even for a President to buck." Newbold Morris, *Let the Chips Fall: My Battles Against Corruption* (New York: Appleton-Century-Crofts, 1955), 33.

170. Statement by the president, January 2, 1952; WHCF OF, 21-D Official File, Truman Papers, Truman Presidential Library, Independence, MO.

171. Robert H. Ferrell. *Harry S Truman: A Life* (Columbia: University of Missouri Press, 1994), 358–362.

Epilogue

1. Former senator Green last appeared in public to greet his friend President Lyndon B. Johnson on September 28, 1964, during the Democratic campaign for the presidency. G. Richmond Carpenter, "Sen. Green Dies at 98 at his Home," *Providence Evening Bulletin*, May 19, 1966, Folder 511, Papers of John O. Pastore, Special and Archival Collections, Providence College, Providence.

2. "Press Conference Transcript," *Providence Journal*, January 31, 1959; "Green Resigns Chairmanship of Senate Body," *Providence Journal*, January 31, 1959, Papers of John O. Pastore, Special and Archival Collections, Providence College, Providence.

3. "Political Leaders Unanimous in Praise of His Dedication," *Evening Bulletin*, January 12, 1960. Papers of John O. Pastore, Special and Archival Collections, Providence College, Providence.

4. "McGrath Reported Set to Enter Senate Race," *Providence Evening Bulletin*, May 3, 1960, Folder 523, Papers of John O. Pastore, Special and Archival Collections, Providence College, Providence.

5. "McGrath Will Fight 'All the Way,'" *Providence Journal*, July 27, 1960, Folder 523, Papers of John O. Pastore, Special and Archival Collections, Providence College, Providence.

6. *Ibid.*

7. Francis M. Stephenson and Jerry Lisker, "A Senate Nor-Easter: Pell of Rhode Island," *Sunday News: New York's Picture Newspaper*, December 26, 1965, Folder 549, Papers of John O. Pastore, Special and Archival Collections, Providence College, Providence.

8. J. Howard McGrath, "An Address by Honorable J. Howard McGrath, Attorney General of the United States before the Friendly Sons of St. Patrick," March 17, 1950.

Appendix

1. Robert J. Donovan, *Conflict and Crisis: The Presidency of Harry S. Truman, 1945–1948*, vol. 1 (New York: W. W. Norton, 1977), 355–356.

2. Robert J. Donovan, *The Tumultuous Years: The Presidency of Harry S. Truman, 1949–1952*, vol. 2 (New York: W. W. Norton, 1982), 374–375.

3. *Ibid.*, 374.

4. *Ibid.*, 375.

5. Bert Cochran, *Harry Truman and the Crisis Presidency*, 223.

6. Harold F. Gosnell, *Truman's Crises: A Political Biography of Harry S Truman* (Westport, CT: Greenwood Press, 1980), 500–501.

7. *Ibid.*, 419–420.

8. "McGrath Boomed for Presidency: Rhode Islander is Honored by 700 Persons at Dinner of B.U. Law School Association," *Providence Journal*, November 13, 1949; "R.I. Democrats Ask If McGrath Plans to Run for Vice President: Friends Say He May Seek Nomination if by 1952 Moment is Propitious for Catholic to Offer Himself for 2nd Highest Office in U.S.," *Providence Journal*, August 2, 1949, 1.

9. David McCullough, *Truman* (New York: Simon & Schuster, 1992), 637–638.

10. *Ibid.*

11. Roger Tubby, diary, as quoted in David McCullough, *Truman*, 895.

12. Robert H. Ferrell, *Harry S Truman: A Life* (Columbia: University of Missouri Press, 1994), 365–366.

13. *Ibid.*, 366.

14. *Ibid.*, 463.

15. Hamby, *Beyond the New Deal*, 462–464.

16. *Ibid.*, 462–464.

17. Alonzo L. Hamby, *Man of the People: A Life of Harry S Truman* (New York: Oxford University Press, 1995), 589.

18. *Ibid.*, 588–593.

19. Jack Redding, with a foreword by J. Howard McGrath, *Inside the Democratic Party* (New York: Bobbs-Merrill, 1958).

20. To give Ross his due, he provided an extensive narrative on McGrath's meeting with the Southern governors in February 1948, and his buoyancy in the face of adversity. For a complete treatment see Irwin Ross, *The Loneliest Campaign: The Truman Victory of 1948* (New York: New American Library, 1968), 4, 64–65.

21. *Ibid.*, 240.

22. Susan M. Hartmann, *Truman and the 80th Congress* (Columbia: University of Missouri Press, 1971), 72–73.

23. Sean J. Savage. *Truman and the Democratic Party* (Lexington: The University Press of Kentucky, 1997), vii.

24. *Ibid.*

25. *Ibid.*, 60.

26. *Ibid.*, 65.

27. *Ibid.*, 66

28. *Ibid.*

29. David Pietrusza, *1948: Harry Truman's Improbable Victory and the Year that Transformed America's Role in the World* (New York: Union Square Press, 2011), 78–79, 383.

30. Zachary Karabell, *The Last Campaign: How Harry Truman Won the 1948 Election* (New York: Vintage, 2000), 7–8.

31. *Ibid.*, 39–40.

32. *Ibid.*, 40.

33. Michael R. Gardner, *Harry Truman and Civil Rights: Moral Courage and Political Risks* (Carbondale: Southern Illinois University Press, 2002), 163–166.

34. *Ibid.*, 172.

35. Kari Frederickson, *The Dixiecrat Revolt and the End of the Solid South, 1932–1968* (Chapel Hill: University of North Carolina Press, 2001), 7–9.

36. *Ibid.*, 9.

37. *Ibid.*

38. *Ibid.*, 195.

39. According to Frederickson in her discussion of federal patronage in Mississippi. Mississippi vice-chairman of the party Philip Mullen stated that Truman rejected McGrath's attempts to reconcile former Dixiecrats within party ranks. *Ibid.*

40. Carol Anderson, *Eyes off the Prize: The United Nations and the African American Struggle for Human Rights, 1944–1955* (New York: Cambridge University Press, 2003), 1–3.

41. *Ibid.*, 5.

42. *Ibid.*, 3.

43. Daniel Yergin, *Shattered Peace: The Origins of the Cold War and the National Security State* (Boston: Houghton Mifflin, 1977), 5.

44. *Ibid.*, 9.

45. *Ibid.*, 9–10.

46. *Ibid.*, 10.

47. Athan Theoharis, *Seeds of Repression: Harry S Truman and the Origins of McCarthyism* (Chicago: Quadrangle Books, 1971), 123.

48. Athan Theoharis, ed., *From the Secret Files of J. Edgar Hoover* (Chicago: Ivan R. Dee, 1993), 121; J. Howard McGrath as quoted in Athan Theoharis, "The Rhetoric of Politics," in Barton J. Bernstein, ed. (Chicago: Quadrangle Books, 1970), 215.

49. Theoharis, *From the Secret Files,* 137.

50. J. Howard McGrath to J. Edgar Hoover, Personal and Confidential Memo, February 26, 1952, as quoted in Athan Theoharis, ed., *From the Secret Files of J. Edgar Hoover* (Chicago: Ivan R. Dee, 1991),136–139.

51. *Ibid.*, 138–143.

52. Richard Gid Powers, *Secrecy and Power: The Life of J. Edgar Hoover* (New York: The Free Press, 1987), 306.

53. Michael J. Devine, "Introduction," in Richard S. Kirkendall, ed., *Civil Liberties and the Legacy of Harry S Truman*, vol. 9, Truman Legacy Series (Kirksville, MO: Truman State University Press, 2013), xv–xvi.

54. *Ibid.*

55. Belknap, "The Smith Act Case," 81–82.

56. Newbold Morris, *Let the Chips Fall: My Battles Against Corruption* (New York: Appleton-Century-Crofts, 1955).

57. *Ibid.*, 25.

58. *Ibid.*

59. Jules Abels. *The Truman Scandals* (Chicago: Henry Regnery Company, 1956), 13–17.

60. *Ibid.*

61. Blair Bolles. *How to Get Rich in Washington: Rich Man's Division of the Welfare State* (New York: W. W. Norton, 1952), 9–11.

62. *Ibid.*, 12.

63. See Truman files. Bolles, *How to Get Rich in Washington*, 264.

64. Andrew J. Dunar, *The Truman Scandals and the Politics of Morality* (Columbia: University of Missouri Press, 1984), 1.

65. *Ibid.*, 21.

66. *Ibid.*, 119–120.

67. *Ibid.*

Bibliography

Unpublished Sources

Archival: Manuscripts and Collections

Biddle, Francis Collection. Franklin Delano Roosevelt Presidential Library, Hyde Park, NY.

Byrnes, James Papers. Clemson Library and Archival Collections, Clemson, SC.

Clark, Thomas Papers. Harry S Truman Presidential Library, Independence, MO.

Clifford, Clark Papers. Harry S Truman Presidential Library, Independence, MO.

Democratic National Committee Papers. Harry S Truman Presidential Library, Independence, MO.

Fogarty, John P. Collection. Special and Archival Collections, Providence College, Providence, RI.

Gerry, Peter G. Papers. Library of Congress, Washington, D.C.

Green, Theodore Francis Papers. Library of Congress, Washington, D.C.

Green, Theodore Francis Papers. John Hay Library, Brown University, Providence, RI.

Hamilton, Henry Dewitt Papers. John Hay Library, Brown University, Providence, RI.

Henderson, Leon Papers. Franklin Delano Roosevelt Presidential Library, Hyde Park, NY.

Hillman, William Papers. Harry S Truman Presidential Library, Independence, MO.

J.D.C. Archives, New York, NY.

League of Women Voters. Rhode Island Historical Society, Providence, RI.

McGrath, James Howard Collection. Special and Archival Collections, Providence College, Providence, RI.

McGrath, James Howard Papers. Harry S Truman Presidential Library, Independence, MO.

NAACP Papers. Boston Public Library, Boston, MA.

Pastore, John O. Collection. Special and Archival Collections. Providence College, Providence, RI.

Redding, John M. Papers. Harry S Truman Presidential Library, Independence, MO.

Roberts, Dennis J. Collection. Special and Archival Collections. Providence College, Providence, RI.

Roosevelt, Eleanor Collection. Franklin Delano Roosevelt Presidential Library, Hyde Park, NY.

Roosevelt, Franklin Delano Collection. Franklin Delano Roosevelt Presidential Library, Hyde Park, NY.

Roosevelt, James Collection. Franklin Delano Roosevelt Presidential Library, Hyde Park, NY.

Snyder, John W. Papers. Harry S Truman Presidential Library, Independence, MO.

Thurmond, Strom Papers. Clemson University, Clemson, SC.

Tobin, Maurice Papers. Harry S Truman Presidential Library, Independence, MO.

Truman, Harry S. Harry S Truman Presidential Library, Independence, MO.

Interviews

Carroll, J. Austin. Telephone interview by author, August 2007.
Clark, Thomas. Interview by Jerry N. Hess, 1972.
Morison, H. Graham. Interview by Jerry N. Hess. Independence, MO, August 16, 1972.
Quinn, Robert Emmet. Interview by Matthew Smith, Providence, RI, July–August 1972.

Dissertations, Theses and Student Papers

Barto, Harold Emery. "Clark Clifford and the Presidential Election of 1948," PhD diss. Rutgers University, October 1970.
Daoust, Norma LaSalle. "The Perils of Providence: Rhode Island's Capital City During the Depression and New Deal." PhD diss. University of Connecticut, Storrs, January 1982.
Dunar, Andrew. "All Honorable Men: The Truman Scandals and the Politics of Morality," PhD diss. University of Southern California, Los Angeles, June 1981.
Honan, Mary Gertrude. "An Inquiry into the Work of the Juvenile Court of the State of Rhode Island." Master's thesis. Rhode Island College of Education, Providence, 1949.
Jennings, William. "The Prince of Pawtucket." PhD diss. Providence College, Providence, 1985.
Lorimer, Madeline. CSA, BA, MA "America's Response to Europe's Displaced Persons, 1948– 1952: A Preliminary Report." PhD diss. Saint Louis University, St. Louis, 1964.
Maiman, Richard John. "'Constitutionalizing' the Juvenile Court: The Impact of *in re Gault* in Rhode Island." PhD diss. Brown University, Providence, 1972.
Slater, Thomas. "The History of Quonset Point Naval Air Station, 1939–1973," Master's thesis. Providence College, Providence, RI, 1983.
Tripp, Eleanor Baldwin. "Displaced Persons: The Legislative Controversy in the United States, 1945–1950." Master's thesis. Columbia University, New York, 1971.

Published Sources

Newspapers and Magazines

Boston Globe
Boston Post
Boston Traveler
Chicago Sun
Hartford Times
Louisville Times
Nation
New York Post
New York Times
Newport Times
News-Tribune
Newsweek
Pawtucket Times

Pawtuxet Valley Daily Times
Providence Journal and Evening Bulletin
Providence Visitor
Saturday Evening Post
Springfield Daily Republican
Magazine
United States News and World Report
U.S. News and World Report
Warwick Beacon
Washington Post
Washington Star
Westerly Sun
Woonsocket Call

Reports, Manuals and Government Documents

Brown, C. Edgar, ed. *Democracy at Work: The Official Report of the Democratic National Convention.* Philadelphia, 1948.
Congressional Quarterly Almanac.
Investigation of the Department of Justice: Report of the Committee on the Judiciary by the Subcommittee to Investigate the Department of Justice. H Res. 50. 83d Cong., 1st Sess., August 1, 1953.
Narragansett Racing Ass'n v. Kiernan et. al. No. 678. *The Atlantic Reporter,* 1938.

Newton, Mortimer, Chairman of the Board. *Ninth Annual Report: 1944 of the Rhode Island Unemployment Compensation Board*, March 27, 1945.

Providence Journal Almanac.

Public Laws of the State of Rhode Island and Providence Plantations. Providence: The Oxford Press, 1936.

Rhode Island Manual with Rules and Orders for the Use of the General Assembly of the State of Rhode Island, 1927–1928, 1929–1930, 1945–1946.

Books and Articles

Acacia, John. *Clark Clifford: The Wise Man of Washington.* Lexington: University Press of Kentucky, 2009.

Allen, Robert, and William V. Shannon. *The Truman Merry-Go-Round.* New York: The Vanguard Press, 1950.

Altschuler, Glenn C., and Stuart M. Blumin. *The G.I. Bill: A New Deal for Veterans.* New York: Oxford University Press, 2009.

Anderson, Carol. *Eyes Off the Prize: The United Nations and the African American Struggle for Human Rights, 1944–1955.* New York: Cambridge University Press, 2003.

Andreson, Robert L. *Providence Shipyard: Walsh-Kaiser Company, Inc. 1943–1945.* Providence: Bank Lithograph Company, 1945.

Bartley, Ernest R. *The Tidelands Oil Controversy: A Legal and Historical Analysis.* Austin: University of Texas Press, 1953.

Behr, Edward. *Prohibition: Thirteen Years that Changed America.* New York: Arcade, 2011.

Bell, Jonathan. *The Liberal State on Trial: The Cold War and American Politics in the Truman Years.* New York: Columbia University Press, 2004.

Bernstein, Barton J., ed. *Politics & Policies of the Truman Administration.* Chicago: Quadrangle Books, 1970.

Blum, John Morton. *V Was for Victory: Politics and American Culture During World War II.* New York: Harcourt Brace, 1976.

Borstelmann, Thomas. *The Cold War and the Color Line: American Race Relations in the Global Arena.* Cambridge: Harvard University Press, 2001.

Bride, Thomas H. "Rhode Island Cash Sickness Compensation Program," *American Journal of Public Health* 39, no. 8 (August 1949): 1011–1015.

Brinkley, Alan. *The End of Reform: New Deal Liberalism in Recession and War.* New York: Vintage, 1995.

Busch, Andrew E. *Truman's Triumphs: The 1948 Election and the Making of Postwar America.* Lawrence: University Press of Kansas, 2012.

Celler, Emanuel. *You Never Leave Brooklyn: The Autobiography of Emanuel Celler.* New York: The John Day Company, 1953.

Chafee, Zechariah, Jr. *State House Versus Pent House: Legal Problems of the Rhode Island Race Track Row.* Cambridge: Crimson Printing Co., 1937.

Cheever, Daniel S. and H. Field Haviland, Jr. *American Foreign Policy and the Separation of Powers.* Cambridge, MA: Harvard University Press, 1952.

Cochran, Bert. *Harry Truman and the Crisis Presidency.* New York: Funk & Wagnalls, 1973.

Cohen, Daniel. *Joseph McCarthy: The Misuse of Political Power.* Brookfield, CT: The Millbrook Press, 1996.

Cohen, Gerard Daniel. *In War's Wake: Europe's Displaced Persons in the Postwar Order.* New York: Oxford University Press, 2012.

Cohodas, Nadine. *Strom Thurmond and the Politics of Southern Change.* New York: Simon & Schuster, 1993.

Conley, Patrick T. *An Album of Rhode Island History, 1636–1986.* Norfolk: The Donning Company, 1986.

_____. *The Irish in Rhode Island: A Historical Appreciation.* Providence: The Rhode Island Heritage Commission, 1986.

_____. *Rhode Island in Rhetoric and Reflection: Public Addresses and Essays.* East Providence: Rhode Island Publications Society, 2002.

Conley, Patrick T., and Paul R. Campbell. *Providence: A Pictorial History.* Norfolk: Donning Company Publishers, 1982.

Cornwell, Elmer E., Jr. "City Bosses and Political Machines." *The Annals of the American Academy of Political and Social Science* 353 (May 1964): 27–39.

_____. "Party Absorption of Ethnic Groups: The Case of Providence, Rhode Island," *Social Forces* 38, no. 3 (March 1960): 205–210.

Davie, Maurice R. *The American Jewish Year Book* 51 (1950): 127–33.

Dinnerstein, Leonard. *America and the Survivors of the Holocaust.* New York: Columbia University Press, 1982.

Donaldson, Gary A. *Truman Defeats Dewey.* Lexington: University Press of Kentucky, 1999.

Dunar, Andrew J. *America in the Fifties.* Syracuse: Syracuse University Press, 2006.

_____. *The Truman Scandals and the Politics of Morality.* Columbia: University of Missouri Press, 1984.

Edwards, India. *Pulling No Punches: Memoirs of a Woman in Politics.* New York: G.P. Putnam's Sons, 1977.

Ferrell, Robert H. *Harry S Truman: A Life.* Columbia: University of Missouri Press, 1994.

Flather, M. Randolph. "Don't Bank on It: Bank Holiday for Rhode Island for Today, March 4 ordered by Acting Governor Quinn." Rhode Island Yearbook 1971: H-198.

Fortin, Marcel P., ed. *Woonsocket RI: A Centennial History, 1888–1988.* Woonsocket: Woonsocket Centennial Committee, 1988.

Frederickson, Kari. *The Dixiecrat Revolt and the End of the Solid South, 1932–1968.* Chapel Hill: University of North Carolina Press, 2001.

Gardner, Michael R. *Harry Truman and Civil Rights: Moral Courage and Political Risks.* Carbondale: Southern Illinois University Press, 2002.

Gentry, Curt. *J. Edgar Hoover: The Man and His Secrets.* New York: W.W. Norton, 1991.

Geselbracht, Raymond H., ed. *The Civil Rights Legacy of Harry S Truman.* Kirksville, MO: Truman State University Press, 2007.

Gosnell, Harold F. *Truman's Crises: A Political Biography of Harry S Truman.* Westport, CT: Greenwood Press, 1980.

Gullan, Harold I. *The Upset That Wasn't: Harry S Truman and the Crucial Election of 1948.* Chicago: Ivan R. Dee, 1998.

Hamby, Alonzo L. *Man of the People: A Life of Harry S Truman.* Oxford: Oxford University Press, 1995.

Hartmann, Susan M. *Truman and the 80th Congress.* Columbia: University of Missouri Press, 1971.

Haynes, John Earl, and Harvey Klehr. *Early Cold War Spies: The Espionage Trials That Shaped American Politics.* New York: Cambridge University Press, 2006.

_____. *Venona: Decoding Soviet Espionage in America.* New Haven: Yale University Press, 1999.

Hechler, Kenneth. *Working with Truman: A Personal Memoir of the White House Years.* New York: G.P. Putnam's Sons, 1982.

Hegarty, Neil. *The Story of the Irish People.* New York: St. Martin's Press, 2011.

Huthmacher, J. Joseph. *Senator Robert F. Wagner and the Rise of Urban Liberalism.* New York: Atheneum, 1971.

Ignatiev, Noel. *How the Irish Became White.* New York: Routledge, 1995.

Karabell, Zachary. *The Last Campaign: How Harry Truman Won the 1948 Election.* New York: Alfred A. Knopf, 2000.

Kellner, George H., and J. Stanley Lemons. *Rhode Island: The Ocean State.* Sun Valley, CA: American Historical Press, 2004.

Kirkendall, Richard S., ed. *Civil Liberties and the Legacy of Harry S Truman.* Kirksville, MO: Truman State University Press, 2013.

Klausen, Jytte. "Did World War II End the New Deal?" in Sidney M. Milkis and Jerome M.

Mileur, eds., *The New Deal and the Triumph of Liberalism*. Boston: University of Massachusetts Press, 2002.

Landis, James J. "Morale and Civilian Defense." *The American Journal of Sociology* 47, no. 30 (November 1941).

Lapomarda, Vincent A. *The Boston Mayor Who Became Truman's Secretary of Labor: Maurice J. Tobin and the Democratic Party*. New York: Peter Lang, 1995.

Lee, J. J., and Marion R. Casey. *Making the Irish American: History and Heritage of the Irish in the United States*. New York: New York University Press, 2006.

Little, Royal. *How to Lose $100,000,000 and Other Valuable Advice*. Boston: Little, Brown, 1979.

Lockard, Duane. *New England State Politics*. Chicago: Henry Regnery and Company, 1959.

Luconi, Stefano. *The Italian-American Vote in Providence, Rhode Island, 1916–1948*. Madison, NJ: Farleigh Dickinson University Press, 2004.

Martin, John Frederick. *Civil Rights and the Crisis of Liberalism: The Democratic Party, 1945 1976*. Boulder, CO: Westview Press, 1979.

McBurney, Christian, Brian L. Wallin, Patrick T. Conley, et al. *World War II Rhode Island*. Charleston, SC: The History Press, 2017.

McCaffrey, Lawrence. *Irish Diaspora in America*. Bloomington: Indiana University Press, 1976.

McCullough, David. *Truman*. New York: Simon & Schuster, 1992.

McFarland, Keith D., and David L. Roll. *Louis Johnson and the Arming of America*. Bloomington: Indiana University Press, 2005.

McGrath, J. Howard. "The Constitutional Convention of 1944." *Rhode Island History* IV, no. 1 (January 1945): 1–6.

Meagher, Timothy J. *Inventing Irish America: Generation, Class, and Ethnic Identity in a New England City, 1880–1928*. Notre Dame: University of Notre Dame Press, 2001.

Miller, G. Wayne. *An Uncommon Man: The Life & Times of Senator Claiborne Pell*. Lebanon, NH: University Press of New England, 2011.

Miller, Kerby, and Paul Wagner. *Out of Ireland: The Story of Irish Emigration to America*. Washington, D.C.: Elliott & Clark, 1994.

Miller, Kerby A. *Emigrants and Exiles: Ireland and the Irish Exodus to North America*. New York: Oxford University Press, 1985.

Milligan, Sean Paul. *Quonset Point Naval Air Station*. Charleston, SC: Arcadia, 1996.

Moakley, Maureen, and Elmer Cornwell. *Rhode Island Politics and Government*. Lincoln: University of Nebraska Press, 2001.

Morison, Samuel Eliot. *The Two-Ocean War: A Short History of the United States in the Second World War*. Boston: Little, Brown, 1963.

Morris, Newbold, and Dana Lee Thomas. *Let the Chips Fall: My Battles Against Corruption*. New York: Appleton-Century-Crofts, 1955.

Morris, Richard B., ed. *Encyclopedia of American History*, 6th ed. New York: Harper & Row, 1982.

Mulligan, Debra A. "The 'Difficult Business' of Wartime Delinquency: Rhode Island and the Establishment of a Juvenile Court." *The New England Journal of History* (Fall 2015).

Names and Places of Nova Scotia. Bellevile, Ontario: Mika Publishing Company, 1974.

O'Neill, William L. *A Democracy at War: America's Fight at Home and Abroad in World War II*. New York: The Free Press, 1993.

O'Reilly, Kenneth. "A New Deal for the FBI: The Roosevelt Administration, Crime Control, and National Security." *The Journal of American History* 69, no. 3 (December 1982): 638–658.

Patten, David. *Rhode Island Story: Recollections of 35 Years on the Staff of the Providence Journal and The Evening Bulletin*. Providence: The Providence Journal Company, 1954.

Phillips, Cabell. *The Truman Presidency: The History of a Triumphant Succession*. New York: Macmillan, 1966.

Pietrusza, David. *1948: Harry Truman's Improbable Victory and the Year that Transformed America*. New York: Union Square Press, 2011.

Potter, Warren, and Robert Oliver. *Fraternally Yours: The Independent Order of Foresters.* London: Queen Anne Press Limited, 1967.

Powers, Richard Gid. *Secrecy and Power: The Life of J. Edgar Hoover.* New York: The Free Press, 1987.

Ray, Alex. *Hired Gun: A Political Odyssey.* New York: University Press of America, 2008.

Reiss, Steven A. *The Sport Kings and the Kings of Crime: Horse Racing, Politics, and Organized Crime in New York, 1865–1913.* Syracuse: Syracuse University Press, 2011.

Rogers, William P. "The Case for Wire Tapping," *The Yale Law Journal* 63, no. 6 (April 1954): 792–798.

Romerstein, Herbert, and Eric Breindel. *The Venona Secrets: The Definitive Expose of Soviet Espionage in America.* Washington, D.C.: Regnery History, 2000.

Ross, Irwin. *The Loneliest Campaign: The Truman Victory of 1948.* New York: The New American Library, 1968.

Savage, Sean J. *Truman and the Democratic Party.* Lexington: University Press of Kentucky, 1997.

Shepard, Ben. *The Long Road Home: The Aftermath of the Second World War.* New York: First Anchor Books, 2012.

Sitkoff, Harvard. "Harry Truman and the Election of 1948: The Coming of Age of Civil Rights in American Politics." *The Journal of Southern History* 37, no. 4 (November 1971): 597–616. Accessed July 27, 2009. http://www.jstor.org/stable/2206548.

Smith, Donald W. "The Wagner-Murray-Dingell Bill: Senate Bill 1050, H.R. 3293." *The American Journal of Nursing* 45, no. 11 (November 1945): 933–936.

Smith, Jean. *FDR.* New York: Random House, 2007.

Sterne, Evelyn Savidge. *Ballots and Bibles: Ethnic Politics and the Catholic Church in Providence.* Ithaca: Cornell University Press, 2004.

Sunstein, Cass. *The Second Bill of Rights: FDR's Unfinished Revolution and Why We Need it More Than Ever.* New York: Basic Books, 2004.

Theoharis, Athan. *Chasing Spies: How the FBI Failed in Counterintelligence but Promoted the Politics of McCarthyism in the Cold War Years.* Chicago: Ivan R. Dee, 2002.

_____. *The FBI & American Democracy.* Lawrence: University Press of Kansas, 2004.

_____. *Seeds of Repression: Harry S Truman and the Origins of McCarthyism.* Chicago: Quadrangle Books, 1971.

Thomas, Dr. A.P. *Woonsocket; Highlights of History: 1800–1876.* Woonsocket: Woonsocket Opera House Society, 1976.

Vaughan, Philip H. *The Truman Administration's Legacy for Black America.* Reseda, CA: Mojave Books, 1976.

Wheeler, Robert A. "Fifth Ward Irish: Immigrant Mobility in Providence, 1850–1870." *Rhode Island History* (Spring 1973): 52–61.

White, Philip. *Whistle Stop: How 31,000 Miles of Train Travel, 352 Speeches, and a Little Midwest Gumption Saved the Presidency of Harry Truman.* Lebanon, NH: University Press of New England, 2014.

Wohl, Alexander. *Father, Son, and Constitution: How Justice Tom Clark and Attorney General Ramsey Clark Shaped American Democracy.* Lawrence: University Press of Kansas, 2013.

Wyman, Mark. *DP: Europe's Displaced Persons, 1945–1951.* New York: Cornell University Publishing, 1998.

Ybarra, Michael J. *Washington Gone Crazy: Senator Pat McCarran and the Great American Communist Hunt.* Hanover, NH: Steerforth Press, 2004.

Yergin, Daniel. *Shattered Peace: The Origins of the Cold War and the National Security State.* Boston: Houghton Mifflin, 1977.

Index